W8-APJ-007

D0020356

Contents at a Glance

To access the online chapters, go to informit.com/myiphone11 and click the Downloads tab below the book description. Click the link to download the chapter.

Table of Contents

3 **Setting Up and Using an Apple ID, iCloud, and Other Online Accounts**   **91**

9   Sending, Receiving, and Managing Texts and iMessages   319

To access the online chapters, go to informit.com/myiphone11
and click the Downloads tab below the book description. Click the
link to download the chapter.

About the Author

Brad Miser has written extensively about technology, with his favorite topics being the amazing "i" devices, especially the iPhone, that make it possible to take our lives with us while we are on the move. In addition to *My iPhone*, Eleventh Edition, Brad has written many other books, including *My iPhone for Seniors*, Fourth Edition. He has also been an author, development editor, or technical editor for more than 50 other titles.

Brad is or has been a sales support specialist, the director of product and customer services, and the manager of education and support services for several software development companies. Previously, he was the lead proposal specialist for an aircraft engine manufacturer, a development editor for a computer book publisher, and a civilian aviation test officer/engineer for the U.S. Army. Brad holds a bachelor of science degree in mechanical engineering from California Polytechnic State University at San Luis Obispo and has received advanced education in maintainability engineering, business, and other topics.

Brad would love to hear about your experiences with this book (the good, the bad, and the ugly). You can write to him at bradmiser@icloud.com.

Dedication

To those who have given the last full measure of devotion so that the rest of us can be free.

Acknowledgments

To the following people on the *My iPhone* project team, my sincere appreciation for your hard work on this book:

Laura Norman, my acquisitions and development editor, who envisioned the original concept for *My iPhone* and works very difficult and long hours to ensure the success of each edition. Laura and I have worked on many books together, and I appreciate her professional and effective approach to these projects. Thanks for putting up with me yet one more time! Frankly, I have no idea how she does all the things she does and manages to be so great to work with given the incredible work and pressure books like this one involve!

Charlotte Kughen, my development and copy editor, who helped craft this book so that it provides useful information delivered in a comprehensible way. Thanks for your work on this book!

Karen Weinstein, the technical editor, who caught a number of mistakes I made and who made useful suggestions along the way to improve this book's content.

Mandie Frank, my project editor, who skillfully managed the hundreds of files and production process that it took to make this book. Imagine keeping dozens of plates spinning on top of poles and you get a glimpse into Mandie's daily life! (And no plates have been broken in the production of this book!)

Chuti Prasertsith for the cover of the book.

Cindy Teeters, who handles the administrative tasks associated with my books. Cindy does her job extremely well and with a great attitude. Thank you!

Que's production and sales team for printing the book and getting it into your hands.

We Want to Hear from You!

As the reader of this book, *you* are our most important critic and commentator. We value your opinion and want to know what we're doing right, what we could do better, what areas you'd like to see us publish in, and any other words of wisdom you're willing to pass our way.

We welcome your comments. You can email or write to let us know what you did or didn't like about this book—as well as what we can do to make our books better.

Please note that we cannot help you with technical problems related to the topic of this book.

When you write, please be sure to include this book's title and author as well as your name and email address. We will carefully review your comments and share them with the author and editors who worked on the book.

Email: feedback@informit.com/register

Mail: Que Publishing
         ATTN: Reader Feedback
         800 East 96th Street
         Indianapolis, IN 46240 USA

Reader Services

Register your copy of *My iPhone* at quepublishing.com for convenient access to downloads, updates, and corrections as they become available. To start the registration process, go to informit.com/register and log in or create an account*. Enter the product ISBN, 9780789758651, and click Submit.

*Be sure to check the box that you would like to hear from us in order to receive exclusive discounts on future editions of this product.

Using This Book

This book has been designed to help you transform an iPhone into *your* iPhone by helping you learn to use it easily and quickly. As you can tell, the book relies heavily on pictures to show you how an iPhone works. It is also task-focused so that you can quickly learn the specific steps to follow to do lots of cool things with your iPhone.

Using an iPhone involves lots of touching its screen with your fingers. When you need to tap part of the screen, such as a button or keyboard, you see a callout with the step number pointing to where you need to tap. When you need to swipe your finger along the screen, such as to browse lists, you see the following icons:

The directions in which you should slide your finger on the screen are indicated with arrows. When the arrow points both ways, you can move your finger in either direction. When the arrows point in all four directions, you can move your finger in any direction on the screen.

To zoom in or zoom out on screens, you unpinch or pinch, respectively, your fingers on the screen. These motions are indicated by the following icons:

When you need to tap once or twice, such as to zoom out or in, you see the following icons matching the number of times you need to tap:

If you use an iPhone 6s/6s Plus or later model, you can use pressure on the screen to activate certain functions. The following icons indicate when you should apply some pressure (called a Peek) or slightly more pressure (called a Pop):

Sometimes, you should touch your finger to the screen and leave it there without applying pressure to the screen. The following icon indicates when you should do this:

When you should rotate your iPhone, you see this icon:

As you can see on its cover, this book provides information iPhone models that can run iOS 11. These models are: 5s, SE, 6, 6 Plus, 6s, 6s Plus, 7, 7 Plus, 8, 8 Plus, and X. Each of these models has specific features and capabilities that vary slightly from the others. Additionally, they have different screen sizes with the SE being the smallest and the Plus models being the largest.

Because of the variations between the models, the figures you see in this book might be slightly different than the screens you see on your iPhone. For example, the iPhone 8 has settings that aren't on the 5s or SE. In most cases, you can follow the steps as they are written with any of these models even if there are minor differences between the figures and your screens.

When the model you are using doesn't support a feature being described, such as the Display Zoom that is on the iPhone 6 and later but not on earlier models, you can skip that information or read it to help you decide if you want to upgrade to a newer model.

The most "different" model of iPhone that runs iOS 11 is the X. To maximize screen space, the X does not have the Touch ID/Home button that all the other models have. It also uses Face ID instead of Touch ID when user authentication is required, such as when you unlock the phone. Most of the tasks in this book are the same on the X as on other models. In some cases, there are minor variations for the X, which are explained in this book. In a few cases, tasks are substantially different on the X than on the other models. If you use an X, please download the online supplement *My iPhone X* by going to www.informit.com/myiphone11 to get the details for these tasks that are unique to the iPhone X.

The iPhone 7 Plus, 8 Plus, and X have additional photographic capabilities because these models have two cameras on their backsides instead of just one. If you have one of these models, check out the online supplement *My iPhone X* (you can download from (www.informit.com/myiphone11) for the detailed step-by-step instructions to use their unique photo-taking features.

You'll soon wonder
how you ever got along
without one!

In this chapter, you get introduced to the amazing iPhone! Topics include the following:

→ Getting to know your iPhone's external features
→ Getting to know your iPhone's software

Getting Started with Your iPhone

Your iPhone is one of the most amazing handheld devices ever because of how well it is designed. It has only a few external features you need to understand. For most of the things you do, you just use your fingers on your iPhone's screen (which just seems natural), and the iPhone's consistent interface enables you to accomplish most tasks with similar steps.

Getting to Know Your iPhone's External Features

Take a quick look at the iPhone's physical attributes. It doesn't have many physical buttons or controls because you mostly use software to control it.

Wake/Sleep button
(5s and SE models)

Camera

Mute switch

Side button
(except 5s and SE
models)

Volume
buttons

Touch ID/Home
button (except X)

Headphone jack (6s and earlier models) Lightning port

- **Cameras**—One of the iPhone's camera lenses is located on its backside near the top-left corner (the iPhone 7 Plus, 8 Plus, and X have two lenses there); the other is on the front at the top near the center of the phone. When you take photos or video, you can choose the cameras on either side. All iPhone models have a flash located near the camera on the backside. The iPhone 6s and later models also have a flash on the front that comes from the screen; for the 5s and SE, there is no flash when you use the camera on the front.

- **Side button**—Press this button (called the Sleep/Wake button on the 5s and SE and located on the top of the phone instead of on the side on those models) to lock the iPhone's screen and put it to sleep. Press it again to wake the iPhone from Sleep mode. You also use this button to shut down the iPhone and to power it up. On the iPhone X, it has other uses, such as activating Siri when you hold it down for a couple of seconds.

- **Mute switch**—This switch determines whether the iPhone makes sounds, such as ringing when a call comes in or making the alert noise for notifications, such as for an event on a calendar. Slide it toward the front of the iPhone to hear sounds. Slide it toward the back of the iPhone to mute all sound. When muted, you see orange in the switch.

- **Volume**—Press the upper button to increase volume; press the lower button to decrease volume. These buttons are contextual; for example, when you are listening to music, they control the music's volume, but when you aren't, they control the ringer volume. When you are using the Camera app, pressing either button takes a photo.

- **Lightning port**—Use this port, located on the bottom side of the iPhone, to plug in the Lightning headphones (iPhone 7/7 Plus or later models) or connect it to a computer or power adapter using the included USB cable. There are also accessories that connect to this port. The Lightning port accepts Lightning plugs that are flat, thin, rectangular plugs. It doesn't matter which side is up when you plug something into this port.

  The iPhone 7/7Plus and later models come with an adapter that enables you to plug devices that have a 3.5 mm plug (such as prior versions of the EarPods) into the Lightning port.

- **Headphone jack (5s, SE, 6/6 Plus, and 6s/6s Plus)**—This standard 3.5 mm jack can be used for headphones (such as the older EarPods) and powered speakers.

- **Touch ID/Home button (all iOS 11 compatible models except the X)**— This serves two functions.

  The Touch ID sensor recognizes your fingerprint, so you can simply touch it to unlock your iPhone, sign in to the iTunes Store, and use Apple Pay, and enter your password in Touch ID-enabled apps. On the iPhone 7/7s and later models, it technically isn't even a button, rather it is a sensor only (though it still works like a button because you press it).

  It also serves as the Home button. When the iPhone is asleep, press it to wake up the iPhone; press it again to unlock the iPhone (if you have Touch ID enabled, this also enters your passcode; if not, you have to manually enter the passcode to unlock the phone). When the iPhone is awake and unlocked, press this button to move to the all-important Home screens; press it twice quickly to open the App Switcher. Press and hold the Home button to activate Siri to speak to your iPhone. You can also configure it so you can use it to perform other actions, such as pressing it three times to open the Magnifier.

Camera

Mute switch

Volume buttons

Side button

Lightning port

One of the most significant hardware changes that Apple made for the iPhone X was to remove the Touch ID/Home button. This enables the iPhone X to have a larger screen than similarly sized iPhone models, such as the 7 or 8. Gestures and different button combinations replace some of the functions of the Touch ID/Home button while Face ID replaces the Touch ID function of this button.

So Many iPhones, So Few Pages

The iPhone is now in its eleventh generation of software that runs on multiple generations of hardware. Each successive generation has added features and capabilities to the previous version. All iPhone hardware runs the iOS operating system. However, this book is based on the current version of this operating system, iOS 11. iOS 11 is compatible with the 5s, SE, 6, 6 Plus, 6s, 6s Plus, 7, 7 Plus, 8, 8 Plus, and X. If you don't have one of these models, this book helps you see why it is time to upgrade, but most of the information contained herein won't apply to your iPhone until you do.

There are also differences even among the models of iPhones that can run iOS 11. For example, the iPhone 7 Plus, 8 Plus, and X have dual cameras on the backside that provide additional photographic features, including telephoto and portrait photographs.

Most of the information in this book is based on iPhone 7, 7 Plus, 8, and 8 Plus. If you don't use one of these models, there might be slight differences between what you see on your screen and the steps and figures in this book (if you use an iPhone X, make sure to read the next sidebar). These differences aren't significant and shouldn't stop you from accomplishing the tasks as described in this book.

X Marks the Spot!

Because of the differences in the iPhone X hardware and the rest of the models, it has an online companion supplement to this book called *My iPhone X*. You can download this supplement by using a web browser to visit www.informit.com/myiphone11. While almost all of the tasks in this book can be followed as written with an iPhone X, the supplement provides detailed steps for those tasks that are unique to the X, such as configuring and using Face ID. Also, some of the photographic tasks that only the 7 Plus, 8 Plus, and X can do are covered in this supplement.

Getting to Know Your iPhone's Software

You might not suspect it based on the iPhone's simple and elegant exterior, but this powerhouse runs very sophisticated software that enables you to do all sorts of great things. The beauty of the iPhone's software is that it is both very powerful and also easy to use—once you get used to its user interface (UI for the more technical among you). The iPhone's UI is so well designed that after a few minutes, you might wish everything worked so well and was so easy to use.

Using Your Fingers to Control Your iPhone

Apple designed the iPhone to be touched. Most of the time, you control your iPhone by using your fingers on its screen to tap icons, select items, swipe on the screen, zoom, type text, and so on. If you want to get technical, this method of interacting with software is called the multi-touch interface.

Going Home

Almost all iPhone activities start at the Home screen, or Home screens, to be more accurate, because the Home screen consists of multiple pages. When your iPhone is unlocked and you are using an app, you get to the Home screen by pressing the Touch ID/Home button once (all models except iPhone X) or touching and swiping up from the bottom of the screen (iPhone X). You move to the Home screen automatically any time you restart your iPhone and unlock it. Along the bottom of the Home screen (or along the side on an iPhone Plus model when held horizontally) is the Dock, which is always visible on the Home screen. This gives you easy access to the icons it contains; up to four icons can be placed on this Dock. Above the Dock are apps that do all sorts of cool things. As you install apps, the number of icons on the Home screens increases. To manage these icons, you can organize the pages of the Home screens in any way you like, and you can place icons into folders to keep your Home screens tidy. At the top of the screen are status icons that provide you with important information, such as whether you are connected to a Wi-Fi network and the current charge of your iPhone's battery.

Status icons

App icons

Folder containing icons

Badge

Home screen

Dock

Touching the iPhone's Screen

The following figures highlight the major ways you control an iPhone:

Tap an app's icon to launch it

- **Tap**— Briefly touch a finger to the iPhone's screen and then lift your finger again. When you tap, you don't need to apply pressure to the screen, simply touch your finger to it. For example, to open an app, you tap its icon.

- **Double-tap**—Tap twice. You double-tap to zoom in on something; for example, you can double-tap on a web page to view something at a larger size.

- **Swipe**—Touch the screen at any location and slide your finger (you don't need to apply pressure, just touching the screen is enough). You use the swipe motion in many places, such as to browse a list of options or to move among Home page screens. Whatever you are swiping on moves in the direction that you swipe.

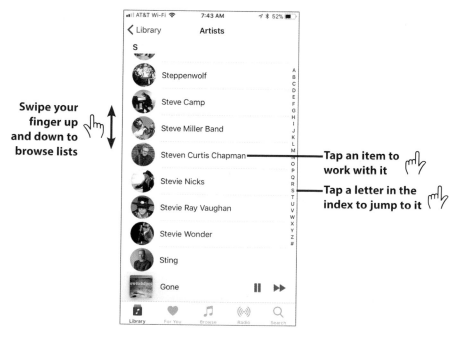

Swipe your finger up and down to browse lists

Tap an item to work with it

Tap a letter in the index to jump to it

- **Drag**—Tap and hold an object and move your finger across the screen without lifting it up; the faster you move your finger, the faster the resulting action happens. (Again, you don't need to apply pressure, just make contact.) For example, you can drag icons around the Home screens to rearrange them.

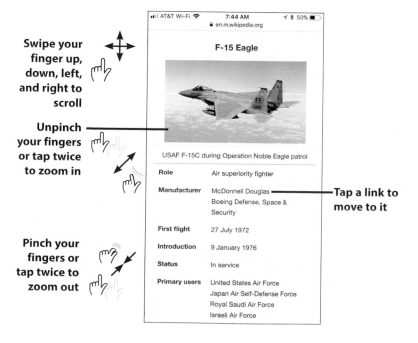

Swipe your finger up, down, left, and right to scroll

Unpinch your fingers or tap twice to zoom in

Pinch your fingers or tap twice to zoom out

Tap a link to move to it

- **Pinch or unpinch**—Place two fingers on the screen and drag them together or move them apart; the faster and more you pinch or unpinch, the "more" the action happens (such as a zoom in). When you are viewing photos, you can unpinch to zoom in on them or pinch to zoom out again.

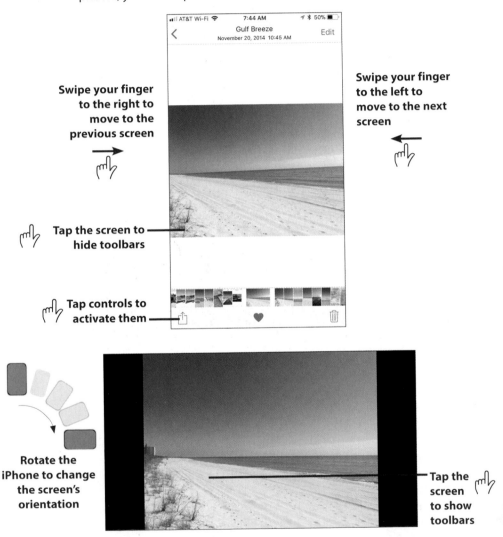

Swipe your finger to the right to move to the previous screen

Swipe your finger to the left to move to the next screen

Tap the screen to hide toolbars

Tap controls to activate them

Rotate the iPhone to change the screen's orientation

Tap the screen to show toolbars

- **Rotate**—Rotate the iPhone to change the screen's orientation.

Tap and press on something to perform a Peek

Swipe up on a Peek to reveal menus with actions you can select to perform them

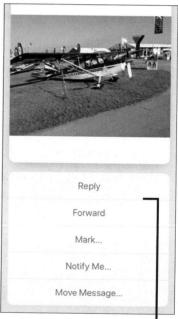

A Peek is a quick way to look at something without actually opening it

When you swipe up on a Peek, you get a menu; tap an action to perform it

- **Peek**—On an iPhone that supports 3D Touch (iPhone 6s and later models), you can take action on something by applying pressure to the screen when you touch it. When you are looking at a preview of something, such as an email, touch and put a small amount of pressure on the screen to perform a Peek. A Peek causes a window to open that shows a preview of the object. You can preview the object in the Peek window; if you swipe up on a Peek, you get a menu of commands related to the object. For example, when you perform a Peek on an email and then swipe up on the Peek, you can tap Reply to reply to the email.

Tap and press on something to perform a Peek

Press slightly harder on a Peek to perform a Pop

When you perform a Pop, the object opens in the associated app

- **Pop**—When you are looking at a Peek, apply slightly more pressure on the screen to perform a Pop, which opens the object in its app. For example, you can perform a Peek on a photo's thumbnail to preview it. Apply a bit more pressure (a Pop) on the preview to "pop" it open in the Photos app (for example, to crop your finger out of the photo).

Working with iPhone Apps

When you tap an app's icon, it opens and fills the iPhone's screen

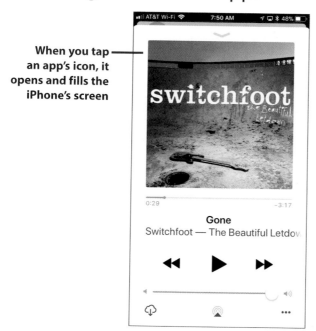

One of the best things about an iPhone is that it can run all sorts of applications, or in iPhone lingo, *apps*. It includes a number of preinstalled apps, such as Mail, Safari, and so on, but you can download and use thousands of other apps, many of which are free, through the App Store. You learn about many of the iPhone's preinstalled apps as you read through this book. And as you learned earlier, to launch an app, you simply tap its icon. The app opens and fills the iPhone's screen. You can then use the app to do whatever it does.

Pressing on an app's icon pops open the Quick Actions menu

Tap a Quick Action to perform it

On an iPhone that supports 3D Touch (iPhone 6s and later models), you can press on an app's icon to open its Quick Actions menu; tap an action to take it. For example, when you open the Quick Actions menu for the Phone app, you can place calls to people you have designated as favorites.

Tap a folder to access its icons

Folder name

Open folder

Tap an icon to open the app

Icons within the folder

Swipe to the right or left to move between a folder's pages

Tap outside a folder or press the Touch ID/ Home button to close it

In Chapter 5, "Customizing How Your iPhone Looks and Sounds," you learn how you can organize icons in folders to keep your Home screens tidy and make getting to icons faster and easier. To access an icon that is in a folder, tap the folder. It opens and takes over the screen. Under its name is a box showing the apps it contains. Like the Home screens, folders can have multiple pages. To move between a folder's pages, swipe to the left to move to the next screen or to the right to move to the previous one. Each time you "flip" a page, you see another set of icons. You can close a folder without opening an app by tapping outside its borders or by pressing the Touch ID/Home button (except the iPhone X).

To open an app within a folder, tap its icon.

When you are done using an app, press the Touch ID/Home button (all models except the iPhone X) or swipe up from the bottom of the screen (iPhone X). You return to the Home screen you were most recently using.

When you move out of an app by pressing the Touch ID/Home button or swiping up from the bottom of the screen (iPhone X only), the app moves into the background but doesn't stop running (you can control whether or not apps are allowed to work in the background using the Settings app, which you use throughout this book). So, if the app has a task to complete, such as uploading photos or playing audio, it continues to work behind the scenes. In some cases, most notably games, the app becomes suspended at the point you move it into the background by switching to a different app or moving to a Home screen. In addition to the benefit of completing tasks when you move into another app, the iPhone's capability to multitask means that you can run multiple apps at the same time. For example, you can run an Internet radio app to listen to music while you switch over to the Mail app to work on your email.

Use the App Switcher to quickly move among open apps

Swipe to the left or right to move among the running apps

The current screen in the app

Tap an app's screen to move into it

Running apps

You can control apps by using the App Switcher. To see this, quickly press the Touch ID/Home button twice (all models except the iPhone X) or swipe up from the bottom of the screen and pause near the middle of the screen (iPhone X). The App Switcher appears.

At the top of the App Switcher, you see icons for apps you have used recently or are currently using. Under each app's icon, you see a thumbnail of that app's screen. You can swipe to the left or right to move among the apps you see. You can tap an app's screen to move into it. That app takes over the screen, and you can work with it, picking up right where you left off the last time you used it.

When you open the App Switcher, the app you were using most recently comes to the center to make it easy to return to. This enables you to toggle between two apps easily. For example, suppose you need to enter a confirmation number from one app into another app. Open the app into which you want to enter the number. Then open the app containing the number you need to enter. Open the App Switcher and tap the previous app to return to it quickly so that you can enter the number.

To close the App Switcher without moving into a different app, press the Touch ID/Home button once (all models except iPhone X) or tap outside the App Switcher (iPhone X). You move back into the app or Home screen you were most recently using.

Swipe up on an app's screen to force it to close

iPhone X App Switching

On the iPhone X, you can switch apps by swiping to the left or right along the bottom of the screen (without opening the App Switcher). Refer to the online supplement *My iPhone X* by going to www.informit.com/myiphone11 for more details about using an iPhone X.

In some cases, you might want to force an app to quit, such as when it's using up your battery too quickly or it has stopped responding to you. To do this, open the App Switcher. Swipe up on the app you want to stop. The app is forced to quit, its icon and screen disappear, and you remain in the App Switcher. You should be careful about this, though, because if the app has unsaved data, that data is lost when you force the app to quit. The app is not deleted from the iPhone—it is just shut down until you open it again (which you can do by returning to the Home screen and tapping the app's icon).

Tap to return to the app you were previously using ──

Sometimes, a link in one app takes you into a different app. When this happens, you see a left-facing arrow with the name of the app you were using in the upper-left corner of the screen. You can tap this to return to the app you came from. For example, you can tap a link in a Mail email message to open the associated web page in Safari. To return to the email you were reading in the Mail app, tap the Mail icon in the upper-left corner of the screen.

Swipe all the way to the right to access widgets

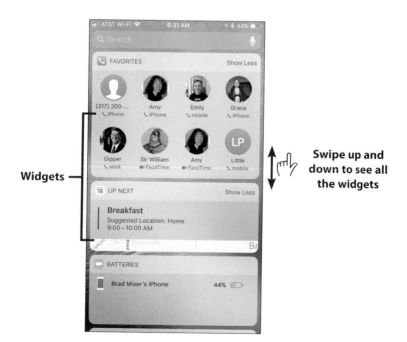

Widgets ──

Swipe up and down to see all the widgets

Music widget ⎯⎯ Tap to show less

Tap an album to play it

Mail widget ⎯⎯ Tap to show more

Tap a VIP to read email from him

Apps can provide widgets, which make it easy to work with those apps from the Widget Center. To access these widgets, swipe all the way to the right from a Home screen or from the Lock screen (more on this later). You see widgets for various apps. Swipe up or down the screen to browse all the widgets available to you. Tap Show Less to collapse a widget or tap Show More to expand it. Tap something inside a widget to use that app. For example, tapping an album in the Music widget plays it. You learn more about how to use widgets in Chapter 2, "Using Your iPhone's Core Features" and how to configure the Widget Center in Chapter 4, "Customizing How Your iPhone Works."

Using the Home Screens

Previously in this chapter, you read that the Home screen is the jumping-off point for many of the things you do with your iPhone because that is where you access the icons you tap to launch things such as apps you've saved there.

Swipe to the left or right to move between pages of your Home screen

The white dot indicates the page you are currently viewing

The Dock showing up to four icons is visible on every page

Tap to the left or right of the current page (white dot) to move to the previous or the next page

When you move to a different page, you see a different set of icons and folders

The Home screen has multiple pages. To change the page you are viewing, swipe to the left to move to later pages or to the right to move to earlier pages. The dots above the Dock represent the pages of the Home screen; the white dot represents the page being displayed. You can also change the page by tapping to the left of the white dot to move to the previous page or to the right of it to move to the next page.

Using the iPhone Plus' Split-Screen

Tap the Bookmark icon when using Safari to open and close split-screen

Web page for bookmark selected in left pane

Swipe to browse the left pane

Tap to open bookmark in the right pane

Swipe to browse the right pane

When you hold an iPhone Plus in the horizontal orientation, you can take advantage of the Split-screen feature in many apps (not all apps support this). In Split-screen mode, the screen has two panes. The left pane is for navigation, whereas the right pane shows the content selected in the left pane. The two panes are independent, so you can swipe up and down on one side without affecting the other. In most apps that support this functionality, there is an icon you can use to open or close the split screen. This icon changes depending on the app you are using. For example, when you are using Safari to browse the Web, tap the Bookmark icon to open the left pane and tap it again to close the left pane (while the left pane is open, you can select bookmarks and see the associated web pages in the right pane). As another example, in the Mail app, you tap the Full Screen icon (two arrows pointing diagonally away from each other) to open or close the left pane.

Preinstalled apps that support this functionality include Settings, Mail, Safari, and Messages; you see examples showing how Split-screen works in those apps later in this book. You should hold your iPhone Plus horizontally when using your favorite apps to see if they support this feature.

Home screen pages

Dock

When you hold a Plus horizontally and move to the Home screen, the Dock moves to the right side of the screen and you see the Home screen's pages in the left part of the window. Though this looks a bit different, it works the same as when you hold an iPhone vertically.

Working with the Control Center

On the Home screen or when you are using apps, swipe up from the bottom of the screen to open the Control Center (except iPhone X)

On an iPhone X, swipe down from the upper-right corner of the screen to open the Control Center

On the Lock screen, swipe up from the bottom of the screen to open the Control Center

The Control Center provides quick access to a number of very useful controls. To access it, swipe up from the bottom of the Home screen (all models except the iPhone X) or swipe down from the upper-right corner of the screen (iPhone X). If your iPhone is asleep/locked, press the Side or Touch ID/Home button or lift the phone to wake it up and then swipe up from the bottom of the Home screen (all models except the iPhone X) or swipe down from the upper-right corner of the screen (iPhone X). When the Control Center opens, you have easy and quick access to a number of controls.

Control Center Tip

Some apps have their own Dock at the bottom of the screen. When you are using such an app, make sure you don't touch an icon on the Dock when you are trying to open the Control Center because you'll do whatever the icon is for instead. Just swipe up on an empty area of the app's Dock and the Control Center opens. On the iPhone X, this isn't an issue because your swipe down from the upper-right corner of the screen instead.

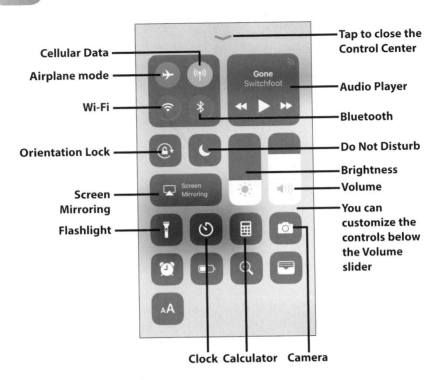

Cellular Data

Airplane mode

Wi-Fi

Orientation Lock

Screen Mirroring

Flashlight

Tap to close the Control Center

Audio Player

Bluetooth

Do Not Disturb

Brightness

Volume

You can customize the controls below the Volume slider

Clock Calculator Camera

In the top-left quadrant of the Control Center are icons you can use to turn on or turn off important functions, which are Airplane mode, Cellular Data, Wi-Fi, Bluetooth, Orientation Lock, and Do Not Disturb mode. To activate a function, tap its icon, which changes color to show the function is active. To disable a function, tap the icon so that it becomes gray to show you it is inactive. For example, to lock the orientation of the iPhone's screen in its current position, tap the Orientation Lock icon so it becomes red. Your iPhone screen's orientation no longer changes when you rotate the phone. To make the orientation change when you rotate the phone again, tap the Orientation Lock icon to turn it off again. You learn about the Airplane and Do Not Disturb modes later in this chapter. Wi-Fi and Cellular Data are explained in Chapter 2. You learn about using Bluetooth in Chapter 15, "Working with Other Useful iPhone Apps and Features."

In the upper-right quadrant, you see the Audio Player. You can use this to control music, podcasts, and other types of audio that are playing in their respective apps (you learn about the Music app in Chapter 15).

Just below the Audio Player are the Brightness and Volume sliders. You swipe up or down on these to increase or decrease the screen's brightness and the volume of whatever you are hearing on your phone.

The controls above the first row of four icons are always on the Control Center; you can't change them in any way. However, below those are a section of controls you can change. By default, you see the Flashlight, Clock, Calculator, Camera, and others in this area. Like the icons toward the top of the screen, tap these icons to perform the associated action, such as using the iPhone's flash as a flashlight, or opening an app—the Clock app, for example. You can configure the controls that are in this area by adding, removing, and organizing them; you learn how to configure your Control Center in Chapter 4.

Tap outside the control to return to the Control Center

Swipe up and down to change brightness

Tap to turn Night Shift on or off

When you press on some of the controls, such as the Brightness slider, you see additional options. You should press the controls you use to see what options are available. For example, when you press the Brightness slider, you see a larger slider and have access to the Night Shift icon (you learn about Night Shift in Chapter 5).

When you're done using the Control Center, tap the downward-facing arrow at the top of the screen and the Control Center is hidden.

Examples of using the controls on the Control Center are throughout the rest of this book.

Working with the Notification Center

Your iPhone has a lot of activity going on, from new emails to reminders to calendar events. The iOS notification system keeps you informed of these happenings through a number of means. Visual notifications include banners and badges. Alert sounds can also let you know something has happened, and vibrations make you feel the new activity.

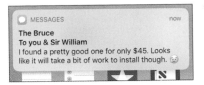

Visual notifications let you know when something of interest has happened, such as receiving a text message

Individual notifications (onscreen alerts, sounds, or vibrations) arrive with the events with which they are associated such as new emails, messages, and updated information from apps. For example, you can have banner notifications and a sound when you receive new text messages.

You learn how to work the notifications your iPhone uses in Chapter 2. Because there is likely to be a lot of activity on your iPhone, you want to customize the notifications you receive so you are aware of important information but not distracted or annoyed by less important activity; configuring notifications is explained in Chapter 4.

Swipe down from the top of the screen to open the Notification Center when your iPhone is unlocked

Swipe up from the middle of the screen to open the Notification Center when your iPhone is locked

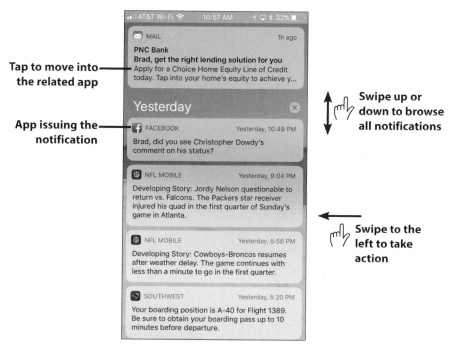

Tap to move into the related app

App issuing the notification

Swipe up or down to browse all notifications

Swipe to the left to take action

You can also access groups of notifications on the Notification Center, which you open by swiping down from the top of the screen when your iPhone is unlocked or swiping up from the middle of the screen when it is locked. The Notification Center opens and displays notifications grouped by day and the app from which they come. You can read the notifications by swiping up and down the screen. You can work with the notifications on the Notification Center just as you work with individual notifications (see Chapter 2). For example, on an iPhone with 3D Touch, press on a notification to pop it open to read more of it or to take action on it; press a little harder to open the associated app. On iPhones without 3D Touch, tap a notification to move into the associated app.

Swipe to the right
to open the app
with which the
notification is
associated

Tap to view the
notification

Tap to delete all of the
notifications for a day

Tap to delete the
notification

Press on a
notification to
read it or delete it

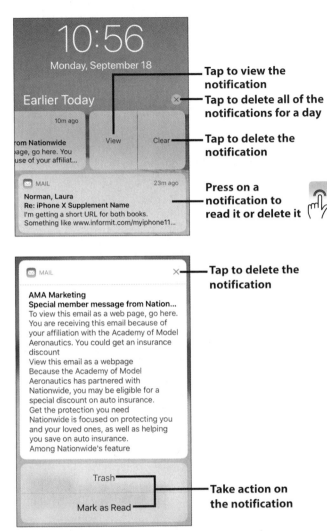

Tap to delete the
notification

Take action on
the notification

When you swipe to the left on a notification, you can tap Clear to delete the notification or View to open it. If you swipe to the right on a notification, you open the app that generated it (if your iPhone is locked, you need to unlock it to move into the app). If you press on a notification, it opens in a window that enables you to read the notification, such as an email, and take action on it.

Tap to delete all of the
notifications for a day

Tap to delete all of the
notifications for a day

You can remove all the notifications for a day by tapping its delete (x) icon and then tapping Clear.

To close the Notification Center when your iPhone is unlocked, move back to the Home screen (press the Touch ID/Home button except on the iPhone X where you swipe up from the bottom of the screen). When the iPhone is locked, just press the Side button to put the phone to sleep to hide the Notification Center.

Using Siri Suggestions

Search your iPhone

Tap to close SIRI
SUGGESTIONS

Tap to show fewer apps

Tap an app to
open it

Tap to run a
suggested search

Earlier, you learned how to access apps from the Home page and App Switcher. Your iPhone can make recommendations about apps that you might want to use based on those you have most recently used, your current activity, and even your location. You can see these suggestions by swiping down from about ¾ up the screen (if you swipe down from the top, you open the Notification Center instead). In the SIRI APP SUGGESTIONS panel, you see the apps being suggested. Tap an app to open it. You can show more apps by tapping Show More, or if the panel is already expanded, tap Show Less to show fewer apps.

At the top of the screen is the Search bar, which you can use to search your phone (this is covered in Chapter 2).

In the SIRI SEARCH SUGGESTIONS panel, you can tap a suggested search to run it (this is also covered in Chapter 2).

If you don't want to use any of the apps shown or perform a search, tap Cancel to return to the previous screen.

Using the Do Not Disturb Mode

All the notifications your iPhone uses to communicate with you are useful, but at times, they can be annoying or distracting. When you put your iPhone in Do Not Disturb mode, its visual, audible, and vibration notifications are disabled so that they won't bother you. For example, the phone won't ring if someone calls you unless you specify certain contacts whose calls you do want to receive while your phone is in this mode.

Tap to keep your iPhone from bothering you

Do Not Disturb is on

Do Not Disturb is on

To put your iPhone in Do Not Disturb mode, open the Control Center and tap the Do Not Disturb icon. It becomes purple and the Do Not Disturb: On status appears at the top of the Control Center. Your iPhone stops notifications. The Do Not Disturb status icon appears at the top of the Home screens so you know your iPhone is silent.

To make your notifications active again, tap the Do Not Disturb icon so it is gray; your iPhone resumes trying to get your attention when it is needed, and the Do Not Disturb status icon disappears from the top of the Home screens.

In Chapter 4, you learn how to set a schedule for Do Not Disturb so that your iPhone goes into this mode automatically at certain times, such as from 10 p.m. to 6 a.m. You can also configure certain exceptions, including whose calls come in even when your iPhone is in Do Not Disturb mode.

Using Airplane Mode

Although there's a debate about whether cellular devices such as iPhones pose any real danger to the operation of aircraft, there's no reason to run any risk by using your iPhone's cellular functions while you are on an airplane. (Besides, not following crew instructions on airplanes can lead you to less-than-desirable interactions with the flight crew.) When you place your iPhone in Airplane mode, its cellular transmitting and receiving functions are disabled, so it poses no threat to the operation of the aircraft. While it is in Airplane mode, you can't use the phone, the Web, Siri, or any other functions that require cellular communication between your iPhone and other devices or networks. You can continue to use Wi-Fi networks to access the Internet and Bluetooth to communicate with Bluetooth devices.

Tap to put your iPhone in Airplane mode

To put your iPhone in Airplane mode, open the Control Center and tap the Airplane mode icon. All connections to the cellular network stop, and your iPhone doesn't broadcast or receive any cellular signals. The Airplane mode icon becomes orange, and you see the Airplane mode status icon at the top of the screen.

This iPhone is in Airplane mode

In Airplane mode, you can use apps that don't require a cellular connection; for example, you can connect to a Wi-Fi network to work with email or browse the Web.

This iPhone is in Airplane mode

Tap to turn off Airplane mode

To turn off Airplane mode, open the Control Center and tap the Airplane mode icon; it becomes gray again and the Airplane mode status icon disappears. The iPhone resumes transmitting and receiving cellular signals, and all the functions that require a cellular connection start working again.

Meeting Siri

Siri is the iPhone's voice-recognition and control software. This feature, which now sounds more natural and less robotic than with previous versions of the iOS, enables you to accomplish many tasks by speaking. For example, you can create and send text messages, reply to emails, make phone calls, get directions, and much more. (Using Siri is explained in detail in Chapter 11, "Working with Siri.")

When you perform actions, Siri uses the related apps to accomplish what you've asked it to do. For example, when you create a meeting, Siri uses the Calendar app.

Siri is a great way to control your iPhone, especially when you are working in handsfree mode.

Your iPhone has to be connected to the Internet for Siri to work. That's because the words you speak are sent over the Internet, transcribed into text, and then sent back to your iPhone. If your iPhone isn't connected to the Internet, this can't happen and Siri reports that it can't connect to the network or simply that it can't do what you ask right now.

Using Siri is pretty simple because it follows a consistent pattern and prompts you for input and direction.

Siri is ready to do your bidding

Activate Siri by pressing and holding down the Touch ID/Home button (all models except iPhone X) or pressing and holding the Side button (iPhone X) until you hear the Siri chime. If so configured (see Chapter 11), you can say "Hey Siri" to activate it, too. And, if those ways aren't enough, you can press and hold down the center part of the buttons on the right EarPod wire.

All of these actions put Siri in "listening" mode, and the "What can I help you with?" text appears on the screen (when you use "Hey Siri" to activate it, the text is skipped and Siri gets right to work). This indicates Siri is ready for your command.

What Siri heard you say — Call Pappy Boyington / Tap to Edit

Siri is going to call Pappy and needs to know which number to call — Which phone number for Gregory Boyington?

Tell Siri which phone number to use by saying "iPhone" — iPhone (317) 805-■■■ / home (555) 555-■■■

Speak your command or ask a question. When you stop speaking, Siri goes into processing mode. After Siri interprets what you've said, it provides two kinds of feedback to confirm what it heard: It displays what it heard on the screen and provides audible feedback to you. Siri then tries to do what it thinks you've asked and shows you what it is doing. If it needs more input from you, you're prompted to provide it and Siri moves into "listening" mode automatically.

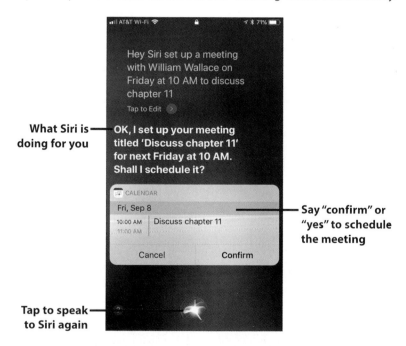

Hey Siri set up a meeting with William Wallace on Friday at 10 AM to discuss chapter 11 / Tap to Edit

What Siri is doing for you — OK, I set up your meeting titled 'Discuss chapter 11' for next Friday at 10 AM. Shall I schedule it?

CALENDAR / Fri, Sep 8 / 10:00 AM Discuss chapter 11 / 11:00 AM

Say "confirm" or "yes" to schedule the meeting

Cancel   Confirm

Tap to speak to Siri again

If Siri requests that you confirm what it is doing or make a selection, do so. Siri completes the action and displays what it has done; it also audibly confirms the result.

Siri isn't quite like using the computer on the Starship Enterprise on *Star Trek*, but it's pretty darn close. Mostly, you can just speak to Siri as you would talk to someone else, and it is able to do what you want or asks you the information it needs to do what you want.

Understanding iPhone Status Icons

At the top of the screen is the Status bar with various icons that provide you with information, such as if you are in Airplane mode, whether you are connected to a Wi-Fi or cellular data network, the time, whether the iPhone's orientation is locked, the state of the iPhone's battery, and so on. Keep an eye on this area as you use your iPhone. The following table provides a guide to the most common of these icons.

Icon	Description	Where to Learn More
	Signal strength—Indicates how strong the cellular signal is.	Chapter 2
AT&T	Provider name—The provider of the current cellular network.	Chapter 2
LTE	Cellular data network—Indicates which cellular network your iPhone is using to connect to the Internet.	Chapter 2
	Wi-Fi—Indicates your phone is connected to a Wi-Fi network.	Chapter 2
Wi-Fi	Wi-Fi calling—Indicates your phone can make voice calls over a Wi-Fi network.	Chapter 2
	Do Not Disturb—Your iPhone's notifications and ringer are silenced.	Chapters 1, 4
	Bluetooth—Indicates if Bluetooth is turned on or off and if your phone is connected to a device.	Chapter 15
79%	Battery percentage—Percentage of charge remaining in the battery.	Chapter 16
	Battery status—Relative level of charge of the battery.	Chapter 16
	Low Battery status—The battery has less than 20% power remaining.	Chapter 16
	Low Power mode—The iPhone is operating in Low Power mode.	Chapter 16

Icon	Description	Where to Learn More
	Orientation Lock—Your iPhone's screen won't change when you rotate your iPhone.	Chapter 1
	Charging—The battery in the iPhone is being charged.	Chapter 16
	Location Services—An app is using the Location Services feature to track your iPhone's location.	Chapter 4
	Airplane mode—The transmit and receive functions are disabled.	Chapter 1

Turning Your iPhone Off or On

Swipe to the right to turn your iPhone off

You seldom need to turn your iPhone off, but when you do, press and hold the Side button until the slider appears at the top of the screen. Swipe the slider to the right to shut down the iPhone. The iPhone shuts down.

To restart your iPhone, press and hold the Side button until the Apple logo appears on the screen, and then let go of the button.

On an iPhone 5s or SE, use the Sleep/Wake button located on the topside of the phone to turn it off or on.

After it starts up, assuming you have a passcode, you see the Enter Passcode screen. Enter your passcode to start using your phone; once your passcode is entered correctly, you move to the Home screen. (Even if you have Touch ID or Face ID enabled to unlock your phone, you must enter your passcode the first time you unlock it after a restart.)

If you don't have a passcode configured (you should have a passcode configured to protect your information), you move directly to the Home screen when the phone starts and it's ready for you to use. Keep in mind, if you do not have a passcode configured, your phone is vulnerable to anyone who gets hold of it. (See Chapter 5 for more information about configuring passcodes and Touch ID or the online supplement *My iPhone X* to learn how to work with Face ID.)

Sleeping/Locking and Waking/Unlocking Your iPhone

When your iPhone sleeps, it goes into a low power mode to extend battery life. Some processes keep working, such as playing music, whereas others stop until your iPhone wakes up. Almost all of the time, you'll put your iPhone to sleep rather than turning it off because it's much faster to wake up than to turn on. Because it uses so little power when it's asleep, there's not much reason to shut it down.

Also, when you put your iPhone to sleep, much of its functionality can't be used until it is unlocked; you can do a number of tasks, such as using widgets and viewing notifications, while the iPhone is awake, but locked. If you configure your iPhone to require a passcode to unlock, this also protects your information. Even when the iPhone is asleep, you can receive and work with notifications, such as when you receive emails or text messages. (See Chapter 4 to configure which notifications you see on the Lock screen and how you can interact with them.)

To put your iPhone to sleep and lock it, press the Side button (on an iPhone 5s or SE, use the Sleep/Wake button). The screen goes dark.

When an iPhone is asleep/locked, you need to wake it up to use it. You can do this in several ways: touch or press the Touch ID/Home button, press the Side button (Sleep/Wake on a 5s or SE) or simply raise the iPhone (on models that support the Raise to Wake feature). The Lock screen appears.

If you want to use app widgets (swipe to the right), access the Notification Center (swipe up from the middle of the screen), open the Control Center (swipe up from the bottom of the Home screen [all models except the iPhone X] or swipe down from the upper-right corner of the screen [iPhone X]), take photos or video (swipe to the left), or control audio playback (when audio is playing the controls appear on the Lock screen), you can do so directly on the Lock screen.

Swipe to the right to access widgets

Swipe up from the middle of the screen to open the Notification Center

Swipe up from the bottom of the screen to open the Control Center (all models except iPhone X)

Swipe down from the top-right corner of the screen to open the Control Center (iPhone X)

This iPhone is awake and locked

Control audio that is playing

Swipe to the left to take photos or video

When you are ready to use apps or access your Home screens, you need to unlock your iPhone. How you unlock your iPhone depends on its state and the model you are using.

If you don't have a passcode, which you should have, you can press the Touch ID/Home button (all models except iPhone X) or swipe up from the bottom of the screen (iPhone X) to unlock it.

If you have configured a passcode (see Chapter 4), there are two states your iPhone can be in; how you unlock it depends on its state.

Enter your passcode to start using your iPhone

If you restarted your iPhone, you need to enter its passcode, even if you have Touch ID or Face ID configured to unlock it.

If you have an iPhone with Touch ID configured to unlock it (see Chapter 4), press the Touch ID/Home button with a finger whose fingerprint has been stored for use; if you are using an iPhone 7 or later model (except the iPhone X), you don't need to press the Touch ID/Home button and can simply touch it instead. When your fingerprint is recognized, your iPhone unlocks and you can start using it.

If you have an iPhone X with Face ID configured to unlock it, you swipe up from the bottom of the screen and look at the screen. When the iPhone recognizes your face, the phone unlocks and you can use it.

If your iPhone doesn't have Touch ID or Face ID configured to unlock it, press the Touch ID/Home button (all models except iPhone X) or swipe up from the bottom of the screen (iPhone X) and enter your passcode to unlock your phone.

Be Recognized

To use the Touch ID, you need to train your iPhone to recognize the fingerprints you want to use. You were prompted to configure one fingerprint when you started your iPhone for the first time. You can change or add fingerprints for Touch ID at any time; see Chapter 4 for the details of configuring Touch ID.

iPhone X Face ID

Refer to the online supplement *My iPhone X* by going to www.informit.com/myiphone11 for the details of configuring and using Face ID on an iPhone X.

However you unlock the phone, when it unlocks, you move to the last screen you were using before it was locked.

The Time Is Always Handy

If you use your iPhone as a watch the way I do, just wake it up. The current time and date appear; if you don't unlock it, the iPhone goes back to sleep after a few seconds.

If you don't use your iPhone for a while, it automatically goes to sleep and locks according to the preference you have set for it (this is covered in Chapter 5).

Working with Touch ID or Face ID

You can use Touch ID and Face ID to quickly, easily, and securely provide a password or passcode in many different situations, such as unlocking your iPhone, downloading apps from the App Store, signing into an account in a banking or other app, and so on.

Touch the Touch ID button to download an app from the App Store

Once configured, using Touch ID is as simple as touching a recorded fingerprint to the Touch ID/Home button when you are prompted to do so. The resulting action is completed, such as downloading an app from the App Store. (As referenced in the prior note, you need to configure your iPhone to recognize your fingerprints to use Touch ID and to enable where it can be used; see Chapter 4 for details.)

Face ID works similarly except that instead of touching the Touch ID/Home button, you look at the screen. When the iPhone recognizes your face, the action is completed.

More iPhone X Face ID

Refer to the online supplement *My iPhone X* by going to www.informit.com/myiphone11 for the details of working with Face ID an iPhone X.

If you don't have the settings configured to enable you to use Touch ID or Face ID or you use an app that doesn't support Touch ID or Face ID, you need to provide your password when prompted to do so. Whatever action you were performing is completed.

Setting Volume

Setting the
ringer volume

To change the iPhone's volume, press the up or down Volume button on the side of the iPhone. When you change the volume, your change affects the current activity. For example, if you are on a phone call, the call volume changes, or if you are listening to music, the music's volume changes. If you aren't on a screen that shows a Volume slider, an icon pops up to show you the relative volume you are setting and the type, such as setting the ringer's volume. When the volume is right, release the Volume button.

Swipe up or
down to change
the volume level

You can also use the Volume slider on the Control Center to change the volume level.

Drag to the
left or right
to change the
volume level

When you are using an audio app, such as the Music app, you can also drag the volume slider in that app or on the Control Center to increase or decrease the volume. Drag the slider to the left to lower volume or to the right to increase it.

When you use the iPhone's EarPods, you can change the volume by pressing the upper part of the switch on the right EarPod's wire to increase volume or the lower part to decrease it.

To mute your phone's sounds, slide the Mute switch, located on the left side of the phone, toward the back of the phone. You see an on-screen indicator that the phone is muted and you see orange within the Mute switch on the side of the iPhone; notification and other sounds won't play. To restore normal sound, slide the switch toward the front of the phone.

Unintentional Muting

If your phone suddenly stops ringing when calls come in or doesn't play notification sounds that you think it should, always check the Mute switch to ensure it hasn't been activated accidentally or that you forgot that you had muted your iPhone. (There's no indication on the screen that the iPhone is currrently muted, so you have to look at the switch to tell.)

Connect to the Internet via Wi-Fi or a cellular network

Use the Settings app to configure your iPhone

Notifications, such as badges, keep you informed

Use the iPhone's great text tools in many apps

Take advantage of an Internet connection in many different apps

Print email and other documents from your phone

In this chapter, you learn to use some of your iPhone's core features. Topics include the following:

→ Working with the Settings app
→ Connecting to the Internet using Wi-Fi networks
→ Connecting to the Internet using cellular data networks
→ Working with text
→ Using widgets
→ Searching on your iPhone
→ Working with Siri Suggestions
→ Working with notifications
→ Printing from your iPhone

2

Using Your iPhone's Core Features

In Chapter 1, "Getting Started with Your iPhone," you learned how to interact with your iPhone including using apps, locking and unlocking it, swiping to open and close things, and zooming in or out. In this chapter, you learn to use some of the iPhone's "core" features, meaning those that apply across multiple apps and functions of your iPhone. For example, an Internet connection is required by many, and used by most, of the apps on your iPhone. As another example, you'll be typing or speaking text in many different situations from emails to messages to searches, so it's fundamental to know how to work with text on your iPhone. Getting comfortable with these core features helps you do the many other things you can do with your iPhone that you learn about throughout the rest of this book.

Working with the Settings App

Aptly named, the Settings app is where you configure the many settings that change how your iPhone looks, sounds, and works. In fact, virtually everything you do on your iPhone is affected by settings in this app. As you use and make an iPhone into *your* iPhone, you frequently visit the Settings app.

Using the Settings App on Any iPhone

You can work with the Settings app on any iPhone as follows:

1. On the Home screen, tap Settings. The Settings app opens. The app is organized in sections starting at the top with your Apple ID information followed by Airplane Mode, Wi-Fi, Bluetooth, and Cellular.

2. Swipe up or down the screen to get to the settings area you want to use.

3. Tap the area you want to configure, such as Sounds & Haptics (iPhone 7 or later) or Sounds (earlier models).

4. Use the resulting controls to con-figure that area. The changes you make take effect immediately.

5. When you're done, you can leave the Settings app where it is (it remains there when you come back to it) or tap the back icon, which is always located in the upper-left corner of the screen (its name changes based on where you are in the app), until you get back to the main Settings screen to go into other Settings areas.

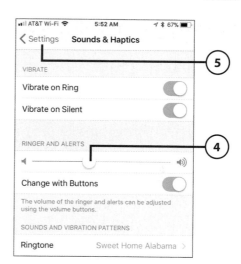

Searching for Settings

You can quickly find settings you need by searching for them:

1. Move into the Settings app. (If you aren't on the main Settings screen, tap the back icon until you get there.)

2. Tap in the Search bar; if you don't see the Search bar, swipe down from the top of the Settings screen until it appears.

3. Type the setting for which you want to search. As you type, potential matches are shown on the list of results. Matches can include a settings area, such as Sounds & Haptics, or specific set-tings, such as the ringtone and vibrations used when you receive a call.

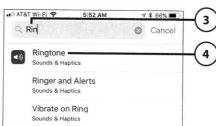

4. Tap the setting you want to use.

5. Configure the setting you select-ed in the previous step.

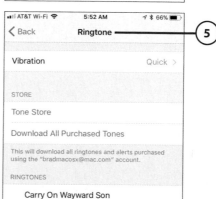

Using the Settings App on an iPhone Plus

When you hold an iPhone Plus in the horizontal orientation and use the Settings app, you can take advantage of the split-screen feature as follows:

1. Hold the iPhone Plus so it is horizontal.

2. Tap the Settings app to open it. In the left pane, you see the areas of the Settings app that you can configure. In the right pane, you see tools you can use to configure the selected setting. The two panes are independent, making navigation easier than with other iPhones.

3. Swipe up or down on the left pane until you see the function, feature, or app you want to configure.

4. Tap the function, feature, or app you want to configure, such as Sounds. Its controls appear in the right pane.

5. Swipe up or down on the right pane until you see the specific setting you want to change.

6. Tap the setting you want to configure, such as Ringtone. Its controls appear in the right pane.

Settings pane   **Tools to configure the selected setting**

Selected setting

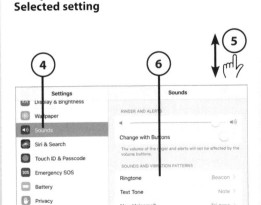

7. Use the tools in the right pane to configure the setting you selected in step 6. These work just as described in the previous task and throughout this chapter except that you move within the right pane instead of changing the entire screen.

8. To move back through the screens in the right pane, use the back icon, which is labeled with the name of the screen you came from.

9. Tap another area in the left pane to configure it. As you can see, the split screen makes it very easy to quickly switch between areas in the Settings app.

Connecting to the Internet Using Wi-Fi Networks

Your iPhone is designed to seamlessly connect to the Internet so apps that use the Internet to work, such as Safari to browse the Web, are always ready when you need them. Wi-Fi networks provide fast Internet connections and you usually have an unlimited amount of data to work with, so you don't have to worry about paying more based on how you are using your iPhone. Because of their speed and unlimited data (usually), Wi-Fi networks are the best way for your iPhone to connect to the Internet.

Wi-Fi networks are available just about everywhere you go, including homes, offices, hotels, restaurants, and other locations. Fortunately, it's very easy to connect your iPhone to the Wi-Fi networks you encounter. (And, if there isn't a Wi-Fi network available, your iPhone uses its cellular data network to connect to the Internet, which is covered later in this chapter.)

Almost all Wi-Fi networks broadcast their information so that you can easily see them with your iPhone; these are called open networks because anyone who is in range can attempt to join one because they appear on Wi-Fi devices automatically. The Wi-Fi networks you can see on your iPhone in public places (such as airports and hotels) are all open. Likewise, any Wi-Fi networks in your home or office are very likely to be open as well. To connect your iPhone to an open network, you tap its name and then enter its password (if required).

Your iPhone remembers Wi-Fi networks you've connected to previously and joins one of them automatically when available; these are called *known* networks. For example, if you have a Wi-Fi network at home and another in your office, when you change locations, your iPhone automatically changes Wi-Fi networks.

If your iPhone can't connect to a known network, it automatically searches for other Wi-Fi networks to join. If one or more are available, a prompt appears showing the networks available to your iPhone. You can select and join one of these networks by tapping its name on the list of networks and entering its password (if one is required, you need to obtain it from the source of the network, such as a hotel or restaurant).

If no Wi-Fi networks are available or you choose not to connect to one, your iPhone automatically switches to its cellular data connection (covered in "Connecting to the Internet Using Cellular Data Networks" later in this chapter).

Connecting to Open Wi-Fi Networks

To connect your iPhone to a Wi-Fi network, perform the following steps:

1. On the Home screen, tap Settings. Next to Wi-Fi, you see the status of your Wi-Fi connection. It is Off if Wi-Fi is turned off, Not Connected if Wi-Fi is turned on and your phone isn't currently connected to Wi-Fi, or the name of the Wi-Fi network to which your iPhone is connected.

2. Tap Wi-Fi.

3. If Wi-Fi isn't enabled already, slide the Wi-Fi switch to on (green) and your iPhone searches for available networks. A list of available networks is displayed in the CHOOSE A NETWORK section (it can take a moment for all the networks available in the area to be shown). Along with each network's name, icons indicating whether it requires a password (the padlock icon) to join and the current signal strength (the radio waves icon) are displayed.

Current Wi-Fi status

Quick Access to the Wi-Fi Switch

You can quickly turn Wi-Fi on or off by swiping up from the bottom of the Home screen (all models except the iPhone X) or swiping down from the upper-right corner of the screen (iPhone X) to open the Control Center. If the Wi-Fi icon (it looks like the signal strength indicator on the Wi-Fi Setting screen) is blue, Wi-Fi is on. Tap that icon to turn Wi-Fi off (the icon becomes gray). Tap it again to turn Wi-Fi on and reconnect to a known network. See Chapter 1 for more information about working with the Control Center.

4. Tap the network you want to join. Of course, when a network requires a password, you must know that password to be able to join it. Another consideration should be signal strength; the more waves in the network's signal strength icon, the stronger the connection.

5. At the prompt, enter the password for the network you selected. If you aren't prompted for a password, skip to step 7. (You're likely to find networks that don't require a password in public places; see the next section for information on these types of networks.)

6. Tap Join. If you provided the correct password, your iPhone connects to the network and gets the information it needs to connect to the Internet. If not, you're prompted to enter the password again. After you successfully connect to the network, you return to the Wi-Fi screen.

7. Review the network information. The network to which you are connected appears just below the Wi-Fi switch and is marked with a check mark. You also see the signal strength for that network.

8. Try to move to a web page, such as www.bradmiser.com, to test your Wi-Fi connection. (See Chapter 12, "Surfing the Web," for details.) If the web page opens, you are ready to use the Internet on your phone. If you are taken to a login web page for a Wi-Fi provider rather than the page you were trying to access, see the next task. If you see a message saying the Internet is not available, there is a problem with the network you joined. Go back to step 4 to select a different network.

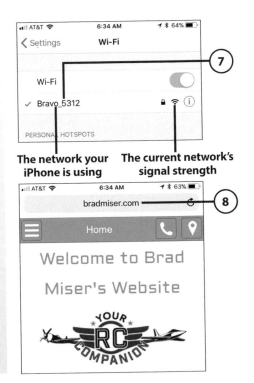

The network your iPhone is using   The current network's signal strength

>>>Go Further
CONNECTING TO WI-FI NETWORKS

As you connect to Wi-Fi networks, consider the following:

- **Typing passwords**—As you type a password, each character is hidden by a dot in the Password field except for the last character you entered, which is displayed on the screen for a moment. Keep an eye on characters as you enter them because you can fix a mistake as soon as you make it rather than finding out after you've entered the entire password and having to start over.

- **Changing networks**—You can use these same steps to change the Wi-Fi network you are using at any time. For example, if you have to pay to use one network while a different one is free, simply choose the free network in step 4.

- **Be known**—After your iPhone connects to a Wi-Fi network successfully, it becomes a known network. This means that your iPhone remembers its information so you don't have to enter it again. Your iPhone automatically connects to known networks when it needs to access the Internet. So unless you tell your iPhone to forget a network (explained later in this chapter), you need to enter its password only the first time you connect to it.

- **Security recommendation**—If you are connected to a network that doesn't use what Apple considers sufficient, you see the words "Security Recommendation" under the network's name. If you tap that network, you see its Info screen. At the top of that screen, you see the type of security the network is using and a recommendation about the type of security it should use. If the Wi-Fi network comes from a router or modem you own or rent, contact your Internet service provider, such as a cable company, to learn how the security provided by that router or modem can be reconfigured to be more secure. If the network is in a public place or business, you just have to use it as is (unless you can contact the administrator of that network to see if better security is available).

- **Personal hotspots**— iPhones and iPads can share their cellular Internet connection (how to do this is covered in a later Go Further sidebar) with other devices by providing a Wi-Fi network to which you can connect your iPhone. The icons for these networks are a bit different, being two connected loops that indicate the network is from a hotspot. You can select and use these networks just like the other types of networks being described in this chapter. The speed of your access is determined mostly by the speed of the device's cellular data connection. Also, the data you use while connected to the hotspot's network counts against the data plan for the device to which you are connected.

Connecting to Public Wi-Fi Networks

Many Wi-Fi networks in public places, such as hotels or airports, require that you pay a fee or provide other information to access the Internet through that network; even if access is free, you usually have to accept terms and conditions for the network to be able to use it.

When you connect to one of these public networks, you're prompted to provide whatever information is required. This can involve different details for different networks, but the general steps are the same. You're prompted to provide whatever information required. Then, follow the instructions that appear.

Following are the general steps to connect to many types of public Wi-Fi networks:

1. Move to the Settings screen.

2. Tap Wi-Fi.

3. Tap the network you want to join. You move to that network's Log In screen. Follow the onscreen prompts to complete the process. This often involves selecting a connection option and providing payment or identification information, as this example of connecting to a hotel's Wi-Fi network shows.

4. Choose the connection option you want to use.

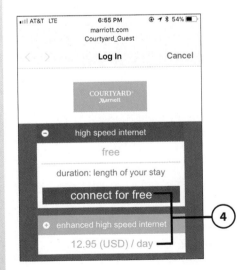

5. Provide the information required to join the network, such as a last name and room number. If a fee is required, you have to provide payment information. In many cases, you at least have to indicate that you accept the terms and conditions for using the network, which you typically do by checking a check box.

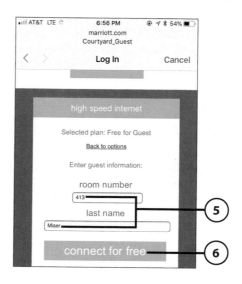

6. Tap the icon to join the network. This icon can have different labels depending on the type of access, such as Connect, Authenticate, Done, Free Access, Login, and so on.

7. Tap Done (if required).

8. Try to move to a web page, such as www.wikipedia.org, to test your Wi-Fi connection (not shown in a figure). (See Chapter 12 for details.) If the web page opens, you are ready to use the Internet on your phone. If you are taken to a login web page for the Wi-Fi network's provider, you need to provide the required information to be able to use the Internet. For example, when access is free, as it is at most airports, you usually just have to indicate you accept the terms of use for that network.

No Prompt?

Not all public networks prompt you to log in as these steps explain. Sometimes, you use the network's website to log in instead. After you join the network (step 3), your iPhone is connected to the network without any prompts. When you try to move to a web page as explained in step 8, you're prompted to log in to or create an account with the network's provider on the web page that appears.

A Closed Network

Some Wi-Fi networks are closed, which means they don't broadcast their names. This means that you don't see closed networks listed in the CHOOSE A NETWORK section on the Wi-Fi screen. To be able to access a closed network, you need to know its name, its password, and the type of security it uses. With this information in hand, tap Other in the CHOOSE A NETWORK section. Then type the network's name. Tap Security, choose the appropriate type, and tap Other Network. Enter the network's password and tap Join.

Disabling Automatic Prompting

When your iPhone can't find a known network—meaning one that you've used before—it presents a prompt showing you the currently available networks. You can use this prompt to select and join one of these networks. This can be useful because you don't have to use the Settings app to find a network to which you are going to connect; instead, you can just tap a network at the prompt to join it.

However, this automatic prompting for networks can be as annoying as it is helpful. It is helpful in that your iPhone prompts you when it comes into range of a network it doesn't know, which can make it easier to know when a network is available to you. It can be annoying when you are moving around a lot because what you are doing can be frequently interrupted by the prompt, even if you don't want to connect to one of the available networks. For example, when you walk through an airport, the prompt can appear multiple times as you move between networks.

To disable automatic network prompting, perform the following steps:

1. Open the Settings app and move to the Wi-Fi screen.

2. Set the Ask to Join Networks switch to off (white). To connect to unknown networks, you need to use the Settings app as described in the previous tasks because your iPhone no longer automatically prompts you to join unknown networks. (Remember that it still joins known networks, meaning those you have used before, automatically.)

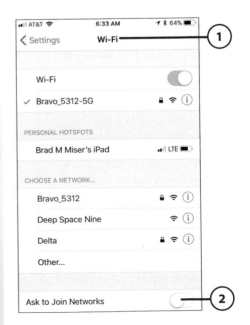

Forgetting Wi-Fi Networks

As you learned earlier, your iPhone remembers networks you have joined and connects to them automatically as needed; these are known networks. Although this is mostly a good thing, there are times when you no longer want to use a particular network any more. For example, when in an airport, you might decide to connect to a network for which you have to pay for faster Internet access, or you might prefer to access the Internet using cellular service. Each time you move through that airport, your iPhone connects to that network again automatically, which might not be what you want it to do.

To have your iPhone forget a network so it doesn't automatically connect to it in the future, do the following:

1. Tap Wi-Fi in the Settings app to view the Wi-Fi screen.

2. Tap the Info icon for the network that you want your iPhone to forget. (You can forget a network only if you are or have previously been connected to it.)

3. Tap Forget This Network.

4. Tap Forget in the resulting prompt. Your iPhone stops using and forgets the network. You return to the Wi-Fi screen. If another known network is available, your iPhone connects to it automatically. If a network you've forgotten is still in range of your iPhone, it continues to appear in the CHOOSE A NETWORK section, but your iPhone no longer automatically connects to it. You can re-join a forgotten network at any time, just as you did the first time you connected to it.

Forget Versus Auto-Join

When you forget a network, your iPhone stops connecting to it automatically and erases the network's password so you have to enter it again if you want to re-join that network. If you just want to stop automatically joining the network but keep its password on your iPhone, set the Auto-Join switch to off (white) instead of performing step 3. Your iPhone stops automatically connecting to that network, but you can re-join it at any time by tapping it on the CHOOSE A NETWORK list (you don't have to re-enter the password as you do if you forget a network).

Cell Phone Provider Wi-Fi Networks

Many cell phone providers also provide other services, particularly public Wi-Fi networks. In some cases, you can access that provider's Internet service through a Wi-Fi network that it provides; often, you can do this at no additional charge. So, you can take advantage of the speed a Wi-Fi connection provides without paying more for it. You connect to these networks just like any other by selecting them on the network list. What happens next depends on the specific network. In some cases, you need to enter your mobile phone number and then respond to a text message to that phone number. Check your provider's website to find out whether it offers this service and where and how you can access it.

Connecting to the Internet Using Cellular Data Networks

When you don't have a Wi-Fi network available or you don't want to use one that is available (such as if it has a fee or is slow), your iPhone can connect to the Internet through a cellular data network.

The provider for your iPhone also provides a cellular data connection your iPhone uses to connect to the Internet automatically when you aren't using a Wi-Fi network (such as when you are in a location that doesn't have one). (Your iPhone tries to connect to an available Wi-Fi network before connecting to a cellular data connection, because Wi-Fi is typically less expensive and faster to use.) These cellular networks cover large geographic areas and the connection to them is automatic; your iPhone chooses and connects to the best cellular network currently available. Access to these networks is part of your monthly account fee; you choose from among various amounts of data per month for different monthly fees.

Most providers have multiple cellular data networks, such as a low-speed network that is available widely and one or more higher-speed networks that have a more limited coverage area. Your iPhone chooses the best connection available automatically.

The cellular data networks you can use are determined based on your provider, your data plan, the model of iPhone you are using, and your location within your provider's networks or the roaming networks available, when you are outside of your provider's coverage area. The iPhone automatically uses the fastest connection available to it at any given time (assuming you haven't disabled that option, as explained later).

In the United States, the major iPhone providers are AT&T, Verizon, T-Mobile, and Sprint. There are also other smaller providers, such as Virgin Mobile. All these companies offer high-speed Long Term Evolution (LTE) cellular networks (these are also referred to as true 4G networks) along with the slower 4G and 3G networks. In other locations, the names and speeds of the networks available might be different.

The following information is focused on LTE networks because I happen to live in the United States and use AT&T as my cell phone provider. If you use another provider, you are able to access your provider's networks similarly, though your details might be different. For example, the icon on the Home screen reflects the name of your provider's network, which might or might not be LTE.

This iPhone is connected to a high-speed LTE cellular network

LTE high-speed wireless networks provide very fast Internet access from many locations. (Note: LTE networks might not be available everywhere, but you can usually access them near populated areas.) To connect to the LTE network, you don't need to do anything. If you aren't connected to a Wi-Fi network, you haven't turned off LTE, and your iPhone isn't in Airplane mode, the iPhone automatically connects to an LTE network when available. When you are connected to the LTE network, you see the LTE indicator at the top of the iPhone's screen. If you can't access the LTE network, such as when you aren't in its coverage area, the iPhone automatically connects to the next fastest network available, such as 4G. If that isn't available, it connects to the next fastest and so on until it finds a network to which it can connect if there is one available. If it can't connect to any network, you see No Service instead of a network's name; this indicates that you currently can't connect to any network, and so you aren't able to access the Internet.

One thing you do need to keep in mind when using a cellular network is that your account might include a limited amount of data per month. When your data use exceeds this limit, you might be charged overage fees, which can be very expensive. Most providers send you warning texts or emails as your data use approaches your plan's limit, at which point you need to be careful about what you do while using the cellular data network to avoid an over-age fee. Some tasks, such as watching YouTube videos or downloading large movie files, can chew up a lot of data very quickly and should be saved for when you are on a Wi-Fi network to avoid exceeding your plan's monthly data allowance. Other tasks, such as using email, typically don't use very much.

Unlimited Data

If you don't already have an account with unlimited data, check with your provid-er periodically to see if an unlimited data plan is available for a reasonable price. As competition has increased among cell providers, unlimited data plans have become more common and less expensive in many areas. If other cell provid-ers are available to you, check to see if they offer unlimited data plans; if so, you can consider changing providers or using a competitor's plan to lower the cost of your plan. Having an unlimited data plan is good because you don't need to worry about overage charges from using more data than your plan allows.

An App for That

Various apps are available in the App Store that you can install on your iPhone that monitor how much data you are using. These apps are a good way to know where your data use is relative to your plan's monthly allowance so that you can avoid an overage situation. To get information on finding, downloading, and installing apps, see the section "Using the App Store App to Find and Install iPhone Apps" in Chapter 4, "Customizing How Your iPhone Works." (To find an app for this purpose, search for "data monitoring app.")

When you move outside your primary network's geographic coverage area, you are in roaming territory, which means a different provider might provide cellular phone or data access, or both. The iPhone automatically selects a roaming provider, if there is only one available, or allows you to choose one, if there is more than one available.

When you are outside of your primary provider's coverage area, roaming charges can be associated with calls or data use. These charges are often very expensive. The roaming charges associated with phone calls are easier to manage, because it's more obvious when you make or receive a phone call in a roaming area. However, data roaming charges are much more insidious, especially if Push functionality (where emails and other updates are pushed to your iPhone from the server automatically) is active. And when you use some applications, such as Maps to navigate, you don't really know how much data is involved. Because data roaming charges are harder to notice, the iPhone is configured by default to prevent data roaming. When data roaming is disabled, the iPhone is unable to access the Internet when you are outside of your cellular network, unless you connect to a Wi-Fi network. (You can still use the cellular roaming network for telephone calls.)

You can configure some aspects of how your cellular network is used, as the following task demonstrates. You can also allow individual apps to use, or prevent them from using, your cellular data network. This is especially important when your data plan has a monthly limit.

In most cases, the first time you launch an app, you're prompted to allow or prevent it from using cellular data. At any time, you can use the Cellular Data options in the Settings app to enable or disable an app's access to your cellular data network.

The options you have for configuring how your iPhone uses its cellular data connection depend on the provider your iPhone is connected to and the model of iPhone you use. For example, if you live in the United States and use Sprint as your cellular provider, the Cellular screens in the Settings app look a bit different than the figures in this section (which are based on AT&T's service). Regardless of the specific options you see on your phone, the basic purpose is the same, which is to configure how your iPhone uses its high-speed network and to enable and disable roaming.

Configuring Cellular Data Use

The following steps show configuring cellular data use on an iPhone using AT&T in the United States; you can use similar steps to configure these options on an iPhone from a different provider:

1. Open the Settings app.

2. Tap Cellular.

3. To use a cellular Internet connection, set the Cellular Data switch to on (green) and move to step 4; if you don't want to use a cellular Internet connection, set this switch to off (white) and skip the rest of these steps. To use the Internet when the Cellular Data switch is off, you have to connect to a Wi-Fi network that provides Internet access.

4. Tap Cellular Data Options.

5. To configure the high-speed network, tap Enable *high-speed network*, where *high-speed network* is the name of the high-speed network your provider has. With some providers, this is a switch that enables or disables the high-speed network; set the switch to be on or off and skip to step 8 (if you set the switch to off, the iPhone can't use the higher-speed network, but can use slower networks).

6. To disable the high-speed network, tap Off; to use it for both voice and data, tap Voice & Data; or to use it only for data, tap Data Only. (When you enable the high-speed network for voice, the quality of the sound of your calls may be better.)

7. Tap the back icon.

8. If you want to allow data roaming, slide the Data Roaming switch to the on (green) position. With some providers, Roaming is an option instead of a switch; tap Roaming and use the resulting switches to enable or disable roaming for voice or data and then tap the back icon.

9. Tap Cellular.

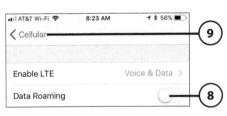

10. Use the controls in the *PROVIDER*, where *PROVIDER* is the name of your provider, to configure how the cellular service interacts with other services, such as to enable Wi-Fi calling, calls on other devices, and so on. These settings are explained in Chapter 7, "Communicating with the Phone and FaceTime Apps."

11. Swipe up the screen until you see the CELLULAR DATA section. This section enables you to allow or prevent individual apps from accessing a cellular data network. To limit the amount of data you use, it's a good idea to review this list and allow only those apps that you rely on to use the cellular data network. (Of course, if you are fortunate enough to have an unlimited cellular data plan, you can leave cellular data for all the apps enabled.) This list can be quite long if you have a lot of apps stored on your iPhone.

12. Set an app's switch to on (green) if you want it to be able to use a cellular data network to access the Internet.

13. Set an app's switch to off (white) if you want it to be able to access the Internet only when you are connected to a Wi-Fi network.

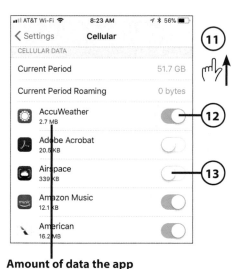

**Amount of data the app
has used since last reset**

Unlimited Data, Limited Speed?

Under an unlimited data plan, some providers limit the speed at which your cellular data service operates if you pass a threshold amount of data used that month. You can continue to use all the data you want, but the performance of the connection might be slower. Check your plan's details to see what the threshold is and what speed reduction is applied.

14. Set the Wi-Fi Assist switch to on (green) if you want your iPhone to automatically switch to its cellular connection when the Wi-Fi connection is weak. If you have a limited cellular data plan, you might want to set this switch to off (white) to minimize cellular data use.

15. If you want to access files on your iCloud drive when you aren't using a Wi-Fi network, set the iCloud Drive switch to on (green). If you set this switch to off, files are synced the next time you connect to a Wi-Fi network.

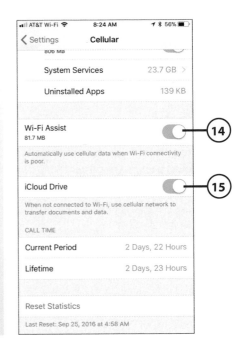

>>>Go Further
MORE ON CELLULAR DATA

Using a cellular network to connect to the Internet means you seldom have to be without a connection unless you choose to be. Here are some things to keep in mind as you keep connected:

- **GSM versus CDMA**—There are two fundamental types of cellular networks, which are GSM (Global System for Mobile Communications) or CDMA (Code-Division Multiple Access). The cellular provider you use determines which type of network your iPhone uses; the two types are not compatible. GSM is used by most of the world whereas some very large carriers in the United States (such as Verizon and Sprint) use CDMA. There are differences between the two, which is why you might see different cellular options than shown in the figures here (which show the options for AT&T, which uses GSM). If your iPhone uses CDMA, you see the International CDMA switch on the Roaming screen. If your phone has poor performance when you are roaming in different countries, set this switch to off (white).

- **Cellular data usage**—In the Cellular Data section, you see how much data you've used for the current period and how much you've used while roaming. This can help you see where your use is compared to your monthly plan allowance (if you have a monthly plan allowance of course) so you know whether you are getting close to exceeding that allowance (thus incurring overage charges). This isn't proactive at all, as you have to remember to check the information. If you are concerned about data use, you're better off getting an app with more active monitoring, as discussed earlier in this chapter in the "An App for That" note.

If you tap System Services at the bottom of the list of apps on the Cellular screen, you see the data usage for core system functions, such as Time & Location, Messaging Services, and Siri. This can be useful information to see how much data these services use, especially when you are in a roaming situation. You can limit the data use by some of these services by not accessing the related function; for example, you can turn off Siri to prevent it from using cellular data.

- **Higher-speed networks use more power**—Using a higher-speed network, such as an LTE network, also uses somewhat more battery power than using a slower network. If getting the absolute maximum time on a charge is important, you might want to disable the high-speed network.

- **Apps' cellular data use**—Just under each app's name in the CELLULAR DATA section, you see how much data the app has used since the counter was reset. This number can help you determine how much data a particular app uses. For example, if an app's use is shown in megabytes (MB), it's used a lot more data than an app whose use is shown in kilobytes (KB).

- **Cellular data use reset**—You can reset all of the statistics on the Cellular screen by swiping up until you reach the bottom of the screen and tapping Reset Statistics. Tap Reset Statistics again.

- **Personal hotspot**—The iPhone can be a personal hotspot, which is when it provides an Internet connection to computers or other devices through its cellular data connection. This is useful when you are in a location where you can't connect a computer or other device to a Wi-Fi or cellular network with Internet access (or don't want to spend the money to do so) but can access the Internet with the iPhone's cellular data connection.

There are a lot of caveats to this service, including whether your provider offers it, additional costs, and so on. Check with your provider to see if the personal hotspot feature is supported and if there are additional fees to use it. If it is provided and the fees are acceptable, this is a good way to provide Internet access to other devices when a Wi-Fi or cellular connection either isn't available or is too expensive.

First, add the personal hotspot service to your cellular account. Second, move to the Cellular screen in the Settings app, and then tap Set Up Personal Hotspot (if you don't see this option, your provider doesn't offer personal hotspot service). Follow the onscreen prompts to complete the configuration of the personal hotspot; the details depend on the specific provider you are using. After your iPhone is configured as a hotspot, it can share its Internet connection with other devices. To allow access to the Internet through your phone's hotspot, provide the name of its network and password (which are both automatically generated when you enable the hotspot) to the people you want to allow to use your hotspot.

Working with Text

You can do lots of things with an iPhone that require you to provide text input. There are a couple of ways you can do this, the most obvious of which is by typing. The iPhone's keyboard is quite amazing. Whenever you need it, whether it's for emailing, messaging, entering a website URL, performing a search, or any other typing function, it pops up automatically.

Tap to enter Predictive Text

Tap to change keyboards

Tap to dictate to your iPhone

Tap and hold to open the Keyboard menu

Tap to type numbers or special characters

Use the iPhone's virtual keyboard to type

To type, just tap the keys. As you tap each key, you hear audio feedback (you can disable this sound if you want to) and the key you tapped pops up in a magnified view on the screen. The keyboard includes all the standard keys, plus a few for special uses. To change from letters to numbers and special characters, just tap the 123 key. Tap the #+= key to see more special characters. Tap the 123 key to move back to the numbers and special characters or the ABC key to return to letters. The keyboard also has contextual keys that appear when you need them. For example, when you enter a website address, the .com key appears so you can enter these four characters with a single tap.

Working with Predictive Text

You can also use Predictive Text, which is the feature that tries to predict text you want to enter based on the context of what you are currently typing and what you have typed before. Predictive Text appears in the bar between the text and the keyboard and presents you with three options. If one of those is what you want to enter, tap it and it is added to the text at the current location of the cursor. If you don't see an option you want to enter, keep typing and the options change as the text changes. You can tap an option at any time to enter it. The nice thing about Predictive Text is that it gets better at predicting your text needs over time. In other words, the more you use it, the better it gets at predicting what you want to type. You can also enable or disable Predictive Text, as you see shortly.

Predictive Text Need Not Apply

When you are entering text where Predictive Text doesn't apply, such as when you are typing email addresses, the Predictive Text bar is hidden and can't be enabled. This makes sense because there's no way text in things such as email addresses can be predicted. When you move back into an area where it does apply, Predictive Text becomes active again.

Working with Keyboards

The great thing about a virtual keyboard like the iPhone has is that it can change to reflect the language or symbols you want to type. As you learn in Chapter 4, you can install multiple keyboards, such as one for your primary language and more for your secondary languages. You can also install third-party keyboards to take advantage of their features (this is also covered in Chapter 4).

By default, two keyboards are available for you to use. One is for the primary language configured for your iPhone (for example, mine is U.S. English). The other is the Emoji keyboard (more on this shortly). How you change the keyboard you are using depends on whether you have installed additional keyboards and the orientation of the iPhone.

If you haven't installed additional keyboards, you can change keyboards by tapping the Emoji key, which has a smiley face on it.

If you have installed other keyboards, you change keyboards by tapping the Globe key.

Each time you tap this key (Globe if available, Emoji if there isn't a Globe), the keyboard changes to be the next keyboard installed; along with the available keys changing, you briefly see the name of the current keyboard in the Space bar. When you have cycled through all the keyboards, you return to the one where you started.

The Keys, They Are A-Changin'

The keys on the keyboard can change depending on the orientation of the iPhone. For example, when you have more than one keyboard installed and hold the iPhone vertically, the Emoji key disappears and you see only the Globe key. Not to worry though, you can still get to the Emoji keyboard by tapping the Globe key until the Emoji keyboard appears, or by opening the Keyboard menu and tapping Emoji. When you have installed additional keyboards and hold the iPhone horizontally, you see both the Globe and Emoji keys. Tap the Emoji key to switch to that keyboard or the Globe key to cycle through all the keyboards.

Tap to configure keyboards and text options ——

Tap a keyboard to use it

You can also select the specific keyboard you want to use and access keyboard and text options by touching and holding on the Globe key (or the Emoji key, if you don't see the Globe key). The Keyboard menu appears. Tap a keyboard to switch to it. Tap Keyboard Settings to jump to the Keyboards screen in the Settings app where you can configure keyboards and enable or disable text options (these settings are covered in Chapter 4).

Tap to use a one-handed keyboard

Tap to use the full-screen keyboard

Tap to use the full-screen keyboard again

Keyboard for typing with the right thumb

Because you often type on your iPhone while you are moving around, it has a one-handed keyboard. This keyboard "squishes" all the keys to the left or right side of the screen to suit typing with a thumb. To use a one-handed keyboard, tap and hold the Globe or Emoji key to open the keyboard menu (this only works when the iPhone is held vertically). Tap the left or right keyboard; the keyboard compresses toward the side you selected and you can more easily tap its keys with one thumb. To return to the full-screen keyboard, tap the right- or left-facing arrow that appears in the "empty" space on the side of the screen not being used for the keyboard or open the Keyboard menu and tap the full-screen keyboard.

Using Emojis

Tap an emoji to enter it

Swipe to browse emojis

Tap to return to the previous keyboard

Tap to see emojis you've used frequently

Tap to see groups of emojis

Emojis are icons you insert into your text to liven things up, communicate your feelings, or just to have some fun (if you don't have this keyboard installed, see Chapter 4). You can open the Emoji keyboard by tapping its key (the smiley face) or by selecting it on the Keyboard menu. You see a palette containing many emojis, organized into groups. You can change the groups of emojis you are browsing by tapping the icons at the bottom of the screen. Swipe to the left or right on the emojis to browse the emojis in the current group. Tap an emoji to enter it at the cursor's location in your message, email, or other type of document. To use an emoji you've used often, tap the Clock icon to see emojis you've used frequently; you'll probably find that you use this set of emojis regularly so this can save a lot of time. To return to the mundane world of letters and symbols, tap the ABC key.

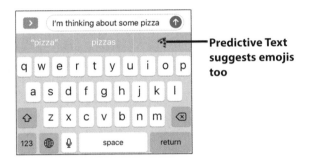

Predictive Text suggests emojis too

The Predictive text feature also suggests emojis when you type certain words; just tap the emoji to replace the word with it.

Emoji Options

If you tap and hold on some emojis, you see options. For example, if you tap and hold on the thumbs-up emoji, you see a menu with the emoji in different flesh tones. Slide your finger over the menu and tap the version you want to use. The version you select becomes the new default for that emoji. You can go back to a previous version by opening the menu and selecting it.

Emojis Galore

Emojis are very widely used in text messages because you can communicate a lot with a single icon. The Messages app enables you to access many kinds of emojis through the apps you can install within the Messages app itself; these are often called stickers, but they work the same way as emojis. See Chapter 9, "Sending, Receiving, and Managing Texts and iMessages," to learn how to add and use sticker apps within the Messages app.

What's Your Typing Orientation?

Like many other tasks, you can rotate the iPhone to change the screen's orientation while you type. When the iPhone is in the horizontal orientation, the keyboard is wider, making it easier to tap individual keys, and you have access to more keys. When the iPhone is in vertical orientation, the keyboard is narrower, but you can see more of the typing area. So, try both to see which mode is most effective for you.

Correcting Spelling as You Type

If you type a word that the iPhone doesn't recognize, that word is flagged as a possible mistake and suggestions are made to help you correct it. How this happens depends on whether or not Predictive Text is enabled.

Suspicious word

Tap to keep the suspicious word

Tap to replace the suspicious word with this one

If you tap the space key, the suspicious word is replaced with this one

If Predictive Text is enabled, potential replacements for suspicious words appear in the Predictive Text bar. When you tap the space key, the suspicious word is replaced with the word in the center of the Predictive Text bar. Tap the word on the far left to keep what you've typed (because it isn't a mistake) or tap the word on the right end of the bar to enter it instead of what you've typed.

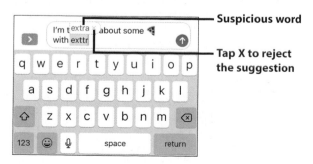

Suspicious word

Tap X to reject the suggestion

If Predictive Text isn't enabled, a suspicious word is highlighted and a suggestion about what it thinks is the correct word appears in a pop-up box. To accept the suggestion, tap the space key. To reject the suggestion, tap the pop-up box to close it and keep what you typed. You can also use this feature for shorthand typing. For example, to type "I've" you can simply type "Ive" and iPhone suggests "I've," which you can accept by tapping the space key.

Typing Tricks

Many keys, especially symbols and punctuation, have additional characters. To see a character's options, tap it and hold down. If it has options, a menu pops up after a second or so. To enter one of the optional characters, drag over the menu until the one you want to enter is highlighted, and then lift your finger off the screen. The optional character you selected is entered. For example, if you tap and hold on the period, you can select .com, .edu, and so on, which is very helpful when you are typing a website or email address.

Your Own Text Replacements

You can create your own text shortcuts so you can type something like "eadd" and it is automatically replaced with your email address. See Chapter 4 for the details.

By default, the iPhone attempts to correct the capitalization of what you type. It also automatically selects the Shift key when you start a new sentence, start a new paragraph, or in other places where its best guess is that you need a capital letter. If you don't want to enter a capital character, simply tap the Shift key before you type. You can enable the Caps Lock key by tapping the Shift key twice. When the key is highlighted (the upward-facing arrow is black), everything you type is in uppercase letters.

Options, Options

Using the Keyboards screen in the Settings app, you can enable or disable text-related functions, such as Auto-Capitalization. See Chapter 4 for details.

Editing Text

2. The magnifying glass shows you where the cursor is

3. Drag the magnifying glass until the cursor is next to the text you want to change

1. Tap and hold on text you want to edit

To edit text you've typed, touch and hold on the area containing the text you want to edit. A magnifying glass icon appears on the screen, and within it you see a magnified view of the location of the cursor. Drag the magnifying glass to position the cursor where you want to start making changes, and then lift your finger from the screen. The cursor remains in that location, and you can use the keyboard to make changes to the text or to add text at that location, or you can make a selection on the menu that appears.

Using 3D Touch with Text

When you are using an iPhone that supports 3D Touch (6s and later models), you can apply slight pressure when you touch the screen to have the closest word selected automatically; it is highlighted in blue to show you that it is selected. To place the cursor without selecting words that are near your finger, just touch the screen without applying any pressure.

Selecting, Copying, Cutting, or Pasting Text

Tap Select All to choose everything in the window

Tap Select to choose a portion of what's in the window

Tap and hold briefly where you want to start selecting

Tap to see more options

You can also select text or images to copy and paste the selected content into a new location or to replace that content. Touch and hold down briefly where you want to start the selection until the magnifying glass icon appears; then lift your finger off the screen. The Select menu appears. Tap Select to select part of the content on the screen, or tap Select All to select everything in the current window.

More Commands

Some menus that appear when you are making selections and performing actions have a right-facing arrow at the right end. Tap this to see a new menu that contains additional commands. These commands are contextual, meaning that you see different commands depending on what you are doing at that specific time. You can tap the left-facing arrow to move back to a previous menu.

The blue markers indicate where the selection starts and stops — **Selected text**

You see markers indicating where the selection starts and stops. (The iPhone attempts to select something logical, such as the word or sentence.) New commands appear on the menu; these provide actions for the text currently selected.

Drag the markers so that they enclose what you want to select

Magnified view of what you are selecting

Selected text (in blue)

Drag the two markers so that the content you want to select is between them; the selected portion is highlighted in blue. As you drag, you see a magnified view of where the selection marker is, which helps you place it more accurately. When the selection markers are located correctly, lift your finger from the screen. (If you tapped the Select All command, you don't need to do this because the content you want is already selected.)

Tap Cut or Copy

Selected text

Tap Cut to remove the content from the current window, or tap Copy to just copy it.

Have I Got a Suggestion for You!

As you select different items, explore the menu to see commands that might be useful to you. These commands are contextual so they change based on what you have selected. For example, when you have a word or phrase selected, one of the suggestions might be Look Up, which opens Siri Suggestions for the word or phrase you selected. The results can include dictionary or Wikipedia entries, suggested apps, and so on. Tap Done to return to the text with which you were working. As you use your iPhone, check out the options on this menu because you'll find some very useful tricks tucked away there.

Format It!

If you tap BIU on the menu, you can tap Bold, Italics, or Underline to apply those formatting options to the selected text. You also can tap multiple format options to apply them at the same time. You might need to tap the right-facing arrow at the end of the menu to see this command, depending on how many commands are on the menu.

**Tap where you
want to paste**

Tap Paste

Move to where you want to paste the content you selected; for example, use the App Switcher to change to a different app. Tap where you want the content to be pasted. For a more precise location, tap and hold and then use the magnifying glass icon to move to a specific location. Lift your finger off the screen and the menu appears. Then tap Paste.

Pasted content

The content you copied or cut appears where you placed the cursor.

Correcting Spelling After You've Typed

**Text that might
be misspelled**

Touch redlined word

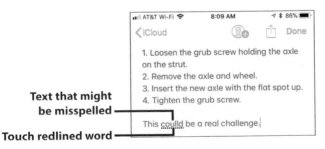

The iPhone also has a spell-checking feature that comes into play after you have entered text (as opposed to the Predictive Text and autocorrect/suggests features that change text as you type it). When you've entered text the iPhone doesn't recognize, it is underlined in red.

Tap the correct word ——

Tap the underlined word. It is shaded in red to show you what is being checked, and a menu appears with one or more replacements that might be the correct spelling. If one of the options is the one you want, tap it. The incorrect word is replaced with the one you tapped.

Contextual Menus and You

In some apps, tapping a word causes a menu with other kinds of actions to appear; you can tap an action to make it happen. For example, in the iBooks app, when you tap a word, the resulting menu enables you to look up the word in a dictionary. Other apps support different kinds of actions, so it's a good idea to try tapping words in apps that involve text to see which commands are available.

Undo

The iPhone has a somewhat hidden undo command. To undo what you've just done, such as typing text, gently shake your phone back and forth a couple of times. An Undo Typing prompt appears on the screen. Tap Undo to undo the last thing you did or tap Cancel if you activated the undo command accidentally.

Dictating Text

You can also enter text by dictating it. This is a fast and easy way to type, and you'll be amazed at how accurate the iPhone is at translating your speech into typed words. Dictation is available almost anywhere you need to enter text. (Exceptions are passcodes and passwords, such as for your Apple ID.)

To start dictating, tap the Microphone key. The iPhone goes into Dictation mode. A gray bar appears at the bottom of the window. As the iPhone "hears" you, the line oscillates.

Tap to put the cursor where you want dictated text to start

Tap the Microphone key to start dictation

The iPhone is taking dictation

Tap when you're done speaking

Start speaking the text you want the iPhone to type. As you speak, the text is entered starting from the location of the cursor. Speak punctuation when you want to enter it. For example, when you reach the end of a sentence, say "period," or to enter a colon say "colon." To start a new paragraph, say "new paragraph."

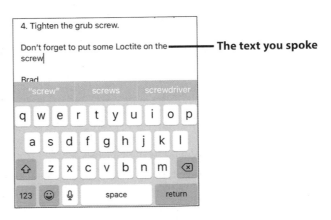

The text you spoke

When you've finished dictating, tap the keyboard icon. The keyboard reappears and you see the text you spoke. This feature is amazingly accurate and can be a much faster and more convenient way to enter text than typing it.

You can edit the text you dictated just like text you typed using the keyboard.

Drawing in Text

Tap where you want the drawing to be inserted   **Tap Insert Drawing**   **Tap the right-facing arrow until you see Insert Drawing**

You can use the iOS drawing tool to create and insert drawings that include shapes, text, colors, and other elements into places where you create text, such as emails. Tap in the window where you want the drawing to be. On the menu, tap the right-facing arrow until you see Insert Drawing and then tap that command.

Tap Done when you're finished

Create a drawing

Tap to insert at the
current cursor location

Use the drawing tool to create the drawing. Tap Add (+) to add shapes, lines, or text. Tap text to edit it. Tap Signature to sign your name. You can tap objects to select them to move or change them. You can use the format tools (color and font) to format objects. When you're done, tap Done. Then tap Insert Drawing to place the drawing where the cursor was located.

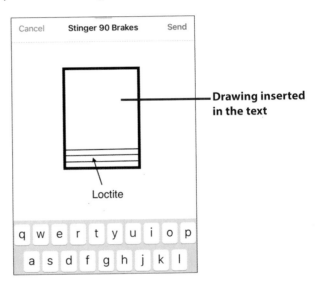

Drawing inserted
in the text

When you move back to the text, you see the drawing you created. You can then complete what you were doing, such as finishing and sending an email message.

Using Widgets

Widgets are "mini" versions of apps installed on your iPhone that you can access easily and quickly from the Widget Center.

Swipe to the right to open the Widget Center

You can open the Widget Center in a number of ways:

- Wake your iPhone and swipe to the right on the Lock screen.

- Move to a Home page and swipe to the right.

- Swipe down the screen to open the Notification Center and then swipe to the right.

Tap to call or FaceTime a favorite

Tap Show Less to collapse a widget

Swipe up and down to browse your widgets

See your next event

Tap to move into the widget's app

Widget name

At the top of the Widget Center, you see the Search tool (more on this later). If you open the Widget Center from the Lock screen, you see the current time and date under the Search tool; if you open it from a Home screen, you don't see the date or time. Beneath that, you see widgets for apps installed on your iPhone. Swipe up and down the screen to browse your widgets.

Configuring the Widget Center

You can choose the widgets that appear in the Widget Center and the order in which those widgets are shown on the screen. See "Configuring the Widget Center" in Chapter 4 for the step-by-step instructions to configure your Widget Center.

Each widget provides information or functions based on its app. For example, you can use the FAVORITES widget to place phone calls using the Phone app or to make FaceTime calls to your contacts you've designated as Favorites (you learn how to do this in Chapter 7). You can see your daily calendar in the CALENDAR widget, get news in the NEWS widget, or listen to music in the MUSIC widget.

You can expand a widget to show all of its information or tools by tapping the Show More command or collapse it to a more minimal state by tapping the Show Less command.

You can interact with widgets in several ways. Some widgets provide information that you can view within the widget, such as CALENDAR, STOCKS, or UP NEXT. Some apps provide options you can tap to perform specific actions; these include FAVORITES and MUSIC. When you tap something within a widget, the associated app opens and either performs the task you indicated or shows more information about what you selected.

Some apps even have multiple widgets. For example, the Calendar app has the UP NEXT widget that shows you the next events on your calendar and the CALENDAR widget that shows the events on the current date.

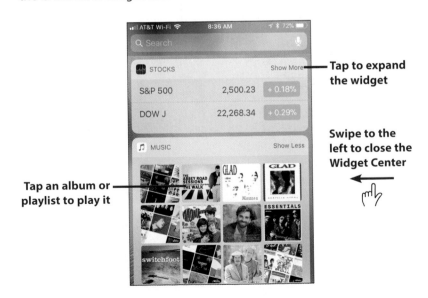

If you don't move into an app from a widget, you can close the Widget Center by swiping to the left. You move back to the screen you came from, such as a Home screen. If you do move into an app from a widget, you work with that app just as if you moved into it from a Home screen.

Searching on Your iPhone

You can use the Search tool to search your iPhone to find many different types of information, including locations, emails, messages, apps, and so on.

Swipe down from the center part of the screen to search your iPhone

There are a couple of ways you can start a search:

- Swipe to the right to open the Widget Center. The Search bar is at the top of the screen.

- On a Home screen, swipe down from the center of the screen. The Search bar appears at the top of the screen.

To perform a search, tap in the Search bar and type the search term using the onscreen keyboard. As you type, recent or suggested searches appear just below the Search bar; tap a search to perform it. Under the search list, you see the current items that match your search. If you don't tap one of the recent or suggested searches, when you finish typing the search term, tap Search to see the full list of results.

Type what you want to search for

Recent or suggested searches

Current results

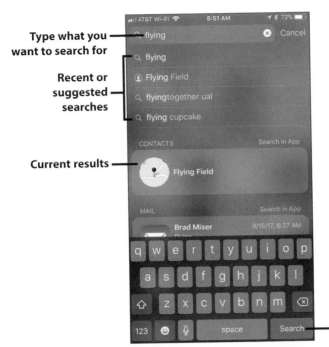

When you're done entering your search term, tap Search

Search results

Location related to the search term

Swipe up and down to browse all of the results

To work with a result, tap it

The results are organized into sections, such as CONTACTS, MAIL, MESSAGES, APPLICATIONS, MAPS, MUSIC, and so on. Swipe up and down the screen to browse all of the results. To work with an item you find, such as to view a location you found, tap it; you move to a screen showing more information or into the associated app and see the search result that you tapped.

Tap to go back to your search ────

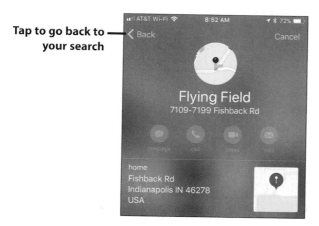

Tap to go back to your search ────

The results remain in the Search tool as you work with them. To move back to the search results, tap the back icon in the upper-left corner of the screen or tap Search (which you see depends on the result you tapped on).

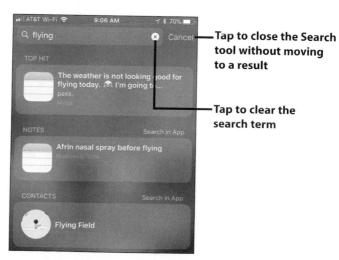

Tap to close the Search tool without moving to a result

Tap to clear the search term

The results of the most recent search are still listed. To clear the search term, tap Clear (x). To close the Spotlight tool without going to one of the results, tap Cancel.

Tell Me More

If one of the categories you find in a search has a lot of entries, you see the Show More command. Tap this to show more of the results for that category. Tap Show Less to collapse the category again. When you can search within an app, you see the Search in App text on the right side of the screen aligned with the results section; tap this to open the app and perform the search within that app.

Working with Siri Suggestions

Siri Suggestions can make it easy to get back to apps, searches, or other items you've used recently. Using Siri Suggestions can also lead you to useful things you weren't necessarily looking for. These suggestions show up in many different areas on your iPhone and you can access them directly at any time.

Swipe down from the center part of the screen to see Siri Suggestions

Tap to open an app

Tap to run a search

To access Siri Suggestions, swipe down from the center of a Home screen. Just under the Search bar, you see the SIRI APP SUGGESTIONS panel. This panel shows you apps you've used recently or apps that might be useful to you based on your location. For example, the Starbucks app may be suggested when you are near a Starbucks location. Tap an app to open it.

There's a Widget for That

You can also use the SIRI APP SUGGESTIONS widget in the Widget Center to quickly access recently used or suggested apps. This widget works just like the SIRI APP SUGGESTIONS panel because it's basically the same thing.

Siri Suggestions can also appear in other apps. Siri monitors your activity and "learns" from what you do in order to improve the suggestions it makes. These suggestions can appear in many different places, such as when you are entering email addresses in a new email, dealing with new contact information, performing searches, editing a text message, and so on. When you see a list of Siri Suggestions, you can tap the suggestion you want to use. For example, if it is an email address, that address is entered for you. If it is a search, the search is performed.

You can enable or disable the apps and services that Siri can access to make these suggestions; the information to do this is provided in Chapter 11, "Working with Siri." For example, if you don't want Siri to be able to make suggestions based on a specific app, you can disable the Search & Siri Suggestions setting for that app.

Working with Notifications

As you learned in Chapter 1, the iPhone's notification system keeps you informed of activity in which you may be interested, such as new emails, events, app updates, and so on. There are a number of types of these notifications that you will experience. Visual notifications include banners and badges. Alert sounds can also let you know something has happened, and vibrations make you feel the new activity.

You can determine which types of notifications are used for specific activity on your iPhone. This might be one of the most important areas to configure because you want to make sure you are aware of activity that is important to you, but too many notifications can be disruptive and annoying. So, you want to strike a good balance between being aware and being annoyed.

Notification Center

In Chapter 1, you learned how to use the Notification Center to work with groups of notifications. This can be a more efficient way to deal with notifications since you can access "batches" of them instead of dealing with each one individually. You might want to configure individual notifications for the activity that is most important to you and access the rest via the Notification Center.

Working with Visual Notifications

There are three types of visual notifications: badges, persistent banners, and temporary banners.

Badge

Badges appear on an app's or a folder's icon to let you know something has changed, such as when you have received new email.

Badges are purely informational, meaning you can't take any action on these directly as you can with the other visual notifications. They inform you about an event so that you can take action, such as to download and install an update to your iPhone's iOS software or read new text messages.

Badges on Folders

In Chapter 5, "Customizing How Your iPhone Looks and Sounds," you learned how to organize apps in folders. When apps in folders have badges enabled, the badge you see on a folder is a total count of the badges on the apps within that folder. The only way to know which apps that are in the folders have badges is to open the folder so you can see the individual app icons and badges.

App the notification is from

Banner notification

Tap to move into the app

Swipe up to close the banner

Press to take action (3D Touch)

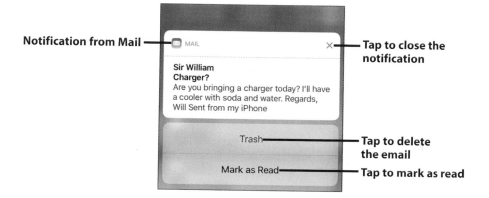

Notification from Mail — MAIL × — **Tap to close the notification**

Sir William
Charger?
Are you bringing a charger today? I'll have
a cooler with soda and water. Regards,
Will Sent from my iPhone

Trash — **Tap to delete the email**

Mark as Read — **Tap to mark as read**

Banner notifications provide information for you, and you can take action related to the event that generated the notification. For example, you can respond to a text message directly from its notification.

There are two types of banner notifications. Persistent banner notifications remain on the screen until you take action on them, which can be closing them, responding to them, etc. Temporary banner notifications appear on the screen for a few seconds and if you don't take action on them, they rotate off the screen to get out of your way.

When your iPhone is unlocked, banner notifications appear at the top of the screen. They provide a summary of the app and the activity that has taken place, such as a new email or text message. When a banner appears, you can view its information; if it is a temporary banner, it rotates off the screen after displaying for a few seconds; if it is a persistent banner, you need to do something to cause it to disappear. You can tap it to move into the app to take some action, such as to read an email. You can swipe up from the bottom of the banner to close it. For some apps, such as Email, you can press on the notification to open a menu of commands.

No 3D Touch?

If your iPhone doesn't support 3D Touch (it's not an iPhone 6s or later model), you can swipe down on a notification to take action on it, such as to reply to a text message.

Banner notification on the Lock screen

Press to take action (3D Touch)

Tap to close the notification

New message

Reply to the message

Banner notifications can also appear on the Lock screen, which is really con-venient because you can read and take action on them directly from that screen. If your phone is asleep, the notifications appear briefly on the screen and then it goes dark again; you can press the Side button or the Touch/ID Home button or raise your phone to see your notifications without unlocking the iPhone. You can swipe up or down the screen to browse the notifications.

To respond to a notification or take other action on it, press it to open it (3D Touch iPhones) or swipe to the right on it (non-3D Touch iPhones) and then take action, such as replying to a message. In some cases, you might need to unlock your phone to complete an action associated with a notification. In those cases, you're prompted to use Touch ID, Face ID, or your passcode to proceed.

If don't want the banners to appear, you can disable them.

Working with Other Types of Notifications

Sounds are audible indicators that something has happened. For example, you can be alerted to a new email message by a specific sound. You can choose global sound notifications, such as a general ringtone, and specific ones, such as a special ringtone when someone in your contacts calls you.

Vibrations are a physical indicator that something has happened. Like sounds, you can configure general vibrations, and you can also configure an app's vibration pattern for its notifications.

Configuring Your Notifications

It's a good idea to configure the notifications your iPhone uses so that you are aware of important activity, such as new work emails, without being distracted by constant notifications for things that don't require your immediate attention (such as a post to Facebook). To learn how to configure your notifications, see "Configuring Notifications" in Chapter 4.

Printing from Your iPhone

You can print directly from your iPhone to AirPrint-compatible printers.

First, set up and configure your AirPrint printer (see the instructions that came with the printer you use).

It Depends

When you tap the Share icon, you might see a menu containing commands instead of the grid of icons shown in the figure. The way it appears is dependent upon the app you are using. If you see a menu, tap Print to move to the Printer Options screen.

AirPrint?

AirPrint is an Apple technology that enables an iOS device to wirelessly print to an AirPrint-compatible printer without installing any printer drivers on the iOS device. To be able to print directly to a printer via Wi-Fi, the printer must support AirPrint (a large number of them do). When an iOS device, such as your iPhone, is on the same Wi-Fi network as an AirPrint printer, it automatically detects that printer and is able to print to it immediately.

When you are in the app from which you want to print, tap the Share icon. Tap Print on the resulting menu. You might need to swipe to the right to expose the Print command. (If you don't see the Share icon or the Print command, the app you are using doesn't support printing.)

Tap to select a printer

Tap the printer you want to use

The first time you print, you need to select the printer you want to use. On the Printer Options screen, tap Select Printer. Then tap the printer you want to use. You move back to the Printer Options screen and see the printer you selected.

Tap the – or + to set the number of copies; the current number of copies is shown to the left of the controls. You can use other controls that appear to configure the print job, such as the Black & White switch to print in black and white on a color printer; the controls you see depend on the capabilities of the printer you selected. Tap Print to print the document.

The next time you print, if you want to use the same printer, you can skip the printer selection process because the iPhone remembers the last printer you used. To change the printer, tap Printer and tap the printer you want to use.

Use iCloud and other accounts to store the data your apps use on the cloud

Go here to configure and manage your Apple ID, iCloud, and other online accounts

Store files on the cloud

In this chapter, you learn how to connect your iPhone to various types of accounts, such as iCloud, Exchange, and Google, so that apps on your iPhone can access data stored on the Internet cloud. Topics include the following:

→ Configuring an Apple ID

→ Configuring and using iCloud

→ Setting up other types of online accounts on your iPhone

→ Configuring other types of online accounts

→ Setting how and when your accounts are updated

Setting Up and Using an Apple ID, iCloud, and Other Online Accounts

No iPhone is an island. Connecting your iPhone to the Internet enables you to share and sync a wide variety of content using popular online accounts such as iCloud, Exchange, and Google. Using iCloud, you can put your email, contacts, calendars, photos, and more on the Internet so that multiple devices—most importantly your iPhone—can connect to and use that information. You can also use Exchange, Google, and other online accounts to store, manage, and use email, calendars, and contact information.

You need to configure these accounts on your iPhone to be able to use them; in this chapter are sections for several different accounts you might want to use. Of course, you only need to refer to the sections related to the accounts you actually use. With all of these services, you need to understand how and when your information is updated along with tasks you might find valuable as you manage the various accounts on your iPhone.

Configuring an Apple ID

An Apple ID is required to access Apple's online services, including iCloud, the App Store, iTunes, and the online store. You can access all of these services with one Apple ID.

An Apple ID has two elements. One is the email address associated with your account; this can be one provided by Apple or you can choose to use an address from a different service (such as Google Gmail). The other element is a password.

In addition to your email address and password, your contact information (such as physical address and phone number) and payment information (if you make purchases through your account, such as apps or storage upgrades) is also part of your Apple ID.

If you have used Apple technology or services before, you probably already have an Apple ID. If you don't already have one, obtaining an Apple ID is simple and free.

If you have any of the following accounts, you already have an Apple ID:

- **iTunes Store**—If you've ever shopped at the iTunes Store, you created an Apple ID.

- **Apple Online Store**—As with the iTunes Store, if you made purchases from Apple's online store, you created an account with an Apple ID.

- **Find My iPhone**—If you obtained a free Find My iPhone account, you also created an Apple ID.

Another way you might have already obtained an Apple ID is during the initial iPhone startup process when you were prompted to sign in to or create an Apple ID.

If you don't have an Apple ID, read the next section to obtain one. If you already have an Apple ID, move to "Signing into Your Apple ID" to learn how to sign into it on your iPhone. If you both have an Apple ID and have already signed into it on your iPhone, skip to the section "Changing the Personal Information Associated with Your Apple ID" to learn how to configure it.

Obtaining an Apple ID

If you don't have an Apple ID, you can use your iPhone to create one by performing the following steps:

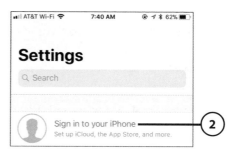

1. On the Home screen, tap Settings.

2. Tap Sign in to your iPhone.

3. Tap Don't have an Apple ID or forgot it?.

4. Tap Create Apple ID.

5. Provide the information required on the following screens; tap Next to move to the next screen after you've entered the required information. You start by entering your birthday, providing your name, and so on. You are guided through each step in the process.

   During the process, you're prompted to use an existing email address or to create a free iCloud email account. You can choose either option. The email address you use becomes your Apple ID that you use to sign in to iCloud. If you create a new iCloud email account, you can use that account from any email app on any device, just like other email accounts you have.

   You also create a password, enter a phone number and verification method, verify the phone number you entered, and agree to license terms. When your account has been created, you sign into iCloud, which you do by entering your iPhone's passcode.

You might then be prompted to merge information already stored on your iPhone, such as Safari bookmarks, onto iCloud. Tap Merge to copy the information that currently is stored on your iPhone to the cloud or Don't Merge to keep it out of the cloud.

When you've worked through merging your information, you're prompted to sign in to the iTunes and App Stores to make sure your new account can work with those services, too. You can choose to review your account information now or skip it and configure it at another time.

When the process is complete, you're signed into your new Apple ID; skip ahead to "Changing the Personal Information Associated with Your Apple ID" to learn how to change its settings.

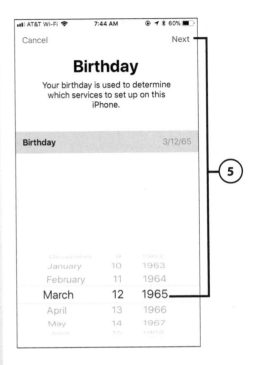

Signing In to Your Apple ID

You can sign in to an existing Apple ID on your iPhone by doing the following:

1. On the Home screen, tap Settings.

2. Tap Sign in to your iPhone.

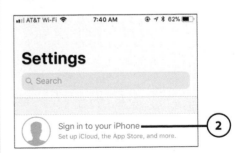

3. Enter your Apple ID (email address).

4. Enter your password.

5. Tap Sign In. If you are using the same Apple ID on another device, you're prompted to enter the verification code sent to those devices. See the sidebar "Two-Factor Authentication" for more information.

6. Enter your verification code; if you weren't prompted to enter a code, skip this step.

7. Enter your iPhone's passcode. You might be prompted to merge existing information on the iPhone onto your iCloud storage.

8. Tap Merge to copy information from your iPhone onto the cloud or Don't Merge if you don't want that information copied to the cloud. You might be prompted to perform this merge step more than once depending on the kind of information already stored on your iPhone. If you don't have any information that can be merged, you skip this step entirely.

When you've finished these steps, you are signed in to your Apple ID and can configure it further using the information in the next section.

Two-Factor Authentication

Apple uses two-factor authentication for its services. This requires that you have two pieces of information to be able to access your Apple accounts. One is your Apple ID login information (email and password). The other is a verification code that is sent to other devices on which the Apple ID is already configured (called trusted devices). This makes using Apple services more secure because even if someone was able to get your Apple ID and password (which is unlikely), he would still need the verification code to be able to sign in to your account (meaning he would also have to be able to access another device on which your Apple ID is already configured, which is very, very unlikely). In general, you should use two-factor authentication when it is available (it requires you have at least two devices that can use your Apple ID, such as an iPhone and a Mac).

You can configure two-factor authentication for your Apple ID in the Password & Security settings, which are described in the next section.

Changing the Personal Information Associated with Your Apple ID

When you create or sign in to your Apple ID, the personal information associated with your account is used on your iPhone. You can change this information on your phone, for example, if you want to change your contact information or how you pay for purchases from Apple. Following are the steps you can use to change the personal information associated with your Apple ID:

1. On the Home screen, tap Settings.

2. Tap your Apple ID, which appears immediately under the Search bar at the top of the Settings screen. The Apple ID screen has four sections. The top section shows your Apple ID and photo (if you have one) and provides access to your account's primary settings, which are contact information, security, and payment information.

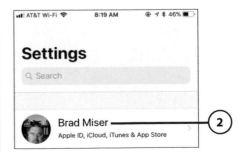

3. To set or change the photo associated with your Apple ID, tap the image shown just above your name.

4. Tap Take Photo to take a new photo for your Apple ID or Choose Photo to use an existing photo; then use the resulting tools to configure the photo for your Apple ID (detailed information about working with the iPhone's photo tools is provided in Chapter 13, "Taking Photos and Video with Your iPhone," and Chapter 14, "Viewing and Editing Photos and Video with the Photos App"). When you're done configuring the photo, you return to the Apple ID screen and see the new photo at the top of the screen.

5. To change your contact information, tap Name, Phone Numbers, Email.

6. To change the name associated with your account, tap the name shown and edit it on the resulting screen; when you're done, tap Back to move to the previous screen (this step is not shown in the figures).

7. To change the email addresses with which you can be contacted in various apps, such as FaceTime, tap Edit.

Address Info

If an email address has the Info icon (i) next to it, you can tap that icon to verify the address or see information about it (such as a message for your primary Apple ID address stating that you can't remove it).

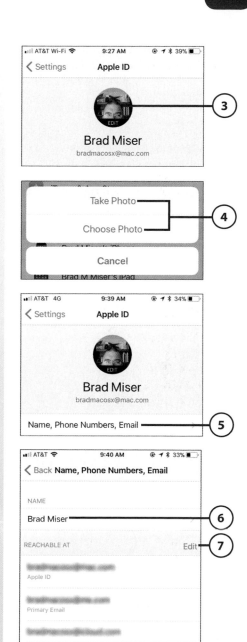

8. To remove an address, tap its unlock icon.

9. Tap Delete. That address is removed from the list and can't be used for associated apps.

10. To add more email addresses or phone numbers, tap Add Email or Phone Number.

11. Tap Add an Email Address to associate a new email or tap Add a Phone Number to add a phone number. Follow the resulting steps to complete the process. For example, enter the new email and then respond to the verification email sent to the address.

Done Is Done

When you make some changes, such as adding a new email address, you exit Edit mode automatically. You have to tap Edit again to make more changes. If a change you make doesn't automatically move you out of Edit mode, tap Done when you are finished making changes.

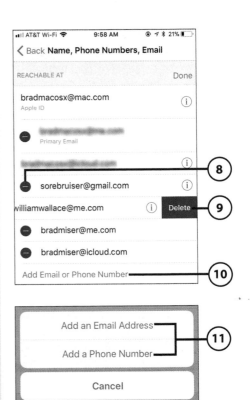

12. If you need to change the birthday for your account, tap it and make the change on the resulting screen.

13. To receive emails from Apple for various types of information, set the associated switch to On (green) or to prevent such messages from being sent, set the switch to Off (white).

14. When you're done making changes to your personal information, tap Back.

Confirmations Galore

Many changes you make to your Apple ID, such as adding a new email address or changing security settings, result in you receiving confirmation emails and notifications from Apple on all of the devices tied to your account. These are helpful because they confirm the actions you are taking. If you ever receive such a notification but you haven't changed your account, carefully review it. In many cases, especially email notifications, these unexpected notifications are attempts to get your information for nefarious purposes. Don't respond to emails you don't expect even if they appear to be from Apple (if you make a change and then receive an email, that is expected). Instead, log in directly to your account on your iPhone or other device to make sure it hasn't been changed by someone else.

Changing Your Apple ID's Password and Security Settings

To access the security settings for your Apple ID, perform the following steps:

1. Move to the Apple ID screen.
2. Tap Password & Security.
3. To change your password, tap Change Password and follow the onscreen instructions to make the change. You need to enter your iPhone's passcode and then you'll be able to change the password.
4. If two-factor authentication isn't currently enabled, tap Turn on Two-Factor Authentication and then tap Continue to complete the process; if it is already enabled, you see the On status (as shown in the figure).
5. To change the phone number used for account verification, tap Edit and use the resulting tools to delete or change existing numbers or add new ones.

Two-factor authentication is enabled

6. If you need a verification code for another device with which you are trying to access your Apple ID information, tap Get Verification Code. The code appears on the screen and you can enter that code on the other device to verify it; tap OK to close the code dialog.

7. When you're done making changes, tap Apple ID.

Changing Your Apple ID's Payment and Shipping Information

To change the payment and shipping information for your Apple ID, perform the following steps:

1. Move to the Apple ID screen.

2. Tap Payment & Shipping.

3. To change your payment information, tap the current payment method (which is what will be used for all purchases made under your account, such as from the App Store).

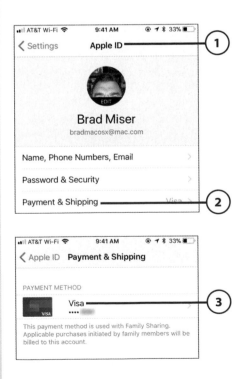

4. Use the fields on the resulting screen to provide or change your name, credit or debit card information, and the address associated with the payment method.

5. Tap Save when you have updated the information.

6. To change your shipping address, tap the current address.

7. Use the fields on the resulting screen to provide or change the address to which items you purchase from Apple should be delivered.

8. Tap Done when you have updated the information.

9. Tap Apple ID to return to the Apple ID screen.

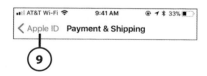

Configuring Services that Use Your Apple ID

In the center part of the Apple ID screen, you see tools you can use to configure iCloud (covered in "Configuring and Using iCloud" later in this chapter) and the iTunes and App Stores (covered in "Customizing How Your iPhone Works with Apps" in Chapter 4, "Customizing How Your iPhone Works"). Family Sharing enables you to configure a group of people with whom you share content related to your Apple ID (such as music you purchase from the iTunes Store and apps you download from the App Store). You can use the Family Sharing option to configure your Family Sharing group and determine the access this group has to your account.

Changing the Devices Using Your Apple ID

You will likely have more than one device that uses your Apple ID. For example, you might have an iPad on which you want to be able to access the same information as you can on your iPhone. You can get information about the devices currently using your Apple ID like so:

1. Move to the Apple ID screen.

2. Tap the device about which you want to get information.

3. Review the information about the device. (If the device is also an iPhone, you can enable or disable some iCloud functions from this screen.)

4. If you don't recognize the device, tap Remove from Account and follow the onscreen prompts to disconnect the device from your Apple ID. You should also immediately change your Apple ID password.

5. To return to the Apple ID screen, tap Apple ID.

Signing Off

If don't want to continue accessing your Apple ID on your iPhone or you want to sign into a different Apple ID, tap Sign Out at the bottom of the Apple ID screen. If Find My iPhone is enabled, you need to enter your password and tap Turn Off to continue the process. You might be prompted to keep some information on your iPhone; if you choose to keep that information, it remains on your iPhone but is no longer synchronized to the information stored on the cloud. After you have completed the process, you can sign in to the same or a different Apple ID using the information in "Signing In to Your Apple ID" earlier in this chapter.

Configuring and Using iCloud

iCloud is a service provided by Apple that provides you with your own storage space on the Internet. You can store content from your computer or devices in your storage space on the cloud, and because it is on the Internet, all your devices are able to access that information at the same time. This means you can easily share your information on your iPhone, a computer, and iPad, so that the same information and content is available to you no matter which device you are using at any one time.

Although your iPhone can work with many types of online/Internet accounts, iCloud is integrated into the iPhone like no other (not surprising because the iPhone and iCloud are both Apple technology). An iCloud account is part of an Apple ID; if you have an Apple ID, you also have an iCloud account.

An iCloud account is useful in a number of ways, including the following:

- **Photos**—You can store your photos in iCloud to back them up and to make them easy to share.

- **Email**—An iCloud account includes an @icloud.com email address. You can configure any device to use your iCloud email account, including an iPhone, an iPad, an iPod, and a computer.

- **Contacts**—You can store your contact information in iCloud.

- **Calendars**—Putting your calendars in iCloud makes it much easier to manage your time.

- **Reminders**—Through iCloud, you can be reminded of things you need to do or anything else you want to make sure you don't forget.

- **Notes**—With the Notes app, you can create text notes, draw sketches, and capture photos for many purposes; iCloud enables you to use these notes on any iCloud-enabled device.

- **Messages**—This puts all of your text messages on the cloud so you can access the same messages from any device.

- **Safari**—iCloud can store your bookmarks, letting you easily access the same websites from all your devices. And you can easily access websites currently open on other devices, such as a Mac, on your iPhone.

- **News**—iCloud can store information from the News app online, making reading news on multiple devices easier.

- **Health**—This causes the information stored using the Health app to be available to multiple devices. For example, you might track information on your Apple Watch and want to be able to analyze it on your iPhone.

- **Wallet**—The Wallet app stores coupons, tickets, boarding passes, and other documents so you can access them quickly and easily. With iCloud, you can ensure that these documents are available on any iCloud-enabled device.

- **Game Center**—This capability stores information from the Game Center app on the cloud.

- **Siri**—It can be helpful to manage Siri information on multiple devices; this setting puts that information on the cloud.

- **Keychain**—The Keychain securely stores sensitive data, such as passwords, so that you can easily use that data without having to remember it.

- **Find My iPhone**—This service enables you to locate and secure your iPhone and other devices.

- **iCloud Backup**—You can back up your iPhone to the cloud so that you can recover your data and your phone's configuration should something ever happen to it.

- **iCloud Drive**—iCloud enables you to store your documents and other files on the cloud so that you can seamlessly work with them using different devices.

- **App Data**—When iCloud Drive is enabled, you can allow or prevent apps from storing data there.

You can also manage your iCloud storage space, share your location, and configure some aspects of iCloud mail.

You learn about iCloud's many useful features throughout this book (such as using iCloud with your photos, which is covered in Chapter 14). The tasks in this chapter show you how to set up and configure the iCloud features you want to use.

Multiple iCloud Accounts

You can have more than one iCloud account. However, you can be signed in to only one iCloud account on your iPhone at a time.

I'm In

To access your iCloud account, sign in to your Apple ID as described in "Signing In to Your Apple ID" earlier in this chapter.

Configuring iCloud to Store Photos

Storing your photos on the cloud provides many benefits, not the least of which is that the photos you take with your iPhone are automatically saved on the cloud so that you can access them from computers and other iOS devices (such as iPads), and your photos remain available even if something happens to your iPhone, such as losing it. Using iCloud also makes it easy for you to share your photos with others. To configure your photos to be stored in iCloud, do the following:

1. Open the Apple ID screen.

2. Tap iCloud.

3. On the iCloud screen, tap Photos.

4. To store your entire photo library on the cloud, set the iCloud Photo Library switch to on (green). This stores all of your photos and video in iCloud, which both protects them by backing them up and makes them accessible on other iOS devices (iPads, iPod touches, iPhones) and computers, (including Macs, Windows PCs, and via the Web).

5. If you enable the iCloud Photo Library feature, tap Optimize iPhone Storage to keep lower-resolution versions of photos and videos on your iPhone (this means the file sizes are smaller so that you can store more of them on your phone), or tap Download and Keep Originals if you want to keep the full-resolution photos on your iPhone. In most cases,

you should choose the Optimize option so that you don't use as much of your iPhone's storage space for photos.

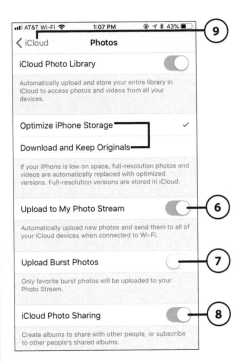

6. Ensure the Upload to My Photo Stream switch is on (green) (if you aren't using the iCloud Photo Library, this switch is called My Photo Stream); if you disabled this, skip to step 8. Any photos you take with the iPhone's camera are copied onto iCloud, and from there they're copied to your other devices on which the Photo Stream is enabled. Note that Photo Stream affects only photos that you take with the iPhone from the time you enable it, whereas the iCloud Photo Library feature uploads all of your photos—those you took in the past and will take in the future.

7. If you want all of your burst photos (photos taken in sequence, such as for action shots) to be uploaded to iCloud, set the Upload Burst Photos switch to on (green). In most cases, you should leave this off (white) because you typically don't want to keep all the photos in a burst. When you review and select photos to keep, the ones you keep are uploaded.

8. To be able to share your photos and to access photos other people share with you, set the iCloud Photo Sharing switch to on (green).

9. Tap iCloud.

Enabling iCloud to Store Information on the Cloud

One of the best things about iCloud is that it stores email, contacts, calendars, reminders, bookmarks, notes, and other data on the cloud so that all your iCloud-enabled devices can access the same information. You can choose the types of data stored on the cloud by performing the following steps:

1. Move to the iCloud screen. Just below the Storage information are the iCloud data options. Some of these have a right-facing arrow that you tap to configure options, and others have a two-position switch. The types of data that have switches are Mail, Contacts, Calendars, Reminders, Notes, Messages, Safari, News, Health, Wallet, Game Center, and Siri. When a switch is green, it means that switch is turned on and the related data is stored to your iCloud account and kept in sync with the information on the iPhone.

2. To store data on the cloud, set an app's switch to On (green). You might be prompted to merge that information with that already stored on the cloud. For example, if you have contacts information on your iPhone already and want to merge that with the contacts already on the cloud, tap Merge. If you don't want the contacts copied to the cloud, tap Don't Merge.

3. If you don't want a specific type of data to be stored on the cloud and synced to your iPhone, tap its switch to turn that data off (the switch becomes white instead of green).

Green means that data is being stored on the cloud

White means the data is not being stored on the cloud

When you turn off a switch because you don't want that information stored on the cloud any more, you might be prompted to keep the associated information on your iPhone or delete it.

If you choose Keep on My iPhone, the information remains on your iPhone but is no longer connected to the cloud; this means any changes you make exist only on the iPhone. If you choose Delete from My iPhone, the information is erased from your iPhone. Whether you choose to keep or delete the information, any information of that type that was previously stored on the cloud remains available there; the delete action affects only the information stored on the iPhone.

After you've configured each data switch on the iCloud screen, you're ready to configure the rest of the data options, which are explained in the following tasks.

Configuring Your iCloud Keychain

A keychain can be used to store usernames, passwords, and credit cards so you can access this information without retyping it every time you need it. Enabling keychain syncing through iCloud makes this information available on multiple devices. For example, if you've configured a website's password on your keychain on a Mac, that password is available in the Safari app if the keychain is synced via iCloud.

Follow these steps to enable keychain syncing through iCloud:

1. On the iCloud screen, tap Keychain.

2. If prompted to do so, enter your Apple ID password and tap OK (not shown in the figures).

3. Set the iCloud Keychain switch to on (green).

Your Experience May Vary

How iCloud Keychain syncing is configured can vary based on the current status of your keychain. These steps assume your keychain is already configured on another device, such as a Mac, and your iPhone is connecting to that keychain. If you don't have any keychain syncing configured, you might see additional steps when you perform step 3. In that case, just follow the onscreen prompts to complete the process.

It's Not All Good

Proceed with Caution

If you store a lot of sensitive information in your keychain on a Mac, such as usernames and passwords to websites, credit cards, and such, be careful about enabling keychain syncing. When you enable this iCloud feature, all this data becomes available on your iPhone and can be used by anyone who can use your phone. Assuming you have a passcode to the phone, you are protected from someone using your phone without you knowing it, but if you let someone use your phone, they can also use your sensitive information. You might choose to leave keychain syncing off and just keep a minimum amount of sensitive information on your phone.

>>>Go Further

CONFIGURING FIND MY iPHONE

Find My iPhone enables you to locate and secure your iPhone if you lose it. This feature is enabled by default when you sign in to your iCloud account. You should usually leave it enabled so that you have a better chance of locating your iPhone should you lose it—or in case you need to delete its data should you decide you won't be getting the iPhone back. There are a couple of configuration tasks you can do for Find My iPhone:

- To disable Find My iPhone, open the iCloud settings screen and tap Find My iPhone. Set the Find My iPhone switch to off (white) and enter your Apple ID password at the prompt. You can no longer access your iPhone via the Find My iPhone feature.

- To send the last known location of the iPhone to Apple when power is critically low, open the Find My iPhone settings screen and set the Send Last Location switch to on (green). When your iPhone is nearly out of power, its location is sent to Apple. You can contact Apple to try to determine where your iPhone was when the battery was almost out of power.

Configuring Your iCloud Backup

Like other digital devices, it is important to back up your iPhone's data so that you can recover should something bad happen to your iPhone. You can back up your iPhone's data and settings to iCloud, which is really useful because that means you can recover the backed-up data using a different device, such as a replacement iPhone. Configure your iCloud backup with the following steps:

1. On the iCloud settings screen, tap iCloud Backup.

2. Set the iCloud Backup switch to on (green). Your iPhone's data and settings are backed up to the cloud automatically.

3. Tap iCloud.

Back Me Up on This

You can manually back up your iPhone's data and settings at any time by tapping Back Up Now on the Backup screen. This can be useful to ensure recent data or settings changes are captured in your backup. For example, if you know you are going to be without a Wi-Fi connection to the Internet for a while, back up your phone to ensure that your current data is saved in the backup.

Configuring iCloud Drive

iCloud Drive, which is enabled by default, stores files (such as Keynote presentations) on the cloud so that you can work with those documents on any device. For example, you can create a Keynote presentation on a Mac and then access it on your iPhone to present it. To configure your iCloud Drive, perform the following steps:

1. On the iCloud settings screen, set the iCloud Drive switch to on (green).

2. Set the switch to on (green) for those apps that you do want to use the iCloud Drive to store data.

3. Set the switch to off (white) for any apps that you don't want to use your iCloud Drive.

Managing Your iCloud Storage

Your iCloud account includes storage space that you can use for your data including photos, documents, and so on. By default, your account includes 5 GB of free storage space. For many people, that is enough, but if you take a lot of photos and video and use the iCloud Photo Library feature, you might find that you need more space. It is easy (and relatively inexpensive) to upgrade the amount of room you have on your iCloud drive. You can use the STORAGE section on the iCloud settings screen to manage your storage space as follows:

1. Move to the top of the iCloud settings screen. Here you see a gauge that displays the amount of space you have and how that space is currently being used. The gray portion of the bar indicates how much free space you have; if this portion of the bar is very small, you might want to consider upgrading your storage space.

2. Tap Manage Storage. At the top of the iCloud Storage screen, you see the same storage information as on the prior screen. Under that, you see the tools you can use to manage your storage.

3. To change the amount of storage space available to you, tap Change and follow the onscreen prompts to upgrade (or downgrade) your storage.

4. If you use the Family Sharing feature, tap Share With Family to enable the people in your sharing group to store content on your iCloud drive.

How much space you are using versus how much is available to you

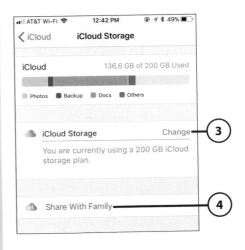

5. When the Share With Family feature is enabled, you can tap Family Usage to see how much space each member of the group is using (you can disable this feature through the Family Sharing option on the Apple ID screen).

6. Swipe up the screen to review all of the apps that are currently using iCloud storage space.

7. Tap an app to get details about how it is using iCloud space.

8. If the app works with documents, you see the list of documents and how much space each is using (if it doesn't use documents, you only see a total).

Delete or Disable?

When you delete documents or data from your iCloud storage, it is removed from the cloud. This also means it is removed from every device using that data on the cloud. If you want the app to stop storing data on the cloud, but keep the data on the devices currently using it, prevent it from using iCloud storage as described in "Configuring iCloud Drive" instead.

9. To remove documents and data from iCloud, tap Delete Documents & Data, Disable & Delete, or Delete Data. After you confirm the deletion, the app's data is deleted from your iCloud storage.

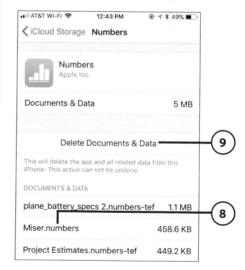

>>>*Go Further*

YET EVEN MORE iCLOUD CONFIGURATION OPTIONS

Most of the time, you can use your iCloud account just fine if you only configure it as described in the previous tasks. However, there are some other configuration options located at the bottom of the iCloud settings screen that you might want to use at some point:

- **Look Me Up**. Some iCloud-aware apps can look you up via your Apple ID; people who do this see your first and last names. You can tap Look Me Up to see which apps and people have accessed this information.

- **Share Your Location**. With this feature, you can share your location with others. You can enable the feature by setting its switch to on (green) and choosing which of your iCloud devices is used to determine your location. You can share your location in Messages, and you can enable people you've included in your Family Sharing group to view your location.

- **Mail**. Use this option to configure certain aspects of your iCloud email. These options are explained in Chapter 8, "Sending, Receiving, and Managing Email."

>>>*Go Further*

EMAIL ALIASES

One of the great features of iCloud is using email aliases. You can create alias addresses for specific purposes, such as avoiding spam or just to use an email address you prefer. Email sent to one of your aliases comes into your normal inbox. When you send email from an alias, it appears to be from the alias address, even though any aliases are still related to the same email account. You can create email aliases for your iCloud account using your iCloud website, available at www.icloud.com. Log in to your iCloud account, and then open the Mail app. Open the Mail Preferences dialog by clicking the gear icon and choosing Preferences. Then, click the Accounts tab, where you can create and manage up to three aliases.

Setting Up Other Types of Online Accounts on Your iPhone

Many types of online accounts provide different services, including email, calendars, contacts, social networking, and so on. To use these accounts, you need to configure them on your iPhone. The process you use for most types of accounts is similar to the steps you used to set up your iCloud account. In this section, you learn how to configure Exchange and Google accounts.

Configuring an Exchange Account

Microsoft Exchange is the most widely used system for corporate email. Your iPhone is compatible with Exchange, which is good news indeed. (You can even configure multiple Exchange accounts on your iPhone if you can't get by with just one.) You can sync Exchange email, contact, calendar, reminder, and notes information on your iPhone; this works similarly to synchronizing with your iPhone using an iCloud account.

Before you can use Exchange on your iPhone, the Exchange server for your account must be configured to support iOS devices. Almost all are these days. You need to have your email address, username, and password; you might also need the server address and domain. If you don't know this information for the Exchange account, you need to contact the IT organization providing the account to get it so you can configure it on your iPhone. With this information in hand, you can use the following steps to configure the Exchange account:

1. On the Home screen, tap Settings.

2. Tap Accounts & Passwords.

3. Tap Add Account.

4. Tap Exchange.

5. Enter your email address.

6. Change the description of the account if you want to use something more specific than Exchange.

7. Tap Next.

8. If you are presented with the option to do so, tap Sign In. This automatic configuration is easiest; if it doesn't work, you need to try the manual method, which is explained in the section "Configuring Other Types of Online Accounts" later in this chapter.

9. Enter your password.

10. Tap Sign In. The information you've entered is verified. If it can't be, you might have entered your password incorrectly, so try again.

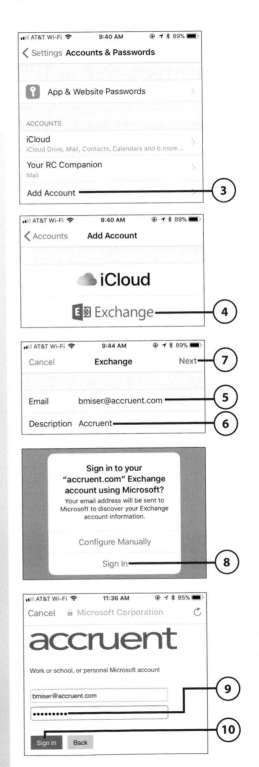

11. Tap Accept. You move back into the Settings app and see the account options screen.

12. If you don't want some of the available items, such as Notes, to be synced onto your iPhone, then set their switches to off (white).

13. Tap Save. You return to the Accounts & Passwords screen and see the Exchange account you just created. Under the account description is the information that is synced with the account, such as Mail, Contacts, Calendars, or Reminders.

14. Tap the new Exchange account.

15. Tap Mail Days to Sync.

16. Tap the time period over which you want emails to be synced; for example, tap 2 Weeks to have email sent to you within the past two weeks synced onto your iPhone.

17. Tap the name of your Exchange account. Your Exchange account information is available in the apps being synced on your iPhone.

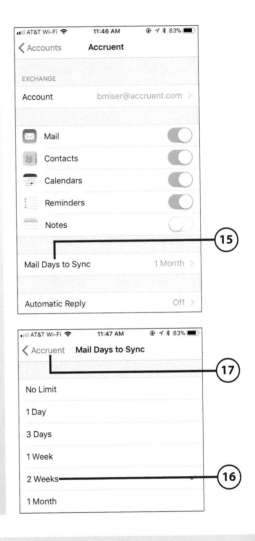

>>>Go Further

MORE ON EXCHANGE CONFIGURATION

There are several other things you might need to do to keep your Exchange account working as you want it to:

- The automatic configuration option, as described in these steps, is the easiest one and is also the one most widely used in the business world today. If it doesn't work for you, check with the IT organization that manages your Exchange account to get the exact configuration steps for your account. If you can't get direct support, you need the details about your account, including username, password, server address, and domain. With that information, you need to manually configure the account. This is similar to configuring other types of accounts, as described in "Setting Up an Online Account That Isn't Built-in."

- Sometimes, you might need to change your account's password if it gets reset (for security purposes most organizations require that Exchange passwords be reset after a certain amount of time, such as 90 days). Because your iPhone won't be able to connect your account with the current password, you see messages telling you the iPhone can't access your account. If you know the new password, enter it and tap OK; your account is updated and works again. However, if you don't have the new password with you, these prompts can be quite annoying as you have to keep clearing them and they keep reappearing immediately. They might even get your Exchange account locked if the iPhone tries and fails to connect a certain number of times. If this happens, you can disable the account by turning off all the data options so your phone won't try to connect to the account. After you get a new password, turn on the data options again and enter the new password at the prompt. Or, use the technique my great acquisitions editor employs; when she encounters a password issue, she puts the iPhone in Airplane mode and turns off Wi-Fi so it won't present annoying warnings until she updates the password.

- You can't change the password for an Exchange account on your iPhone. You have to change the password elsewhere, such as through your company's process or via the Outlook app on a Mac or Windows PC. After your Exchange password has been changed, you're prompted to enter the new password the first time your iPhone attempts to access your account.

- You can have a reply automatically sent in response to email you receive. To configure an automatic reply, move to the Exchange account's Settings screen. Tap Automatic Reply at the bottom of the screen. Set the Automatic Reply switch to on (green) and type the text to be sent in the automatic reply. Swipe down the screen and tap End Date at the top of the screen. Use the resulting date and time wheels to set when you want the automatic reply to stop being sent. Tap Save. From the current time until the one you set as the End Date, the automatic reply is sent to any email that is received by your Exchange account. You can stop the reply at any time by moving to the Automatic Reply screen and setting the Automatic Reply switch to off (white). You can also edit the text in the automatic reply on this screen.

Configuring a Google Account

A Google account provides email, contacts, calendar, and note syncing that are similar to iCloud and Exchange. To set up a Google account on your iPhone, do the following:

1. On the Home screen, tap Settings.

2. Tap Accounts & Passwords.

3. Tap Add Account.

4. Tap Google.

5. Enter your Google email address.

6. Tap Next.

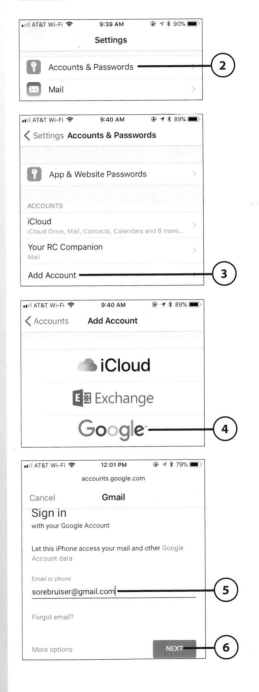

7. Enter your Google account password.

8. Tap Next.

9. Enable the features of the account you want to access on the iPhone—which are Mail, Contacts, Calendars, and Notes—by setting the switch to on (green) for the types of data you do want to use or to off (white) for the types of data you don't want to use.

10. Tap Save. The account is saved, and the data you enabled becomes available on your iPhone.

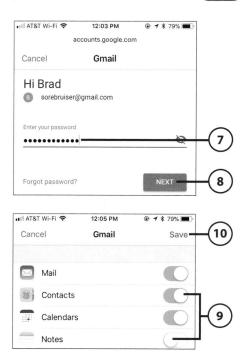

Advanced Google

Similar to iCloud and Exchange, a Google account has some settings you aren't likely to use, but it's good to know how to get to them in case you do. To access these settings, move to the tap Accounts & Passwords screen and tap your Google account. On the Gmail account's screen, you can change the types of data you are syncing by setting the switches to on or off. Tap Account, and then tap Advanced to see additional settings. Working with these is similar to working with iCloud and Exchange. For example, you can determine where draft email messages are stored, such as on the Gmail server or on your iPhone.

You can't change the password for a Google account in the Settings app on your iPhone. You have to change the password elsewhere, such as by accessing your Google account via the Google website. After your Google password has been changed, you're prompted to enter the new password the first time your iPhone attempts to access your account.

Configuring Other Types of Online Accounts

You can access many types of online accounts on your iPhone. These include accounts that are "built in," which are iCloud, Exchange, Google, Yahoo!, AOL, and Outlook.com. Setting up a Yahoo!, AOL, or Outlook.com account is similar to iCloud, Exchange, and Google. Just select the account type you want to use and provide the information for which you are prompted.

There are other types of accounts you might want to use that aren't "built in." An email account included with an Internet access account, such as one from a cable Internet provider, is one example. Support for these accounts isn't built in to the iOS; however, you can usually set up such accounts on your iPhone fairly easily.

When you obtain an account, such as email accounts that are part of your Internet service, you should receive all the information you need to configure those accounts on your iPhone. If you don't have this information, visit the provider's website and look for information on configuring the account in an email application. You need to have this information to configure the account on the iPhone.

Setting Up an Online Account that Isn't Built In

With the configuration information for the account you want to use on your iPhone in hand, you're ready to set it up:

1. On the Home screen, tap Settings.

2. Tap Accounts & Passwords.

3. Tap Add Account.

4. Tap Other.

5. Tap the type of account you want to add. For example, to set up an email account, tap Add Mail Account.

6. Enter the information by filling in the fields you see; various types of information are required for different kinds of accounts. You just need to enter the information you received from the account's provider.

7. Tap Next. If the iPhone can set up the account automatically, its information is verified and it's ready for you to use (if the account supports multiple types of information, you can enable or disable the types with which you want to work on your iPhone). If the iPhone can't set up the account automatically, you're prompted to enter additional information to complete the account configuration. When you're done, the account appears on the list of accounts and is ready for you to use.

8. Configure the switches for the data sync options you see. For example, to use the account for email, set the Mail switch to on (green).

9. Tap Save. The account you configured is available in the related app, such as Mail if you set up an email account.

Multiple Accounts

There is no limit (that I have found so far) on the number of online accounts (even of the same type, such as Gmail) that you can access on your iPhone. (You can only have one iCloud account configured on your iPhone at the same time.)

Setting How and When Your Accounts Are Updated

The great thing about online accounts is that their information can be updated any time your iPhone can connect to the Internet. This means you have access to the latest information, such as new emails, changes to your calendars, and so on. There are three basic ways information gets updated:

- **Push**—When information is updated via Push, the server pushes (thus the name) updated information onto your iPhone whenever that information changes. For example, when you receive a new email, that email is immediately sent (or pushed) to your iPhone. Push provides you with the most current information all the time but uses a lot more battery than the other options.

- **Fetch**—When information is updated via Fetch, your iPhone connects to the account and retrieves the updated information according to a schedule, such as every 15 minutes. Fetch doesn't keep your information quite as current as Push does, but it uses much less battery than Push does.

- **Manual**—You can cause an app's information to be updated manually. This happens whenever you open or move into an app or by a manual refresh. For example, you can get new email by moving onto the Inboxes screen in the Mail app and swiping down from the top of the screen.

You can configure the update method that is used globally, and you can set the method for specific accounts. Some account types, such as iCloud and Exchange, support all three options whereas others might support only Fetch and Manual. The global option for updating is used unless you override it for individual accounts. For example, you might want your work account to be updated via Push so your information there is always current, whereas configuring Fetch on a personal account might be frequent enough.

Configuring How New Data Is Retrieved for Your Accounts

To configure how your information is updated, perform the following steps:

1. Move to the Accounts & Passwords screen of the Settings app.

2. Tap Fetch New Data.

3. To enable data to be pushed to your iPhone, slide the Push switch to on (green). To disable push to extend battery life, set it to off (white). This setting is global, mean-ing that if you disable Push here, it is disabled for all accounts even though you can still configure Push to be used for individual accounts. For example, if your Exchange account is set to use Push but Push is globally disabled, the Exchange account's setting is ignored and data is fetched instead.

4. To change how an account's information is updated, tap it. The account's screen displays. The options on this screen depend on the kind of account it is. You always have Fetch and Manual; Push is displayed only for accounts that support it.

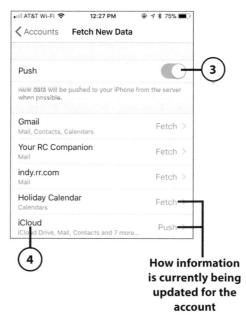

How information is currently being updated for the account

5. Tap the option you want to use for the account: Push, Fetch, or Manual.

If you choose Manual, information is retrieved only when you manually start the process by opening the related app (such as Mail to get your email) or by using the refresh gesture, regardless of the global setting.

If you choose Fetch, information is updated according to the schedule you set in step 9.

6. If you choose the Push option in step 5 and are working with an email account, choose the mailboxes whose information you want to be pushed by tapping them so they have a check mark; to prevent a mailbox's information from being pushed, tap it so that it doesn't have a check mark. (The Inbox is selected by default and can't be unselected.)

7. Tap Fetch New Data.

8. Repeat steps 5–7 until you have set the update option for each account. (The current option is shown to the right of the account's name.)

9. Tap the amount of time when you want the iPhone to fetch data when Push is turned off globally or for those accounts for which you have selected Fetch or that don't support Push; tap Manually if you want to manually check for information for Fetch accounts or when Push is off. Information for your accounts is updated according to your settings.

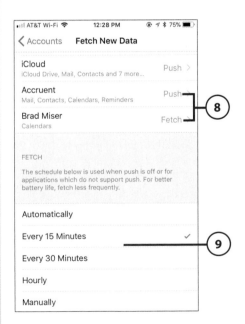

>>>Go Further

TIPS FOR MANAGING YOUR ACCOUNTS

As you add and use accounts on your iPhone, keep the following points in mind:

- You can temporarily disable any data for any account by moving to the Accounts & Passwords screen and tapping that account. Set the switches for the data you don't want to use to off (white). You might be prompted to keep or delete that information; if you choose to keep it, the data remains on your iPhone but is disconnected from the account and is no longer updated. If you delete it, you can always recover it again by simply turning that data back on. For example, suppose you are going on vacation and don't want to deal with work email, meeting notifications, and so on. Move to your work account and disable all its data. That data disappears from the related apps; for example, the account's mailboxes no longer appear in the Mail app. When you want to start using the account again, simply re-enable its data.

- If you want to completely remove an account from your iPhone, move to its configuration screen, swipe up the screen, and tap Delete Account. Tap Delete in the confirmation dialog box and the account is removed from your iPhone. (You can always sign in to the account to start using it again.)

- You can have different notifications for certain aspects of an account, such as email. See Chapter 2, "Using Your iPhone's Core Features," for the details about using notifications, and Chapter 4 for the steps to configure the notifications your online accounts use. For example, you might want to hear a different sound when you receive work emails versus those sent to your personal account.

- You can change how information is updated at any time, too. If your iPhone is running low on battery, disable Push and set Fetch to Manually so you can control when the updates happen. When your battery is charged again, you can re-enable Push or set a Fetch schedule.

Tap to personalize your iPhone to make it your own

Install apps so you can do all kinds of useful and fun things with your iPhone

Configure notifications from apps so they provide the right amount of information at the right times

In this chapter, you learn how to make an iPhone into *your* iPhone. Topics include the following:

→ Configuring notifications
→ Scheduling Do Not Disturb
→ Configuring the Control Center
→ Configuring the Widget Center
→ Setting keyboard, language, and format options
→ Setting Privacy and Location Services preferences
→ Setting passcode, Touch ID, and content restrictions
→ Customizing how your iPhone works with apps

Customizing How Your iPhone Works

As you've seen in previous chapters, the Settings app enables you to configure various aspects of your iPhone, such as connecting your iPhone to a Wi-Fi network and configuring iCloud and other online accounts. The Settings app provides many other configuration tools that you can use to tailor how your iPhone works to suit your preferences.

Perhaps the most important settings are related to the security of your iPhone, which you can configure by setting a passcode and fingerprint recognition using Touch ID along with your privacy and location settings. Also very important is configuring the notifications your iPhone uses so you get the information you need without being constantly bombarded; setting a Do Not Disturb schedule helps prevent your iPhone from bothering you when you don't want it to. You can also configure the Control Center, Widget Center, keyboards, privacy and location services options, and how content on your phone can be accessed.

Although the Settings app enables you to customize how your iPhone works in many ways, installing apps on your iPhone enables it to do so much more than it can "out of the box." You'll want to explore and download apps to completely customize how you use your iPhone; the possibilities of what your phone can do with apps are limitless!

Configuring Notifications

In Chapter 2, "Using Your iPhone's Core Features," you learned how to work with the various types of notifications your iPhone presents to keep you informed of important (and at times, not-so-important) information. Notifications can become distracting or overwhelming because the apps on your phone can provide notifications about all manner of things—incoming mail, messages, news updates, and so on. If an app manages a lot of activity, it can generate multiple notifications over a short period of time.

You can configure how apps can provide notifications and, if you allow notifications, which type. You can also configure other aspects of notifications, such as whether an app's notifications appear in the Notification Center or if they appear on the Lock screen. Apps can support different notification options; some apps, such as Mail, support notification configuration by account (for example, you can set a different alert sound for new mail in each account). You can follow the same general steps to configure notifications for each app; you should explore the options for the apps you use most often to ensure they work the best for you.

The steps in the following task show you how to configure Mail's notifications, which is a good example because it supports a lot of notification features; the notification settings for other apps might have fewer features or might be organized slightly differently. But configuring the notifications for any app follows a similar pattern as exemplified by the steps for Mail's notification settings.

To configure notifications from the Mail app, perform the following steps:

1. Tap Settings on the Home screen.

2. Tap Notifications.

3. Tap Show Previews. As you may recall from Chapter 2, alerts from an app can contain a preview of the information related to the alert, such as part of an email message.

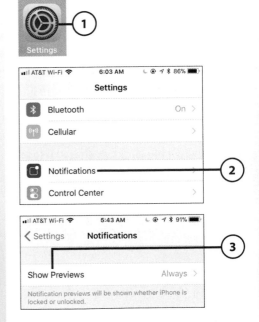

4. To have alerts always show the preview, tap Always; tap When Unlocked to show previews only when your iPhone is unlocked; or tap Never to hide previews. This is a global setting for all apps. You can override this for individual apps as you see in later steps.

5. Tap Notifications. In the Notification Style section, you see all the apps installed on your phone. Along with the app name and icon, you see the current status of its notifications.

6. Swipe up or down the screen to locate the app whose notifications you want to configure. (The apps are listed in alphabetical order.)

7. Tap the app whose notifications you want to configure.

8. If you want the app to provide notifications, set the Allow Notifications switch to on (green) and move to step 9. If you don't want notifications from the app, set the Allow Notifications switch to off (white) and skip to step 25.

9. Tap the account for which you want to configure notifications; if the app doesn't support accounts, skip this step.

10. Tap Sounds.

Notification options enabled

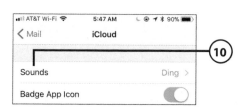

11. Use the resulting Sounds screen to choose the alert sound and vibration for new email messages to the account (see "Choosing the Sounds and Vibratory Feedback Your iPhone Uses" in Chapter 5, "Customizing How Your iPhone Looks and Sounds," for the details about configuring sounds and vibrations).

12. Tap the back icon located in the upper-left corner of the screen (how it is labeled depends on what you are working with; for example, it shows the account name when you are working with a Mail account).

13. To display the app's badge (which shows the number of new items in that app or account), set the Badge App Icon switch to on (green). (If you set this to off (white) for an account, new items sent to that account won't be included in the count of new items shown on the badge.)

14. If you want the app's or account's notifications to appear on the Lock screen, slide the Show on Lock Screen switch to on (green). If you receive sensitive information to the account, you might want to leave this off so that this information isn't displayed on the Lock screen, which anyone who has access to your iPhone can view.

15. To show notifications from the app/account in the Notification Center, set the Show in History switch to on (green); if you set this to off (white), notifications from the app/account are not shown in the Notification Center.

16. If you want to receive banner notifications for the account, set the Show as Banners switch to on (green); if you don't want banner notifications, leave this set to off (white) and skip to step 18.

17. Tap Temporary if you want banners to appear on the screen for a few seconds and then disappear or Persistent if you want them to remain on the screen until you take action on them (such as reading the associated email). You know which type is currently selected because its name appears in an oblong.

18. Tap Show Previews.

19. Tap Always (Default) if you always want previews to appear in notifications; When Unlocked if you want them to appear only when your iPhone is unlocked; or Never if you don't want previews to be displayed at any time. This setting overrides the global setting you configured earlier.

20. Tap the back icon, which is located in the upper-left corner of the window.

21. Tap the back icon, which is located in the upper-left corner of the window.

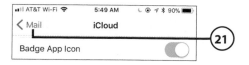

22. Configure notifications for the other accounts used in the app.

23. Configure notifications for VIP email and threads.

24. Tap Notifications.

25. Repeat steps 6 through 24 for each app shown on the Notifications screen. Certain apps might not have all the options shown in these steps, but the process to configure their notifications is similar.

26. Swipe up until you reach the bottom of the screen.

27. Configure any special notifications you see. What you see here depends on the country or region your phone is associated with. For example, where I live in the United States, the GOVERNMENT ALERTS section includes two notifications. AMBER Alerts are issued when a child is missing and presumed abducted, whereas Emergency Alerts are issued for things such as national crises, local weather, and so on. You can use the switches to enable (green) or prevent (white) these types of alerts, but you can't configure them.

More Options

Some apps provide notifications for the types of activity they manage. For example, the Calendar app enables you to configure notifications for upcoming events, invitations, and so on. Open the Notification Settings screen for the apps you use frequently to explore the notification options they offer.

>>>Go Further

NOTIFY THIS

Here are some other hopefully useful notification tidbits for your consideration:

- **VIPS**—Mail supports VIPs, which are people from whom email messages are treated specially, such as having a dedicated mailbox in the Mail app. You can apply specific notification settings to VIP messages using the VIP notification option. These override the notification settings for the email account to which messages from VIPs are sent.

- **Threads**—Mail can keep related messages together as threads. Like VIP messages, you can override Mail's notifications for messages that are part of threads using the Thread Notifications option.

- **Special sounds and vibrations for contacts**—You can override some app's sounds and vibration notification settings for individuals in your Contacts app. For example, you can configure a specific ringtone, new text tone, and vibrations for calls or texts from a contact. You do this using the contact information screen as explained in Chapter 6, "Managing Contacts."

- **Installed app not shown**—You must have opened an app at least once for it to appear on the Notifications screen.

- **Initial notification prompt**—The first time you open many apps, you are prompted to allow that app to send you notifications. If you allow this, the app is able to send notifications about its activity. If you deny this, the app isn't able to send notifications. You can always configure the app's notifications using the steps in this task regardless of your initial decision.

- **Lots of apps**—If you have a lot of apps or activity on your iPhone, notifications can become disruptive. It can take a little time to set each app's notifications, but making sure you receive only the notifications that are important to you prevents your iPhone from bothering you unnecessarily.

Scheduling Do Not Disturb

As you learned in Chapter 1 "Getting Started with Your iPhone," the Do Not Disturb feature enables you to temporarily silence notifications; you can also configure quiet times during which notifications are automatically silenced by performing the following steps:

1. Open the Settings app and tap Do Not Disturb.

2. To activate Do Not Disturb manually, set the Manual switch to on (green). (This does the same thing as activating it from the Control Center as explained in Chapter 1.)

3. To configure Do Not Disturb to activate automatically on a schedule, set the Scheduled switch to on (green).

4. Tap the From and To box.

5. Tap From.

6. Swipe on the time selection wheels to select the hour and minute (AM or PM) when you want the Do Not Disturb period to start.

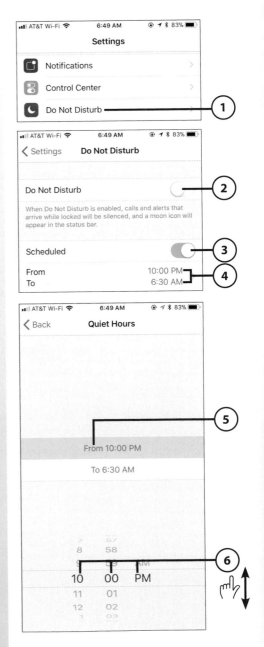

7. Tap To.

8. Swipe on the time selection wheels to set the hour and minute (AM or PM) when you want the Do Not Disturb period to end.

9. Tap Back.

10. If you want notifications to be silenced during the Do Not Disturb period only when your phone is locked, tap While iPhone is locked. Tap Always if you want notifications to be silenced regardless of the Lock status. This setting presumes that if your iPhone is unlocked, you won't mind taking calls or having notifications even if it is within the Do Not Disturb period because you are probably using the phone.

11. Tap Allow Calls From.

12. Tap the option for the group of people whose calls should be allowed during the Do Not Disturb period. The options are Everyone, which allows all calls to come in; No One, which sends all calls directly to voicemail; Favorites, which allows calls from people on your Favorites lists to come through but calls from all others go to voicemail; or one of your contact groups, which allows calls from anyone in the selected group to come through while all others go to voicemail.

13. Tap Back.

14. Set the Repeated Calls switch to on (green) if you want a second call from the same person within three minutes to be allowed through. This feature is based on the assumption that if a call is really important, the person calling you will try again immediately.

15. Tap Activate in the DO NOT DISTURB WHILE DRIVING section.

16. To have Do Not Disturb activate automatically when you are driving, tap Automatically to have this based on your iPhone's motion (once the iPhone's accelerometer detects that the phone has reached a particular speed) or When Connected to Car Bluetooth to have Do Not Disturb active whenever your iPhone is connected to your car's Bluetooth system; to prevent this type of automatic activation, tap Manually.

17. Tap Do Not Disturb.

18. Tap Auto-Reply To.

19. Configure when you want auto-matic replies to be sent when Do Not Disturb is on (regardless of how it was activated) by tapping No One to prevent automatic replies; Recents to send replies to people on your recent lists (such as calls you have recently received); Favorites to send replies to your favorites; or All Contacts to automatically reply to anyone on your Contacts lists.

20. Tap Back.

21. Tap Auto-Reply.

22. Type the message you want to be automatically sent.

23. Tap Do Not Disturb. During the Do Not Disturb period or based on the DO NOT DISTURB WHILE DRIVING setting, your iPhone is silent, except for any exceptions you configured. Automatic replies are sent accord-ing to your configuration. When the scheduled Do Not Disturb period ends, your iPhone resumes its nor-mal notification activity.

Configuring the Control Center

As you learned in Chapters 1 and 2, the Control Center provides quick access to a number of your iPhone's features and tools. The top part of the Control Center screen always contains the same controls, but you can configure the controls toward the bottom of the Control Center by performing the following steps:

1. Open the Settings app and tap Control Center.

2. To be able to access the Control Center while you are using apps, set the Access Within Apps switch to on (green). If you set this to off, you need to move back to the Home or Lock screen to use the Control Center.

3. Tap Customize Controls. The Customize screen has two sections: INCLUDE shows the tools installed in your Control Center, whereas MORE CONTROLS shows tools that are available for you to add to the Control Center.

4. To remove a tool from the Control Center, tap its unlock (–) icon.

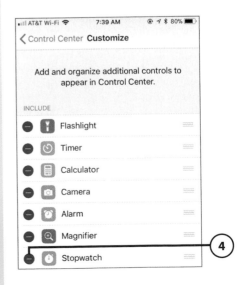

5. Tap Remove. The tool is moved from the INCLUDE list to the MORE CONTROLS list.

6. To add a control to the Control Center, tap its add (+) icon. The control moves to the bottom of the INCLUDE list.

7. Move a control higher on the Control Center by dragging its order (three lines) icon up the INCLUDE list or move it lower by dragging its order icon down the list. The top four controls on the list appear first in the customizable part of the Control Center; the next four are below those, and so on.

8. Repeat steps 4 through 7 until you have all the controls you want on the Control Center in the order you want them. The next time you open the Control Center, it reflects the changes you made.

Your Control Center Options Are Limited

There are more controls on the Control Center than you see on the Customize screen. You can't change some of the Control Center's options. For example, you always see the Airplane Mode, Cellular Data, Wi-Fi, and Bluetooth icons on the Control Center. The area you can customize is below the Screen Mirroring, Brightness, and Volume controls.

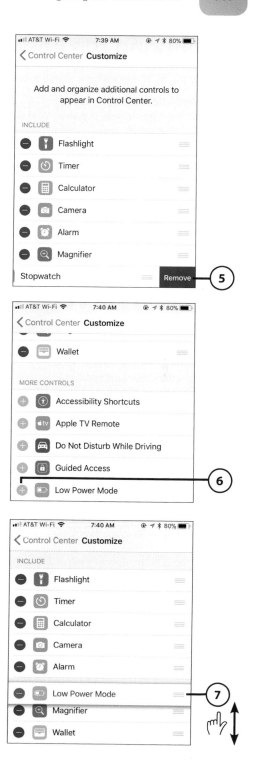

Configuring the Widget Center

As described in Chapters 1 and 2, the Widget Center provides quick access to widgets that enable you to take action or to view information. You can determine which widgets are shown in the Widget Center and the order in which those widgets appear on the screen; for example, you might want your most frequently used widgets to be at the top of the screen.

To configure the Widget Center, perform the following steps:

1. Open the Widget Center by moving to the Home screen and swiping all the way to the right.

2. Swipe all the way up the screen.

3. Tap Edit. You see the Add Widgets screen. This screen has two sections. At the top are the currently installed widgets; installed widgets have the unlock (–) icon next to their icons. Toward the bottom of the screen, you see the MORE WIDGETS section that shows you available widgets that aren't currently in your Widget Center.

4. To remove a widget, tap its unlock (–) icon.

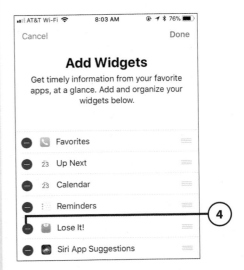

5. Tap Remove. The widget is removed from your Widget Center and moved onto the MORE WIDGETS list.

6. Swipe up the screen until you see the MORE WIDGETS section. Widgets that are new since the last time you viewed this list are marked with a blue circle.

7. To add a widget to the Widget Center, tap its add (+) icon. The widget jumps up the screen to become the last widget on the list of widgets in the Widget Center.

8. To change where a widget appears in the Widget Center, drag its order icon up or down the screen. When it is in the position you want, take your finger off the screen and the widget is placed there.

9. Repeat steps 4 through 8 until the Widget Center contains the widgets you want to access, in the order in which you want them to be shown.

10. When you're done making changes to the Widget Center, tap Done. You return to the Widget Center and see the results of the changes you've made.

New Widgets

When new widgets become available, you see a message under Edit on the Widget Center screen. Tap this to move into Edit mode, so you can see the new widgets and add them to the Widget Center if you want to use them.

New widget

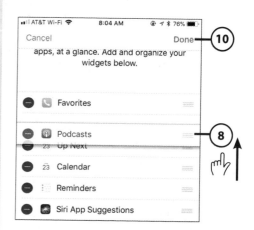

Setting Keyboard, Language, and Format Options

You'll be working with text in many apps on your iPhone. You can customize a number of keyboard- and format-related options so text appears and behaves the way you want it to.

Setting Keyboard Preferences

You use the iPhone's keyboard to input text in many apps, including Mail, Messages, and so on. A number of settings determine how the keyboard works.

1. On the Settings screen, tap General.

2. Swipe up the screen.

3. Tap Keyboard.

4. Tap Keyboards. This enables you to activate more keyboards so that you can choose a specific language's keyboard when you are entering text. At the top of the screen, you see the keyboards that are available to you.

5. Tap Add New Keyboard.

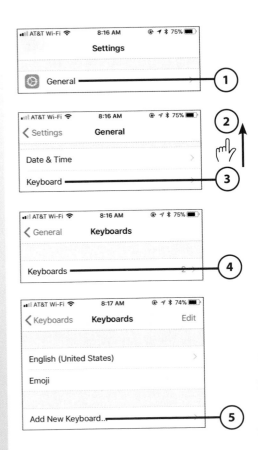

Fun in Text

The Emoji keyboard allows you to include a huge variety of smiley faces, symbols, and other icons whenever you type. The Emoji keyboard is active by default; however, if you don't see it on the list of active keyboards, you can use these steps to activate it.

---

6. Swipe up and down the screen to browse the available keyboards.

7. Tap the keyboard you want to add.

8. Tap the keyboard you added in step 7.

9. Tap the keyboard layout you want to use. (Not all keyboards support options; if the one you are configuring doesn't, skip this step.)

10. Tap Keyboards.

11. Repeat steps 5–10 to add and configure additional keyboards.

12. Tap Keyboards.

>>>Go Further

THIRD-PARTY KEYBOARDS

You can install and use keyboards from third parties (meaning not Apple) on your iPhone. To do this, open the App Store app and search for "keyboards for iPhone" or you can search for a specific keyboard by name if you know of one you want to try. (See "Using the App Store App to Find and Install iPhone Apps," later in this chapter for help using the App Store app.) After you have downloaded the keyboard you want to use, use steps 1–5 to move back to the Keyboards Settings screen. When you open the Add New Keyboard screen, you see a section called THIRD-PARTY KEY-BOARDS in which you see the additional keyboards you have installed. Tap a keyboard in this section to activate it as you do with the default keyboards. When you move back to the Keyboards screen, you see the keyboard you just activated. Tap it to configure its additional options. Then you can use the new keyboard just like the others you have activated. Make sure you check out the documentation for any keyboards you download so you take advantage of all of their features.

13. Tap One Handed Keyboard.

14. To be able to use the one-handed keyboard (which squishes all the keys toward one side of the screen), tap Left to place it on the left side or Right to put it on the right side of the screen; tap Off if you don't want to use the one-handed keyboard.

15. Tap Back.

16   To prevent your iPhone from automatically capitalizing as you type, set Auto-Capitalization to off (white).

17. To disable the automatic spell checking/correction, set Auto-Correction to off (white).

18. To disable the iPhone's Spell Checker, set the Check Spelling switch to off (white).

19. To disable the Caps Lock function, set the Enable Caps Lock to off (white).

20. To disable the iPhone's Predictive Text feature (see Chapter 2), set the Predictive switch to off (white).

21. To prevent the iPhone from automatically trying to correct your punctuation, set the Smart Punctuation switch to off (white).

22. To prevent the character you type from being shown in a magnified pop-up as you type it, set the Character Preview switch to off (white).

23. To disable the shortcut that types a period followed by a space when you tap the space bar twice, set the "." Shortcut switch to off (white). You must tap a period and the spacebar to type these characters when you end a sentence.

24. To disable the iPhone's dictation feature, set the Enable Dictation switch to off (white). The microphone key won't appear on the keyboard and you won't be able to dictate text.

25. If dictation is enabled, tap Dictation Languages.

26. If you don't want to be able to use dictation with a language, tap it so that it doesn't have a check mark. If you do want to be able to dictate in a listed language, ensure it has a check mark (if it doesn't, tap it).

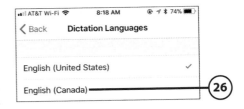

Language Options

The keyboard options you see depend on the language being used. For example, if settings apply only to a specific language, you see them in that language's section.

Changing Keyboards

To delete a keyboard, move to the Keyboards Settings screen and swipe to the left on the keyboard you want to remove. Tap Delete. The keyboard is removed from the list of activated keyboards and is no longer available to you when you type. (You can always activate it again later.) To change the order in which keyboards appear, move to the Keyboards screen, tap Edit, and drag the keyboards up and down the screen. When you've finished, tap Done. (An explanation of how to switch between keyboards when you type is provided in Chapter 2.)

Creating and Working with Text Replacements

Text replacements are useful because you can use just a few letters to type a series of words. You type the replacement, and it is replaced by the phrase with which it is associated. To configure your text replacements, do the following:

1. Move to the Keyboards screen as described in steps 1–3 in the previous task.

2. Tap Text Replacement.

3. Review the current replacements.

4. To add a replacement, tap Add (+).

5. Type the phrase for which you want to create a replacement.

6. Type the shortcut you want to be replaced by the phrase you created in step 5.

7. Tap Save. If the replacement doesn't contain any disallowed characters, it is created and you move back to the Text Replacement screen where you see your new text replacement. If there is an error, you see an explanation of the error; you must correct it before you can create the replacement.

8. Repeat steps 4–7 to create other text replacements.

9. When you've created all the replacements you want, tap Keyboards.

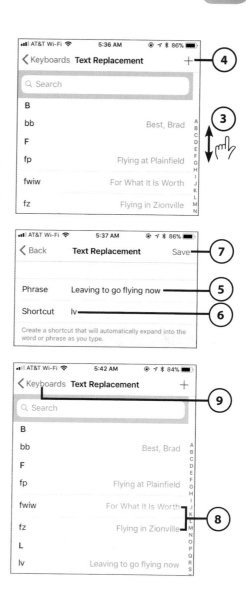

Shortcuts to Replacements

To change a replacement, tap it. Use the resulting screen to change the phrase or shortcut, and tap Save to update the replacement. To remove a replacement, swipe to the left on it and tap Delete. To search for a replacement, tap in the Search bar at the top of the screen and type the replacements you want to see; you can also use the index along the right side of the screen to find replacements. You can also tap Edit on the Shortcuts screen to change your replacements. And, yes, you can create a phrase without a replacement, but I don't really see much use for that!

Setting Language and Region Preferences

There are a number of formatting preferences you can set that determine how information is formatted in various apps. For example, you can choose how addresses are formatted by default by choosing the region whose format you want to follow.

1. On the Settings screen, tap General.

2. Swipe up the screen.

3. Tap Language & Region.

4. Tap iPhone Language.

5. Swipe up and down the screen to view the languages with which your iPhone can work or tap in the Search bar and type a language you want to use to find it. The current language is marked with a check mark.

6. Tap the language you want to use.

7. Tap Done.

8. Tap to confirm the change in language you indicated. Your iPhone screen goes dark while the iPhone switches to the new language. When it comes back, you return to the Language & Region screen, and the language you selected starts being used.

9. Tap Add Language.

10. Using steps 5–7, find and tap a secondary language. This language is used when your primary language can't be, such as on websites that don't support your primary language.

11. Tap Done.

12. Tap the language you want to be primary to confirm it. The language you selected is configured and you move back to the Language & Region screen. The new language is shown on the list in the center of the screen.

Order, Order!

To change the order of preference for the languages you have configured, tap Edit, drag the languages up or down the screen to set their order, and tap Done to save your changes.

---

13. To add more languages, tap Add Language and follow steps 10–12 to add more languages.

14. Tap Region.

15. Swipe up and down the regions available to you. The current region is marked with a check mark.

16. Tap the region whose formatting you want to use; if there are options within a region, you move to an additional screen and can tap the specific option you want to use.

17. Tap Done.

18. If you've changed the region, tap the language you want to use as the primary iPhone language. Your iPhone starts using the formatting associated with the region you selected.

19. Tap Calendar.

20. Tap the calendar you want your iPhone to use.

21. Tap Back.

22. Tap Temperature Unit.

23. Tap the unit in which you want temperatures to be displayed.

24. Tap Back.

25. Swipe up until you see the bottom of the screen where there are examples of the format options you have selected, such as the time and date format.

>>>Go Further

THE ACCESSIBLE iPHONE

If you tap the Accessibility option on the General Settings screen, you see a large number of options you can configure to make your iPhone more accessible. For example, you can enable VoiceOver to have the iPhone guide you through screens by speaking their contents. Zoom magnifies the entire screen. Magnifier enables you to use the iPhone's camera to quickly magnify things. Under the Speech option, Speak Selection has the iPhone speak text you have selected, and Speak Auto-text has the iPhone speak corrections it suggests to you, such as auto-capitalizations. There are other options you can configure; explore this screen to find settings of interest to you. If your iPhone starts looking or behaving quite differently, move back to this screen to make sure an Accessibility option hasn't been enabled accidentally. There are many options here, and sometimes one or more of them is turned on accidentally, and it can be confusing if you aren't expecting it. Even if you don't have any type of physical challenges, some of these options can still be quite useful. For example, the Magnifier comes in really handy when you need to look at something too small to see comfortably without an aid (you can put the Magnifier on your Control Center for quick access).

Setting Privacy and Location Services Preferences

Using its GPS or network connection, your iPhone's Location Services feature can determine where the phone is. This is useful in many situations, such as in the Maps app when you want to generate directions. Lots of other apps use this capability, too, such as apps that provide you location-specific information (the Uber app uses it to determine your location when you request a ride, for example). You can configure certain aspects of how these services work. And, if you don't want specific apps to be able to access your iPhone's current location, you can disable this feature for those apps. Of course, if you do, apps that rely on this capability don't work properly (they prompt you to allow access to this service as you try to use them).

You can also determine which apps can access certain kinds of information, such as the apps that are able to access your contact information in the Contacts app.

To configure privacy settings, do the following:

1. Move to the Settings screen and tap Privacy.

2. Tap Location Services.

3. To disable Location Services for all apps, set the Location Services switch to off (white); to leave it enabled, skip to step 5.

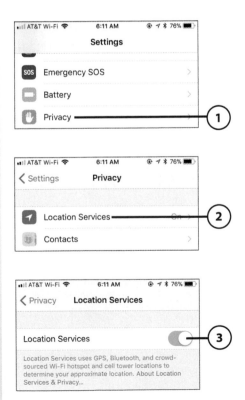

4. Tap Turn Off at the prompt. No apps are able to identify your location; skip the rest of these steps because they don't apply when Location Services is disabled.

5. Tap Share My Location. You can share your location with others in several areas, such as the Messages app.

6. To prevent your location from being shared, set the Share My Location switch to off (white) and skip to step 10. If you leave this switch on (green), move to the next step.

7. Tap From.

8. Tap the device that should be used to identify your location (this only applies if you have multiple devices configured with your Apple ID).

9. Tap Back.

10. Tap Back.

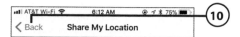

11. Swipe up and down the list of apps on the Location Services screen. These are all the apps that have requested access to your iPhone's location. Along the right side of the screen, you see the current status of Location Sharing for the app. Always means that the app can always access your location. While Using means the app can only access your location information while you are using it. Never means that using location information for the app has been disabled (some apps don't work properly when set to this status). Apps marked with a purple arrow have recently accessed your location; those that have done so within the past 24 hours are marked with a gray arrow. An outline purple arrow indicates that the app is using a geofence, which is a perimeter around a location that defines an area that is used to trigger some event, such as a reminder.

12. Tap an app to configure its access to Location Services.

13. Tap the status in which you want to place the app's access to your location. Some apps only have the Always or Never options, whereas others also have the While Using the App option.

14. Tap Back.

Share with Family?

The iPhone's Family Sharing feature enables you to designate up to five other people as a family (they don't actually have to be related to you in any way). When you do this, you can allow members of this group to share content you have downloaded, such as music or movies, from the iTunes Store. You can also share your location information with them. When Family Sharing is enabled, you see the members of the family group on the Share My Location screen. You can tap each person and tap Share My Location to share your location with that person. The people in your family with whom you share your location can see it in the Find Friends app.

15. Repeat steps 12–14 for each app whose access to your location you want to configure.

16. Tap System Services.

17. Enable or disable Location Services for the System Services you see. As with apps, if you disable Location Services for a system function, it might not work properly.

18. Tap Back.

19. Tap Privacy. Next, allow or prevent apps or other services from accessing data stored on your iPhone.

20. Tap an app or service on the list; this example shows Bluetooth Sharing. A list of apps that have requested to use the app's data or a service (in this example, Bluetooth) is displayed. If the requesting app or service is able to use the app's data, its switch is on (green).

>>>Go Further

MORE ON SYSTEM SERVICES

One of the System Services is Significant Locations. This service tracks places you visit. This information is used to improve the performance of some apps. If you want to prevent this, tap Significant Locations, enter your passcode or touch the Touch ID/Home button, and then set the Significant Locations switch to off (white).

You can use the switches in the PRODUCT IMPROVEMENT section to enable or disable various types of information from being collected, such as what is popular near you.

Use the Status Bar Icon switch to enable or disable the Location Services arrow at the top of the screen when a system service is accessing location information. (This arrow always appears when apps use location information.)

21. Prevent a requesting app or service from accessing the app's data by setting its switch to off (white). That app is no longer able to use the data it requested (which can inhibit some of its functionality).

22. Tap Privacy.

23. Repeat steps 20–22 for each app or service on the list. Most of time, you can just leave the permissions with the default setting (unless you want to block a specific app from using a certain kind of data).

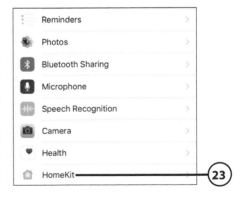

>>>*Go Further*

MORE ON PRIVACY

At the bottom of the Privacy screen, you see Analytics. Under this section, you can determine if information about performance of apps and your device is communicated back to Apple. You can also determine if information about the performance of apps is shared with app developers.

You also see the Advertising option. If you tap this, you can limit the tracking of ads you view by setting the Limit Ad Tracking switch to on (green). Typically, this tracking is used by advertisers to present ads that are related to ads you have viewed (the point being to make the ads more effective). You can reset the identifier used to identify you by tapping Reset Advertising Identifier and then tapping Reset Identifier. You can tap View Ad Information to see your status with respect to advertising in Apple apps.

Configuring Passcode, Touch ID, and Content Restrictions

Your iPhone contains data you probably don't want others to access. You can (and should) require a passcode so your iPhone can't be unlocked without the proper passcode being entered. This gives you a measure of protection should you lose control of your phone. If you have an iPhone 5s or later, you can record your fingerprints so that you can unlock your phone (by automatically entering the passcode) and enter your Apple ID password by touching the Touch ID/ Home button. The capability can also be used in other apps and services that require confirmation, such as Apple Pay, banking apps, and others.

You can also restrict the access to specific content and apps on your phone. Suppose you let other people borrow your iPhone but don't want them to use certain apps or to see data you'd rather keep to yourself. You can enable a restriction to prevent someone from accessing these areas without entering the restriction code. You can also restrict the use of apps, movies, music, and other content based on the age rating that the app or other content has.

Configuring Your Passcode and Touch ID

To configure the passcode you have to enter to unlock your iPhone, perform the following steps (note these steps show an iPhone that supports Touch ID; if your model doesn't have this, the steps are slightly different as you will only be configuring a passcode):

iPhone X and Face ID

The iPhone X uses Face ID instead of Touch ID. For help configuring and working with Face ID, download the online supplement *My iPhone X* by going to www.informit.com/myiphone11.

1. On the Settings screen, tap Touch ID & Passcode.

2. Tap Turn Passcode On.

3. Enter a six-digit passcode.

4. Re-enter the passcode. If the two passcodes match, the passcode is set.

Already Have a Passcode?

When you first turned your iPhone on, you were prompted to create a passcode and to record a fingerprint for Touch ID. If your iPhone already has a passcode set, when you perform step 1, you're prompted to enter your current passcode. When you enter it correctly, you move to the Passcode Lock screen, and you can make changes to the current passcode, add new fingerprints, and so on. In that case, you can skip directly to step 5. If you want to change your current passcode, tap Change Passcode and follow steps 3 and 4 to change it. Then continue with step 5.

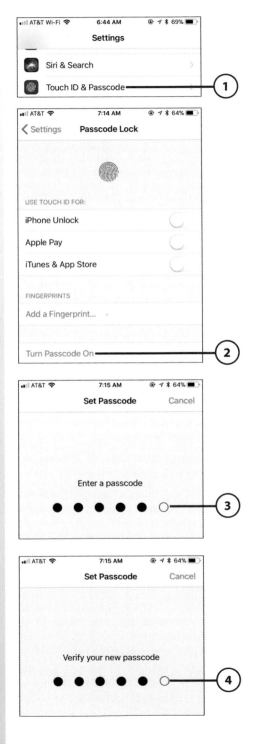

5. If you have an Apple ID configured, enter your Apple ID password; if you don't have an Apple
   ID configured, skip to step 7.

6. Tap Continue.

7. Tap Require Passcode; when
   you use Touch ID to unlock your
   iPhone, you don't have an option
   for when the passcode is required,
   so if you are going to or already
   use Touch ID, skip to step 10.

8. Tap the amount of time the iPhone
   is locked before the passcode
   takes effect. The shorter this time
   is, the more secure your iPhone is,
   but also the more frequently you'll
   have to enter the passcode if your
   iPhone locks frequently.

9. Tap Back.

10. If you have an iPhone 5s or later,
    tap Add a Fingerprint and con-
    tinue to step 11; if you have a
    model that doesn't support Touch
    ID, skip to step 25.

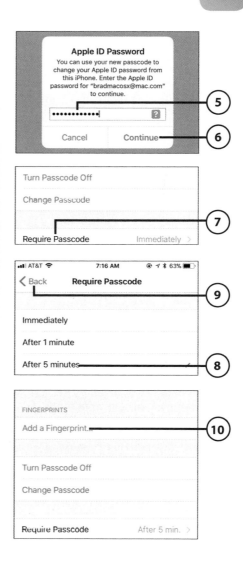

Are You Complex?

By default, your passcode is a simple six-digit number. If you want to have a more
complex (and more secure) passcode, on the Create or Change Passcode screen,
tap Passcode Options. You are prompted to create a new, complex passcode.
You can choose Custom Alphanumeric Code, Custom Numeric Code, or 4-Digit
Numeric Code (this is a less secure option and I don't recommend it). Choose the
option you want and then follow the onscreen prompts to create it. The Alphanumeric Code option is the most secure, especially if you use a code that is eight
characters or longer that includes both letters and numbers. The steps to set a
complex passcode are similar; the difference is that you use the keyboard and
numeric keypad to configure the passcode instead of just the numeric keypad.

11.   Touch the finger you want to record to the Touch ID/Home button, but don't press it. An image of a fingerprint appears.

12.   Leave your finger on the Touch ID/Home button until you feel the phone vibrate, which indicates part of your fingerprint has been recorded and you see some segments turn red. The parts of your fingerprint that are recorded are indicated by the red segments; gray segments are not recorded yet. This step captures the center part of your finger.

13.   Lift your finger off the Touch ID/Home button and touch the button again, adjusting your finger on the button to record other parts that currently show gray lines instead of red ones. Other segments of your fingerprint are recorded.

14.   Repeat step 13 until all the segments are red. You are prompted to change your grip so you can record more of your fingerprint.

15. Tap Continue.

16. Repeat step 13, again placing other areas of your finger to fill in more gray lines with red. This step captures the fingerprints more toward the edges of your fingers. When the entire fingerprint is covered in red lines, you see the Complete screen.

17. Tap Continue. The fingerprint is recorded and you move back to the Touch ID & Passcode screen. You see the fingerprint that has been recorded.

18. Tap the fingerprint you recorded.

19. Give the fingerprint a name.

20. Tap Passcode Lock.

21. Repeat steps 10–20 to record up to five fingerprints. These can be yours or someone else's if you want to allow another person to access your iPhone.

22. To be able to use Touch ID to unlock your iPhone, ensure the iPhone Unlock switch is set to on (green).

23. To use your fingerprint to make Apple Pay payments, set the Apple Pay switch to on (green). (Refer to Chapter 15, "Working with Other Useful iPhone Apps and Features," for more information about Apple Pay.)

24. If it isn't enabled already and you want to also be able to enter your Apple ID password by touching your finger to the Touch ID/Home button, set the iTunes & App Store switch to on (green). You need to enter your Apple ID password and tap Continue to complete this configuration.

25. Swipe up the screen until you see the Voice Dial switch.

26. To prevent Voice Dial from working, set the Voice Dial switch to off (white). (Voice Dial enables you to make calls by speaking even if you don't use Siri.)

27. Use the switches in the ALLOW ACCESS WHEN LOCKED section to enable or disable the related functions when your iPhone is locked. The options include Today View (the Today section of the Notification Center), Recent Notifications, Control Center, Siri, Reply with Message, Home Control, Wallet, and Return Missed Calls. If you set a switch to off (white), you won't be able to access the corresponding function when your iPhone is locked.

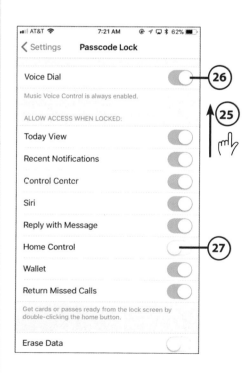

28. If you want the iPhone to auto-
     matically erase all your data after
     an incorrect passcode has been
     entered 10 times, set the Erase
     Data switch to on (green).

29. Tap Enable.

Touch ID and Apps

The first time you launch an app that supports Touch ID, you're prompted to enable
Touch ID in that app. If you allow this, you can log into the associated account by
touching the Touch ID button, just like unlocking your phone or using Apple Pay.

Automatic Erase

When you have enabled the Erase Data function and you enter an incorrect
passcode when unlocking your iPhone, you see a counter showing the number
of unsuccessful attempts. When this reaches 10, all the data on your iPhone is
erased on the next unsuccessful attempt.

Making Changes

Any time you want to make changes to your passcode and fingerprint (iPhone
5s or later) settings, move back to the Passcode Lock screen by tapping Touch
ID & Passcode and entering your passcode. To disable the passcode (not recommended), tap Turn Passcode Off, tap Turn Off, and enter the passcode. To
change your passcode, tap Change Passcode. You then enter your current
passcode and enter your new passcode twice. You return to the Passcode Lock
screen, and the new passcode takes effect. You can change the other settings
similar to how you set them initially as described in these steps. For example,
you can add new fingerprints. To remove a fingerprint, move to the Fingerprints
screen, swipe to the left on the fingerprint you want to remove, and tap Delete.

Automatic Locking

For security purposes, you should configure your iPhone so that it locks automatically after a specific amount of idle time passes. To do this, you use the Auto-Lock
setting on the Display & Brightness settings screen as explained in Chapter 5.

Setting Restrictions for Content and Apps

To restrict access to content or apps, perform the following steps:

1. On the Settings screen, tap General.

2. Swipe up the screen until you see Restrictions.

3. Tap Restrictions.

4. Tap Enable Restrictions.

5. Create a Restrictions Passcode. You have to enter this passcode to change the content restrictions or to be able to access restricted content.

6. Re-enter your Restrictions Passcode. You return to the Restrictions screen, and the Allow switches are enabled.

Dueling Passcodes

Your iPhone can have two passcodes: the Lock passcode and the Restrictions passcode. Each controls access to its respective functions. Limiting access to content and apps likely means you will be letting someone else use your phone. The person who will be using your iPhone might need to be able to unlock it unless you want to have to unlock it for them. If you want to allow them to unlock the phone but want to restrict access to your Apple Pay information or Apple ID, create a fingerprint for that person, but disable Touch ID for Apple Pay and iTunes & App Stores (see the previous task for details). This enables the person to unlock and use your iPhone; you can control what they can do by setting a Restrictions passcode and configuring permissions as described in these steps. (You don't want to give the person the passcode to the phone as that defeats the purpose of configuring restrictions.)

7. In the ALLOW section, set the switch next to each function you want to disable to off (white). For example, to prevent FaceTime calls, set the FaceTime switch to off (white); the FaceTime icon is removed from the Home screen and can't be used. With the other controls, you can prevent access to Safari, the Camera, Siri & Dictation, AirDrop, CarPlay, the iTunes Store, and so on.

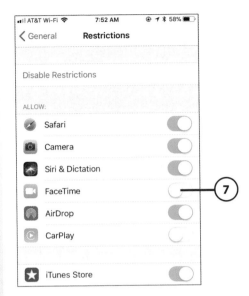

In-App Purchases

Some apps, especially games, allow you to make purchases while you are using the app. For example, you can buy additional levels for a game. To prevent in-app purchases, set the In-App Purchases switch to off (white). This is especially important if you let your phone be used by children or others who might inadvertently make purchases you don't want made.

8. Swipe up to see the ALLOWED CONTENT section.

9. Tap Ratings For.

10. Tap the country whose rating system you want to use for content on your iPhone.

Whose Ratings?

The country you select in step 10 determines the options you see in the remaining steps because the restrictions available depend on the location you select. These steps show the United States rating systems; if you select a different country, you see rating options for that country instead.

11. Tap Restrictions.

12. Tap Music, Podcasts & News.

13. To prevent content tagged as explicit from being played, set the EXPLICIT switch to off (white). Explicit content will not be available in the associated apps, such as Music or News.

14. Tap Back.

15. Tap Movies.

16. Tap the highest rating of movies that you want to be playable (for example, tap PG-13 to prevent R and NC-17 movies from playing); tap Allow All Movies to allow any movie to be played; or tap Don't Allow Movies to prevent any movie content from playing. Prevented movie ratings are highlighted in red.

17. To prevent movies from being streamed to the iPhone, set the Show Movies in the Cloud switch to off (white).

18. Tap Restrictions.

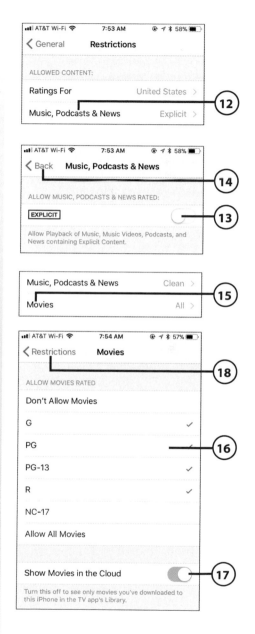

19. Tap TV Shows and use the resulting screen to set the highest rating of TV shows that you want to be playable (for example, tap TV-14 to prevent TV-MA shows from playing); tap Allow All TV Shows to allow any show to be played; or tap Don't Allow TV Shows to prevent any TV content from playing. Prevented ratings are highlighted in red. Use the Show TV Shows in the Cloud switch to allow or prevent TV content from streaming on the iPhone. Tap Restrictions to return to the Restrictions screen.

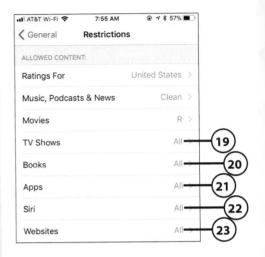

20. Use the Books option to enable or disable access to sexually explicit books.

21. Tap Apps and set the highest rating of app that you want to be available (for example, tap 12+ to prevent 17+ applications from working); tap Allow All Apps to allow any application to be used; or tap Don't Allow Apps to prevent all applications. Tap Restrictions to return to the Restrictions screen.

22. Use the Siri option to restrict explicit language or content during web searches.

23. Use the Websites option to control the websites that can be accessed. The options are to limit sites with adult content or to allow only specific websites to be visited. When you select the Specific Websites Only option, you can create a list of sites and only those sites can be visited.

24. Swipe up the screen until you see the PRIVACY section.

25. Use the settings in the PRIVACY section to determine whether apps can access information stored in each area and whether they should be locked in their current states. For example, you can prevent apps from accessing your calendars or photos. Configuring these is similar to the Privacy settings you read about earlier in this chapter.

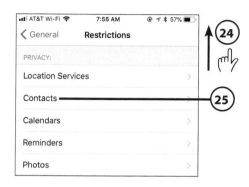

26. Swipe up the screen until you see the ALLOW CHANGES section.

27. Tap areas that you want to restrict, such as Cellular Data or Volume Limit, and then tap Don't Allow Changes to prevent changes to that area.

28. To prevent multiplayer games in the Game Center, set the Multiplayer Games switch to off (white). Users will no longer be able to play games against other people.

29. To prevent new friends from being added in the Game Center, set the Adding Friends switch to off (white). Players will be restricted to the friends already allowed.

30. To prevent the screen from being recorded during game play associated with the Game Center, set the Screen Recording switch to off (white).

Removing Restrictions

To remove all restrictions, move to the Restrictions screen (your Restrictions passcode is required) and tap Disable Restrictions. Enter your Restrictions passcode, and all restrictions are removed.

Customizing How Your iPhone Works with Apps

Installing apps on your iPhone enables you to add more functionality than you can probably imagine. As the old Apple ad use to proclaim, "There's an app for that." And in all likelihood, there probably is an app for a lot of what you would like to use your iPhone for. The App Store app enables you to find, download, and install apps onto your iPhone.

Before you jump into the App Store, take a few moments to ensure your iPhone is configured for maximum ease and efficiency of dealing with new apps.

Configuring Your iPhone to Download and Maintain Apps

To download apps from the App Store, you need an Apple ID (if you need help getting or configuring an Apple ID, see Chapter 3, "Setting Up and Using an Apple ID, iCloud, and Other Online Accounts"). With your Apple ID configured on your phone in the iCloud area, make sure it is also ready to go for the App Store and ensure you can use Touch ID when you download apps (instead of typing your password).

1. Open the Settings app.

2. Tap iTunes & App Store.

3. Ensure the Apple ID you want to use to download apps is shown at the top of the screen; if it isn't tap the Apple ID shown, tap Sign Out, and then sign into your Apple ID.

4. Ensure the Apps switch is on (green); this causes any apps you download to your iPhone to also automatically be downloaded to other devices (with which the apps are compatible, of course) that use the same Apple ID.

5. Ensure the Updates switch is on (green); this causes any updates to apps you have installed on your iPhone to be downloaded and installed automatically. I recommend you use this option so you can be sure you are always running the most current versions of your apps.

6. If you don't have an unlimited cellular data plan, you might want to set Use Cellular Data to off (white) so apps and other content are downloaded only when you are on a Wi-Fi network. If this is enabled (green), apps and content are downloaded to your iPhone when you are using a cellular network, which can consume significant amounts of your data plan. (Some apps or content are so large, they can only be downloaded when you are using a Wi-Fi connection.)

7. Use the information in the task "Configuring Your Passcode and Touch ID" to ensure the iTunes & App Store switch is enabled (green) so that you can use Touch ID to download apps instead of typing your password. (If it isn't enabled, tap the switch, enter your Apple ID password, and tap OK to enable it.)

Using the App Store App to Find and Install iPhone Apps

The App Store app enables you to quickly and easily browse and search for apps, view information about them, and then download and install them on your iPhone with just a few taps.

When you use the App Store app, you can find apps to download using any of the following options:

- **Today**—This tab takes you to apps featured in the App Store on the day you go into the store. They are grouped in various ways, such as APP OF THE DAY, based on what is trending, and so on. When you tap any of the items on the Today screen, you move into the group or app on which you tapped.

- **Games**—Easily the most popular category of apps, Games enables you to find those critical games you need to prove your skills and pass the time. When you move into the Games area, the games are also grouped in various ways, such as Top Paid, Top Free, Top Categories, etc.

- **Apps**—This category leads you to apps that aren't games. On this screen, in addition to the Top Paid and Top Free lists, you see apps organized by category. Tap a category to explore the apps it contains.

- **Updates**—Through this option, you can update your apps (if you don't have automatic updates set as described earlier) or if you have automatic updates enabled, you see the list of updates made to the apps on your iPhone along with those that are pending.

- **Search**—This tool enables you to search for apps. You can search by name, developer, and other keywords.

Finding and downloading any kind of app follows this same pattern:

1. **Find the app you are interested in.** You can use the options described in the previous list to find apps by browsing for them, or you can use the search option to find a specific app quickly and easily.

2. **Evaluate the app.** The information screen for apps provides lots of information that you can use to decide whether you want to download an app (or not). The information available includes a text description, screenshots, ratings and reviews from users, and so on.

3. **Download and install the app.**

The following tasks provide detailed examples for each of these steps.

Searching for Apps

If you know something about an app, such as its name, its developer, its purpose, or just about anything else, you can quickly search the App Store to find the app. Here's how to search for an app:

1. Move to the Home screen and tap App Store.

2. Tap Search.

3. Tap in the Search box.

4. Type a search term. This can be the type of app you are looking for based on its purpose (such as *travel apps*) or the name of someone associated with the app, its title, its developer, or even a topic. As you type, the app suggests searches that are related to what you are typing.

5. Tap the search you want to perform or tap the Search key on the keyboard to search for the term you entered in step 4. The apps that meet your search term appear.

6. Swipe up and down on the screen to review the apps in the search results.

7. If none of the apps are what you are looking for, tap Clear (x) in the Search box and repeat steps 4–6.

8. When you find an app of interest to you, tap it. You move to the app's information screen.

9. Use the app's information on the information screen to evaluate the app and decide if you want to download it. You can read about the app, see screenshots, and read other peoples' reviews to help you decide. If you want to download the app, see "Downloading Apps" later in this chapter for the details.

Follow the Trends?

Before you enter a search term on the Search screen, you see the Trending Searches, which are the searches that are being performed most frequently. You can tap one of these to use it to search for apps.

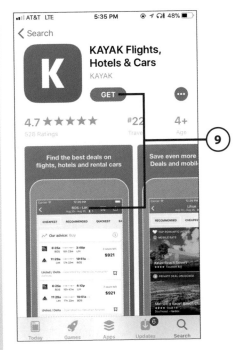

Browsing for Apps

If you don't know of a specific app you want, you can browse the App Store. To browse, you can tap any graphics or links you see in the App Store app. One of the most useful ways to browse for apps is by using categories:

1. Open the App Store app.

2. Tap Apps (browsing for games or using the Today option works very similarly).

3. Swipe up the screen until you see the Top Categories section.

4. Tap See All to browse all available categories.

5. Tap a category in which you are interested.

6. Swipe up and down to browse the groupings of apps, such as Apps We Love, Top Paid, and so on.

7. Tap See All for a grouping to browse the apps it contains.

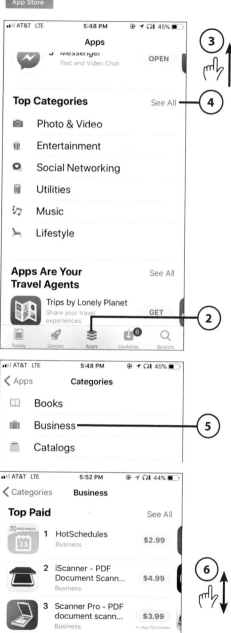

8. Swipe up and down to browse the apps in the group you selected in step 7.

9. Tap an app in which you are interested. You move to that app's information screen.

10. Use the information on the information screen to decide whether you want to download the app. You can read about the app, see screenshots, and read other peoples' reviews to help you decide. If you want to download the app, see "Downloading Apps" later in this chapter for the details. Or, you can continue browsing by tapping the Back icon in the top-left corner of the screen to return to the category list.

>>>Go Further

MORE ON FINDING APPS

Following are a few pointers to help you use the App Store:

- When you see a + inside an app's price or Get button, that means the app is a universal app, which means it runs equally as well on iPhones, iPads, and iPod touches.

- Some apps include video previews. When you see the Play icon on an image, it is a video preview. Tap the Play icon to watch it. Tap Done in the upper-left corner of the screen to move back to the screenshots.

- After you have used an app, you can add your own review by moving back to its Reviews tab and tapping Write a Review. You move to the Write a Review screen where you have to enter your iTunes Store account information before you can write and submit a review.

- You can read user reviews of the apps in the App Store. You should take these with a grain of salt. Some people have an issue with the developer or the type of app; are reviewing an older version of the app; or are commenting on issues unrelated to the app itself; and these issues can cause them to provide unfairly low ratings. The most useful individual user reviews are very specific, as in "I wanted the app to do x, but it only does y." It can be more helpful to look at the number of reviews and the average user rating than reading the individual reviews.

Downloading Apps

Downloading and installing apps is about as easy as things get, as you can see:

1. In the App Store, view the app you want to download.

2. Tap GET (for free apps) or the price (for apps that have a license fee). The icon then becomes INSTALL, if it is a free app, or BUY if it has a license fee.

3. Tap Install or Buy. Depending on your iTunes & App Store settings, you might be prompted to sign in with your Apple ID and password to start the download. If you aren't prompted to confirm the download, you can skip the next step because the app starts downloading immediately.

4. If you are prompted to confirm the download, and you are using an iPhone 5s or later and have enabled Touch ID for store downloads, touch the Touch ID/Home button at the prompt; if you are using another model, or you don't use Touch ID for store downloads, type your Apple ID password, and then tap Sign In.

Face ID

If you have an iPhone X, you can configure Face ID so that you can confirm an app download by looking at your phone. See the online supplement *My iPhone X* by going to www.informit.com/myiphone11 for the details.

You see the progress of the process.

When the process is complete, the status information is replaced by the OPEN button.

App being downloaded

App is ready to use

>>>Go Further

MORE ON APPS

As you use the App Store app to install apps on your iPhone, keep the following hints handy:

- Like other software, apps are updated regularly to fix problems, add features, or make other changes. If you set the iTunes & App Store Updates setting to on (green) as described earlier in this chapter, updates to your apps happen automatically in the background. Your apps are always current so you don't have to update them manually. (More information on updating apps is in Chapter 16, "Maintaining and Protecting Your iPhone and Solving Problems.")

- If you see the Download icon next to an app rather than Get or Buy, that means you have previously downloaded (and paid for if it isn't free) the app but it is not currently installed on your iPhone. Tap the icon to download and install it.

- To let someone else know about an app, tap the Share icon and then tap how you want to let him know; the options include AirDrop, Message, Mail, Twitter, and Facebook. To buy an app for someone, tap Gift.

- Apps can work in the background to keep their information current, such as Weather and Stocks. To configure this, open the Settings app, tap General, and tap Background App Refresh. Tap Background App Refresh and tap Off to disable this, Wi-Fi to enable it only when your iPhone is connected to a Wi-Fi network, or Wi-Fi & Cellular Data to allow it any time your iPhone is connected to the Internet. Tap the Back icon, located in the upper-left corner of the screen, to see the list of apps installed on your iPhone. To enable an app to work in the background, set its switch to on (green). To disable background activity for an app, set its switch to off (white).

- After you install an app, move to the Settings screen and look for the app's icon. If it is there, the app has additional settings you can use to configure the way it works. Tap the app's icon in the Settings app and use its Settings screen to configure it.

Tap to configure your iPhone's
screen and sounds

Customize the
layout of the
icons on your
Home screens
by placing icons
where you want
them

Place icons
in folders to
keep your
Home screens
organized

Choose the
image you
want as
wallpaper

In this chapter, you learn how to make an iPhone look and sound the way you want it to. Topics include the following:

→ Customizing your Home screens
→ Setting the Screen's Brightness, Lock/Wake, Text, View, and Wallpaper Options
→ Choosing the sounds and vibratory feedback your iPhone uses

Customizing How Your iPhone Looks and Sounds

There are lots of ways that you can customize an iPhone to make it *your* iPhone so that it looks and sounds the way you want it to. You can design your Home screens; set the screen's brightness, text size, and wallpaper; and choose the sounds your iPhone makes.

Customizing Your Home Screens

The iPhone's Home screens are the starting point for anything you do because these screens contain the icons and folders of icons that you tap to access the apps that you want to use. You see and use the Home screens constantly, so it's a good idea to customize them to your preferences.

In the background of the Lock screen and every Home screen is the wallpaper image. In the section called "Setting the Wallpaper on the Home and Lock Screens," you learn how to configure your iPhone's wallpaper in both locations.

As you know, you can access apps on your Home screens by tapping them. The Home screens come configured with icons in default locations. You can change the location of these icons to be more convenient for you. As you install more apps on your iPhone, it's a good idea to organize your Home screens so that you can quickly get to the apps you use most frequently. You can move icons around the same screen, move icons between the pages of the Home screen, and organize icons within folders. You can even change the icons that appear on the Home screen Dock. You can also delete icons you no longer need.

Moving Icons Around Your Home Screens

You can move icons around on a Home screen, and you can move icons among screens to change where they are located.

1. Move to a Home screen by pressing the Touch ID/Home Button (except iPhone X) or swiping up from the bottom of the screen (iPhone X).

2. Swipe to the left or right across the Home screen until the page containing an icon you want to move appears.

3. Touch (don't tap because if you do, the app opens instead) and hold on any icon. After a moment, the icons begin jiggling, which indicates that you can move icons on the Home screens. You also see the Delete symbol (x) in the upper-left corner of some icons, which indicate that you can delete both the icon and app (more on this later in this section).

4. Touch and hold an icon you want to move; it becomes darker to show that you have selected it.

Touch But Don't Press (3D Touch Models)

If you are working with an iPhone 6s/6s Plus or later model that supports 3D Touch, don't press on icons when you want to move them; just touch your finger lightly to the screen. If you apply pressure, you might open the Quick Action menu instead. When you just touch an icon and leave your finger on the screen without any pressure, the icons become fuzzy briefly, and then start jiggling to indicate you can move them.

5. Drag the icon to a new location on the current screen; as you move the icon around the page, other icons separate and are reorganized to enable you to place the icon in its new location.

6. When the icon is in the location you want, lift your finger. The icon is set in that place. (You don't have to be precise; the icon automatically snaps into the closest position when you lift your finger off the screen.)

7. Tap and hold on an icon you want to move to a different page.

8. Drag the icon to the left edge of the screen to move it to a previous page or to the right edge of the screen to move it to a later page. As you reach the edge of the screen, you move to the previous or next page.

9. Drag the icon to its location on the new Home screen and lift your finger off the icon.

10. Continue moving icons until you've placed them in the locations you want; then press the Touch ID/Home button once. The icons are locked in their current positions, they stop jiggling, and the Delete symbols disappear.

---

iPhone X

Because it doesn't have a Touch ID/Home button, arranging icons and folders on an iPhone X is a bit different. Refer to the online supplement *My iPhone X* on www.informit.com/myiphone11 for the specifics for the iPhone X.

Creating Folders to Organize Apps on Your Home Screens

You can place icons into folders to keep them organized and to make more icons available on the same page. To create a folder, do the following:

1. Move to the Home screen containing icons you want to place in a folder.

2. Touch and hold an icon until the icons start jiggling; the Delete symbols appear.

3. Drag one icon on top of another one that you want to be in the new folder together.

4. When the first icon is on top of the second and a folder appears, lift your finger. The two icons are placed into the new folder, which is named based on the type of icons you place within it. The folder opens and you see its default name.

5. Edit the name by tapping in the name field.

6. Delete the current name by tapping the Delete icon.

7. Change the default name for the folder or type a completely new name if you deleted the previous one.

8. Tap Done.

9. Tap outside the folder to close it.

10. If you're done organizing the Home screen, press the Touch ID/Home button. The icons stop jiggling.

Locating Folders

You can move a folder to a new location in the same way you can move any icon. Touch and hold (don't tap or it opens instead) the folder's icon until the icons start jiggling. Drag the folder icon to where you want it to be.

The new folder

Placing Icons in Existing Folders

You can add icons to an existing folder like so:

1. Move to the Home screen containing an icon you want to place in a folder.

2. Touch and hold an icon until the icons start jiggling and the Delete symbols appear.

3. Drag the icon you want to place into a folder on top of the folder's icon so that the folder opens. (The icon doesn't have to be on the same Home screen page; you can drag an icon from one page and drop it on a folder on a different page.)

4. When the folder opens, lift your finger from the screen. The icon is placed within the folder.

Adding Apps to Folders Quickly

If you don't want to change the icon's location when you place it in the folder, lift your finger as soon as the folder's icon is highlighted; this places the icon in the folder but doesn't cause the folder to open. This is faster than waiting for the folder to open, but doesn't allow you to position the icon within the folder.

5. Drag the new icon to its location within the folder.

6. Tap outside the folder. The folder closes.

7. When you're done adding icons to folders, press the Touch ID/Home button.

The folder now contains the app you placed in it

Removing Icons from Folders

To remove an icon from a folder, tap the folder from which you want to remove the icon to open it. Touch and hold the icon you want to remove until it starts jiggling. Drag the icon you want to remove from inside the folder to outside the folder. When you cross the border of the folder, the folder closes and you can place the icon on a Home screen.

Folders and Badges

When you place an icon that has a badge notification (the red circle with a number in it that indicates the number of new items in an app) in a folder, the badge transfers to the folder so that you see it on the folder's icon. When you place more than one app with a badge notification in the same folder, the badge on the folder becomes the total number of new items for all the apps in the folder. You need to open a folder to see the badges for the individual apps it contains.

Configuring the Home Screen Dock

The Dock on the bottom of the Home screen appears on every page. You can place any icons on the Dock that you want, including folder icons.

1. Move to the Home screen containing an icon you want to place on the Dock.

2. Touch and hold an icon until the icons start jiggling and the Delete symbols appear.

3. Drag an icon that is currently on the Dock from the Dock onto the Home screen to create an empty space on the Dock.

4. Drag an icon or folder from the Home screen onto the Dock.

5. Drag the icons on the Dock around so they are in the order you want them to be.

6. Press the Touch ID/ Home button to set the icons in their current places.

New icon on the Dock

Deleting Icons

You can delete icons from a Home screen to remove them from your iPhone. When you delete an app's icon, its data is also deleted and you won't be able to use the app anymore (of course, you can download it again if you change your mind).

1. Move to the Home screen containing an icon you want to delete.

2. Touch and hold an icon until the icons start jiggling and the Delete symbols appear (you can delete icons that are inside folders, too).

3. Tap the icon's Delete symbol.

4. Tap Delete. The app and any associated data on your iPhone are deleted.

>>>*Go Further*

MORE ON ORGANIZING HOME SCREENS

Organizing your Home screens can make the use of your iPhone more efficient. Here are a few more things to keep in mind:

- You can place many icons in the same folder. When you add more than nine, any additional icons are placed on new pages within the folder. As you keep adding icons, pages keep being added to the folder to accommodate the icons you add to it. You can swipe to the left or right within a folder to move among its pages, just as you can to move among your Home screens. You can also drag icons between pages in a folder, just like on a Home screen.

- To change an existing folder's name, move to a screen showing the folder whose name you want to change. Touch and hold an icon until the icons jiggle. Tap the folder so that it opens, and then tap the current name. Edit the name, tap Done, and tap outside the folder to close it. Press the Touch ID/Home button to complete the process.

- To delete a folder, remove all the icons from it. The folder is deleted as soon as you remove the last icon from within it.

- You can delete icons for apps you've added to your iPhone or some of the default apps, such as the Stocks app. You can't delete some of the default apps, which is why their icons don't have Delete symbols like apps that you install do. If you don't use some of these default apps that you can't delete, move them to pages of your Home screen that you don't use very often so they don't get in your way, or create a folder for unused icons and store them there, out of your way.

- To return your Home screens to how they were when you first started using your iPhone, open the Settings app, tap General, Reset, Reset Home Screen Layout, and Reset Home Screen. The Home screens return to their default configurations. Icons you've added are moved onto the later pages.

Setting the Screen's Brightness, Lock/ Wake, Text, View, and Wallpaper Options

There are a number of settings you can configure to suit your viewing preferences and how your iPhone locks/wakes:

- **Brightness**—Because you continually look at your iPhone's screen, it should be the right brightness level for your eyes. However, the screen is also a large user of battery power, so the dimmer an iPhone's screen is, the longer its battery lasts. You should find a good balance between viewing comfort and battery life.

- **Night Shift**—This feature changes the color profile of the screen after dark. It is supposed to make the light produced by the iPhone more suitable to darker conditions. You can set the color temperature to your preferences and can set a schedule if you want Night Shift to be activated automatically.

- **Auto-Lock**—The Auto-Lock setting causes your iPhone to lock and go to sleep after a specific amount of inactivity. This is good for security as it is less likely someone can pick up and use your phone if you let it sit for a while. It also extends battery life because it puts the iPhone to sleep when you aren't using it.

- **Raise to Wake**—This setting, available on iPhone 6s/6s Plus and later models, enables you to wake up the iPhone by lifting it up. This is useful because you don't even need to press a button, just lift the phone and you see the Lock screen, giving you quick access to the current time, the Audio Player, notifications, and widgets. However, some people find this feature more annoying than helpful so if the phone waking when you lift it up bothers you, disable this setting on your phone.

- **Text Size/Bold**—As you use your iPhone, you'll be constantly working with text so it's also important to configure the text size to meet your preferences. You can use the Bold setting to bold text to make it easier to read.

- **View**—The iPhone 6 and later models offer two views. The Standard view maximizes screen space and the Zoomed view makes things on the screen larger, making them easier to see, but less content fits on the screen. You can choose the view that works best for you.

- **Wallpaper**—Wallpaper is the image you see "behind" the icons on your Home screens. Because you see this image so often, you might as well have an image that you want to see or that you believe makes using the Home screens easier and faster. You can use the iPhone's default wallpaper images, or you can use any photo available on your iPhone. You can also set the wallpaper you see on the iPhone's Lock screen (you can use the same image as on the Home screens or a different one). Although it doesn't affect productivity or usability of the iPhone very much, choosing your own wallpaper to see in the background of the Home and Lock screens makes your iPhone more personal to you and is just plain fun.

Setting the Screen Brightness and Night Shift Using the Settings App

To set the screen brightness and Night Shift, perform the following steps:

1. In the Settings app, tap Display & Brightness.

2. Drag the slider to the right to raise the brightness or to the left to lower it. A brighter screen uses more power but is easier to see.

3. Tap Night Shift.

4. To have Night Shift activate automatically, set the Scheduled switch to on (green); if you don't want it to activate automatically, skip to step 11.

5. Tap the From/To setting.

6. To have Night Shift on between sunset and sunrise, tap Sunset to Sunrise and skip to step 10.

7. To set a custom schedule for Night Shift, tap Custom Schedule.

8. Tap Turn On At and swipe up or down on the hour, minute, and AM/PM wheels to set the time when you want Night Shift to activate.

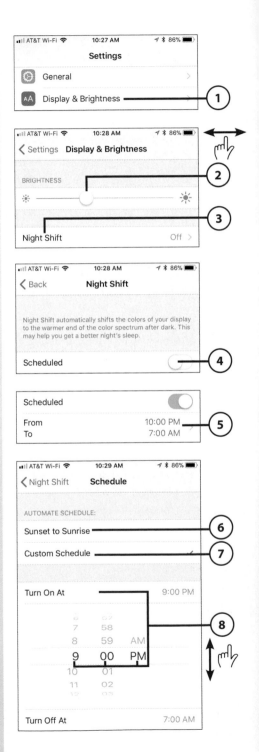

9. Tap Turn Off At and use the time wheels to set when you want Night Shift to turn off.

10. Tap Night Shift.

11. To manually turn Night Shift on at any time, set the Manually Enable Until Tomorrow switch to on (green). Night Shift activates and remains on until sunrise when it shuts off automatically. (You can manually turn off Night Shift by setting the Manually Enable Until Tomorrow switch to off [white]).

12. Drag the COLOR TEMPERATURE slider to the right to make the Night Shift effect more pronounced or to the left to make it less warm. If Night Shift isn't active when you drag the slider, it goes into effect as you move the slider so you can see the effect the temperature you select has.

13. Tap Back.

Setting the Screen Brightness and Night Shift Using the Control Center

You can use the Control Center to quickly adjust brightness and Night Shift as follows:

1. Swipe up from the bottom of the Home screen (all models except the iPhone X) or swipe down from the upper-right corner of the screen (iPhone X, not shown in the figure) to open the Control Center.

2. Swipe up or down on the Brightness slider to increase or decrease the brightness, respectively.

3. To turn Night Shift on or off, press and hold on the Brightness slider.

4. Use the Brightness slider to change the screen's brightness (this does the same thing as using the slider on the Control Center, but since it is larger here, it is a bit easier to use).

5. Tap the Night Shift icon to turn Night Shift on. When on, the Night Shift icon is orange.

6. Tap the Night Shift icon to turn Night Shift off. When off, the Night Shift icon is white.

7. Tap outside the tools to return to the Control Center.

8. Tap the downward-facing arrow at the top of the Control Center to close it. .

Setting Auto-Lock and Raise to Wake

To set the screen brightness, perform the following steps:

1. In the Settings app, tap Display & Brightness to open the Display & Brightness settings screen.

2. Tap Auto-Lock.

3. Tap the amount of idle time you want to pass before the iPhone automatically locks and goes to sleep. You can choose from 30 seconds or 1 to 5 minutes; choose Never if you want to only manually lock your iPhone. I recommend that you keep Auto-Lock set to a relatively small value to conserve your iPhone's battery and to make it more secure. Of course, the shorter you set this time to be, the more frequently you have to unlock your iPhone.

4. Tap Back.

5. If you want to be able to wake your phone by lifting it, set the Raise to Wake switch to on (green); to disable this feature, set the switch to off (white).

Setting Text Size and Bold

To change the text size or make all text bold, perform the following steps:

1. In the Settings app, tap Display & Brightness to open the Display & Brightness settings screen.

2. Tap Text Size. This control changes the size of text in all the apps that support the iPhone's Dynamic Type feature.

3. Drag the slider to the right to increase the size of text or to the left to decrease it. As you move the slider, the text at the top of the screen resizes so you can see the effect of the change you are making.

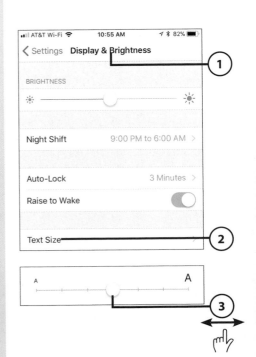

4. When you are happy with the size of the text, tap Back.

5. If you want to make all of the text on your iPhone bold, set the Bold Text switch to on (green) and move to step 6. If you don't want to bold the text, skip the next step.

6. Tap Continue. Your iPhone restarts. All the text is in bold, making it easier to read.

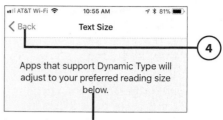

As you change the size of the text, you see the results in this sample

Setting Text Size Using the Control Center

To change the text size with the Control Center, perform the following steps:

1. Swipe up from the bottom of the Home screen (all models except the iPhone X) or swipe down from the upper-right corner of the screen (iPhone X, not shown in the figure) to open the Control Center.

2. Tap the Text Size icon. (If you don't see this icon, you need to add it to the Control Center. See Chapter 4, "Customizing How Your iPhone Works," for details.)

3. Tap above the shaded area to increase the text size.

4. Tap below the shaded area to decrease the text size.

5. Tap outside the tool to return to the Control Center.

6. Tap the downward-facing arrow at the top of the Control Center to close it.

Choosing a View

To configure the view you use, perform the following steps:

1. In the Settings app, tap Display & Brightness to open the Display & Brightness settings screen.

2. Tap View; if you don't see this option, your iPhone doesn't support it and you can skip the rest of these steps.

As you change the size of the text, you see the results this sample

3. Tap Standard.

4. Look at the sample screen.

5. Swipe to the left or right to see examples of what other screens look like in the Standard view.

6. Look at the next sample screen.

7. Swipe to the left or right to see examples of what other screens look like in the Standard view.

8. Tap Zoomed. The sample screens change to reflect the Zoomed view.

What this screen looks like in Standard view

9. Swipe to the left and right to preview the other sample screens in the Zoomed view.

10. If you want to keep the current view, tap Cancel and skip the rest of these steps.

11. To change the view, tap the view you want.

12. Tap Set (if Set is grayed out, the view you selected is already set and you can skip the rest of these steps).

13. Tap Use Zoomed (this is Use Standard if you are switching to the Standard view). Your iPhone restarts and uses the new view.

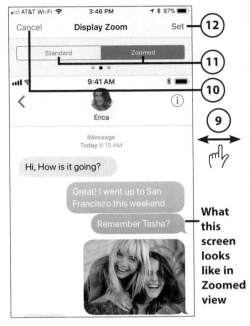

What this screen looks like in Zoomed view

Setting the Wallpaper on the Home and Lock Screens

To configure your wallpaper, perform the following steps:

1. In the Settings app, tap Wallpaper. You see the current wallpaper set for the Lock and Home screens.

2. Tap Choose a New Wallpaper. The Choose screen has two sections. The top section enables you to choose one of the default wallpaper images (Dynamic, Stills, or Live), whereas the lower section shows you the photos available on your iPhone. If you don't have any photos stored on your iPhone, you can only choose from the default images. To choose a default image, continue with step 3; to use one of your photos as wallpaper, skip to step 8.

3. Tap Dynamic if you want to use dynamic wallpaper, Stills if you want to use a static image, or Live if you want to use a Live Photo. These steps show selecting a Live Photo, but using a dynamic or still image is similar.

4. Swipe up and down the screen to browse the images available to you.

5. Tap the image you want to use as wallpaper.

Current wallpaper on your Lock screen

Current wallpaper on your Home screens

6. Tap Perspective to use the Perspective view of the wallpaper, tap Still if you want a static version of the image, or tap Live Photo to use a Live Photo. (See the sidebar "More on View Options" for an explanation of these terms.)

7. Tap Set and move to step 15.

Wallpaper Options Explained

Dynamic wallpaper has motion (kind of like a screen saver on a computer). Stills are static images. Live Photos show motion when you tap and hold on them. Live Photos are available only on iPhone 6s/6s Plus or later models. On other models, you see only the Dynamic and Stills options.

8. To use a photo as wallpaper, swipe up the screen to browse the sources of photos available to you; these include All Photos, Favorites, Selfies, albums, and so on.

Working with Photos

To learn how to work with the photos on your iPhone, see Chapter 14, "Viewing and Editing Photos and Video with the Photos App."

9. Tap the source containing the photo you want to use.

10. Swipe up and down the selected source to browse its photos.

11. Tap the photo you want to use. The photo appears on the Move and Scale screen, which you can use to resize and move the image around.

More on View Options

The Perspective view can be a bit difficult to describe because it is subtle. This view magnifies the wallpaper image when you tilt your iPhone. It is sometimes noticeable and sometimes not, depending on the image you are using for wallpaper. The best thing to do is to enable it to see if you notice any difference or disable it if you prefer not to use it for the specific images you use as wallpaper. You can enable or disable it at any time for your wallpaper on the Lock and Home screens. To change the view without changing the wallpaper, move to the Wallpaper screen and tap the wallpaper (tap the Lock or Home screen) you want to change. Tap Perspective to use the Perspective view or Still if you want the image to be static. To save the view, tap Set or to leave it as it is, tap Cancel.

When you choose a Live Photo as wallpaper, you can touch and hold on the screen to see the image's motion. Note that when you apply a Live Photo to the Home screen wallpaper, it becomes a static image for which you can choose the Still or Perspective view.

12. Use your fingers to unpinch to zoom in or pinch to zoom out, and hold down and drag the photo around the screen until it appears how you want the wallpaper to look.

13. Tap Perspective to use the Perspective view of the wallpaper (see the sidebar "More on View Options"), tap Still to use a static version of the image, or tap Live Photo to use a Live Photo (available only when you are working with a Live Photo on iPhone 6s or iPhone 6s Plus or later models).

14. Tap Set.

15. Tap Set Lock Screen or Set Home Screen to apply the wallpaper to only one of those screens; tap Set Both to apply the same wallpaper in both locations. The next time you move to the screen you selected, you see the wallpaper you chose.

New wallpaper on the Home screen

16. If you set the wallpaper in only one location, tap Choose (not shown on a figure) to move back to the Choose screen and repeat steps 3–15 to set the wallpaper for the other location.

New wallpaper on the Lock screen

Choosing the Sounds and Vibratory Feedback Your iPhone Uses

Sound and vibrations are two ways your iPhone uses to communicate with you. You can configure the sounds and vibrations the phone uses in two ways. One is by choosing the general sounds and vibrations your iPhone makes, which is covered in this section. You can also configure the sounds and vibrations that apps use for notifications about certain events; this is covered Chapter 4.

If you have an iPhone 7 or later model, it offers haptic feedback, which means the phone vibrates slightly when something happens, such as when you make a choice on a selection wheel. You can determine whether you want to feel this feedback or not. If you don't have one of these models, you won't see references to haptics on your Sounds screens.

To configure your iPhone's general sounds, do the following:

1. On the Settings screen, tap Sounds & Haptics (iPhone 7 and later) or Sounds (earlier models).

2. Set the Vibrate on Ring switch to on (green) if you want your iPhone to also vibrate when it rings.

3. Set the Vibrate on Silent switch to on (green) if you want your iPhone to vibrate when you have it muted.

4. Set the volume of the ringer and alert tones by dragging the slider to the left or right.

5. Set the Change with Buttons switch to on (green) if you want to also be able to change the ringer and alert volume using the Volume buttons on the side of the phone.

6. Tap Ringtone. On the resulting screen, you can set the sound and vibration your iPhone uses when a call comes in.

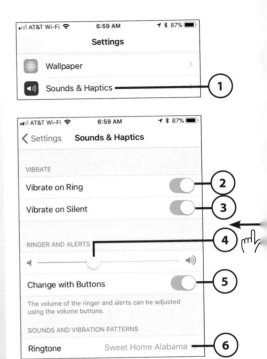

7. Swipe up and down the screen to see all the ringtones available to you. There are two sections of sounds on this screen: RINGTONES and ALERT TONES. These work in the same way; alert tones tend to be shorter sounds. At the top of the RINGTONES section, you see any custom ringtones you have configured on your phone; a dark line separates those from the default ringtones that are below the custom ones.

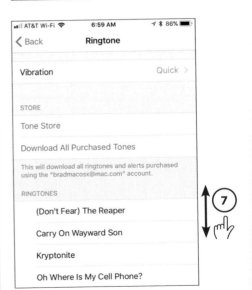

Individual Ringtones and Vibrations

The ringtone and vibration you set in steps 6–14 are the default or general settings. These are used for all callers except for people in your Contacts app for whom you've set specific ringtones or vibrations. In that case, the contact's specific ringtone and vibration are used instead of the defaults. See Chapter 6, "Managing Contacts," to learn how to configure specific ringtones and vibrations for contacts.

8. Tap a sound, and it plays; tap it again to stop it.

9. Repeat steps 7 and 8 until you have selected the sound you want to have as your general ringtone.

10. If necessary, swipe down the screen so you see the Vibration section at the top.

11. Tap Vibration. A list of Standard and Custom vibrations is displayed.

12. Swipe up and down the screen to see all the vibrations available. The STANDARD section contains the default vibrations, and in the CUSTOM section you can tap Create New Vibration to create your own vibration patterns, as discussed in the "Sounding Off" sidebar at the end of this section.

13. Tap a vibration. It "plays" so you can feel it; tap it again to stop it.

14. Repeat steps 12 and 13 until you've selected the general vibration you want to use; you can tap None at the bottom of the Vibration screen (not shown in the figure) below the CUSTOM section if you don't want to have a general vibration.

15. Tap Ringtone.

16. Tap Back. The ringtone you selected is shown on the Sounds and Haptics (or Sounds) screen next to the Ringtone label.

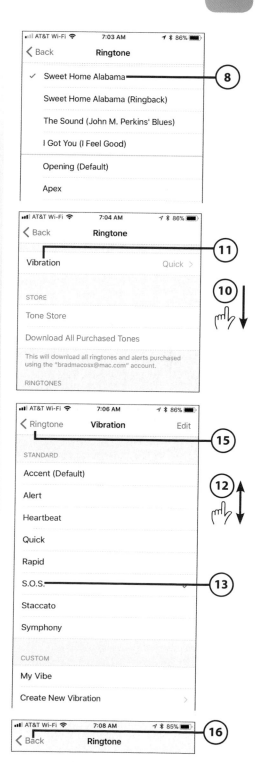

17. Tap Text Tone.

18. Use steps 7–14 with the Text Tone screen to set the sound and vibration used when you receive a new text. The process works the same as for ringtones, though the screens look a bit different. For example, the ALERT TONES section is at the top of the screen because you are more likely to want a short sound for new texts.

19. When you're done setting the text tone, tap Back.

20. Using the same process as you did for ringtones and text tones, set the sound and vibrations for the rest of the events on the list.

21. If you don't like the audible feedback when you tap keys on the iPhone's virtual keyboard, slide the Keyboard Clicks switch to off (white) to disable that sound. The keyboard is silent as you type on it.

22. If you don't want your iPhone to make a sound when you lock it, slide the Lock Sound switch to off (white). Your iPhone no longer makes this sound when you press the Side button to put it to sleep and lock it.

23. Set the System Haptics switch to off (white) if you prefer not to experience vibratory feedback for events. (System Haptics are available on iPhone 7 or later models.)

Current ringtone

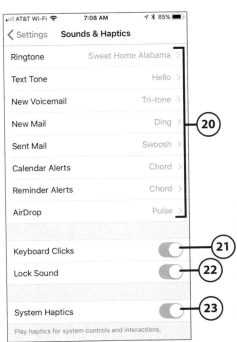

>>>Go Further

SOUNDING OFF

Following are two more sound- and vibration-related pointers:

- You can tap the Store icon on the Ringtone, Text Tone, and other screens to move to the iTunes Store, where you can purchase and download ringtones and other sounds to your iPhone.

- You can create custom vibration patterns, too. On the Vibration screen, tap Create New Vibration. Tap the vibration pattern you want to create; when you're done tapping, tap Stop. Tap Record to start over if you don't like the one you created. When you're done, tap Save. Name the pattern and tap Save. The patterns you create are available in the CUSTOM section on the Vibration screen, so you can use them just like the iPhone's default vibration patterns. To remove a custom pattern, swipe to the left on it and tap Delete.

Use Settings to configure how contacts are displayed

Tap here to work with your contact information

Use your contact information in many apps

In this chapter, you learn how to ensure that your iPhone has the contact information you need when you need it. Topics include the following:

→ Setting your Contacts preferences
→ Creating contacts on your iPhone
→ Working with contacts on your iPhone
→ Managing contacts on your iPhone

6

Managing Contacts

Contact information, including names, phone numbers, email addresses, and physical addresses, is useful to have on your iPhone. When you want to contact someone, you don't need to remember an email address or phone number; instead, just tap the name of the person you want and tap how you want to communicate with them. Or, you might want to see a contact's address in the Maps app.

The Contacts app enables you to do all these things plus much more. This app makes using your contact information seamless. You can access contact information directly in the Contacts app and take action on it (such as placing a call), or you can use your contact information within other apps, such as Mail, Phone, and Messages.

To use contact information, it first must be stored in the Contacts app. You can add this information to your iPhone via iCloud, Exchange, and other similar accounts; by capturing it when you perform tasks (such as reading email); or by entering information manually. You'll also need to manage your contact information over time, such as adding to it or changing it.

Setting Your Contacts Preferences

Use the Accounts & Passwords settings to configure the online accounts in which you store contact information. Refer to Chapter 3, "Setting Up and Using an Apple ID, iCloud, and Other Online Accounts," for help setting up online accounts.

Using the Contacts settings, you can determine whether contact information can be used in Siri and other apps, how contacts are sorted and displayed, if or how names are shortened on various screens, your contact information, and which account should be the default for contact information. You can probably work with these settings just fine without making any changes to these Contacts settings, but if you want to make adjustments, open the Settings app and tap Contacts. Use the information in the following table to configure your contact settings.

Settings App Explained

To get detailed information on using the Settings app, see "Working with the Settings App" in Chapter 2, "Using Your iPhone's Core Features."

Contacts Settings

Setting	Description
Accounts & Passwords	Use the Accounts & Passwords settings to configure the online accounts you use to store contact information.
Siri & Search	Set the Search & Siri Suggestions switch to off (white) if you don't want to use contact information in searches or to allow Siri to access your contact information. Set Find Contacts in Other Apps to off (white) if you don't want contact information in the various apps to be suggested to you, such as to automatically complete addresses when you create emails, or try to identify callers when a number calling you is unknown. You typically should leave both of these on (green) unless you find the automatic contact suggestions annoying or not helpful.
Sort Order	Tap First, Last to have contacts sorted by first name and then last name or tap Last, First to have contacts sorted by last name and then first name.
Display Order	To show contacts in the format *first name, last name,* tap First, Last. To show contacts in the format *last name, first name,* tap Last, First.
Short Name	You can choose whether short names are used and, if they are, what form they take. Short names are useful because more contact information can be displayed in a smaller area, and they look "friendlier." To use short names, move the Short Name switch to the on position (green). Tap the format of the short name you want to use. You can choose from a combination of initial and name or just first or last name. If you want nicknames for contacts used for the short name when available, set the Prefer Nicknames switch to on (green).

My Info	Use this setting to find and tap your contact information in the Contacts app, which it can insert for you in various places and which Siri can use to call you by name; your current contact information is indicated by the label "me" next to the alphabetical index.
Default Account	Tap the account in which you want new contacts to be created by default (which is then marked with a check mark). If you have only one account configured for contacts, you don't have this option.

Where Contacts Are Stored Matters

You should store your contacts in an online account (for example, iCloud or Google), because the information is accessible on many devices and it is also backed up. If you don't have an online account, contact information is stored only on your iPhone. This is not good because, if something happens to your phone, you can lose all of your contacts.

Creating Contacts on Your iPhone

You can create new contacts on an iPhone in a number of ways. You can start with some information, such as the email address on a message you receive, and create a contact from it, or you can create a contact by manually filling in the contact information. In this section, you learn how to create a new contact starting with information in an email message and how to create a new contact manually.

Creating New Contacts from Email

When you receive an email, you can easily create a contact to capture the email address. (To learn how to work with the Mail app, see Chapter 8, "Sending, Receiving, and Managing Email.")

1. On the Home screen, tap Mail.

2. Use the Mail app to read an email message (see Chapter 8 for details).

3. Tap the email address from which you want to create a new contact; if the address isn't in blue as shown, tap Details before tapping the address. The contact's Info screen appears. You see as much information as could be gleaned from the email address, which is typically the sender's name and email address.

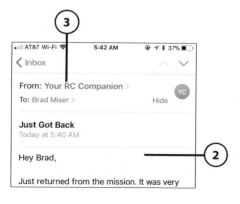

4. Tap Create New Contact. The New Contact screen appears. The name, email address, and any other information that can be identified are added to the new contact. The email address is labeled with iPhone's best guess, such as other or home.

5. Use the New Contact screen to enter more contact information or update the information that was added (such as the label applied to the email address) and save the new contact by tapping Done. This works just like when you create a new contact manually, except that you already have some information—most likely, a name and an email address. For details on adding and changing more information for the contact, see the next task, "Creating Contacts Manually."

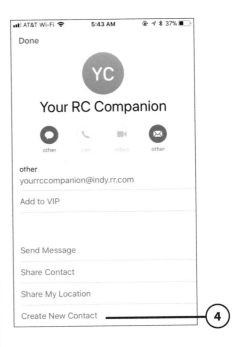

More Information for New Contacts

In some cases, such as when an email comes from an email server that includes full contact information (such as email from an Exchange account), you see a bar at the top of the email message above the From and To section. This bar shows the sender's name and phone number. Under this, you see Ignore and Add to Contacts. Tap Ignore to ignore this additional contact information. Tap Add to Contacts to create a new contact with all of the information available; this does the same thing as steps 3 through 5 except the resulting new contact contains more information with the name and email address; for example, phone numbers.

>>>*Go Further*

MORE ON CREATING CONTACTS FROM APPS

It's useful to be able to create contact information by starting with some information in an app. Keep these points in mind:

- Mail is only one of the apps from which you can create contacts. You can start a contact in just about any app you use to communicate, such as Messages, or get information, such as Maps. The steps to start a contact in these apps are similar to those for Mail. Tap the Info icon (i) for the person or address for which you want to create a contact, and then tap Create New Contact. The Contacts app fills in as much of the information as it can, and you can complete the rest yourself.

- You can also add more contact information to an existing contact from an app you are currently using. You can do this by viewing the contact information (such as a phone number) and tapping Add to Existing Contact (instead of Create New Contact). You then search for and select the contact to which you want to add the additional information. After it's saved, the additional information is associated with the contact you selected. For example, suppose you have created a contact for a company but all you have is its phone number. You can quickly add the address to the contact by using the Maps app to look it up and then add the address to the company's existing contact information by tapping the location, tapping Add to Existing Contact, and selecting the company in your contacts.

Creating Contacts Manually

Most of the time, you'll want to get some basic information for a new contact from an app, as the previous task demonstrated, or through an online account, such as contacts stored in your Exchange account. If these aren't available, you can also start a contact from scratch and manually add all the information you need to it. Also, you use the same steps to add information to or change information for an existing contact that you do to create a new one, so even if you don't start from scratch often, you do need to know how to do so.

The Contacts app leads you through creating each type of information you might want to capture. You can choose to enter some or all of the default information on the New Contact screen, or add additional fields as needed.

The following steps show creating a new contact containing the most common contact information you are likely to need:

1. On the Home screen, tap Contacts. (If you don't see the Contacts app on the Home screen, tap the Extras folder to open it and you should see the app's icon. You might want to move the Contacts icon from this folder to a more convenient location on your Home screen; see Chapter 5, "Customizing How Your iPhone Looks and Sounds," for the steps to do this.) The Contacts screen displays.

   If you see the Groups screen instead, tap Done to move to the Contacts screen. (Groups are covered later.)

2. Tap the Add (+) icon. The New Contact screen appears with the default fields. (You can add more data fields as needed using the add field command.)

3. To associate a photo with the contact, tap add photo. You can choose a photo already on your phone or take a new photo. These steps show using an existing photo. See the "Taking Photos" note for the steps to take a new photo.

4. Tap Choose Photo.

5. Use the Photos app to move to, select, and configure the photo you want to associate with the contact (see Chapter 14, "Viewing and Editing Photos and Video with the Photos App," for help with the Photos app).

6. Tap Choose. You return to the New Contact screen where the photo you selected is displayed.

7. Tap in the First name field and enter the contact's first name; if you are creating a contact for an organization only, leave both name fields empty. (The Display Order preference determines whether the First name or Last name field appears at the top of the screen.)

8. Tap in the Last name field and enter the contact's last name.

9. Enter the organization, such as a company, with which you want to associate the contact, if any.

10. Tap add phone to add a phone number. A new phone field appears along with the numeric keypad.

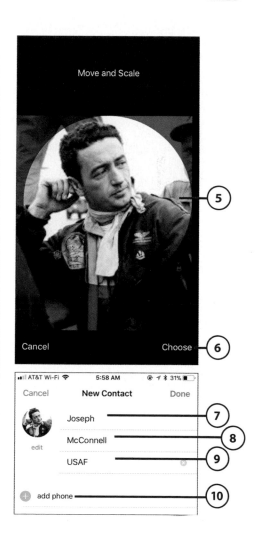

Taking Photos

To take a new photo for a contact, tap Take Photo in step 4 instead of Choose Photo. The Camera app's screen appears. Use the iPhone's camera to capture the photo you want to associate with the new contact (taking photos is covered in Chapter 13, "Taking Photos and Video with Your iPhone"). Use the Move and Scale screen to adjust the photo so it is what you want to use. Then, tap Use Photo. The photo is pasted into the image icon on the New Contact screen.

11. Use the numeric keypad to enter the contact's phone number. Include any prefixes you need to dial it, such as area code and country code. The Contacts app formats the number for you as you enter it.

12. Tap the label for the phone number, such as home, to change it to another label. The Label screen appears.

13. Swipe up and down the Label screen to see all the options available.

14. Tap the label you want to apply to the number, such as iPhone. That label is applied and you move back to the New Contact screen.

15. Repeat steps 10–14 to add more phone numbers to the contact.

16. Swipe up the screen until you see add email.

17. Tap add email. The keyboard appears.

A Rose by Any Other Name Isn't the Same

The labels you apply to contact information, such as phone numbers, become important when a contact has more than one type of that information. For example, a person might have several phone numbers, such as for home, an iPhone, and work. Applying a label to each of these numbers helps you know which number is for which location. This is especially useful when you use Siri as you can tell Siri which number to use to place a call, such as "Call Sir William Wallace home" to call the number labeled as home on William's contact card.

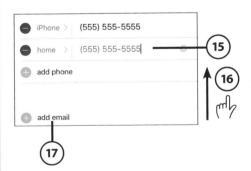

18. Type the contact's email address.

19. Tap the label for the email address to change it.

20. Tap the label you want to apply to the email address. You move back to the New Contact screen.

21. Repeat steps 17–20 to add more email addresses.

22. If necessary, swipe up the screen until you see Ringtone.

23. Tap Ringtone. The list of ringtones and alert tones available on your iPhone appears.

24. Set the Emergency Bypass switch to on (green) if you want sounds and vibrations for phone calls or new messages associated with the contact you are creating to play even when Do Not Disturb is on. (For more about Do Not Disturb, see Chapter 1, "Getting Started with Your iPhone" and for information about working with notifications, see Chapter 2, "Using Your iPhone's Core Features.")

25. Swipe up and down the list to see all of the tones available.

26. Tap the ringtone you want to play when the contact calls you. When you tap a ringtone, it plays so you can experiment to find the one that best relates to the contact. Setting a specific ringtone helps you identify a caller without looking at your phone. (For more on working with sounds and vibrations, see Chapter 5.)

27. Tap Vibration and use the resulting screen if you want to set a specific vibration for the contact.

28. Tap Done. You return to the New Contact screen.

29. Using the pattern you have learned in the previous steps, move to the next item you want to set and tap it.

30. Use the resulting screens to enter the information you want to configure for the contact. After you've done a couple of the fields, it is easy to do the rest because the same pattern is used throughout.

31. When you've added all the information you want to capture, tap Done. The New Contact screen closes and the new contact is created and ready for you to use in Contacts and other apps. It is also moved onto other devices with which your contact information is synced. See the "Creating Contacts Expanded" Go Further sidebar for additional information on syncing and maintaining contacts.

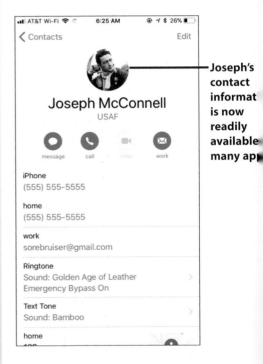

Joseph's contact informat is now readily available many ap

>>>*Go Further*

CREATING CONTACTS EXPANDED

Contacts are useful in many ways, so you should make sure you have all the contact information you need. Here are a few points to ponder:

- You can (and should) sync contacts on multiple devices (computers and other iOS devices) by using iCloud, Exchange, Gmail, or other similar online accounts to store your contact information on the cloud from where all your devices can access it. Refer to Chapter 3 for the details of setting up online accounts.

- Syncing your contacts works in both directions. Any new contacts you create or any changes you make to existing contact information on your iPhone move back to your other devices through the sync process.

- To remove a field in which you've entered information, tap Edit, tap the red circle with a dash in it next to the field, and then tap Delete. If you haven't entered information into a field, just ignore it because empty fields don't appear on a contact's screen.

- The address format on the screens in the Contacts app is determined by the country you associate with the address. If the current country isn't the one you want, tap it and select the country in which the address is located before you enter any information. The fields appropriate for that country's addresses appear on the screen.

- If you want to add a type of information that doesn't appear on the New Contact screen, swipe up the screen and tap add field to see a list of fields you can add. Tap a field to add it; for example, tap Nickname to add a nickname for the contact. Then, enter the information for that new field.

- When you add more fields to contact information, those fields appear in the appropriate context on the Info screen. For example, if you add a nickname, it is placed at the top of the screen with the other "name" information. If you add an address, it appears with the other address information.

- As you learn in Chapter 7, "Communicating with the Phone and FaceTime Apps," you can configure the Phone app to announce the name of callers when you receive calls. This can be even more useful than setting a specific ringtone for your important contacts.

Working with Contacts on Your iPhone

There are many ways to use contact information. The first step is always finding the contact information you need, typically by using the Contacts app. Whether you access it directly or through another app (such as Mail), it works the same way. Then, you select the information you want to use or the action you want to perform.

Using the Contacts App

You can access your contact information directly in the Contacts app. For
example, you can search or browse for
a contact and then view the detailed
information for the contact in which you
are interested.

1. On the Home screen, tap
   Contacts. (If you don't see the
   Contacts app on the Home screen,
   tap the Extras folder to open it
   and you see the Contacts app.
   You might want to move the
   Contacts icon from this folder to a
   more convenient location on your
   Home screen; see Chapter 5 for
   the steps to do this.) The Contacts
   screen displays with the contacts
   listed in the view and sort format determined by the Contacts
   settings. (If the Groups screen
   appears, tap Done. You move back
   to the Contacts screen.)

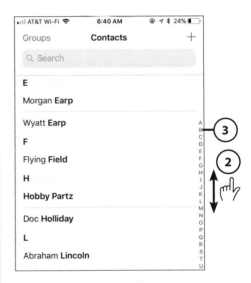

   You can find a contact to view by
   browsing (step 2), using the index
   (step 3), or searching (step 4). You
   can use combinations of these, too,
   such as first using the index to get
   to the right area and then browsing to find the contact in which
   you are interested.

2. Swipe up or down to scroll the
   screen to browse for contact
   information; swipe up or down
   on the alphabetical index to
   browse rapidly.

3. Tap the index to jump to contact
   information organized by the first
   letter of the format you selected
   in the Contact Preferences (last
   name or first name).

4. Use the Search tool to search for a specific contact; tap in the tool, type the name (you can type last, first, company, and nickname), and then tap the contact you want to view on the results list.

5. Tap a contact to view that contact's information.

6. Swipe up and down the screen to view all the contact's information.

7. Tap the data or icons on the screen to perform actions, including the following:

- **Phone numbers**—Tap a phone number to call it. You can also tap one of the phone icons just under the contact's image to call that number. For example, to call the number labeled as mobile, tap the mobile icon.

- **Email addresses**—Tap an email address or the icon with the address's label (such as other for the email address labeled as other) on it to create a new message to that address.

- **URLs**—Tap a URL to open Safari and move to the associated website.

- **Addresses**—Tap an address to show it in the Maps app.

- **FaceTime**—Tap video or FaceTime to start a FaceTime call with the contact. (If an icon, such as video, is disabled, you don't have that type of information stored for the contact.)

- **Text**—Tap the message icon or tap Send Message and choose the phone number or email address to which you want to send a text message.

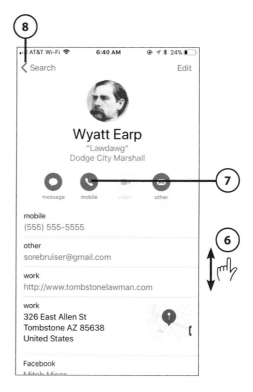

- **Share Contact**—Tap Share Contact. The Share menu appears. To share the contact via email, tap Mail; to share it via a text, tap Message; or to share it using AirDrop, tap AirDrop. You can also share via Twitter or Facebook. Then, use the associated app to complete the task.

- **Favorites**—Tap Add to Favorites and choose the phone number or email address you want to designate as a favorite. You can use this in the associated app to do something faster. For example, if it's the Phone app, you can tap the Favorites tab to see your favorite contacts and quickly dial one by tapping it. You can also quickly access favorites from the FAVORITES widget by swiping to the right when you are on the Locked screen. You can add multiple items (such as cell and work phone numbers) as favorites for one contact.

8. To return to the prior screen without performing an action, tap the back icon located in the upper-left corner of the screen.

>>>Go Further
MAKE CONTACT

When working with your contacts, keep the following points in mind:

- **Last known contact**—The Contacts app remembers where you last were and takes you back there whenever you move into the Contacts app. For example, if you view a contact's details and then switch to a different app to send a message, and then back to Contacts, you are returned to the screen you were last viewing. To move back to the main Contacts screen, tap the back icon (it is labeled with the previous screen's name, such as Search or Contacts) in the upper-left corner of the screen.

- **Groups**—In a contact app on a computer, such as Contacts on a Mac, contacts can be organized into groups, which in turn can be stored in an online account, such as iCloud. When you sync, the groups of contacts move onto the iPhone. You can limit the contacts you browse or search; tap Groups on the Contacts screen.

  The Groups screen displays the accounts (such as iCloud or Exchange) with which you are syncing contact information; under each account are the groups of contacts stored in that account. If a group has a check mark next to it, its contacts are displayed on the Contacts screen. To hide a group's contacts, tap it so that the check mark disappears. To hide or show all of a group's contacts, tap All *account*, where *account* is the name of the account in which those contacts are stored. To make browsing contacts easier, tap Hide All Contacts to hide all the groups and contacts; then, tap each group whose contacts you want to show on the Contacts screen.

Tap Done to move back to the Contacts screen.

• **Speaking of contacts**—You can use Siri to speak commands to work with contacts, too. You can get information about contacts by asking for it, such as "What is William Wallace's work phone number?" If you want to see all of a contact's information, you can say "Show me William Wallace." When Siri displays contact information, you can tap it to take action, such as tapping a phone number to call it. (See Chapter 11, "Working with Siri," for more on using Siri.)

It's Not All Good

Managing Contact Groups

When you create a new contact, it is associated with the account you designated as the default in the Contacts settings and is stored at the account level (not in any of your groups). You can't create groups in the Contacts app, nor can you change the group with which contacts are associated. You have to use a contacts app on a computer to manage groups and then sync your iPhone (which happens automatically when you use an online account, such as iCloud) to see the changes you make to your contact groups.

Accessing Contacts from Other Apps

You can also access contact information while you are using a different app. For example, you can use a contact's email address when you create an email message. When you perform such actions, you use the Contacts app to find and select the information you want to use. The following example shows using contact information to send an email message, and using your contact information in other apps (such as Phone or Messages) is similar.

1. Open the app from which you want to access contact information (this example uses Mail).

2. Tap the Compose icon.

3. Tap the Add (+) icon in the To field.

4. Search, browse, or use the index to find the contact whose information you want to use. You see the results of your search under the Search bar. The text that matches your search is shown in bold. For example, if you search for Wal, you see people named Wallace, Walker, Walken, etc., and "Wal" is shown in bold in each result.

5. Tap the contact whose information you want to use. (If a contact doesn't have relevant information; for example, if no email address is configured when you are using the Mail app, that contact is grayed out and can't be selected.)

   If the contact has only one type of the relevant information (such as a single email address, if you started in the Mail app), you immediately move back to the app and the appropriate information is entered, and you can skip to step 7.

6. If the contact has multiple entries of the type you are trying to use, tap the information you want to use—in this case, the email address. The information is copied into the app and entered in the appropriate location.

7. Complete the task you are doing, such as sending an email message.

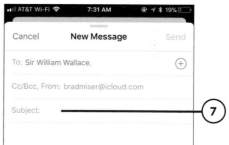

Managing Your Contacts on Your iPhone

When you sync contacts with an iCloud, Exchange, or other account, the changes go both ways. For example, when you change a contact on the iPhone, the synced contact manager application, such as Outlook, makes the changes for those contacts on your computer. Likewise, when you change contact information in a contact manager on your computer, those changes move to the iPhone. If you add a new contact in a contact manager, it moves to the iPhone, and vice versa. You can also change contacts manually in the Contacts app on your iPhone.

Updating Contact Information

You can change any information for an existing contact, such as adding new email addresses, deleting outdated information, and changing existing information.

1. Use the Contacts app to find and view the contact whose information you want to change.

2. Tap Edit. The contact screen moves into Edit mode, and you see Unlock icons.

3. Tap current information to change it; you can change a field's label by tapping it, or you can change the data for the field by tapping the information you want to change. Use the resulting tools, such as the phone number entry keypad, to make changes to the information. These tools work just like when you create a new contact (refer to "Creating Contacts Manually," earlier in this chapter).

4. To add more fields, tap add (+) in the related section, such as add phone in the phone number section; then, select a label for the new field and complete its information. This also works just like adding a new field to a contact you created manually.

5. Tap a field's Unlock (–) icon to remove that field from the contact.

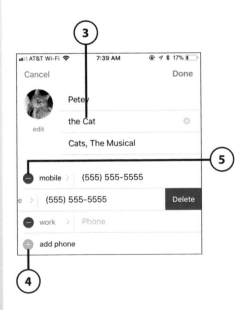

6. Tap Delete. The information is removed from the contact.

7. To change the contact's photo, tap the current photo, or the word *edit* under the current photo, and use the resulting menu and tools to select a new photo, take a new photo, delete the existing photo, or edit the existing one.

8. When you finish making changes, tap Done. Your changes are saved, and you move out of Edit mode.

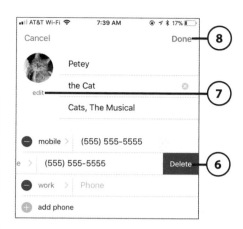

No Tones or Vibes?

If you leave the default tones or vibration patterns set for a contact, you won't see those fields when you view the contact. However, when you edit a contact, all the fields you need to add these to a contact become available.

Adding Information to an Existing Contact While Using Your iPhone

As you use your iPhone, you'll encounter information related to a contact that isn't currently part of that contact's information. For example, a contact might send you an email from a different email address than the one you have stored for her. When this happens, you can easily add the new information to the existing contact. Just tap the information to view it (such as an email address), and then tap Add to Existing Contact. Next, select the existing contact to which you want to add the new information. The new information is added to the contact. Depending on your iPhone model, tap Update or Done (or Cancel, if you decide not to keep the new information) to return to the app you're working in.

Deleting Contacts

To get rid of contacts, you can delete them from the Contacts app.

1. Find and view the contact you want to delete.

2. Tap Edit.

3. Swipe up to get to the bottom of the Info screen.

4. Tap Delete Contact.

5. Tap Delete Contact to confirm the deletion. The app deletes the contact, and you return to the Contacts screen.

>>>Go Further

LINKING CONTACTS

When you enter Edit mode in a contact, the Linked Contacts section appears at the bottom of the screen. You can use this to combine contacts. For example, if you end up with two contacts for the same person, you can link them to combine their information into one contact. Or, you might want to link multiple people to a company. When you link contacts, information from all the linked contacts appears on one contact, which is the contact from which you start the link process.

To link a contact, tap Edit and then tap link contacts. Find and tap the contact you want to link to the one you are editing. That contact's information displays. Tap Link.

The information from the second contact is linked to the first. You can repeat this as many times as you want. (Note that you have to have the group within which a contact is stored displayed to be able to link it.) When you are finished linking contacts, tap Done. The contact to which the others are linked is known as the *unified contact* (or card). It is labeled with the contact from which you started the linking process.

You can change how the information in the unified contact is displayed by viewing the unified contact, and then tapping one of the linked contacts. Tap the command you want to use, such as Use This Photo for Unified Card, which uses the image for the main contact in the unified contact.

To unlink contacts, edit the unified contact, tap the Unlock icon next to a linked contact, and tap Unlink. The contact information is separated as it was before you linked them.

Tap to configure
Phone and
FaceTime
settings

Tap to hear *and*
see the person
you want to
talk to

Tap to make
calls, listen to
voicemail, and
more

In this chapter, you explore all the cell phone and FaceTime functionality that your iPhone has to offer. Topics include the following:

→ Configuring phone settings
→ Making voice calls
→ Managing in-process voice calls
→ Receiving voice calls
→ Managing voice calls
→ Using visual voicemail
→ Communicating with FaceTime

Communicating with the Phone and FaceTime Apps

Although it's also a lot of other great things, such as a music player, web browser, email tool, and such, there's a reason the word phone is in iPhone. It's a feature-rich cell phone that includes some amazing features, two of which are visual voicemail and FaceTime. Other useful features include a speakerphone, conference calling, and easy-to-use onscreen controls. Plus your iPhone's phone functions are integrated with its other features. For example, when using the Maps application, you might find a location, such as a business, that you're interested in contacting. You can call that location just by tapping the number you want to call directly on the Maps screen.

Configuring Phone Settings

Of course, we all know that your ringtone is the most important phone setting, and you'll want to make sure your iPhone's ringtones are just right. Use the iPhone's Sounds settings to configure custom or standard ringtones and other phone-related sounds, including the new voicemail sound. You can also configure the way your phone vibrates when you receive a call. These are explained in Chapter 5, "Customizing How Your iPhone Looks and Sounds."

You can also have different ringtones and vibrations for specific people so you can know who is calling just by the sound and feel when a call comes in (configuring contacts is explained in Chapter 6, "Managing Contacts").

And you'll want to configure notifications for the Phone app. These include alerts, the app's badge, sounds, and vibrations. Configuring notifications is explained in Chapter 4, "Customizing How Your iPhone Works."

It is likely that you can use the Phone app with its default settings just fine. However, you might want to take advantage of some of its features by configuring the settings described in the following table. To access these settings, open the Settings app and tap Phone.

Provider Differences

The settings for the Phone app depend on the cell phone provider you use. The table lists most, but certainly not all, of the options you might have available. Depending on the provider you use, you may see more, fewer, or different settings than shown in the table. It's a good idea to open your Phone settings to see the options available to you.

Phone Settings

Section	Setting	Description
N/A	My Number	Shows your phone number for reference purposes.
CALLS	Announce Calls	When you enable this setting, the name of the caller (when available) is announced when the phone rings. Tap Always to always have the name announced, Headphones & Car to have the caller announced only when you are using headphones or your car's audio system, Headphones Only to have announcements only when you are using headphones, or Never if you don't want these announcements.
CALLS	Call Blocking & Identification	Tap this to see a list of people who you are currently blocking. You can tap someone on the list to see more information or swipe to the left and tap Unblock to unblock someone. Tap Block Contact to block someone in your Contacts app.
CALLS	Wi-Fi Calling	When enabled, you can place and receive calls via a Wi-Fi network. This is particularly useful when you are in a location with poor cellular reception, but you have access to a Wi-Fi network. When you set the Wi-Fi Calling on This iPhone switch to on (green), you're prompted to confirm your information. When you do, the service starts and you see the Update Emergency Address option; this is used to record your address so if you can place emergency calls via Wi-Fi, your location can be determined.

Section	Setting	Description
CALLS	Calls on Other Devices	When enabled, and your iPhone is on the same network as other iOS devices (such as iPads) or Macs configured with your information, you can take incoming calls and place calls from those devices. This can be useful when you aren't near your phone or simply want to use a different device to have a phone conversation. It can also be annoying because when a call comes in, all the devices using this feature start "ringing." When the Allow Calls on Other Devices switch is on (green), you can choose the specific devices calls are allowed on by setting their switches to on (green).
CALLS	Respond with Text	When calls come in, you have the option to respond with text. For example, you might want to say "Can't talk now, will call later." There are three default text responses or you can use this setting to create your own custom text responses.
CALLS	Call Forwarding	Enables you to forward incoming calls to a different phone number. Set the Call Forwarding switch to on (green) and enter the number to which you want calls forwarded. Set the switch to off (white) to stop your calls from being forwarded.
CALLS	Call Waiting	Enables or disables the call waiting feature.
CALLS	Show My Caller ID	Shows or hides your caller ID information when you place a call.
N/A	Change Voicemail Password	Use this option to change your voicemail password.
N/A	Dial Assist	Enable the Dial Assist feature, if you want the correct country code to be added to numbers in your country when dialing those numbers from outside your country or if you want the correct area codes to be added when you dial a local number. For example, if you live in the United States and don't want the correct prefixes added to U.S. phone numbers when you dial them from outside the United States, turn off Dial Assist. You then have to add any prefixes manually when dialing a U.S. number from outside the United States.
N/A	SIM PIN	Your iPhone uses a Subscriber Identity Module (SIM) card to store certain data about your phone; the SIM PIN setting enables you to associate a personal ID number (PIN) with the SIM card in an iPhone. To use your account with a different phone, you can remove the SIM card from your iPhone and install it in other phones that support these cards. If you set a PIN, that PIN is required to use the card in a different phone.
N/A	*Provider* Services, where *Provider* is the name of your provider	This area provides information about your account, such as the numbers you can dial for checking balances, paying bills, and other account management. You can also access your account by tapping the link at the bottom of the screen.

Making Voice Calls

There are a number of ways to make calls with your iPhone; after a call is in progress, you can manage it in the same way no matter how you started it.

Signal strength (more filled in bars indicates stronger signal)

Provider name

You can tell you are able to make a call or receive calls using your cellular network when you see your provider's information at the top of the screen along with the strength of the signal your phone is receiving. As long as you see at least one bar shaded in, you should be able to place and receive calls via the cellular network. More shaded bars are better because they mean you have a stronger signal, meaning the call quality will be better.

Wi-Fi calling is available

If the Wi-Fi calling feature is enabled and your phone is connected to a Wi-Fi network, you see the Wi-Fi calling icon for your provider at the top of the screen.

With a reasonably strong cellular signal or connection to a Wi-Fi network with Wi-Fi calling enabled, you are ready to make calls.

Which Network?

When you leave the coverage area for your provider and move into an area that is covered by another provider that supports roaming, your iPhone automatically connects to the other provider's network. When you are roaming, you see a different provider near the signal strength indicator at the top of the screen. For example, if AT&T is your provider and you travel to Toronto, Canada, the provider might become Rogers instead of AT&T, which indicates you are roaming. (In most cases, your provider sends a text message to you explaining the change in networks, including information about roaming charges.) Although the change to a roaming network is automatic, you need to be very aware of roaming charges, which can be significant depending on where you use your iPhone and what your default network is. Before you travel outside of your default network's coverage, check with your provider to determine the roaming rates that apply to where you are going. Also, see if there is a discounted roaming plan for that location. If you don't do this before you leave, you might get a nasty surprise when the bill arrives because roaming charges can be substantial.

Dialing with the Keypad

The most obvious way to make a call is to dial the number.

1. On the Home screen, tap Phone. The Phone app opens.

2. If you don't see the keypad on the screen, tap Keypad.

3. Tap numbers on the keypad to dial the number you want to call. If you dial a number associated with one or more contacts, you see the contact's name and the type of number you've dialed just under the number. (If you make a mistake in the number you are dialing, tap the Delete icon to the right of the call icon to delete the most recent digit you entered.)

4. Tap the call icon. The app dials the number, and the Call screen appears.

5. Use the Call screen to manage the call (not shown in the figure); see "Managing In-Process Voice Calls" later in this chapter for the details.

Number you are calling

Contact name and type of number you have dialed

Delete

Dialing with Contacts

As you saw in Chapter 6, the Contacts app is a complete contact manager so you can store various kinds of phone numbers for people and organizations. To make a call using a contact, follow these steps.

1. On the Home screen, tap Phone.

2. Tap Contacts.

3. Browse the list, search it, or use the index to find the contact you want to call. (Refer to Chapter 6 for information about using the Contacts app.)

4. Tap the contact you want to call.

5. Tap the number you want to dial; or tap the call Icon that is labeled with the type of number under the contact's name (if the person has more than one phone number, you are then prompted to tap the number you want to call). The app dials the number, and the Call screen appears.

Call Icon

At the top of a contact's screen, you see the call icon (the receiver icon). If a contact has only one number, this icon is labeled with the label applied to that number, such as iPhone or Work; tap the icon to call that number. If the person has more than one number, the icon is labeled with call; when you tap the call icon, you see all of the person's numbers and can tap the number you want to dial.

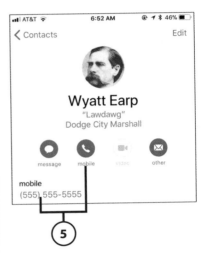

6. Use the Call screen to manage the call (not shown in the figure); see "Managing In-Process Voice Calls" later in this chapter for the details.

Dialing with Favorites

You can save contacts as favorites to make calling or videoconferencing them even simpler. (You learn how to save favorites in various locations later in this chapter. You learn how to make a contact into a favorite in Chapter 6.)

1. On the Home screen, tap Phone.

2. Tap the Favorites icon.

3. Browse the list until you see the favorite you want to call. Under the contact's name, you see the type of favorite, such as a phone number (identified by the label in the Contacts app, for example, iPhone or mobile) or FaceTime.

4. Tap the favorite you want to call; to place a voice call, tap a phone number (if you tap a FaceTime contact, a FaceTime call is placed instead). The app dials the number, and the Call screen appears.

5. Use the Call screen to manage the call (not shown in the figure); see "Managing In-Process Voice Calls" later in this chapter for the details.

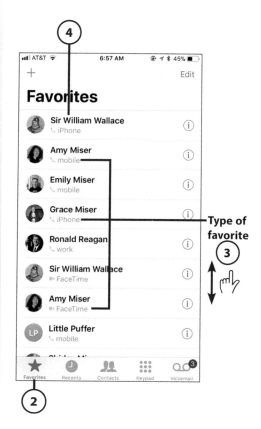

Type of favorite

Nobody's Perfect

If your iPhone can't complete the call for some reason, such as not having a strong enough signal, the Call Failed screen appears. Tap Call Back to try again and maybe try moving to another location that might have a stronger signal or tap Done to give up. When you tap Done, you return to the screen from which you came.

Dialing with Recents

As you make, receive, or miss calls, your iPhone keeps tracks of all the numbers on the Recents list. You can use the Recents list to make calls.

1. On the Home screen, tap Phone.

2. Tap Recents.

3. Tap All to see all calls.

4. Tap Missed to see only calls you missed.

5. If necessary, browse the list of calls.

6. To call the number associated with a recent call, tap the title of the call, such as a person's name, or the number if no contact is associated with it. The app dials the number, and the Call screen appears. Skip to step 10.

7. To get more information about a recent call, for example, to see exactly what time yesterday they called, tap its Info icon. The Info screen appears.

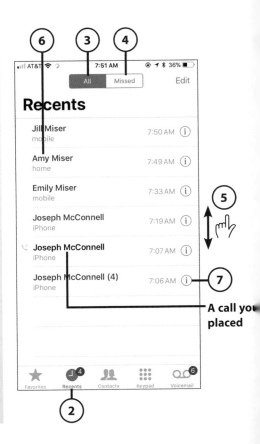

A call you placed

Info on the Recents Screen

If you have a contact on your iPhone associated with a phone number, you see the person's name and the label for the number (such as mobile). If you don't have a contact for a number, you see the number itself. If a contact or number has more than one call associated with it, you see the number of recent calls in parentheses next to the name or number. If you initiated a call, you see the phone icon next to the contact's name and label.

8. Read the information about the call or calls. For example, if the call is related to someone in your Contacts list, you see detailed information for that contact. If there are multiple recent calls, you see information for each call, such as its status (Missed Call, Canceled Call, or Outgoing Call, for example) and time.

9. Tap a number on the Info screen. The app dials the number, and the Call screen appears.

Going Back

To return to the Recents screen without making a call, tap Recents.

10. Use the Call screen to manage the call (not shown in the figure); see "Managing In-Process Voice Calls" later in this chapter for the details.

Dialing from the FAVORITES Widget

Using the FAVORITES widget, you can quickly call a favorite. Use the following steps.

Managing Widgets

If you don't see the FAVORITES widget, you need to add it. See Chapter 4 for the steps to manage your widgets.

1. From the Home or Lock screen, swipe to the right to open your widgets.

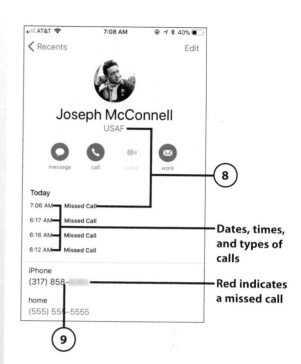

Dates, times, and types of calls

Red indicates a missed call

2. Swipe up or down until you see the FAVORITES widget.

3. Tap Show More to see the full list of favorites. The list expands.

4. Tap the person you want to call.

5. Use the Call screen to manage the call (not shown in the figure); see the next section for the details.

You've Got the Touch

If your iPhone supports 3D Touch (iPhone 6s/6s Plus and later), you can also place calls to favorites by pressing on the Phone app. The FAVORITES pane appears; tap a favorite to place a call. You can also access the most recent voicemail or see the most recent call.

Managing In-Process Voice Calls

When you place a call, there are several ways to manage it. The most obvious is to place your iPhone next to your ear and use your iPhone like any other phone you've ever used. As you place your iPhone next to your ear, the controls on its screen become disabled so you don't accidentally tap onscreen icons with the side of your face or your ear. When you take your iPhone away from your ear, the Call screen appears again and the Phone app's controls become active again.

When you are on a call, press the Volume buttons on the left side of the iPhone to increase (top button) or decrease (bottom button) its volume. Some of the other things you can do while on a call might not be so obvious, as you learn in the next few tasks.

Following are some of the icons on the Call screen that you can use to manage an active call:

Tap to mute your side of the call

Tap to change the call into a FaceTime call

Tap to put the call on speaker

Tap to end the call

- Mute your side of the call by tapping mute. You can hear the person on the other side of the call, but he can't hear anything on your side.

- Tap speaker to use the iPhone's speakers to hear the call. You can speak with the phone held away from your face, too.

- Tap FaceTime to convert the voice call into a FaceTime call (read more on FaceTime later in this chapter).

- When you're done with the call, tap the receiver icon to end it.

Contact Photos on the Call Screen

If someone in your contacts calls you, or you call her, the photo associated with the contact appears on the screen. Depending on how the image was captured, it either appears as a small icon at the top of the screen next to the contact's name or fills the entire screen as the background wallpaper.

Entering Numbers During a Call

You often need to enter numbers during a call, such as to log in to a voicemail system, access an account, or enter a meeting code for an online meeting.

1. Place a call using any of the methods you've learned so far.

2. Tap keypad.

3. Tap the numbers you want to enter.

4. When you're done, tap Hide. You return to the Call screen.

Making Conference Calls

Your iPhone makes it easy to talk to multiple people at the same time. You can have two separate calls going on at any point in time. You can even create conference calls by merging them together. Not all cell providers support two on-going calls or conference calling, though. If yours doesn't, you won't be able to perform the steps in this section.

1. Place a call using any of the methods you've learned so far.

2. Tap add call.

3. Tap the icon you want to use to place the next call. Tap Favorites to call a favorite, tap Recents to use the Recents list, tap Contacts to place the call using the Contacts app, or tap Keypad to dial the number. These work just as they do when you start a new call.

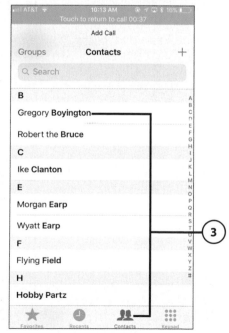

4. Place the call using the option you selected in step 3. Doing so places the first call on hold and moves you back to the Call screen while the Phone app makes the second call. The first call's information appears at the top of the screen, including the word hold so you know the first call is on hold. The app displays the second call just below that, and it is currently the active call.

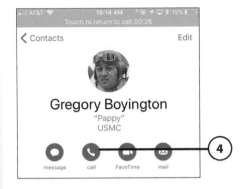

Similar but Different

If you tap contacts instead of add call, you move directly into the Contacts screen. This might save you one screen tap if the person you want to add to the call is in your Contacts app.

5. Talk to the second person you called; the first remains on hold.

6. To switch to the first call, tap it on the list or tap swap. This places the second call on hold and moves it to the top of the call list, while the first call becomes active again.

The first call is placed on hold

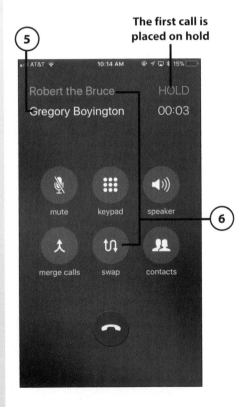

7. Tap merge calls to join the calls so all parties can hear you and each other. The iPhone combines the two calls, and you see a single entry at the top of the screen to reflect this.

Merging Calls

As you merge calls, your iPhone attempts to display the names of the callers at the top of the Call screen. As the text increases, your iPhone scrolls it so you can read it. Eventually, the iPhone replaces the names with the word Conference.

Number of Callers

Your provider and the specific technology of the network you use can limit the number of callers you place in a conference call. When you reach the limit, the add call icon is disabled.

8. To add another call, repeat steps 2–7. Each time you merge calls, the second line becomes free so you can add more calls.

9. To manage a conference call, tap the Info icon (i) at the top of the screen.

The first call is now active while the second is on hold

10. To speak with one of the callers privately, tap Private (if the Private icons are disabled, you can't do this with the current calls). Doing so places the conference call on hold and returns you to the Call screen showing information about the active call. You can merge the calls again by tapping merge calls.

11. Tap End to remove a caller from the call. The app disconnects that caller from the conference call. When you have only one person left on the call, you return to the Call screen and see information about the active call.

12. Tap Back to move back to the Call screen. You move to the Call screen and can continue working with the call, such as adding more people to it.

13. To end the call for all callers, tap the receiver icon.

It's Not All Good

Watch Your Minutes

When you have multiple calls combined into one, depending on your provider, the minutes for each call can continue to count individually. So if you've joined three people into one call, each minute of the call might count as three minutes against your calling plan. Before you use this feature, check with your provider to determine what policies govern conference calling for your account.

Using Another App During a Voice Call

Tap to return to the call

A call is active, and you can use other apps while still talking

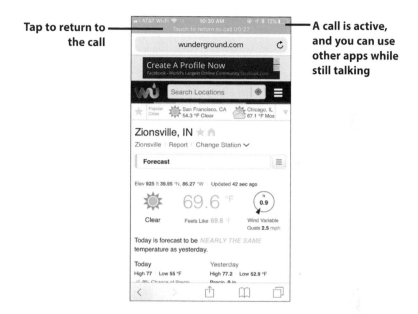

If your provider's technology supports it, you can use your iPhone for other tasks while you are on a call. When you are on a call, press the Touch ID/ Home button (all models except iPhone X) or swipe up from the bottom of the screen (iPhone X) to move to a Home screen, and then tap a different app (placing the call in speaker mode before you switch to a different app or using the headphones are best for this). Or, you can use the App Switcher to move into a different app. The call remains active and you see the active call information in a green bar at the top of the screen. You can perform other tasks, such as looking up information, sending emails, and visiting websites. You can continue to talk to the other person just like when the Call screen is showing. To return to the call, tap the green bar.

Receiving Voice Calls

Receiving calls on your iPhone enables you to access the same great tools you can use when you make calls, plus a few more for good measure.

Answering Calls

Person calling you ————

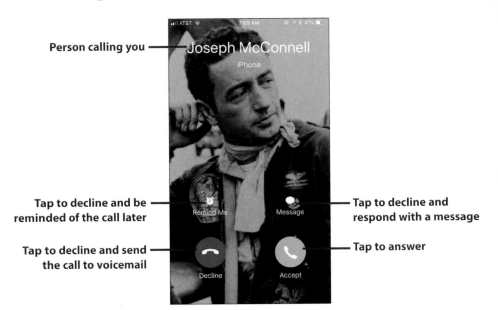

Tap to decline and be reminded of the call later

Tap to decline and respond with a message

Tap to decline and send the call to voicemail

Tap to answer

When your iPhone rings, it's time to answer the call—or not. If you configured the ringer to ring, you hear your default ringtone or the one associated with the caller's contact information when a call comes in. If vibrate is turned on, your iPhone vibrates whether the ringer is on or not. If you enabled the announce feature, the name of the caller is announced (if available). And if those ways aren't enough, a message appears on iPhone's screen to show you information about the incoming call. If the number is in your Contacts app, you see the contact with which the number is associated, the label for the number, and the contact's image if there is one. If the number isn't in your contacts, you see the number only.

Wallpaper

If the photo associated with a contact was taken with your iPhone or came from a high-resolution image, you see the contact's image at full screen when the call comes in, instead of the small icon at the top of the screen.

Calls on Other Devices

By default, when you receive a call on your iPhone, it also comes to any iOS 8 or later devices or Macs running Yosemite or later that are on the same Wi-Fi network, and you can take the call on those devices. To disable this, set the Calls on Other Devices setting to off as described earlier in this chapter.

Person calling you — Robert the Bruce
Scottish Federation

Tap to decline
and be reminded — Remind Me
of the call later

Tap to decline and
respond with a message — Message

slide to answer

Swipe to the right
to answer

If your iPhone is locked when a call comes in, swipe the slider to the right to answer it or use the Remind Me and Message icons, which work just like they do when a call comes in when the iPhone isn't locked.

When you receive a call, you have the following options:

- **Answer**—Tap Accept (if the iPhone is unlocked) or swipe the slider to the right (if the iPhone is locked) to take the call (you don't have to unlock the phone to answer a call). You move to the Call screen and can work with the call just like calls you place. For example, you can add a call, merge calls, place the call on hold, or end the call.

- **Decline**—If you tap Decline (when the iPhone is unlocked), the Phone app immediately routes the call to voicemail. You can also decline a call by quickly pressing the Side button twice.

- **Silence the ringer**— To silence the ringer without sending the call directly to voicemail, press the Side button once or press either volume button. The call continues to come in, and you can answer it even though you shut off the ringer.

- **Respond with a message**—Tap Message to send the call to voicemail and send a message back in response. You can tap one of the default messages, or you can tap Custom to create a unique message (the table at the beginning of the chapter explains where to find the setting to create custom messages). Of course, the device the caller is using to make the call must be capable of receiving messages for this to be useful.

- **Decline the call but be reminded later**—Tap Remind Me and the call is sent to voicemail. Tap When I leave, When I get home, When I get to work, or In 1 hour to set the timeframe in which you want to be reminded. A reminder is created in the Reminders app to call back the person who called you, and it is set to alert you at the time you select.

Silencio!

To mute your iPhone's ringer, slide the Mute switch located above the Volume switch toward the back so the orange line appears. The Mute icon (a bell with a slash through it) appears on the screen to let you know you turned off the ringer. To turn it on again, slide the switch forward. The bell icon appears on the screen to show you the ringer is active again. To set the ringer's volume, use the Volume controls (assuming that setting is enabled) when you aren't on a call and aren't listening to an app, such as the Music app.

Answering Calls During a Call

As mentioned earlier, your iPhone can manage multiple calls at the same time. If you are on a call and another call comes in, you have a number of ways to respond.

- **Decline incoming call**—Tap Send to Voicemail to send the incoming call directly to voicemail.

- **Place the first call on hold and answer the incoming call**—Tap Hold & Accept to place the current call on hold and answer the incoming one. After you do this, you can manage the two calls just as when you call two numbers from your iPhone. For example, you can place the second call on hold and move back to the first one, merge the calls, and add more calls.

- **End the first call and answer the incoming call**—Tap End & Accept to terminate the active call and answer the incoming call.

- **Respond with message or get reminded later**—These options work just as they do when you are dealing with any incoming phone call.

Auto-Mute

If you are listening to music or video when a call comes in, the app providing the audio, such as the Music app, automatically pauses. When the call ends, that app picks up right where it left off.

Managing Voice Calls

You've already learned most of what you need to know to use your iPhone's cell phone functions. In the following sections, you learn the rest.

Clearing Recent Calls

Previously in this chapter, you learned about the Recents tool that tracks call activity on your iPhone. As you read, this list shows both completed and missed calls; you can view all calls by tapping the All tab or only missed calls by tapping Missed. On either tab, missed calls are always in red, and you see the number of missed calls since you last looked at the list in the badge on the Recents tab. You also learned how you can get more detail about a call, whether it was missed or made.

Over time, you'll build a large Recents list, which you can easily clear.

1. Tap Phone.

2. Tap Recents.

3. Tap Edit.

4. Tap Clear to clear the entire list; to delete a specific recent call, skip to step 6.

5. Tap Clear All Recents. The Recents list is reset.

Delete Faster

On the Recents screen, you can delete an individual recent item by swiping to the left on it (starting to the left of the i icon) and tapping Delete.

6. Tap a recent item's unlock (–) icon.

7. Tap Delete. The recent item is deleted.

8. When you are done managing your recent calls, tap Done.

Adding Calling Information to Favorites

Earlier you learned how simple it is to place calls to someone on your Favorites list. There are a number of ways to add people to this list, including adding someone on your Recents list.

1. Move to the Recents list.

2. Tap the Info icon (i) for the person you want to add to your favorites list. The Info screen appears. If the number is associated with a contact, you see that contact's information.

3. Swipe up to move to the bottom of the screen.

4. Tap Add to Favorites. If the person has multiple types of contact information, such as phone numbers, email addresses, and so on, you see each type of information available.

5. Tap the type of information you want to add as a favorite, such as Call to make a phone number a favorite.

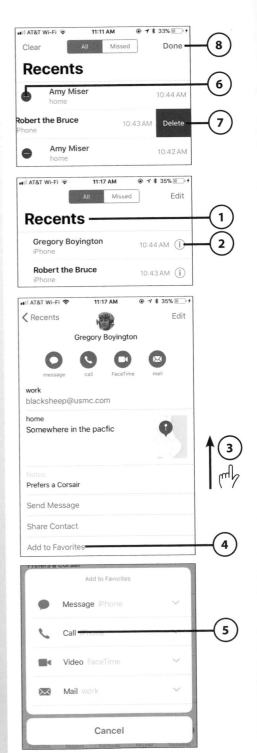

6. Tap the number or email address you want to add as a favorite.

7. Repeat steps 5 and 6 if you want to add the contact's other numbers or addresses to the favorites list. (If all the numbers and email addresses are assigned as favorites, the Add to Favorites icon doesn't appear on the contact's screen.)

Make Contact First

To make someone a favorite, he needs to be a contact in the Contacts app. Refer to Chapter 6 to learn how to make someone who has called you into a contact.

Using the iPhone's Headset for Calls

Your iPhone includes an EarPods headset with a microphone on one of its cords. The mic includes a button in the center of the switch on the right side of the EarPods' cable that you can use to do the following:

- **Answer**—Press the mic button once to answer a call.

- **End a call**—Press the mic button while you are on a call to end it.

- **Decline a call**—Press and hold the mic button for about two seconds. Two beeps sound when you release the button to let you know that your iPhone sent the call to voicemail.

- **Put a current call on hold and switch to an incoming call**—Press the mic button once and then press again.

- **End a current call on hold and switch to an incoming call**—Press the mic button once and hold for about two seconds. Release the button and you hear two beeps to let you know you ended the first call. The incoming call is ready for you.

- **Activate Siri**—Press and hold the mic button until you hear the Siri chime. This is useful when you want to make a call to someone without looking at or touching your phone.

Oh, That Ringing in My Ears

When you have EarPods plugged into your iPhone and you receive a call, the ringtone plays on both the iPhone's speaker (unless the ringer is muted, of course) and through the EarPods.

Using Visual Voicemail

Visual voicemail just might be the best of your iPhone's many great features. No more wading through long, uninteresting voicemails to get to one in which you are interested. You simply jump to the message you want to hear. If that isn't enough for you, you can also jump to any point within a voicemail to hear just that part, such as to repeat a phone number that you want to write down. Even better, the iPhone creates a transcript of voicemails, so you can read them instead of listening to them.

The Phone app can access your voicemails directly so don't need to log in to hear them.

Recording a New Greeting

The first time you access voicemail, you are prompted to record a voice-mail greeting. Follow the onscreen instructions to do so.

You can also record a new greeting at any time.

1. Move to the Phone screen and tap Voicemail. If badge notifications are enabled for the Phone app, you see the number of voice-mails you haven't listened to yet in the badge on the Voicemail icon.

2. Tap Greeting.

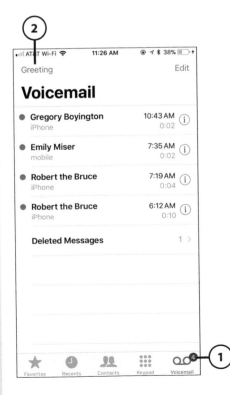

3. To use a default greeting that provides only the iPhone's phone number, tap Default and skip to step 10.

4. Tap Custom to record a personalized greeting. If you have previously used a custom greeting, it is loaded into the editor. You can replace it by continuing with these steps.

5. Tap Record. Recording begins.

6. Speak your greeting. As you record your message, the red area of the timeline indicates (relatively) how long your message is.

7. When you're done recording, tap Stop.

For the Very First Time

Some providers require that you dial into your voicemail number the first time you use it. If you tap Voicemail and the phone starts to dial instead of you seeing Visual Voicemail as shown in these figures, this is your situation. You call the provider's voicemail system, and you're prompted to set up your voicemail. When you've completed that process, you can use these steps to record your greeting.

8. Tap Play to hear your greeting.

9. If you aren't satisfied, drag the Playhead to the beginning and repeat steps 5–8 to record a new message.

10. When you are happy with your greeting, tap Save. The Phone app saves the default or custom greeting as the active greeting and returns you to the Voicemail screen.

Your message being recorded

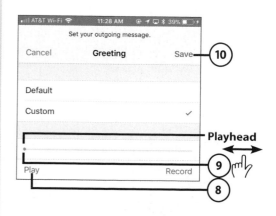

Playhead

Adding to a Custom Message

To add onto an existing greeting, drag the playhead to where you want to start recording and tap Record. Tap Stop when you're done.

No Visual Voicemail?

If your voicemail password isn't stored on your iPhone when you tap Voicemail, your phone dials into your voicemail instead of moving to the Voicemail screen. If that happens, something has gone wrong with your password and you need to reset it. Follow your provider's instructions to reset the password. When you have the new password, open the Phone Settings screen, tap Change Voicemail Password, enter the reset password, create a new password, and re-enter your new password. (You need to tap Done after each time you enter a password.)

Change Greeting

To switch between the default and the current custom greeting, move to the Greeting screen, tap the greeting you want to use (which is marked with a check mark), and tap Save. When you choose Custom, you use the custom greeting you most recently saved.

Listening to, Reading, and Managing Voicemails

Unless you turned off the voicemail sound, you hear the sound you selected each time a caller leaves a voicemail for you. The number in the badge on the Phone icon and on the Voicemail icon on the Phone screen increases by 1 (unless you've disabled the badge). (Note that the badge number on the Phone icon includes both voicemails left for you and missed calls, whereas the badge number on the Voicemail icon indicates only the number of voicemails left for you.) (A new voicemail is one to which you haven't listened, not anything to do with when it was left for you.) If you've configured visual notifications for new voicemails (see Chapter 4), you see those on the screen as well.

If you receive a voicemail while your iPhone is locked, you see a message on the screen alerting you that your iPhone received a voicemail (unless you have disabled these notifications from appearing on the Lock screen). (It also indicates a missed call, which is always the case when a call ends up in voicemail.) Press (3D Touch iPhones) or swipe to the right (non-3D Touch models) on the notification to jump to the Voicemail screen so that you can work with your messages.

And in yet another scenario, if you are using your iPhone when a message is left, you see a notification (unless you have turned off notifications for the Phone app) that enables you to deal with the new message.

Missing Password

If something happens to the password stored on your iPhone for your voice-mail, such as if you restore the iPhone, you are prompted to enter your pass-word before you can access your voicemail. Do so at the prompt and tap OK. The iPhone signs you in to voicemail, and you won't have to enter your pass-word again (unless something happens to it again of course).

Contacts or Numbers?

Like phone calls, if a contact is associated with a number from which you've received a voicemail, you see the contact's name associated with the voicemail message. If no contact exists for the number, you see the number only.

Finding and Listening to Voicemails

Working with voicemails is simple and quick.

Voicemail you haven't listened to

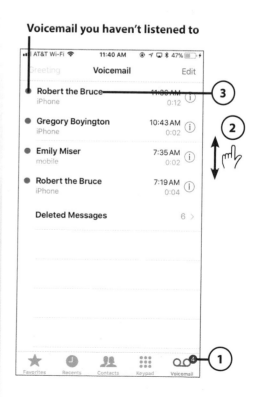

1. Move into the Phone app and tap Voicemail (if you pressed or swiped on a new message noti-fication, you jump directly to the Voicemail screen).

2. Swipe up and down the screen to browse the list of voicemails. Voicemails you haven't listened to are marked with a blue circle.

3. To listen to or read a voicemail, tap it. You see the timeline bar and controls and the message plays.

4. Read the message if you don't want to listen to it.

5. Tap the Pause icon to pause a message.

6. Tap Speaker to hear the message on your iPhone's speaker.

7. To move to a specific point in a message, drag the Playhead to the point at which you want to listen.

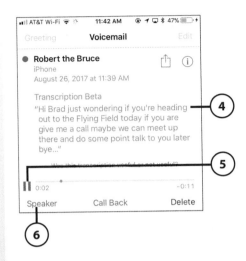

Moving Ahead or Behind

You can also drag the Playhead while a message is playing to rewind or fast-forward it. This is also helpful when you want to listen to specific information without hearing the whole message again.

8. Tap Call Back to call back the person who left the message.

9. Tap Delete to delete the message.

10. Tap the Share icon to share the message, and then tap how you want to share it, such as Message or Mail. For example, when you tap Mail, you send the voicemail to someone else using the Mail app, so he can listen to the message.

11. Tap the Info icon (i) to get more information about a message. The Info screen appears. If the person who left the message is on your contacts list, you see her contact information. The number associated with the message is highlighted in blue.

Time elapsed in the message

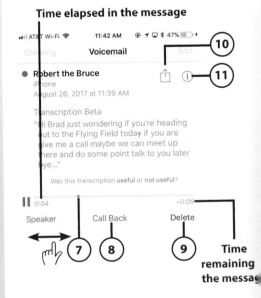

Time remaining the message

12. Swipe up or down the screen to review the caller's information.

13. Tap Voicemail.

14. To listen to a message you have listened to before (one that doesn't have a blue dot), tap the message and then tap the Play icon. It begins to play. You can also read its transcript (if available).

Deleting Messages

To delete a voicemail message that isn't the active message, tap it so it becomes the active message and then tap Delete. Or swipe to the left on the message you want to delete and tap Delete. Or swipe quickly all the way to the left on the message to delete it.

Listening to and Managing Deleted Voicemails

When you delete messages, they are moved to the Deleted Message folder. You can work with deleted messages as follows:

1. Move to the Voicemail screen.

2. If necessary, swipe up the screen until you see the Deleted Messages option.

3. Tap Deleted Messages.

Message you've listened to

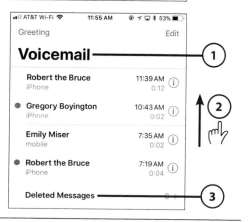

What's Missed?

In case you're wondering, your iPhone considers any call you didn't answer to be a missed call. So if someone calls and leaves a message, that call is included in the counts of both missed calls and new voicemails. If the caller leaves a message, you see a notification informing you that you have a new voicemail and showing who it is from (if available). If you don't answer and the caller doesn't leave a message, it's counted only as a missed call and you see a notification showing a missed call along with the caller's identification (if available).

4. Swipe up or down the screen to browse all the deleted messages.

5. Tap a message to listen to it or to read its transcript.

6. Tap the Play icon to hear the message. You can use the other playback tools just like you can with undeleted messages.

7. Tap Undelete to restore the deleted message. The iPhone restores the message to the Voicemail screen.

8. Tap Clear All to remove all deleted messages permanently. (If this is disabled, close the open message by tapping it.)

9. Tap Clear All at the prompt. The deleted messages are erased and you return to the Deleted screen.

10. Tap Voicemail to return to the Voicemail screen.

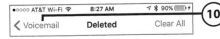

Lost/Forgot Your Password?

If you have to restore your iPhone or it loses your voicemail password for some other reason and you can't remember it, you need to have the password reset to access your voicemail on the iPhone. For most cell phone providers, this involves calling the customer support number and accessing an automated system that sends a new password to you via a text message. For AT&T, which is one of the iPhone providers in the United States, call 611 on your iPhone and follow the prompts to reset your password (which you receive via a text). No matter which provider you use, it's a good idea to know how to reset your voicemail password because it is likely you will need to do so at some point.

Communicating with FaceTime

FaceTime enables you to see, as well as hear, people with whom you want to communicate. This feature exemplifies what's great about the iPhone; it takes complex technology and makes it simple. FaceTime works great, but there are two conditions that have to be true for you and the people you want some FaceTime with. To be able to see each other, both sides have to use a device that has the required cameras (this includes iPhone 4s and newer, iPod touches third generation and newer, iPad 2s and newer, and Macs running Snow Leopard and newer), and have FaceTime enabled (via the settings on an iOS device that are explained on the next page or via the FaceTime application on a Mac). And each device has to be able to communicate over a network; an iPhone or cellular iPad can use a cellular data network (if that setting is enabled) or a Wi-Fi network while Macs have to be connected to the Internet through a Wi-Fi or other type of network. When these conditions are true, making and receiving FaceTime calls are simple tasks.

In addition to making video FaceTime calls, you can also make audio-only FaceTime calls. These work similarly to making a voice call except the minutes don't count against your voice plan when you use a Wi-Fi network (if you are making the call over the cellular network, the data does count against your data plan, so be careful about this).

Assuming you are in a place where you don't have to pay for the data you use, such as when you use a Wi-Fi network, you don't have to pay for a Face-Time call (video or audio-only) either.

Configuring FaceTime Settings

FaceTime is a great way to use your iPhone to hear and see someone else. There are a few FaceTime settings you need to configure for FaceTime to work. You can connect with other FaceTime users via your phone number or an email address.

1. Move to the Settings screen.

2. Tap FaceTime.

3. If the FaceTime switch is off (white), tap the FaceTime switch to turn it on (green). If the FaceTime switch is on and you see an Apple ID, you are already signed into an account; in this case, you see the current FaceTime settings and can follow along starting with step 7 to change these settings. You can sign out of the current account by tapping it, and then tapping Sign Out; proceed to step 4 to sign in with a different account.

4. To use your Apple ID for FaceTime calls, tap Use your Apple ID for FaceTime (if you haven't signed into an Apple ID account, see Chapter 3, "Setting Up and Using an Apple ID, iCloud, and Other Online Accounts" to do so and then come back here to enable FaceTime). If you don't sign in to an Apple ID, you can still use FaceTime, but it is always via your cellular connection, which isn't ideal because then FaceTime counts under your voice minutes on your calling plan or as data on your data plan.

5. Configure the email addresses you want people to be able to use to contact you for FaceTime sessions by tapping them to enable each address (enabled addresses are marked with a check mark) or to disable addresses (these don't have a check mark). (If you don't have any email addresses configured on your iPhone, you are prompted to enter email addresses.)

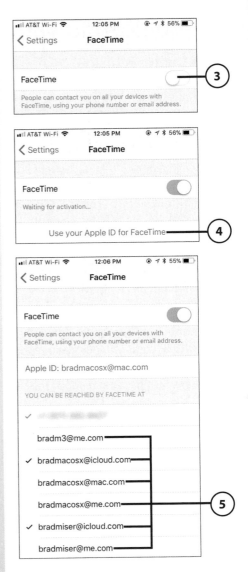

6. Tap the phone number or email address by which you will be identified to the other caller during a FaceTime call.

7. If you want to allow Live Photos to be captured while you are in a FaceTime session, set the FaceTime Live Photos switch to on (green). (To learn more about Live Photos, see Chapter 13, "Taking Photos and Video with Your iPhone.")

Blocking FaceTime

If you tap Blocked at the bottom of the FaceTime Settings screen, you see the names, phone numbers, and email addresses that are currently blocked from making calls, sending messages, or making FaceTime requests to your iPhone. To block someone else, tap Add New and then tap the contact you want to block.

Making FaceTime Calls

FaceTime is a great way to communicate with someone because you can hear and see him (or just hear him if you choose an audio-only FaceTime call). Because iPhones have cameras facing each way, it's also easy to show something to the person you are talking with. You make FaceTime calls starting from the FaceTime, Contacts, or Phone apps and from the FAVORITES widget. No matter which way you start a FaceTime session, you manage it in the same way.

Careful

If your iPhone is connected to a Wi-Fi network, you can make all the FaceTime calls you want (assuming you you have unlimited data on that network). However, if you are using the cellular data network, be aware that FaceTime calls may use data under your data plan. If you have a limited plan, it's a good idea to use FaceTime primarily when you are connected to a Wi-Fi network. (Refer to Chapter 2, "Using Your iPhone's Core Features," for information on connecting to Wi-Fi networks.)

To start a FaceTime call from the Contacts app, do the following:

1. Use the Contacts app to open the contact with whom you want to chat (refer to Chapter 6 for information about using the Contacts app).

Playing Favorites

If you've set a FaceTime contact as a favorite, you can open the Phone app, tap Favorites, and tap the FaceTime favorite to start the FaceTime session.

2. To place an audio-only FaceTime call, tap the FaceTime audio icon. (The rest of these steps show a FaceTime video call, but a FaceTime audio-only is very similar to voice calls described earlier in this chapter.)

3. Tap the contact's FaceTime video icon. The iPhone attempts to make a FaceTime connection. You hear the FaceTime "chirping" and see status information on the screen while the call is attempted. When the connection is complete, you hear a different tone and see the other person in the large window and a preview of what she is seeing (whatever your iPhone's front-side camera is pointing at— most likely your face) in the small window. If the person you are trying to FaceTime with isn't available for FaceTime for some reason (perhaps she doesn't have a FaceTime-capable device or is not connected to the Internet), you see a message saying that the person you are calling is unavailable for FaceTime, and the call terminates.

4. After the call is accepted, manage the call as described in the "Managing FaceTime Calls" task later in this chapter.

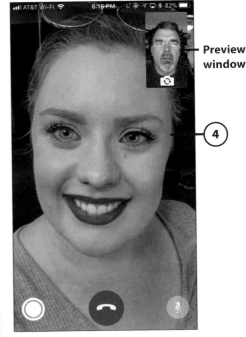

Preview window

>>>Go Further

MORE INFORMATION ABOUT FACETIME CALLS

As you make FaceTime calls, following are some other bits of information for your consideration:

- **Failing FaceTime**—If a FaceTime request fails, you can't really tell the reason why. It can be a technical issue, such as none of the contact information you have is FaceTime-enabled, the person is not signed into a device, or the person might have declined the request. If you repeatedly have trouble connecting with someone, contact him to make sure he has a FaceTime-capable device and that you are using the correct FaceTime contact information.

- **Leave a Message**—On the FaceTime Unavailable screen, you can tap Leave a Message to send a text or iMessage message to the person with whom you are trying to FaceTime.

- **Transform a call**—You can transform a voice call into a FaceTime session by tapping the FaceTime icon on the Call screen. When you transform a call into a FaceTime session, the minutes no longer count against the minutes in your calling plan because all communication happens over the Wi-Fi network or your cellular data plan if you enabled that option and aren't connected to a Wi-Fi network. (The voice call you started from automatically terminates when you make the switch.)

- **FaceTime app**—To use the FaceTime app to start a call, tap the FaceTime icon on the Home screen. Tap the Video tab to make a video call or the Audio tab to make an audio-only call. Tap the Add (+) icon to use your contacts to start the call. You can also enter a name, email address, or phone number in the bar at the top of the screen (if you haven't made or received any FaceTime calls before, you won't see the tabs until you make your first call). Tap a person on the Recents list to place a FaceTime call to that person. Once you've connected, you manage the FaceTime session as described in the rest of this chapter.

- **FaceTime with Siri**—You can also place a FaceTime call using Siri by activating Siri and saying "FaceTime *name*" where *name* is the name of the person with whom you want to FaceTime. If there are multiple options for that contact, you must tell Siri which you want to use. After you've made a selection, Siri starts the FaceTime call.

- **FaceTime with the FAVORITES widget**—You can open the FAVORITES widget and tap the FaceTime icon for the person with whom you want to have a FaceTime conversation.

Receiving FaceTime Calls

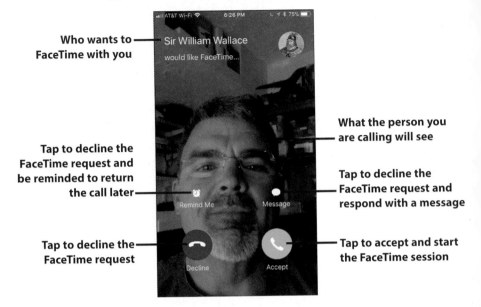

Who wants to — FaceTime with you

What the person you — are calling will see

Tap to decline the FaceTime request and be reminded to return the call later —

Tap to decline the — FaceTime request and respond with a message

Tap to decline the — FaceTime request

Tap to accept and start — the FaceTime session

When someone tries to FaceTime with you, you see the incoming FaceTime request screen message showing who is trying to connect with you and the image you are currently broadcasting. Tap Accept to accept the request and start the FaceTime session. Manage the FaceTime call as described in the "Managing FaceTime Calls" task.

Tap Remind Me to decline the FaceTime request and create a reminder or Message to decline the request and send a message. These options work just as they do for a voice call (you have the same custom message options). You can also press the Side button to decline the request.

When a FaceTime request comes in while your iPhone is locked, you swipe to the right on the slider to accept the call or use the Remind Me or Message options if you don't want to take the call (this is the same as when you receive a voice call via the Phone app).

If you decline the FaceTime request, the person trying to call you receives a message that you're not available (and a message if you choose that option). She can't tell whether there is a technical issue or if you simply declined to take the call.

Tracking FaceTime Calls

FaceTime calls are tracked just as voice calls are. Open the FaceTime app and tap Video to see recent video FaceTime calls or Audio to see recent audio FaceTime calls. On the recents list, FaceTime calls are marked with the video camera icon. FaceTime audio-only calls are marked with a telephone receiver icon. FaceTime calls that didn't go through are in red and are treated as missed calls. You can do the same tasks with recent FaceTime calls that you can with recent voice calls.

Managing FaceTime Calls

During a FaceTime call (regardless of who placed the call initially), you can do the following:

Drag to change the location of the preview window

Tap to change the camera you are using

Tap to take a photo

Tap to mute your side of the call

- Drag the preview window, which shows the image that the other person is seeing, around the screen to change its location. It "snaps" into place in the closest corner when you lift your finger up.

- Move your iPhone and change the angle you are holding it to change the images you are broadcasting to the other person. Use the preview window to see what the other person is seeing.

- Tap Mute to mute your side of the conversation. Your audio is muted and you see the Mute icon in the preview window. Video continues to be broadcast so the other person can still see you.

The other person
is seeing what the
backside camera is
showing

Tap to change the
camera you are using

Tap to take a photo

- To use the camera on the backside of the iPhone, tap the Change Camera icon. The other person now sees whatever you have the camera on the back of the iPhone pointed at. If the other person changes her camera, you see what her backside camera is pointing at.

- Tap the shutter icon to take a Live Photo (if that setting is enabled) of the image you are seeing in the FaceTime window.

Tap the screen to make
the controls appear

- After a few moments, the controls disappear. Tap the screen to make them reappear.

Preview shows the landscape orientation

FaceTime works in landscape orientation, too

Tap to end the FaceTime session

- Rotate your iPhone to change the orientation to horizontal. This affects what the other person sees (as reflected in your preview), but you continue to see the other person in her iPhone's current orientation.

- Tap the receiver icon to end the FaceTime call session.

FaceTime Break

Just like when you are in a voice call, you can move into and use other apps (if your provider's technology supports this functionality). You see the green FaceTime in progress bar at the top of the screen. The audio part of the session continues, but the other person sees a still image with a camera icon and the word "Paused." As soon as you move back into the FaceTime session, the video resumes. Likewise, if the other person moves out of the FaceTime app, you see the Paused icon.

Tap to
configure
email
settings

Tap to use
email

In this chapter, you explore all the email functionality that your iPhone has to offer. Topics include the following:

→ Configuring email accounts
→ Setting Mail app preferences
→ Working with email
→ Managing email

Sending, Receiving, and Managing Email

For most of us, email is an important way we communicate with others, both in our professional and personal lives. Fortunately, your iPhone has great email tools so you can work with email no matter where you are. Of course, you need to be connected to the Internet through a Wi-Fi or cellular data connection to send or receive email—although you can read downloaded messages, reply to messages, and compose messages when you aren't connected.

To use email on your iPhone, you use the Mail app. This app has lots of great features that help you really take advantage of email from all your accounts. Before jumping into the app, you need to have one or more email accounts configured on your iPhone. As you work with your email, there are a number of Mail settings that you might want to configure to tailor how the app works to suit your preferences.

Configuring Email Accounts

Before you can start using an iPhone for email, you have to configure the email accounts you want to access with it. The iPhone supports many kinds of email accounts, including iCloud, Exchange, Gmail, and so on. Setting up the most common types of email accounts is covered in Chapter 3, "Setting Up and Using an Apple ID, iCloud, and Other Online Accounts," so if you haven't done that already, go back to that chapter and get your accounts set up. Then come back here to start using those accounts for email.

Setting Mail App Preferences

There are a number of settings that affect how the Mail app works. The good news is that you can use the Mail app with its default settings just fine. However, you might want to tweak how it works for you by making changes using the Settings app; you can use the information in the table that follows to understand the options available to you.

To access the settings in the table, first tap the Settings icon on the Home screen, tap the option listed in the Settings Area column, and then move to the location to make changes to the setting (for example, to change the amount of text shown in email previews, open the Settings app; tap Mail; move to the MESSAGE LIST section; and then tap Preview). For each setting, you see a description of what it does along with options (if applicable).

Settings App Explained

To get detailed information on using the Settings app, see "Working with the Settings App" in Chapter 2, "Using Your iPhone's Core Features."

Mail and Related Settings

Settings Area	Location	Setting	Description
Accounts & Passwords	ACCOUNTS	Email accounts	You can configure the accounts used in the Mail app to determine which account can receive or send email on your iPhone (see Chapter 3 for details).
Accounts & Passwords	N/A	Fetch New Data	Determines when new email is downloaded to your iPhone (see Chapter 3 for an explanation of the options).

Settings Area	Location	Setting	Description
Mail	ALLOW MAIL TO ACCESS	Siri & Search	When enabled (green), Search, Siri, and other elements of the iOS can use information in the Mail app. For example, when you search for a person, the Search tool can search your email for relevant information. If you don't want your email information to be used, set the switch to off (white).
Mail	ALLOW MAIL TO ACCESS	Notifications	Configure the type of notifications the Mail app uses. See "Configuring Notifications" in Chapter 4, "Customizing How Your iPhone Works," for a detailed explanation.
Mail	ALLOW MAIL TO ACCESS	Cellular Data	When enabled (green), Mail can send and receive email when your iPhone is connected to the Internet using the cellular data network. Email typically doesn't use a lot of data, but if you receive many emails with very large attachments and have a limited data plan, you might want to set this switch to off (white).
Mail	MESSAGE LIST	Preview	Determines the number of lines you want to display for each email when you view the Inbox and in other locations, such as alerts. This preview enables you to get the gist of an email without opening it. More lines give you more of the message but take up more space on the screen.
Mail	MESSAGE LIST	Show To/Cc Label	Slide the switch to on (green) to always see a To or Cc label next to the subject line on messages in your inboxes. This helps you know when you are included in the To line or as a Cc, which usually indicates whether you need to do something with the message or if it is just for your information.
Mail	MESSAGE LIST	Swipe Options	Changes what happens when you swipe to the left or right on email when you are viewing an Inbox. You can set the Swipe Left motion to be None, Mark as Read, Flag, or Move Message. When you do a partial swipe to the left, you see the More icon, which leads to a menu of actions, and the option you configure for the Left Swipe setting. When you do a full swipe to the left, a message is deleted. You can set the Swipe Right motion to be None, Mark as Read, Flag, Move Message, or Archive. When you swipe all the way to the right on a message, the action you configure for the Swipe Right is performed. When you do a partial swipe, you see an icon that you can tap to perform the action. Note that you can't have the same option configured for both directions.

Settings Area	Location	Setting	Description
Mail	MESSAGE LIST	Flag Style	Determines how messages you flag are marked; you can choose a colored circle or a flag icon. Flagging messages marks messages that you want to know are important or that need your attention.
Mail	MESSAGES	Ask Before Deleting	When this switch is on (green), you're prompted to confirm when you delete or archive messages. When this switch is off (white), deleting or archiving messages happens without the confirmation prompt.
Mail	MESSAGES	Load Remote Images	When this switch is on (green), images in HTML email messages are displayed automatically. When this switch is off (white), you have to manually load images in a message. (If you receive a lot of spam, you should turn this off so that you won't see images in which you might not be interested.)
Mail	THREADING	Organize By Thread	When this switch is on (green), messages in a conversation are grouped together as a "thread" on one screen. This makes it easier to read all the messages in a thread. When this switch is off (white), messages are listed individually. (You learn more about working with threads in the "Working with Email" task later in this chapter.)
Mail	THREADING	Collapse Read Messages	When enabled and you read messages in a thread, the thread collapses so you see the thread rather than the individual messages in the thread.
Mail	THREADING	Most Recent Message on Top	With this switch set to on (green), the most recent message in a thread appears at the top of the thread and the messages move backward in time as you move down the list of messages. When disabled (white), the first message in the thread displays at the top with the next oldest message appearing next, and so on until the last message, which is the most recent message in the thread.
Mail	THREADING	Complete Threads	With this switch enabled (green), all the messages in a thread are displayed when you view the thread, even if you've moved messages to a different folder (other than the inbox).
Mail	COMPOSING	Always Bcc Myself	When this switch is on (green), you receive a blind copy of each email you send; this means that you receive the message, but you are hidden on the list of recipients. When this switch is off (white), you don't receive a blind copy. (Email you send is automatically saved in the Sent folder so you always have a record of emails you send.)

Settings Area	Location	Setting	Description
Mail	COMPOSING	Mark Addresses	This feature highlights addresses in red that are not from domains that you specify. You enter the domains (everything after the @ in email addresses, such as icloud.com) from which you do not want addresses to be marked (highlighted in red) when you create email. You can add multiple domains to the list by separating them with commas. All addresses from domains not listed will be marked in red. To disable this feature, delete all the domains from the list.
Mail	COMPOSING	Increase Quote Level	When this option is enabled (green), the text of an email you are replying to or forwarding (quoted content) is automatically indented. Generally, you should leave this enabled so it is easier for the recipients to tell when you have added text to an email, versus what is from the previous email messages' quoted content.
Mail	COMPOSING	Signature	Signatures are text that is automatically added to the bottom of new email messages that you create. For example, you might want your name and email address added to every email you create. You can configure the same signature for all your email accounts or have a different signature for each account. If you don't want to use a signature, delete any signatures that are currently configured. (Note that the default signature is "Sent from my iPhone.")
Mail	COMPOSING	Default Account	Determines which email account is the default one used when you send an email (this setting isn't shown if you have only one email account). You can override the default email account for an email you are sending by choosing one of your other email addresses in the From field.
Display & Brightness	N/A	Text Size	Changes the size of text in all apps that support Dynamic Type (Mail does). Drag the slider to the right to make text larger or to the left to make it smaller.
Display & Brightness	N/A	Bold Text	Changes text to be bold when the Bold Text switch is set to on (green).
Control Center	N/A	Text Size	Changes the size of text; you can add the Text Size tool to your Control Center to make it quicker and easier to use. See "Configuring the Control Center" in Chapter 4 for the steps to configure your Control Center.

More on Marking Addresses

When you configure at least one address on the Mark Addresses screen, all addresses from domains except those listed on the Mark Addresses screen are in red text on the New Message screen. This is useful to prevent accidental email going to places where you don't want it to go. For example, you might want to leave domains associated with your workplace off this list so that whenever you send email to addresses associated with your workplace, the addresses appear in red to remind you to pay closer attention to the messages you are sending.

Email Notifications and Sounds

If you want to be alerted whenever new email is received and when email you create is sent, be sure to configure notifications for the Mail app. These include whether unread messages are shown in the Notification Center, the type of alerts, whether the badge appears on the Mail icon, whether the preview is shown, the alert sound, and whether new messages are shown on the Lock screen. For a detailed explanation of configuring notifications, refer to Chapter 4.

Working with Email

The Mail app offers lots of great features and is ideally suited for working with email on your iPhone. This app offers a consolidated Inbox, so you can view email from all your accounts at the same time. Also, the Mail app organizes your email into threads (assuming you didn't disable this feature), which makes following a conversation convenient.

You've got email

When you move to a Home screen, you see the number of new email messages you have in the badge on the Mail app's icon (assuming you haven't disabled this); tap the icon to move to the app. Even if you don't have any new email, the Mail icon still leads you to the Mail app. Other ways Mail notifies you of new messages include by displaying visual notifications and the new mail sound. (You determine which of these options is used for each email account by configuring its notifications as explained in the "Email Notifications and Sounds" note earlier in this chapter.)

If you are using an iPhone that supports 3D Touch (6s/6s Plus or later models), you can press on the Mail icon to open the Quick Actions menu and choose an action you want to perform. For example, you can start a new email message by tapping New Message or move directly to your VIP email by tapping VIP. You can move to the most recent messages from one of your VIPs by tapping him in the MAIL widget.

VIP

You can designate people with whom you correspond as a Very Important Person (VIP). Mail has options specifically for your VIPs, such as a dedicated inbox, the MAIL widget, and so on. You learn more about working with VIPs later in this chapter.

About Assumptions

The steps and figures in this section assume you have more than one email account configured and are actively receiving email from those accounts on your iPhone. If you have only one email account active, your Mailboxes screen contains that account's folders instead of mailboxes from multiple accounts and the Accounts sections that appear in these figures and steps. Similarly, if you disable the Organize by Thread setting, you won't see messages in threads as these figures show. Instead, you work with each message individually.

The Mail app enables you to receive and read email for all the email accounts configured on your iPhone. The Mailboxes screen is the top-level screen in the app and is organized into two sections.

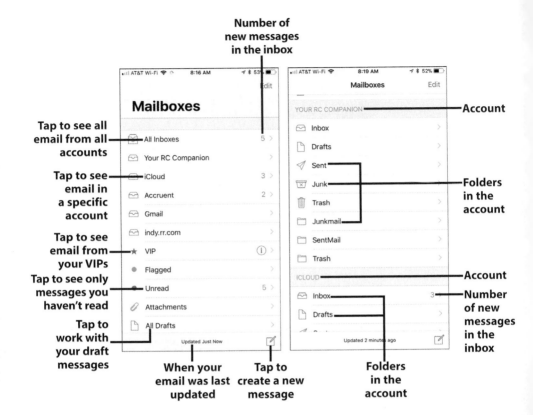

Number of new messages in the inbox

Tap to see all email from all accounts

Tap to see email in a specific account

Tap to see email from your VIPs

Tap to see only messages you haven't read

Tap to work with your draft messages

When your email was last updated

Tap to create a new message

Account

Folders in the account

Account

Number of new messages in the inbox

Folders in the account

The Inboxes section shows the Inbox for each account along with folders for email from people designated as VIPs, your unread messages, and your draft messages (those you've started but haven't sent yet). Next to each Inbox or folder is the number of new emails in that Inbox or folder. (A new message is simply one you haven't viewed yet.) At the top of the section is All Inboxes, which shows the total number of new messages to all accounts; when you tap this, the integrated Inbox containing email from all your accounts is displayed.

The Accounts section, which is underneath the Inboxes section on the screen, shows the set of inboxes and folders within each email account. The difference between these sections is that the Inbox options take you to just the Inbox for one or all of your accounts or specific folders (such as the VIP folder), whereas the Account options take you to all the folders under each account. You can tap any folder or inbox under an account to view the emails stored in that folder or inbox.

Receiving and Reading Email

To read email you have received, perform the following steps:

1. On the Home screen, tap Mail. When you open Mail (assuming you didn't use the App Switcher to quit the app when you left it), you move back to the screen you were last on, for example, if you were reading an email you return to it. If the Mailboxes screen isn't showing, tap the back icon in the upper-left corner of the screen until you reach the Mailboxes screen.

2. To read messages, tap the Inbox that contains messages you want to read, or tap All Inboxes to see the messages from all your email accounts. Various icons indicate the status of each message, if it has attachments, if it is from a VIP, or if it is part of a thread. A message is part of a thread when it has double right-facing arrows along the right side of the screen—individual messages have only one arrow.

3. Swipe up or down the screen to browse the messages. You can read the preview of each message to get an idea of its contents.

4. If a message you are interested in is in a thread, tap its arrows. (If it isn't part of a thread, skip to step 6.) The thread expands (the double arrows point down instead of to the right) and you can see the messages it contains. The first message in the thread appears in a gray bar. The responses to the message appear under it in a lighter shade of gray; the responses don't have a subject because they are all related to the subject of the thread.

Pulling on Threads

A thread is a group of emails that are related to the same subject. For example, if someone sends an email to you saying how wonderful the *My iPhone* book is, and you reply with a message saying how much you agree, those two messages would be grouped into one thread. Other messages with the same subject are also placed in the thread.

Collapsing Threads

To collapse an expanded thread, tap the downward-facing arrows. You see only the most recent message in the thread again.

5. Swipe up or down the screen to browse the messages in the thread.

6. To read a message (whether in a thread or not), tap it. As soon as you open a message, it's marked as read and the new mail counter reduces by one. You see the message screen with the address information at the top, including whom the message is from and whom it was sent to. Under that the message's subject along with time and date it was sent are displayed. Below that is the body of the message. If the message has an attachment or is a reply to another message, the attachment or quoted text appears toward the bottom of the screen.

7. Swipe up and down the screen to read the entire message.

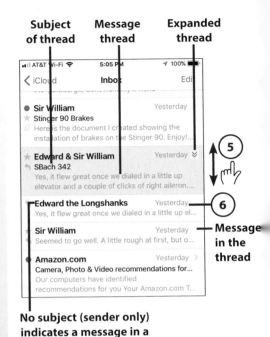

Subject of thread · Message thread · Expanded thread

No subject (sender only) indicates a message in a thread

Message in the thread

Quoted message

Standard Motions Apply

You can use the standard finger motions on email messages, such as unpinching or tapping to zoom, swiping directions to scroll, and so on. You can also rotate the phone to change the orientation of messages from vertical to horizontal; this makes it easier to type.

8. If the message contains an attachment, swipe up the screen to get to the end of the message. Some types of attachments, most notably photos, appear directly in the message and you don't have to download them to the device. If an attachment hasn't been downloaded yet, it starts to download automatically (unless it is a large file). If the attachment hasn't been downloaded automatically, which is indicated by "Tap to Download" in the attachment icon, tap it to download it into the message. When an attachment finishes downloading, its icon changes to represent the type of file it is. If the icon remains generic, it might be of a type the iPhone can't display, and you would need to open it on a computer or other device.

9. Tap the attachment icon to view it.

Tap to download an attachment (large files)

Attachment downloading

10. Scroll the document by swiping up, down, left, or right on the screen.

11. Unpinch or double-tap to zoom in.

12. Pinch or double-tap to zoom out.

13. Tap the Share icon to see the available actions for the attachment.

14. Swipe to the left or right to see all the available options.

15. Tap the action you want to take, such as opening the attachment in a different app, printing it, sharing it via email, and so on. Tap Cancel to return to the attachment if you don't want to do any of these. If you open the attachment in an app, work with the attachment in that app. To return to the email, tap Mail in the top-left corner of the screen to return to the Mail app (not shown in the figures).

16. Tap Done (depending on the type of attachment you were viewing, you might tap the back icon instead).

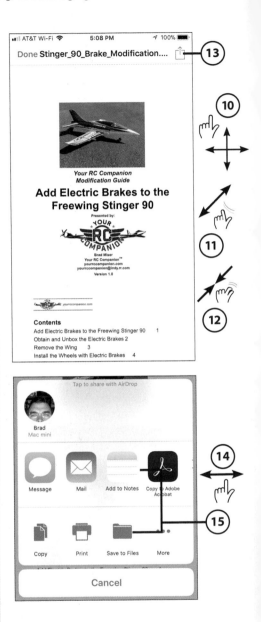

17. To view information for an email address, such as who sent the message, tap it. The Info screen appears. On this screen, you see as much information for the person as is available. If it is someone in the Contacts app, you see all of the information stored there, and you can place a call, send a message, etc. If it is not someone in the Contacts app, you see the person's email address along with actions you might want to perform, such as creating a contact for him or adding new information to an existing contact. (See Chapter 6, "Managing Contacts," for information about working with contacts.)

18. Tap Done to return to the message.

19. To read the next message in the current Inbox, tap the down arrow. (If the arrow is disabled, you are viewing the most recent email in the inbox.)

20. To move to a previous message in the current Inbox, tap the up arrow. (If the arrow is disabled, you are viewing the oldest message in the inbox.)

21. To move back to see the entire Inbox, tap the back icon, which shows the number of unread messages in the inbox from which you came (all your inboxes if you were viewing them all).

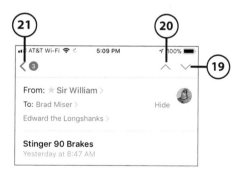

Reading Threads

If you want to read all the messages in a thread instead of individual messages it contains, tap the thread (instead of tapping its arrows to expand it). The thread opens, and you see the title of the thread at the top of the screen in a gray bar. You can browse up and down the thread's screen to read all of the messages it contains. When you are done with the thread, tap the back icon located in the upper-left corner of the screen.

Two Other Ways to Open New Email

You can view a preview of email messages in notifications you receive and press or swipe on the notification to get to the full message. You can also use Siri to get and read new email. If that isn't enough ways, you can also use the MAIL widget to quickly get to email from your VIPs.

Receiving and Reading Email on an iPhone Plus

The larger screens on the iPhone Plus models (6, 7, and 8) provide some additional functionality that is unique to those models. You can access this by holding the Plus horizontally when you use the Mail app.

Full Screen View

Navigation pane

Content pane

1. Open the Mail app and hold the iPhone so it is oriented horizontally. The mail window splits into two panes. On the left is the Navigation pane, where you can move to and select items you want to view. When you select something in the left pane, it appears in the Content pane on the right, which shows the email message you were most recently reading.

2. In the left pane, navigate to the Mailboxes screen by tapping the back icon until it disappears.

3. Swipe up or down the Navigation pane to browse the mailboxes and accounts available to you. Notice that the two panes are independent. When you browse the left pane, the right pane doesn't change.

4. Tap the mailbox or account whose contents you want to view.

5. Swipe up and down the messages to browse all of them in the mailbox you selected.

6. Tap the message or thread that you want to read. If you tap a thread, the messages it contains appear in the left pane; browse the messages in the thread by swiping up and down the screen and then tap the message in the thread that you want to read. The message currently selected is highlighted in gray.

7. Read the message.

8. Use the other tools to work with it; these work just like they do on other models and when you hold the iPhone vertically. For example, tap the up arrow to move to the previous message in the current Inbox.

9. To read the message in full screen, tap the Full Screen icon. The Content pane uses the entire screen.

10. Work with the message.

11. When you're done, tap the back icon, which shows the number of unread messages in the selected inbox from which you came (all your inboxes if you were viewing them all).

12. Select and read other messages.

13. When you're done, tap the back icon, which is labeled with the name of the inbox or folder whose contents you are browsing.

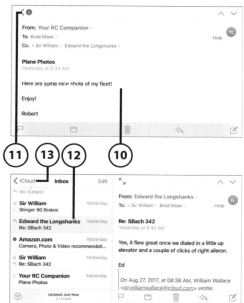

Using 3D Touch for Email

You can use the 3D Touch feature (iPhone 6s/6s Plus or later models) for email as follows:

1. Browse a list of email messages.

2. Press and hold on an email in which you are interested. A Peek of that email appears.

3. Review the preview of the email that appears in the Peek.

4. To open the email so you can read all of it, press down slightly harder until it pops open and use the steps in the earlier task to read it (skip the rest of these steps).

5. To see actions you can perform on the email, swipe up on the Peek.

6. Tap the action you want to perform, such as Reply All, to reply to the email.

>>>Go Further

MORE ON RECEIVING AND READING EMAIL

Check out these additional pointers for working with email you receive:

- If more messages are available than are downloaded, tap the Load More Messages link. The additional messages download to the inbox you are viewing.

- You can change the amount of detail you see at the top of the message screen by tapping Details to show all of the detail, such as the entire list of recipients, or Hide to collapse that information.

- A thread is started based on its subject and sender. As replies are made, the messages continue to be categorized by subject because Re: is appended to it. It even remains in the thread if the initial subject continues to be in the message but other words are added.

- If a message includes a photo, Mail displays the photo in the body of the email message if it can (if the image is large, you might have to download it to see it). You can zoom in or out and scroll to view it just as you can for photos in other apps.

- If you tap a PDF attachment in a message and the iBooks app is installed on your iPhone, you're prompted to select Quick Look or Open in iBooks. If you select Open in iBooks, the document opens in the iBooks app where you can read it using the powerful features it offers for reading ebooks and other documents.

- Some emails, especially HTML messages, are large and don't immediately download in their entirety. When you open a message that hasn't been fully downloaded, you see a message stating that this is the case. Tap the link to download the rest of the message.

- If you have other apps with which an attachment is compatible, you can open the attachment in that app. For example, if you have Pages installed on your iPhone and are viewing a Word document attachment, you can tap the Share icon and tap Open in Pages to open the document in the Pages app. You can get the same options by touching and holding on the attachment's icon in the body of a message until the Share menu appears.

Sending Email

You can send email from any of your accounts. Follow these steps for a basic walk-through of composing and sending a new email message:

1. Tap the Compose icon at the bottom of any Mail screen. (If you are using an iPhone that supports 3D Touch, you can press down on the Mail app's icon and choose New Message to create a new email from a Home page.) A new email message containing your signature is created. (For an explanation of where to configure a signature, see the table at the beginning of the chapter.)

2. Tap the To field and type the first recipient's email address. As you type, Mail attempts to find matching addresses in your Contacts list, or in emails you've sent or received, and displays the matches it finds. These can include individuals or groups with which you've emailed. To select one of those addresses, tap it. Mail enters the rest of the address for you. Or, just keep entering information until the address is complete.

3. Address the email using your Contacts app by tapping the Add (+) icon.

4. Use the Contacts app to find and select the contact to whom you want to address the message. (Refer to Chapter 6 for the details about working with contacts.) When you tap a contact who has only one email address, that address is pasted into the To field and you return to the New Message window. When you tap a contact with more than one email address, you move to that contact's screen, which shows all available addresses; tap the address to which you want to send the message.

Have Multiple Email Accounts?

If you have more than one email account, it's important to know from which account you are sending a new message. If you tap the Compose icon while you are on the Mailboxes screen or the Inboxes screen, the From address is the one for the account you set as your default; otherwise, the From address is the email account associated with the Inbox you are in.

5. Repeat steps 2–4 to add other recipients to the message.

6. Tap the Cc/Bcc, From line. The Cc and Bcc lines expand.

Removing Addresses

To remove an address, tap it so it is highlighted in a darker shade of blue; then tap the Delete (x) icon on the iPhone's keyboard.

7. Follow the same procedures from steps 2–4 to add recipients to the Cc field.

8. Follow the same procedures from steps 2–4 to add recipients to the Bcc field.

9. If the correct account is shown, skip to step 11; to change the account from which the email is sent, tap the From field. The account wheel appears at the bottom of the screen.

10. Swipe up or down the wheel until the From address you want to use is shown between the lines.

11. Tap in the Subject line. The account selection wheel closes.

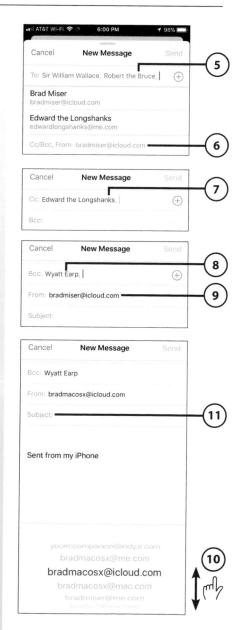

12. Type the subject of the message.

13. If you want to be notified when someone replies to the message you are creating, tap the bell; if not, skip to step 16.

14. Tap Notify Me. When anyone replies to the message, you are notified.

15. If you don't see the body of the message, swipe up the screen and it appears.

16. Tap in the body of the message, and type the message above your signature. Mail uses the iOS's text tools, attempts to correct spelling, provides Predictive Text, and makes suggestions to complete words. (Refer to Chapter 2 for the details of working with text.)

17. To make the keyboard larger, rotate the iPhone so that it is horizontal.

18. When you finish the message, tap Send. The progress of the send process is shown at the bottom of the screen; when the message has been sent, you hear the send mail sound you configured, which confirms that the message has been sent. If you enabled the reply notification for the message, you are notified when anyone replies to it.

Start Writing Now, Finish Writing and Send Later

If you want to save a message you are creating without sending it, tap Cancel. A prompt appears; select Save Draft to save the message; if you don't want the message, tap Delete Draft instead. When you want to work on a draft message again, touch and hold down the Compose icon. After a moment, you see your most recent draft messages; tap the draft message you want to work on. You can make changes to the message and then send it or save it as a draft again. (You can also move into the Drafts folder to select and work with draft messages; moving to this folder is covered later in this chapter.)

Using Mail's Suggested Recipients

As you create messages, Mail suggests recipients based on the new message's current recipients. For example, if you regularly send emails to a group of people, when you add two or more people from that group, Mail suggests others you might want to include. As you add others to the message, Mail continues suggesting recipients based on the current recipient list. You can use these suggestions to quickly add more recipients to a new message.

1. Create a new message.

2. Add at least two recipients. Just below the To line, Mail suggests additional recipients for the new message based on other messages you have created.

3. Tap the additional recipients you want to add to the new message. (Mail sometimes suggests multiple recipients as a group if you have emailed that group before.) As you select these recipients, Mail keeps making suggestions and new people appear in the gray bars.

4. When you're done adding To recipients, tap in the next field you want to complete and continue creating the new message.

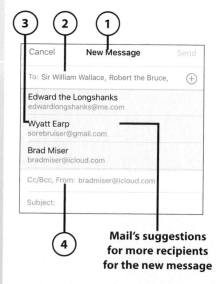

Mail's suggestions for more recipients for the new message

Replying to Email

Email is all about communication, and Mail makes it simple to reply to messages.

1. Open the message you want to reply to.

2. Tap the arrow icon.

3. Tap Reply to reply to only the sender or, if there was more than one recipient, tap Reply All to reply to everyone who received the original message. The Re: screen appears showing a new message. Mail pastes the contents of the original message at the bottom of the body of the new message below your signature. The original content is in blue and is marked with a vertical line along the left side of the screen.

4. Use the message tools to add or change the To, Cc, or Bcc recipients.

5. Write your response.

6. Tap Send. Mail sends your reply.

Including a Photo or Video in a Message

To add a photo or video to a message you create (new, reply, or forward), tap twice in the body. Swipe to the left on the resulting toolbar (if you don't see it immediately) until you see the Insert Photo or Video command, and then tap it. Use the Photos app (see Chapter 14, "Viewing and Editing Photos and Video with the Photos App," for information about this app) to move to and select the photo or video you want to attach. Tap Choose. The photo or video you selected is added to the message.

Sending Email from All the Right Places

You can send email from a number of places on your iPhone. For example, you can share a photo with someone by viewing the photo, tapping the Share icon, and then tapping Mail. Or you can tap a contact's email address to send an email from your contacts list. In all cases, the iPhone uses Mail to create a new message that includes the appropriate content, such as a photo or link; you use Mail's tools to complete and send the email.

Print Email from Your iPhone

If you need to print a message, tap the arrow icon at the bottom of the screen and tap Print. To learn about printing from your iPhone, refer to Chapter 2.

Forwarding Emails

When you receive an email you think others should see, you can forward it to them.

1. Read the message you want to forward.

2. If you want to include only part of the current content in the message you forward, tap where you want the forwarded content to start. This is useful (and considerate!) when only a part of the message applies to the people to whom you are forwarding it. If you want to forward the entire message, skip to step 4.

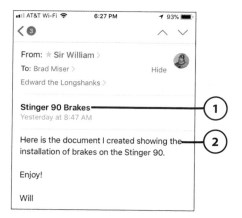

3. Use the text selection tools to select the content you want to include in your forwarded message.

4. Tap the arrow icon.

5. Tap Forward.

6. If the message includes attachments, tap Include at the prompt if you also want to forward the attachments, or tap Don't Include if you don't want them included. The Forward screen appears. Mail pastes the contents of the message that you selected, or the entire content if you didn't select anything, at the bottom of the message below your signature. If you included attachments, they are added to the new message as well.

7. Address the forwarded message using the same tools you use when you create a new message.

8. Type your commentary about the message above your signature.

9. Tap Send. Mail forwards the message.

Large Messages

Some emails, especially HTML messages, are so large that they don't immediately download in their entirety. When you forward a message whose content or attachments haven't fully downloaded, Mail prompts you to download the "missing" content before forwarding. If you choose not to download the content or attachments, Mail forwards only the downloaded part of the message.

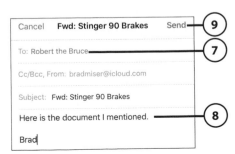

Managing Email

Following are some ways you can manage your email. For example, you can check for new messages, see the status of messages, delete messages, and organize messages using the folders associated with your email accounts.

Checking for New Email

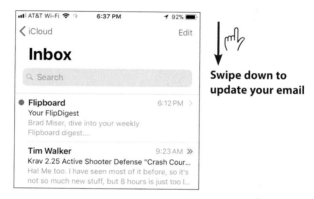

Swipe down to update your email

To manually retrieve messages, swipe down from the top of any Inbox or the Mailboxes screen. The screen "stretches" down and when you lift your finger, the Mail app checks for and downloads new messages.

Mail also retrieves messages whenever you move into the app or into any Inbox or all your Inboxes. Of course, it also retrieves messages according to the selected Fetch New Data option. It downloads new messages immediately when they arrive in your account if Push is enabled or automatically at defined intervals if you've set Fetch to get new email periodically. (Refer to Chapter 3 for an explanation of these options and how to set them.)

How many unread messages you have in the current Inbox

When your email was last updated

The bottom of the Mailboxes or an Inbox screen always shows when email was most recently downloaded to your iPhone; on the bottom of Inbox screens, you also see the number of new email messages (if there are any unread messages).

Understanding the Status of Email

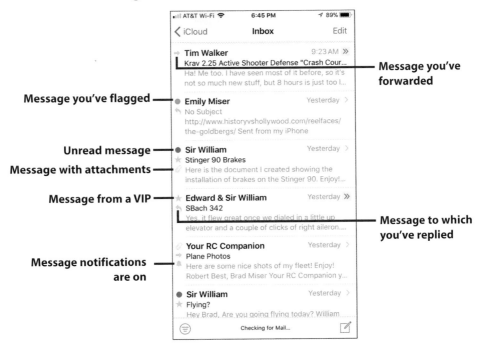

Message you've flagged

Unread message

Message with attachments

Message from a VIP

Message notifications are on

Message you've forwarded

Message to which you've replied

When you view an Inbox or a message thread, you see icons next to each message to indicate its status (except for messages that you've read but not done anything else with and that aren't from a VIP, which aren't marked with any icon).

Managing Email from the Message Screen

Tap to delete a message

To delete a message while reading it, tap the Trash icon. If you enabled the warning preference, confirm the deletion and the message is deleted. If you disabled the confirmation prompt, the message is deleted immediately.

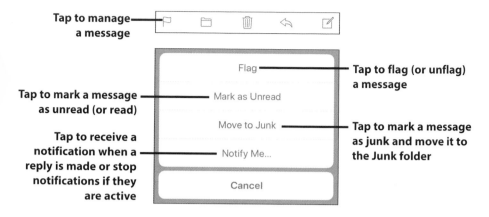

Tap to manage a message

Tap to mark a message as unread (or read)

Tap to receive a notification when a reply is made or stop notifications if they are active

Flag

Mark as Unread

Move to Junk

Notify Me...

Cancel

Tap to flag (or unflag) a message

Tap to mark a message as junk and move it to the Junk folder

To take other action on a message you are reading, tap the Flag icon. On the menu that opens, you can choose a number of commands. The action you select is performed on the message you are viewing.

Dumpster Diving

As long as an account's trash hasn't been emptied, you can work with a message you've deleted by moving to the account's screen and opening its Trash folder. Over time, a lot of deleted messages can accumulate in the Trash folder. To get rid of these messages, open the Trash folder under the account. Tap Delete All and tap Delete All again at the prompt. The deleted messages are removed from the folder and are gone forever. This frees up space on the cloud as well as on your iPhone.

Where Has My Email Gone?

When you send an email to the Archive folder, it isn't deleted. To access messages you've archived, tap the back icon in the upper-left corner of the screen until you get to the Mailboxes screen. Tap the Archive folder under the account to which email you've archived was sent.

Managing Email from an Inbox

Previously in this chapter, you saw the settings options for swipe actions for email. You can use those to configure how right and left swipes affect your email from an Inbox screen, such as flagging a message with a left swipe. (Depending on the choices you set for the swipe preferences, the results you see when you swipe might be different than shown here. However, the swipe right or swipe left actions still reveal commands you can use unless you chose None in the settings, in which case nothing happens when you swipe on a message.)

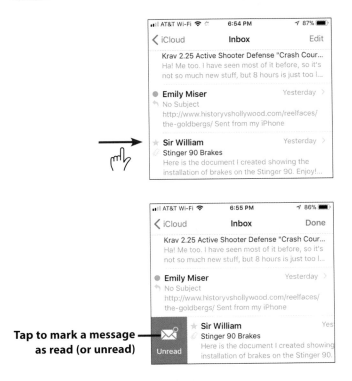

Tap to mark a message as read (or unread)

Swipe to the right on a message to change its read status. If the message has been read, you can reset its status to unread, or, if it hasn't been read, you can mark it as read.

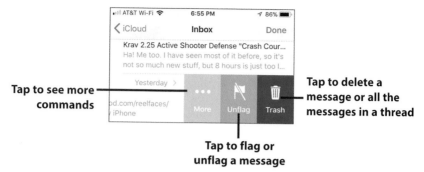

Tap to see more commands

Tap to flag or unflag a message

Tap to delete a message or all the messages in a thread

Swipe to the left on a message to see several options. Tap Trash to delete the message or messages if you swiped on a thread (the number of messages that will be deleted is shown in parentheses). Tap Flag to flag the message or Unflag to remove the flag. Tap More to open a menu of additional commands.

Tap to reply to a message

Tap to mark a message as unread (or read)

Tap to stop receiving a notification when a reply is made or start notifications if they aren't currently active

Tap to forward a message

Tap to view related messages

Tap to move the message or messages to a different folder

When you tap More, you see other commands for actions you can take on the message, such as replying to it or moving it to a different folder.

No-Stop Swiping to Delete

If you quickly swipe all the way to the left on a message on an Inbox screen, the message is deleted in one fell swipe.

Managing Multiple Emails at the Same Time

You can also manage email by selecting multiple messages on an Inbox screen, which is more efficient because you can take action on multiple messages at the same time.

1. Move to an Inbox screen showing messages you want to manage.

2. Tap Edit. A selection circle appears next to each message, and actions appear at the bottom of the screen.

3. Select the message(s) you want to manage by tapping their selection circles. As you select each message, its selection circle turns blue and is marked with a check mark. At the top of the screen, you see how many messages you have selected.

   When you use an iPhone Plus in the horizontal orientation, you see the selection screen on the left and a preview of what you have selected in the right pane. Even though it looks a bit different, it works in the same way.

4. To delete the selected messages, tap Trash. Mail deletes the selected messages and exits Edit mode. (If you enabled the warning prompt, you have to confirm the deletion.)

5. To change the status of the selected messages, tap Mark.

Selected messages

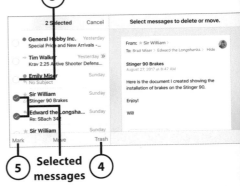

Selected messages

6. Tap the action you want to take on the selected messages. You return to the Inbox screen and exit Edit mode.

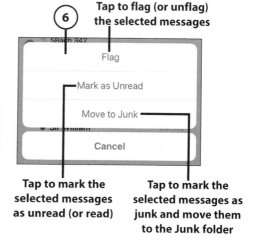

Tap to flag (or unflag) the selected messages

Tap to mark the selected messages as unread (or read)

Tap to mark the selected messages as junk and move them to the Junk folder

Organizing Email from the Message Screen

You can have various folders to organize email, and you can move messages among these folders. For example, you can recover a message from the Trash by moving it from the Trash folder back to the Inbox.

1. Open a message you want to move to a different folder.

2. Tap the Mailboxes icon. You're prompted to move the messages into the folder you most recently moved messages into or to choose a different folder.

3. To move the messages into a folder you have previously used, tap Move to "*foldername*" where *foldername* is the name of that folder and skip the rest of these steps.

4. To move the message into a folder that wasn't the one you used most recently, tap Other Mailbox. The Mailboxes screen appears. At the top of this screen is the message you are moving. Under that are the mailboxes available under the current account.

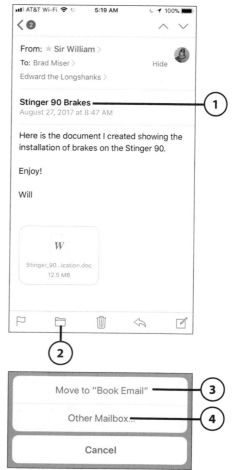

Move to Other Accounts

If you want to move selected messages to a folder under a different account, tap Accounts in the upper-left corner of the screen. Tap the account to which you want to move the message (not all accounts will be available; if an account is grayed out, you can't move a message to it). Then tap the mailbox into which you want to move the message.

5. Swipe up and down the screen to browse the mailboxes available in the current account.

6. Tap the mailbox to which you want to move the message. The message moves to that mailbox, and you move to the next message in the list you were viewing.

   When you use an iPhone Plus in the horizontal orientation, you see the list of folders you are navigating in the left pane and a preview of the messages you have selected in the right pane.

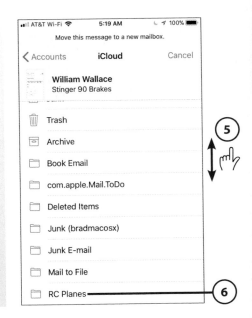

Makin' Mailboxes

You can create a new mailbox to organize your email. Move to the Mailboxes screen and tap Edit. Then, tap New Mailbox located at the bottom of the screen. Type the name of the new mailbox. Tap the Mailbox Location and then choose where you want the new mailbox located (for example, you can place the new mailbox inside an existing one). Tap Save. You can then store messages in the new mailbox.

Organizing Email from the Inbox

Like deleting messages, organizing email from the Inbox can be made more efficient because you can move multiple messages at the same time.

1. Move to an Inbox screen showing messages you want to move to a folder.

2. Tap Edit. A selection circle appears next to each message. Actions appear at the bottom of the screen.

3. Select the messages you want to move by tapping their selection circles. As you select each message, its selection circle turns blue and is marked with a check mark.

4. Tap Move. You're prompted to move the messages into the folder you most recently moved messages into or to choose a different folder.

5. To move the messages into a folder you have previously used, tap Move to "foldername" where foldername is the name of that folder and skip the rest of these steps.

6. To move the message into a folder that wasn't the one you used most recently, tap Other Mailbox. The Mailboxes screen appears. At the top of this screen is the message you are moving. Under that are the mailboxes available under the current account.

7. Swipe up and down the screen to browse the mailboxes available in the current account.

   On an iPhone Plus held horizontally, you see the list of folders in the left pane and a preview of the selected messages in the right pane.

8. Tap the mailbox to which you want to move the selected messages. They are moved into that folder, and you return to the previous screen, which is no longer in Edit mode.

Threading Your Way Through Email

When you select a thread, you select all the messages in that thread. Whatever action you select is taken on all the thread's messages at the same time.

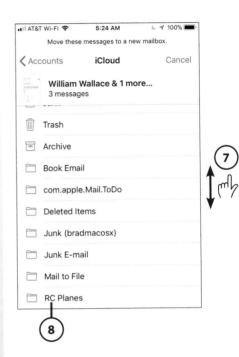

Viewing Messages in a Mailbox

You can open a mailbox within an account to work with the messages it contains. For example, you might want to open the Trash mailbox to recover a deleted message.

1. Move to the Mailboxes screen.

2. If necessary, swipe up the screen to see the email accounts you are using. Each account has its own section showing the mailboxes stored on that account.

3. If you don't see an account's mailboxes, expand the account by
   tapping its arrow.

4. Tap the folder or mailbox containing the messages you want to
   view. You see the messages it contains. In some cases, this can take
   a few moments for the messages
   to be downloaded if that folder
   or mailbox hasn't been accessed
   recently.

5. Tap a message or thread to view
   it. (If you want to move messages,
   such as to recover messages that
   are in the Trash, see "Organizing
   Email from the Inbox.")

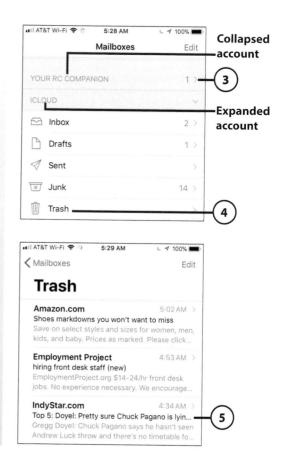

Collapsed
account

Expanded
account

Changing Mailboxes

You can change the mailboxes that appear on the Mailboxes screen. For
example, you can display the Attachments mailbox to make messages with
attachments easier to get to. Move to the Mailboxes screen and tap Edit. To
cause a mailbox to be visible, tap it so that it has a check mark in its circle. To
hide a mailbox, tap its check mark so that it shows an empty circle. Drag the
Order icon for mailboxes up or down the screen to change the order in which
mailboxes appear. Tap Add Mailbox to add a mailbox not shown on the list. Tap
Done to save your changes.

Saving Images Attached to Email

Email is a great way to share photos. When you receive a message that includes photos, you can save them on your iPhone.

1. Move to the message screen of an email that contains one or more photos or images.

2. Swipe up the message to see all the images it contains.

3. Touch and hold on an image (if you are using an iPhone that supports 3D Touch, don't press down when you touch or you Peek at the image instead).

4. Swipe to the left until you see the Save Image icons.

5. Tap Save Image to save just the image you touched or tap Save *X* Images, where *X* is the number of images attached to the message, to save all the attachments. (If there is only one image, the command is just Save Image.) The images are saved in the Photos app on your iPhone. (See Chapter 14 for help working with the Photos app.)

Filtering Email

You can quickly filter the email messages in an inbox as follows:

1. Open the inbox you want to filter.

2. Tap the Filter icon. The contents of the inbox are filtered by the current criteria, which is indicated by the terms under "Filtered by." The Filter icon is highlighted in blue to show the inbox is filtered.

3. Tap the current filter criteria.

4. Set the criteria by which you want to filter the messages in the inbox; the current criteria are indicated by check marks or green switches. For example, tap To: Me to only show messages on which you are included in the To block.

5. Tap Done. You return to the inbox and only messages that meet your filter criteria are shown.

6. Tap the Filter icon to display all the messages again.

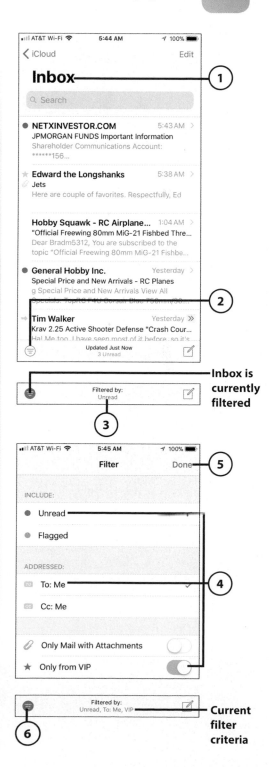

Inbox is currently filtered

Current filter criteria

Searching Your Email

As you accumulate email, you might want to find specific messages. For example, suppose you want to retrieve an email message that was related to a specific topic, but you can't remember where you stored it. Mail's Search tool can help you find messages like this quite easily.

1. Move to the screen you want to search, such as an account's Inbox or a folder's screen. (This is optional as you can choose an area to search later in the process.)

2. If necessary, swipe down to move to the top of the screen to display the Search tool.

3. Tap in the Search tool.

4. Enter the text for which you want to search. As you type, Mail makes suggestions about what you might be searching for. These appear in different sections based on the type of search Mail thinks you are doing, such as People, Subjects, and more.

5. To use one of Mail's suggestions to search, such as a person, tap their name; or continue typing your search term and when you are done, tap Search. Mail searches for messages based on your search criterion and you see the results.

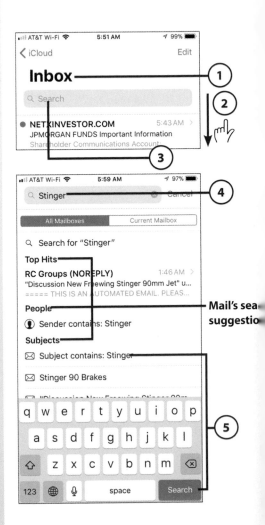

Mail's sea[rch] suggestio[ns]

6. To search for the term in the sub-ject field, tap Subject, or to search in the body, tap Message.

7. Tap Search.

8. To search in all your mailboxes, tap All Mailboxes, or to search in only the current mailbox, tap Current Mailbox.

9. Work with the messages you found, such as tapping a message to read it. Tap the back icon in the upper-left corner of the screen to return to the search results.

10. To clear a search and exit Search mode, tap Cancel.

11. To clear a search but remain in Search mode, tap the Clear icon (x).

When you use an iPhone Plus hori-zontally, searching is even better, because you can select a found message in the search results in the left pane and read it in the right pane.

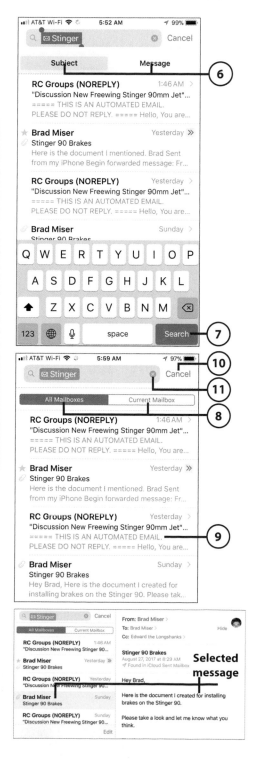

Working with VIPs

The VIP feature enables you to indicate specific people as your VIPs. When a VIP sends you email, it is marked with a star icon and goes into the special VIP mailbox so you can access these important messages easily. You can also create specific notifications for your VIPs, such as a unique sound when you receive email from a VIP (see Chapter 4).

Designating VIPs

To designate someone as a VIP, perform the following steps:

1. View information about the person you want to be a VIP by tapping his name in the From or Cc fields as described earlier in the chapter.

2. On the Info screen, tap Add to VIP. The person is designated as a VIP and any email from that person receives the VIP treatment.

Accessing VIP Email

To work with VIP email, do the following:

1. Move to the Mailboxes screen.

2. Tap VIP.

3. Work with the VIP messages you see.

>>>*Go Further*

MORE ON VIPS

Here are a few more tidbits on VIPs:

- Messages from VIPs are marked with the star icon no matter in which mail-box you see the messages. If you haven't read a VIP message, the star is blue. If you have read it, the star is gray.

- To see the list of your current VIPs, move to the Mailboxes screen and tap the Info icon (i) for the VIP mailbox. You see everyone currently designated as a VIP. Tap Add VIP to add more people to the list. Tap VIP Alerts to create special notifications for VIPs.

- To return a VIP to normal status, view his information and tap Remove from VIP.

Managing Junk Email

Junk email, also known as spam, is an unfortunate reality of email. No matter what precautions you take, you are going to receive some spam emails. Of course, it is good practice to be careful about where you provide your email address to limit the amount of spam you receive.

Consider using a "sacrificial" email account when you shop, post messages, and in the other places where you're likely to get spammed. If you do get spammed, you can stop using the sacrificial account and create another one to take its place. Or you can delete the sacrificial account from your iPhone and continue to use it on your computer where you likely have better spam tools in place. If you have an iCloud account, you can set up and use email aliases for this purpose.

The Mail app on the iPhone includes a very basic junk management tool. However, if you use an account or an email application on a computer that features a junk mail/spam tool, it acts on mail sent to your iPhone, too. For example, if you configure spam tools for a Gmail account, those tools act on email before it reaches your iPhone. Similarly, if you use the Mail app on a Mac, its rules and junk filter work on email as you receive it; the results of this are also reflected on your iPhone. To change how you deal with junk email on your iPhone, change the junk email settings for your account online (such as for Gmail) or by changing how an email app on a computer deals with junk mail. The results of these changes are reflected in the Mail app on your iPhone.

Many email accounts, including iCloud and Google, have Junk folders; these folders are available in the Mail app on your iPhone. You can open the Junk folder under an account to see the messages that are placed there.

Marking Junk Email

You can perform basic junk email management on your iPhone by doing the following:

1. When you view a message that is junk, tap the Flag icon.

2. Tap Move to Junk. The message is moved from the inbox to the Junk folder for the account to which it was sent. Future messages from the same sender go into the Junk folder automatically.

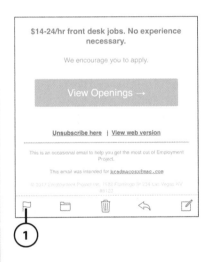

Junk It

You can also move a message to the Junk folder by swiping slowly to the left on it, tapping More, and then tapping Move to Junk. If you swipe quickly all the way to the left side of the screen, you'll delete the message instead.

Junk It or Trash It?

The primary difference between moving a message to the Junk folder or deleting it is that when you mark a message as junk, future messages from the same sender are moved to the Junk folder automatically. When you delete a message, it doesn't change how future messages from the same sender are handled.

Send messages from
other apps too, such
as to share photos

Tap to configure
Messages

Tap to
send and
receive text
messages,
photos, video,
and more

In this chapter, you'll explore the texting and messaging functionality your iPhone has to offer. Topics include the following:

→ Preparing the Messages app for messaging
→ Sending messages
→ Receiving, reading, and replying to messages
→ Working with messages

Sending, Receiving, and Managing Texts and iMessages

You can use the iPhone's Messages app to send, receive, and converse; you can also send and receive images, videos, and links with this app. You can enhance your messages in a number of ways, such as creating dynamic messages, sending Digital Touches, and using apps. You can maintain any number of conversations with other people at the same time, and your iPhone lets you know whenever you receive a new message via audible and visible notifications that you can configure. In addition to conversations with other people, many organizations use text messaging to send important updates, such as airlines communicating flight status changes.

The Messages app can send and receive text messages via your cell network based on telephone numbers—this is the texting function that almost all cell phones support. Using this option, you can send text messages to and receive messages from anyone who has a cell phone capable of text messaging.

You can also use iMessages within the Messages app to send and receive messages via an email account to and from other iOS

devices (iOS 5 or newer) or Macs (running OS X Lion or newer). This is especially useful when your cell phone account has a limit on the number of texts
you can send via your cell account; when you use iMessage for texting, there
is no limit on the amount of data you can send and so you incur no additional costs for your messages. The iMessages option is also really useful because
you can send messages to and receive messages from iPod touch, iPad, and
Mac users even if these devices don't have cell phone capability.

Preparing the Messages App for Messaging

Like most of the apps described in this book, there are settings for the Messages app you can configure to choose how the app works for you. For
example, you can configure iMessage so you can communicate via email
addresses, configure how standard text messages are managed, and so on.
You can also choose to block messages from specific people.

Setting Your Text and iMessage Preferences

Perform the following steps to set up
Messages on your iPhone:

1. Move to the Settings app and tap
   Messages.

2. Set the iMessage switch to on
   (green).

3. Set the Show Contact Photos switch to on (green) if you want images associated with your contacts to appear in messages.

4. Slide the Send Read Receipts switch to on (green) to notify others when you read their messages. Be aware that receipts apply only to iMessages (not texts sent over a cellular network).

5. Slide the Send as SMS switch to on (green) to send texts via your cellular network when iMessage is unavailable. If your cellular account has a limit on the number of texts you can send, you might want to leave this set to off (white) so you use only iMessage when you are texting. If your account has unlimited texting, you should set this to on (green).

6. Tap Send & Receive.

7. Tap Use your Apple ID for iMessage. You sign into your Apple ID. At the top of the iMessage screen, you see your Apple ID. You also see the phone number of your iPhone and the email addresses associated with your Apple ID that can be used in the Messages app.

Apple ID?

These steps assume you are already signed into an Apple ID on your iPhone (see Chapter 3, "Setting Up and Using an Apple ID, iCloud, and Other Online Accounts" for help with an Apple ID). If you haven't, when you perform step 7, you're prompted to provide an Apple ID and password to sign into that Apple ID. If you are already signed into an Apple ID for Messages and see your Apple ID at the top of the iMessage screen, you can skip step 7. If you want to change the Apple ID currently being used for iMessage, tap Send & Receive, tap the Apple ID shown at the top of the iMessage screen, and then tap Sign Out. You can then sign in to a different Apple ID for Messages.

8. To prevent an email address from being available to others to send you messages, in the YOU CAN BE REACHED BY IMESSAGE AT section, tap it so it doesn't have a check mark.

9. To enable an address so it can be used for messages, tap it so it does have a check mark.

10. Tap the phone number or email address you want to use by default when you start a new text conversation in the START NEW CONVERSATIONS FROM section. Because there are no data or media limitations with iMessages, you usually want to choose your email address as the default way to start a conversation.

11. Tap Messages.

12. Tap Text Message Forwarding; if you don't see this option, your cell phone carrier doesn't support it and you can skip to step 14.

13. Set the switch to on (green) for devices on which you want to be able to receive and send text messages using your iPhone's cell phone function (this doesn't affect messages sent via iMessages because they go to all the devices on which your Apple ID is being used for iMessages automatically).

14. Tap Back.

Code Required?

In some cases, when you perform step 13, you are prompted to enter a code for that device. This code appears on the device you are enabling; for example, if you turned the switch for a Mac on, the code appears on that Mac. You need to enter that code at the prompt on your iPhone and tap Allow to finish the process.

15. Swipe up the screen to see the SMS/MMS section.

16. Set the MMS Messaging switch to off (white) if you don't want to allow photos and videos to be included in messages sent via your phone's cellular network. You might want to disable this option if your provider charges more for these types of messages—or if you simply don't want to deal with anything but text in your messages.

17. Set the Group Messaging switch to on (green) to keep messages you send to a group of people organized by the group. When enabled, replies you receive to messages you send to groups (meaning more than one person on a single message) are shown on a group message screen where each reply from anyone in the group is included on the same screen. If this is off (white), when someone replies to a message sent to a group, the message is separated out as if the original message was just to that person. (The steps in this chapter assume Group Messaging is on.)

18. Set the Show Subject Field switch to on (green) to add a subject field to your messages. This divides text messages into two sections; the upper section is for a subject, and you type your message in the lower section. This is not commonly used in text messages, and the steps in this chapter assume this setting is off.

19. Set the Character Count switch to on (green) to display the number of characters you've written compared to the number allowed (such as 59/160). When it is off, you don't see a character count for messages you send. Technically, text messages you send via the cellular network are limited to 160 characters, so showing the character count helps you see where you are relative to this limit (iMessages don't have a limit). I don't use this setting so you won't see it in the figures in this chapter, but if character count is important to you, you should enable this.

20. Use the Blocked option to block people from texting you (see the next task).

21. Tap Keep Messages.

22. Tap the length of time for which you want to keep messages.

23. If you tapped something other than Forever, tap Delete. The messages on your iPhone older than the length of time you selected in step 22 are deleted.

24. Tap Messages.

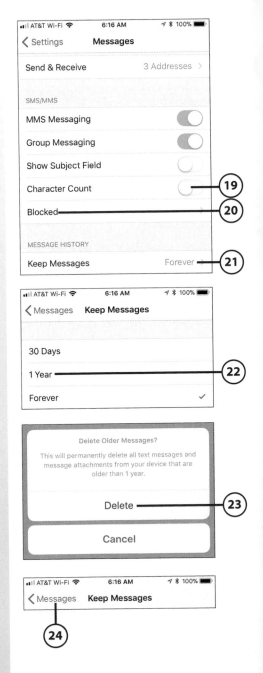

25. If you want messages from people or organizations not in the Contacts app to be put on a separate list, set the Filter Unknown Senders switch to on (green). When this switch is on, you see a separate tab for messages from people you might not know; notifications for those messages are also disabled. This can be useful if you receive a lot of messages from people you don't know and don't want to be annoyed by notifications about those messages. (This feature is explained in the section "Working with Messages from People You Might Not Know" later in this chapter.)

26. Tap Expire.

27. Choose the time after which you want audio messages to expire and be deleted from your iPhone. The options you see depend on your cell phone provider. For example, if you tap After 2 Minutes, audio messages are automatically deleted two minutes after you listen to them. This is good because audio messages require a lot of storage space, and deleting them keeps that space available for other things. Other choices might be After 1 Year or Never (if you don't want audio messages to ever be deleted).

28. Tap Messages.

29. To be able to listen to audio messages by lifting the phone to your ear, set the Raise to Listen switch to on (green). If you set this to off (white), you need to manually start audio messages.

30. To have the images in your messages sent at a lower quality level, set the Low Quality Image Mode switch to on (green). This can be a useful setting if you or the other recipients of your messages have limited data plans because lower quality images require less data to transmit and receive. If you tend to use all or most of your data allowance each month and send a lot of images, you might want to enable this setting and see if that reduces your data use.

Audio Messages

There are two types of audio messages you can send via the Messages app. Instant audio messages are included as part of the message itself. Audio, such as voice memos, can also be attached to messages. The Expire settings only affect instant audio messages. Audio that is attached to messages is not deleted automatically.

Blocking People from Messaging or Texting You

If you want to block someone before they send messages to you, configure that person's contact information so you can easily block his messages. Refer to Chapter 6, "Managing Contacts," for the steps to create contacts. (You can also block someone after you have received messages you don't want, which doesn't require that there be a contact first; those steps are provided later in this chapter.) Use the following steps to block a contact from sending messages to you:

1. Move to the Messages screen in the Settings app.

2. Swipe up the Messages screen.

3. Tap Blocked.

4. If necessary, swipe up the screen.

5. Tap Add New.

6. Use the Contacts app to find and tap the contact you want to block. (Note that contacts without email addresses or phone numbers that don't have the potential to send messages to you are grayed out and cannot be selected.) You return to the Blocked screen and see the contact on your Blocked list. Any messages, phone calls, and FaceTime requests from the contact, as long as they come from an email address or phone number included in his contact information, won't be sent to your iPhone.

>>>Go Further

MORE ON MESSAGES CONFIGURATION

Following are a few more Messages configuration tidbits for your consideration:

- You can use only one Apple ID for iMessages at a time. To change the account you are using, move to the iMessage screen by tapping Send & Receive on the Messages Settings screen. Then tap the Apple ID shown. Tap Sign Out. You can then sign in to a different Apple ID.

- SMS stands for Short Message Service, which is what text messages use. MMS stands for Multimedia Messaging Service, which adds the ability to include multimedia elements (photos, video, sound, and so on) in text messages. All text devices and accounts support SMS, but they don't all support MMS.

>>>*Go Further*

- In the Notifications settings, you can configure the notifications the Messages app uses to communicate with you. You can configure the alert styles (none, temporary banners, or persistent banners), badges on the Messages icon to show you the number of new messages, sounds and vibrations when you receive messages, and so on. Messages also supports repeated alerts, which by default is to send you two notifications for each message you receive but don't read. Configuring notifications is explained in detail in Chapter 4, "Customizing How Your iPhone Works."

- To unblock someone so you can receive messages from them again, move to the Messages screen in the Settings app, tap Blocked, swipe to the left across the contact you want to unblock, and tap Unblock.

- You can also block someone without having a contact for them. To do this, move to the details screen for the conversation containing the person you want to block (you learn how to work with conversations later in this chapter). Tap the person, email address, or number you want to block. On the resulting screen, tap Block this Caller. Tap Block Contact at the prompt. That person is blocked from sending you messages.

Sending Messages

You can use the Messages app to send messages to people using a cell phone number (as long as the device receiving it can receive text messages) or an email address that has been registered for iMessage. If the recipient has both a cell number and iMessage-enabled email address, the Messages app assumes you want to use iMessage for the message.

When you send a message to more than one person and at least one of those people can use only the cellular network, all the messages are sent via the cellular network and not as an iMessage.

More on Mixed Recipients

If one of a message's recipients has an email address that isn't iMessage-enabled (and doesn't have a phone number), the Messages app attempts to send the message to that recipient as an email message. The recipient receives the email message in an email app on his phone or computer instead of through the Messages app.

Whether messages are sent via a cellular network or iMessage isn't terribly important, but there are some differences. If your cellular account has a limit on the number of texts you can send, you should use iMessage when you can because those messages won't count against your limit. Also, when you use iMessage, you don't have to worry about a limit on the number of characters in a message. When you send a message via a cellular network, your messages might be limited to 160 characters.

When you send messages to or receive messages from a person or a group of people, you see those messages in a conversation. Every message sent among the same people is added to that conversation. When you send a message to a person or group you haven't messaged before, a new conversation is created. If you send a message to a person or group you have messaged before, the message is added to the existing conversation.

Messages on an iPhone running iOS 10 or later can include lots of different elements, including effects, Digital Touches, content from apps, and more. When you include these items in your messages sent to other people using devices running iOS 10 or later, they'll be received as you intended. If they are using devices that aren't running iOS 10 or later or Macs running macOS Sierra or later, messages with these enhancements might or might not be what you intended. For example, if the recipient is using an older version of the iOS, a Digital Touch message comes in as a static image. If the recipient is using a device not running the iOS at all, such as an Android device, it can be hard to predict what will happen to messages if you enhance them. So, keep the recipients of your messages in mind and adjust the content you send to them accordingly.

Creating a New Message and Conversation

You can send messages by entering a number or email address manually or by selecting a contact from your contacts list.

1. On the Home screen, tap Messages.

2. Tap the Compose icon (if you don't see this icon, tap the back icon in the upper-left corner of the screen until you do). If you haven't used the Messages app before, you skip this step and move directly to the New Message screen in the next step.

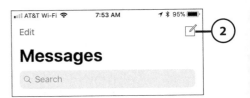

3. Type the recipient's name, email address, or phone number. As you type, the app attempts to match what you type with a saved contact or to someone you have previously messaged and shows you a list of suggested recipients. You see phone numbers or email addresses for each recipient on the list. Phone numbers or addresses in blue indicate the recipient is registered for iMessages and your message is sent via that means. Messages to phone numbers in green are sent as text messages over the cellular network. If a number or email address is gray, you haven't sent any messages to it yet; you can tap it to attempt to send a message. You also see groups you have previously messaged.

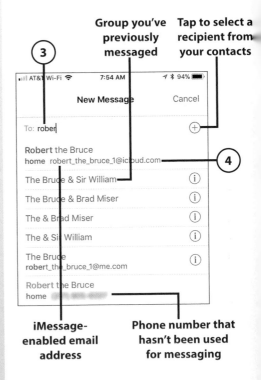

4. Tap the phone number, email address, or group to which you want to send the message. The recipients' names are inserted into the To field. Or, if the information you want to use doesn't appear, just type the complete phone number (as you would dial it to make a call to that number) or email address.

Straight to the Source

You can tap the Add icon (+) in the To field to use the Contacts app to select a contact to whom you want to address the message (see Chapter 6 for the details of using the Contacts app).

Go to the Group

You can tap the Info icon (i) next to a group on the suggested recipients list to see the people that are part of that group.

5. If you want to send the message to more than one recipient, tap in the space between the current recipient and the Add (+) icon and use steps 3 and 4 to enter the other recipients' information, either by selecting contacts using the Add icon (+), or by entering phone numbers or email addresses. As you add recipients, they appear in the To field. (If you addressed the message to a number or email address that matches a number in your contacts, the contact's name replaces the number in the To field. If not, the number or email address remains as you entered it.)

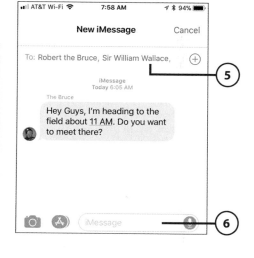

Change Your Mind?

To remove a contact or phone number from the To box, tap it once so it becomes highlighted in blue and then tap the Delete key on the keyboard.

6. Tap in the Message bar, which is labeled iMessage if you entered iMessage addresses or Text Message if you entered a phone number. The cursor moves into the Message bar and you are ready to type your message.

7. Type the message you want to send in the Message bar.

8. Tap the Send icon (circle with an upward-facing arrow), which is blue if you are sending the message via iMessage or green if you are sending it via the cellular network. The Send status bar appears as the message is sent; when the process is complete, you hear the message sent sound and the status bar disappears.

If the message is addressed to iMessage recipients, your message appears in a blue bubble in a section labeled iMessage. If the person to whom you sent the message enabled his read receipt setting, you see when he reads your message.

If you sent the message via the cellular network instead of iMessage, you see your message in a green bubble in a section labeled Text Message.

When you send a message, you see a new conversation screen if the message was not sent to someone or a group of people with whom you were previously messaging. If you have previously sent messages to the same recipient or recipients, you move back to the existing conversation screen and your new message is added to that conversation instead.

In a group conservation, you see icons and the names of each person who received the message; if there are more than two or three people, the icons "stack" on top of each other. (If you sent a message via a cellular text, you only see the person's name or number.)

Recipients of the message   Message sent to more than one person

When the message was sent   This message has been sent via iMessage

Recipient of the message   This message has been sent via a cellular network

>>>*Go Further*

TEXT ON

Following are some additional points to help you take your texting to the next level (where is the next level, anyway?):

- **iMessage or cell**—If the recipient has an iOS device or Mac that has been enabled for iMessage, text messages are sent via iMessage when possible even if you choose the recipient's phone number.

- **Group messaging**—If you've enabled the Group Messaging setting, when you include more than one recipient, any messages sent in reply are grouped in one conversation. If this setting isn't enabled, each reply to your message appears in a separate conversation.

- **Larger keyboard**—Like other areas where you type, you can rotate the iPhone to be horizontal where the keyboard is larger as is each key. This can make texting easier, faster, and more accurate.

- **Recents**—When you enter To information for a new message, included on the list of potential recipients are people being suggested to you by your iPhone. When a suggested recipient has an Info icon (i), tap that icon, tap Ignore Contact, and then tap Ignore at the prompt to prevent that person from being suggested in the future.

Sending Messages in an Existing Conversation

As you learned earlier, when you send a message to or receive a message from one or more people, a conversation is created. You can add new messages to a conversation as follows:

1. On the Home screen, tap Messages. You see a list of conversations on the Messages screen. If you were previously in a conversation, you see the messages in that conversation and the people involved at the top of the screen instead. Tap the back icon, which is the left-facing arrow in the top-left corner of the screen to return to the conversation list on the Messages screen.

   On the list, the conversation containing the most recent message you've sent or received is at the top; conversations get "older" as you move down the screen.

2. Swipe up or down the screen or tap in the Search bar and type names, numbers, or email addresses to find the conversation to which you want to add a message.

3. Tap the conversation to which you want to add a message. At the top of the screen, you see the people involved in the conversation. Under that, you see the current messages in the conversation.

4. Tap in the Message bar.

5. Type your message.

6. Tap the Send icon. Your new message is added to the conversation and sent to everyone participating in the conversation.

Who sent the message (group message only)

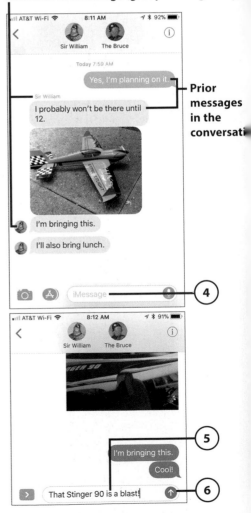

Prior messages in the conversati

Applying Effects to Messages You Send

The Messages app enables you to apply effects to your messages. Bubble effects apply to the message you send, whereas Screen effects fill the screen when your message is read. There are quite a few effects you can use, and they are easy to apply using the following steps:

1. Create a new message or add a message to an existing conversation.

2. Tap and hold on the Send icon. The Send with effect screen appears.

No iOS 10 or later?

Recipients must be using devices running iOS 10 or later or Macs running macOS Sierra for these effects to play as you see them when you send them. You can send messages with effects to people not using iOS 10 or later devices or Macs not running macOS Sierra; the messages are delivered, but the effects are not.

3. Tap Bubble to apply a Bubble effect; to apply a Screen effect instead, skip to step 7.

4. Tap an effect. It is applied to the current message so you see how it will look.

5. Tap other effects to see what they do.

Ah, Forget It

If you decide you don't want to add an effect, tap the Delete icon (x) at the bottom of the screen and you return to your unadorned message, which you can then send without any bells or whistles.

6. To send the message with the current Bubble effect, tap the Send icon and skip the rest of these steps. Your message is sent and the recipient sees the effect on the message's bubble when he opens the message.

7. Tap Screen to apply a Screen effect.

8. Swipe to the left or right. Each time you swipe, a new Screen effect is applied and you see it on the screen.

9. When you find the effect you want to use, tap the Send icon. Your message is sent and each recipient sees the effect in the background of the Messages screen when she opens the message. You also see the effect applied to the message on your iPhone.

Including Photos or Video You've Recently Taken in Messages You Send

It's easy to use Messages to quickly send photos or video you've taken recently to other people as you see the following steps:

1. Move into the conversation with the person or people to whom you want to send a photo, or start a new conversation.

2. Tap the Camera icon. In the photo pane, you see the photos and video you've taken recently.

Send a Video? No Problemo.

The steps in this task and the following two tasks show including photos in messages you send. You can send videos using very similar steps.

---

3. Swipe to the left on the photo panel to browse the recent photos and videos.

4. Tap the first photo or video you want to send. It is marked with a check mark and is added to the message you are sending.

5. Swipe to left or right to review more recent photos and videos.

6. Tap the next photo or video you want to send. It is also marked with a check mark and added to the message.

7. Repeat steps 6 and 7 until you've added all the photos and videos you want to send.

Limitations, Limitations

Not all cell carriers support MMS messages (the type that can contain images and video), and the size of messages can be limited. Check with your carrier for more information about what is supported and whether there are additional charges for using MMS messages. If you're using iMessage, you don't have this potential limit and are always able to include images and video in your texts. Also be sure your recipient can receive MMS messages before you send one.

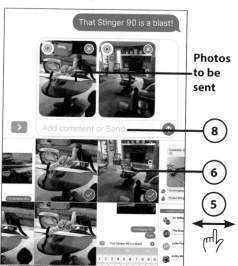

Photos to be sent

8. Tap in the Message bar.

9. Type the comments you want to send with the photos or videos.

10. Tap the Send icon. The photos, videos, and comments are added to the conversation.

This message includes Live Photos

Photos to be sent

Including Photos or Video Stored on Your iPhone in Messages You Send

You can add any image, photo, or video stored on your iPhone in a conversation by performing the following steps:

1. Move into the conversation with the person or people to whom you want to send a photo or video, or start a new conversation.

2. Tap the Camera icon.

3. Swipe to the right until you see the Photos icon.

4. Tap Photos.

5. Swipe up or down the screen to find the source containing the photos or videos you want to send. (For more information about using the Photos app to find and select photos, see Chapter 14, "Viewing and Editing Photos and Video with the Photos App.")

6. Tap the source containing the photos or videos you want to send.

7. Swipe up or down the screen until you see the photo or video you want to send.

8. Tap the photo or video you want to send.

9. Tap Choose. You move back to the conversation and see the image or video in the message bar.

10. Tap in the Message bar.

11. Type the message you want to send with the photo or video.

12. Tap the Send icon.

Taking Photos or Video and Sending Them in Messages

You can capture new photos and video using the iPhone's cameras and immediately send them to others via messages as follows:

1. Move into the conversation with the person or people to whom you want to send a photo or video, or start a new conversation.

2. Tap the Camera icon.

2. If you don't see the camera window or the Camera icon, swipe to the right until you do.

3. To use the full Camera app to take the photo or video, go on to step 4; to take a photo using the small camera window you see on the screen, position the image that you want to take and tap the Shutter icon. The photo is taken and added to the message; skip to step 10.

4. Tap the Camera icon.

5. Use the Camera app to take the photo or video you want to send. (For more information about taking photos or videos, see Chapter 13, "Taking Photos and Video with Your iPhone.")

6. Use the tools you see to modify the photo or video, such as to add markups or edit it (see Chapter 14 for details).

7. Use the tools you selected in the previous step to make changes to the photo or video. This example shows adding a markup to a photo.

8. Tap Save.

9. Tap Done.

10. Tap in the Message bar.

11. Type the message you want to send with the photo.

12. Tap the Send icon. The photo and message are added to the conversation.

This Isn't Houston, but There Is a Problem

If a message you try to send is undeliverable or has some other problem, it is marked with an error icon, which is an exclamation point inside a red circle. The most common cause of this issue is a poor Internet connection. Tap the error icon and tap Try Again to attempt to resend the message. If it doesn't work again, you might need to wait until you have a better connection.

Sharing with Messages

You can share all sorts of information via Messages from many apps, such as Safari, Contacts, Maps, and so on. From the app containing the information you want to share, tap the Share icon. Then tap Messages. The information with which you are working is automatically added to a new message. Use the Messages app to complete and send the message.

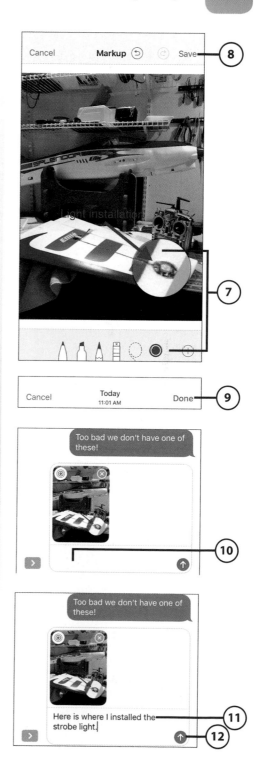

Using Digital Touches in Messages You Send

You can enhance your messages with Digital Touches, which are dynamic images you draw with your fingers, or you can use the default images.

1. Move into the conversation with the person or people to whom you want to send a Digital Touch.

2. If you see the Digital Touch icon, skip to step 3; if not, tap the app icon.

3. Tap the Digital Touch icon. The Digital Touch panel opens.

4. Tap the upward-facing arrow to open the Digital Touch screen in full screen mode.

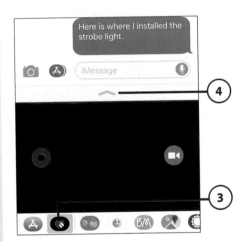

Use the Small Screen

You can create Digital Touches directly in the small Digital Touch panel that appears when you tap the Digital Touch icon. Putting it in full screen mode gives you more room to work but takes slightly longer. To create a touch directly in the panel, use the Digital Touch drawing tools directly in the small window and then tap the Send icon to send it.

5. To send one of the default Digital Touches, move to step 8; to create your own Digital Touch, tap the color you want to use. The current color's icon has a dot in the center to show it's selected.

6. Use your finger to draw or write on the screen. You can change the color at any time; for example, you can use different colors in a drawing or for each letter in a word. Drawing on the Digital Touch screen is much like using colored pencils on paper.

7. Tap the Send icon to send it. The full screen mode digital pane collapses and you see a preview of your Digital Touch as it sends.

8. Tap the Info icon. You see a list of all the gestures you can use to add a Digital Touch to a conversation. (This step is optional. If you know the gesture to create the Digital Touch you want to send, skip to step 11.)

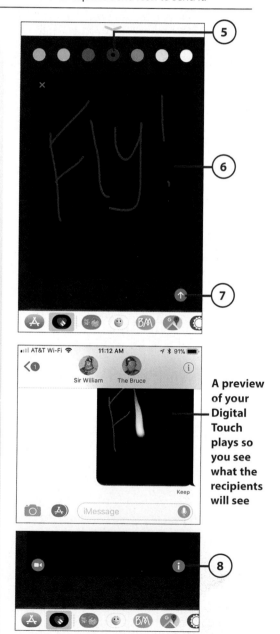

A preview of your Digital Touch plays so you see what the recipients will see

9. Review the default Digital Touches.

10. Tap the Close icon (x) to close the list.

iOS 10 Required

Like effects, the recipient must be using a device running iOS 10 or later or a Mac running macOS Sierra to receive Digital Touches as you see them when you send them. If you send a Digital Touch message to devices not running iOS 10 or later, they appear as a static image in the message.

Start Over

To get rid of the contents of the Digital Touch screen, tap the Delete icon (x).

11. Use the finger gesture to add the default Digital Touch you want to the conversation. You see a preview in the Digital Touch pane, and the Digital Touch is immediately sent to the recipients and added to the conversation.

>>>Go Further
YOU'VE GOT THE TOUCH

Here are a few more touch-related tidbits:

- You can collapse the full screen Digital Touch pane by tapping the downward-facing arrow in the top-right corner of the screen.

- By default, Digital Touch messages you send or receive expire after two minutes. If you want to keep a Digital Touch message, tap Keep, which appears at the bottom of the message as soon as you send it. The Digital Touch message remains until you delete it manually or it is deleted with the other messages based on the Messages app's settings.

- You can't stop a default Digital Touch once you make its gesture. As soon as you make the gesture, it is sent.

- You can take a video or photo and create a Digital Touch on top of it by tapping the Video Camera icon in the Digital Touch pane. The camera view opens and you can take a photo or video. You can draw on or apply a Digital Touch before or during a video capture. You can send the photo or video by tapping the Send icon.

Adding Apps to Messages

You can use apps to add content to your messages. You can use the default apps installed in Messages (examples are provided later in this chapter) and you can add more apps as follows:

1. Open Messages and move into a conversation.

2. Tap the Apps icon. The App Drawer opens and you see the installed apps at the bottom of the screen. The app you used most recently is selected automatically.

3. Tap the App Store app (if you don't see this app, swipe to the left or right on the App Drawer until you do).

4. Tap Visit Store. You move into the App Store and see apps that work within Messages.

5. Browse or search within the App Store to find apps you want to add to Messages, such as stickers you can insert into your messages. This works very similarly to using the App Store app, which is covered in Chapter 4. Note that if you just browse you only see Messages-compatible apps, but if you search you see both "regular" apps and Messages apps.

6. Tap the Get icon for a free app or the price icon for an app with a license fee. You might have to touch the Touch ID button, use Face ID, or enter your Apple ID password to complete the process. Just like other apps, it is downloaded to your iPhone, but it's installed in the Messages App Drawer instead of on a Home screen.

After the app is downloaded, it appears in the App Drawer, and you can use it.

App installed in the App Drawer

Managing Apps in Messages

You can configure the apps in the App Drawer by performing the following steps:

1. Open Messages and move into a conversation.

2. Tap the Apps icon. The App Drawer opens.

3. Swipe to the left on the App Drawer until you see the More icon. As you swipe on the App Drawer, it enlarges so you can more clearly see the app icons.

4. Tap More. You see apps currently installed on the App Drawer. There are two sections. FAVORITES are apps you've tagged as your favorites; these appear on the left end of the App Drawer and so are easier to access. In the MORE APPS section, you see the other apps in the App Drawer. You can use the apps in either section.

5. Tap Edit.

6. If you don't want to see an app in the App Drawer, set its switch to off (white). It no longer appears in the App Drawer, but remains available so you can re-enable it again.

Get Rid of It

If you want to remove an app from the App Drawer, perform steps 1 through 4. Swipe to the left on the app you want to remove. Tap Delete. The app is removed from the App Drawer.

7. To move an app into the FAVORITES section, tap the Add (+) icon. It jumps up to the FAVORITES section.

8. To move an app from FAVORITES to MORE APPS, tap its unlock (–) icon.

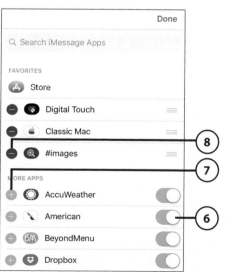

9. Tap Remove from Favorites. The app moves to the lower section, but remains in the App Drawer.

10. To change the order of the apps in the FAVORITES section, drag apps up or down the list by their Order (three lines) icon.

11. When you're done managing apps, tap Done.

12. Tap Done.

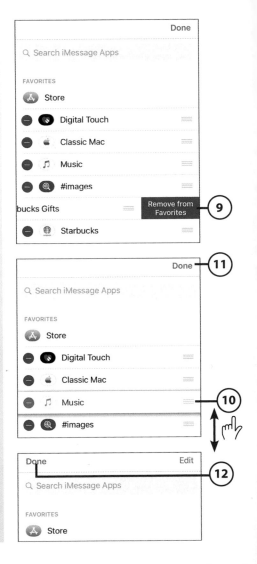

Adding Content from Apps to Messages You Send

You can use the apps on the Messages' App Drawer to add content to the messages you send. As you saw in the previous task, there are many different types of apps available and each works according to the type of content you can use. Some are quite simple, such as providing icons or images (sometimes called stickers) you can easily add to messages. Others are a bit more complicated, for example, you can use the #images app to search for and add images to your messages. Using any of these apps to add content to your messages follows a similar pattern, so once you see how to use one of them, you can use any of them fairly easily.

This example shows you how to use the #images app to add static images and animated gifs to your messages:

1. Move into a conversation or start a new one.

2. If you don't see the app you want to use, swipe to the left or right until you do. (If you don't see the App Drawer, tap the Apps icon to open it.)

3. Tap the app you want to use.

4. Tap the up-facing arrow to expand the app to full screen; this step is optional because you can use the app in the collapsed view in the same way.

5. Type a search term. Search terms that match what you type are listed.

6. Tap the search you want to perform. (If you don't see a search you want to use, complete your search phrase and tap the Search icon on the keyboard.)

7. Swipe up and down the screen to browse all the images that match your search.

8. Tap the image you want to add to the conversation.

9. Tap in the Message bar. In many cases, you'll skip adding a message (steps 9 and 10) and just send the content by skipping to step 11.

10. Type a comment you want to send with the content you added.

Delete It

To delete the content without sending it, tap the Delete icon (x) that appears on the content you've added to the conversation.

Tap to delete content

11. Tap the Send icon to send the app content you've added.

Including Instant Audio in Messages You Send

You can send audio messages that you record via a message by performing the following steps:

1. Move to the conversation to which you want to add an audio message, or start a new conversation.

2. Tap and hold on the Microphone in the Message bar (not the one on the keyboard). Recording starts.

3. Speak your message; keep your finger touching the Microphone while you speak.

4. When you're done recording, take your finger off the screen.

5. Tap the Play icon to replay your message.

6. If you don't want to send the message, delete it by tapping the Delete icon (x).

7. Tap the Send icon to send the message. The audio message is added to the conversation and the recipients are able to listen to it.

Adding Your Location to Messages You Send

Location information can be available for the participants in a conversation so you can see where others are, and they can see where you are. You can add your location information to a conversation as follows:

1. Move to the conversation to which you want to add your location information.

2. Tap the Info icon (i).

3. To share your current location as a snapshot, tap Send My Current Location. Your current location is captured and sent to the recipients of the message.

4. To dynamically share your location so that it updates as you move around, tap Share My Location.

Your message is being recorded

Who you will be sharing your location with

Current Locations

When a current location is added to a conversation, it is static, meaning it is only the location at that point in time. It appears as a map thumbnail in the conversation. Recipients can tap it to zoom in on the location, and then tap Directions to Here to generate directions from their location to the one sent as the current location.

Which Device?

If you have multiple devices that can provide your location, you can configure which device is used to determine your location by opening the Settings app, tapping Privacy, tapping Location Services, tapping Share My Location, tapping From, and then tapping the device that should be used for your position.

5. Tap how long you want your location information to be shared.

6. To stop sharing your location, tap Stop Sharing My Location. If you selected to share it for one hour or until the end of the day, location sharing stops automatically at the time you selected.

7. Tap Done to return to the conversation.

Using Quick Actions to Send Messages

You can use the Quick Actions feature on iPhones that support 3D Touch with the Messages app as follows:

1. Press on the Messages icon. The Quick Actions menu appears.

2. Tap the person to whom you want to send a message or tap New Message to send a message to someone not shown on the list. If you choose a person, you move into an existing conversation with that person or a new conversation is started. If you choose New Message, you move to the New Message screen.

3. Complete and send the message.

Receiving, Reading, and Replying to Messages

Text messaging is about communication, so when you send messages you expect to receive responses. People can also send new messages to you. As you learned earlier, the Messages app keeps messages grouped as a conversation consisting of messages you send and replies you receive to the same person or group of people.

Receiving Messages

Swipe to the right on the notification to move into the Messages app to read the entire message

Message alert notification on the Lock screen

Press the notification to read all of it and respond (3D Touch only)

Tap to open the message in the Messages app

Message alert notification on the Home screen

Press the notification to read all of it and respond (3D Touch only)

When you aren't currently using the Messages screen in the Messages app and receive a new message (as a new conversation or as a new message in an ongoing conversation), you see, hear, and feel the notifications you have configured for the Messages app. (Refer to Chapter 4 to configure your message notifications.)

If you are on the Messages screen in the Messages app when a new message comes in, you hear and feel the new message notification sound and/or vibration, but a notification does not appear. On the conversation list, any conversations containing a new message are marked with a blue circle showing the number of new messages in that conversation.

If a new message is from someone with whom you have previously sent or received a message, and you haven't deleted all the messages to or from those recipients (no matter how long it has been since a message was added to that conversation), the new message is appended to an ongoing conversation. That conversation then moves to the top of the list of conversations in the Messages app. If there isn't an existing message to or from the people involved in a new message, a new conversation is started and the message appears at the top of that list.

Speaking of Texting

Using Siri to hear and speak text messages is extremely useful. Check out Chapter 11, "Working with Siri," for examples showing how you can take advantage of this great feature. One of the most useful Messages commands is to activate Siri and say "Get new messages." Siri reads any new messages you have received.

Reading Messages

You can get to new messages you receive by doing any of the following:

Read the message in its alert ──

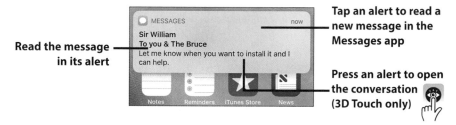

Tap an alert to read a new message in the Messages app

Press an alert to open the conversation (3D Touch only)

- Read a message in its alert. Tap a banner alert notification from Messages to move into the message's conversation in the Messages app.

When you use 3D Touch and press a message, you move into the conversation

Reply to the message

- If you are using an iPhone that supports 3D Touch, you can press on an alert to open the conversation to which the message was added. You can read all the messages it contains and reply to those messages.

Conversations with new messages are marked with a blue dot

Tap a conversation with a new message to read the new message

- Open the Messages app and tap a conversation containing a new message; these conversations appear at the top of the Messages list and are marked with a blue circle. The conversation opens and you see the new message.

- Swipe to the right on a message notification when it appears on the Lock screen. You move into the conversation to which the message was sent (you might need to unlock your phone first).

- If you receive a new message in a conversation that you are currently viewing, you immediately see the new message.

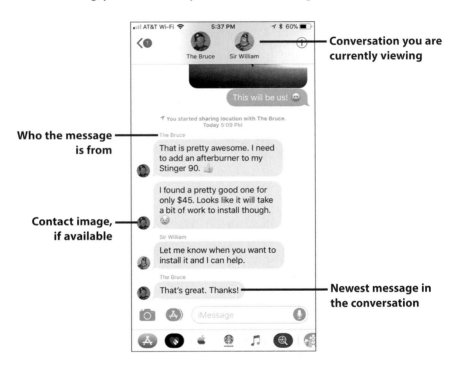

Conversation you are currently viewing

Who the message is from

Contact image, if available

Newest message in the conversation

However you get to a message, you see the new message in either an existing conversation or a new conversation. The newest messages appear at the bottom of the screen. You can swipe up and down the screen to see all of the messages in the conversation. As you move up the screen, you move back in time.

Messages sent to you are on the left side of the screen and appear in gray bubbles. Just above the bubble is the name of the person sending the message; if you have an image for the contact, that image appears next to the bubble. The color of your bubbles indicates how the message was sent: blue indicates an iMessage while green indicates a cellular message.

Viewing Images or Video You Receive in Messages

Photo sent to you

Tap and hold to pop a photo open (3D Touch only)

Tap to view

When you receive a photo or video as an attachment, it appears in a thumbnail along with the accompanying message.

Tap to return to the conversation

Number of photos in the conversation

Tap to bring up a list of recent photos in the conversation

Tap to share

Swipe to see other photos or videos in the conversation

To view a photo or video attachment, tap it. You see the photo or video at a larger size. You can rotate the phone, zoom, and swipe around the photo just like viewing photos in the Photos app (see Chapter 14 for details). You can watch a video in the same way, too.

Tap the Share icon to share the photo with others via a message, email, tweet, Facebook, and so on. (When you hold an iPhone Plus horizontally, all the icons are at the top of the screen.)

If there is more than one photo or video in the conversation, you see the number of them at the top of the screen. Swipe to the left or right to move through the available photos.

Tap the List icon to see a list of the recent photos in the conversation (this only appears if there is more than one photo in the conversation).

Swipe up and down to browse all the photos in the conversation

Tap to view

Tap to close the list

Tap a photo on the list to view it. Tap Close to return to the photo you were viewing.

To move back to the conversation, tap Done.

Swipe up for options

Press to view

When you use an iPhone that supports 3D Touch and you press on a photo, it opens in a Peek. If you continue pressing on the photo, it opens in the view window just like when you tap on it in the conversation.

When you are peeking at a photo, swipe up on it to reveal options. You can copy the photo so you can paste it elsewhere, save the photo in the Photos app, or forward it to others.

No 3D Touch?

If your iPhone doesn't support 3D Touch, you can save a photo by touching the photo (don't apply pressure) and using the Save Image command on the resulting menu. You can also copy or forward it from this menu.

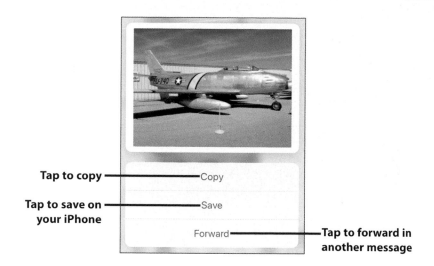

Tap to copy ————————Copy

Tap to save on ————————Save
your iPhone

Forward————————————Tap to forward in
another message

Listening to Audio in Messages You Receive in Messages

Audio message

Tap to listen via the speakerphone

Tap to play

When you receive an audio message, you can tap the Play icon to play it, or, if you enabled the Raise to Listen option, lift the phone to your ear and the message plays automatically. Tap the Speaker icon to hear the message via the iPhone's speakerphone.

Tap to pause

While the message is playing, you see its status along with the Pause icon, which you can tap to pause the audio message. After the message finishes, you see a message saying that it expires in 2 minutes or 1 year, depending on your settings. That message is quickly replaced by Keep.

Tap to save the
audio message

Tap Keep to save the message on your phone. (Keep disappears indicating the audio is saved.)

Kept Audio Messages

When one or more of the recipients of an audio message that you sent keeps it, a status message is added to the conversation on your phone, so you know who keeps audio messages you have sent. And, others know when you keep their messages, too.

Replying to Messages from the Messages App

To reply to a message, read the message and do the following:

1. Read, watch, or listen to the most recent message.

2. Use the photos, Digital Touch, or App tools to reply with content of that type as you learned about earlier in this chapter.

3. Tap in the Message bar if you want to reply with text.

4. Type your reply or use the Dictation feature to speak your reply (this is translated to text; it's not recording and embedding an audio message).

5. Tap the Send icon.

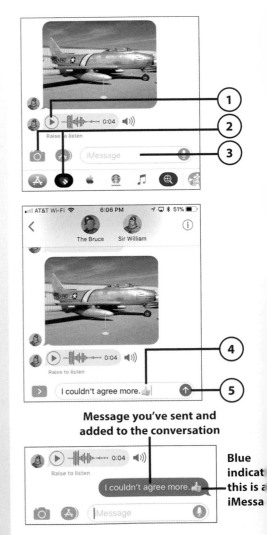

Message you've sent and
added to the conversation

Blue
indicat
this is a
iMessa

Mix and Match

The Messages app can switch between types of messages. For example, if you have an iMessage conversation going but can't access the iMessage service for some reason, the app can send messages as a cellular text. It can switch the other way, too. The app tries to send iMessages first if it can but chooses whichever method it needs to get the messages through. (If you disabled the Send as SMS option, messages are only sent via iMessage.)

More Tricks of the Messaging Trade

My Acquisitions Editor Extraordinaire pointed out that people can't receive messages when their phones aren't connected to the Internet (via Wi-Fi or cell). You don't see a warning in this case; you can only tell the message wasn't delivered because the Delivered status doesn't appear under the message. The message is delivered as soon as the other person's phone is connected to the Internet again, and its status is updated accordingly on your phone. Also, when an iMessage can't be delivered, you can tap and hold on it; then tap Send as Text Message. The app tries to send the message via SMS instead of iMessage.

Replying to Messages from a Banner Alert

If you have banner alerts configured for your messages, you can reply directly from the alert from either the Home or Lock screens:

1. Press on the notification (3D Touch) or swipe to the right (non-3D Touch). The conversation opens.

2. Type your reply or tap the right-facing arrow to add other types of content to your response.

3. Tap the Send icon. Your message is added to the conversation.

Having a Messages Conversation

Messaging is all about the back-and-forth communication with one or more people. You've already learned the skills you need, so put them all together. You can start a new conversation by sending a message to one or more people with whom you don't have an ongoing conversation; or you can add to a conversation already underway.

1. Send a new message to a person or add a new message to an existing conversation. You see when your message has been delivered. If you sent the message to an individual person via iMessages and he has enabled his Read Receipt setting, you see when he has read your message and you see a bubble as he is composing a response. (If you are conversing with more than one person, the person doesn't have her Read Receipt setting enabled, or the conversation is happening via the cellular network, you don't see either of these.)

As the recipient composes a response, you see a bubble on the screen where the new message will appear when it is received (again, only if it is an iMessage with a single individual). Of course, you don't have to remain on the conversation's screen waiting for a response. You can move to a different conversation or a different app. When the response comes in, you are notified per your notification settings.

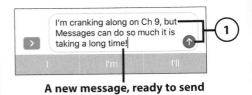

A new message, ready to send

Your message has been delivered

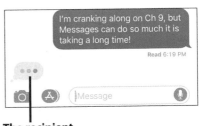

Your message has been read

The recipient is composing a response

Seen But Not Read

Don't take the Read status too literally. All it means is that the conversation to which your message was added has been viewed. Of course, the Messages app can't know whether the recipient actually read the message.

2. Read the response.

3. Send your next message.

4. Repeat these steps as long as you want. Conversations remain in the Messages app until you remove them. Messages within conversations remain forever (unless you delete them, for one year, or for 30 days depending on your Keep Messages setting as shown earlier in this chapter).

The iMessage Will Be With You…Always

Messages that are sent with iMessage move with you from device to device, so they appear on every device configured to use your iMessage account. Because of this, you can start a conversation on your iPhone while you are on the move and pick it up on your iPad or Mac later.

Working with Messages

As you send and receive messages, the interaction you have with each person or group becomes a separate conversation. A conversation consists of all the messages that have gone back and forth. You manage your conversations from the Messages screen.

Multiple Conversations with the Same People

The Messages app manages conversations based on the phone number or email address associated with the messages in that conversation rather than the people (contacts) involved in the conversation. So, you might have multiple conversations with the same person if that person used a different means, such as a phone number and an email address, to send messages to you.

Managing Messages Conversations

Use the Messages screen to manage your messages.

1. On the Home screen, tap Messages. The Messages screen showing conversations you have going appears, or you move into the conversation you were most recently using (tap the left-facing arrow at the top of the screen to move back to the conversation list). Conversations containing new messages appear at the top of the list. The name of the conversation is the name of the person or people associated with it, or it might be labeled as Group if the app can't display the names. If a contact can't be associated with the person, you see the phone number or email address you are conversing with instead of a name.

2. Swipe up and down the list to see all the conversations.

3. Tap a conversation you want to read or reply to. The conversation screen appears; the name of the screen is the people with whom you are conversing, either by name if they are a contact or email address or phone number if they aren't.

If you have the badge enabled, you see the number of new messages on the Messages icon

Day or time of most recent message

Who is involved in the conversation

Conversation with new messages

Information Messages

Many organizations use messages to keep you informed. Examples are airlines that send flight status information, retailers that use messages to keep you informed about shipping, and so on. These messages are identified by a set of numbers that don't look like a phone number. You can't send a response to most of these messages; they are one-way only. In some cases, you can issue commands related to the texts from that organization, such as "Stop" to stop further texts from being sent.

4. Read the new messages or view other new content in the conversation. Your messages are on the right side of the screen in green (cell network) or blue (iMessage), whereas the other people's messages are on the left in gray. Messages are organized so the newest message is at the bottom of the screen.

5. Swipe up and down the conversation screen to see all the messages it contains.

6. To add a new message to the conversation, tap in the Message bar, type your message or use an app to add content, and tap the Send icon.

7. Swipe down to scroll up the screen and move back in time in the conversation.

8. To see details about the conversation, tap the Info icon (i). The Details screen appears. At the top of the screen, you see location information for the people with whom you are texting if it is available.

See the Time of Every Message

To see the time or date associated with every message in the conversation being displayed, swipe to the left and hold your finger down on the screen. The messages shift to the left and the time of each message appears along the right side of the screen. The date associated with each message appears right before the first message on that date.

9. If you are working with a group message and want to give it a name, tap Enter a Group Name. If you are working with a conversation involving one other person or don't want to name the group, skip to step 11.

— Location of other participan (if availab

9

What's in a Name?

When you name a group (conversation), that name is applied to the conversation for all the participants.

10. Enter the name of the group, and tap Done.

10

11. To place a voice call or audio-only FaceTime call to one of the participants in the conversation, tap the phone icon. If the person has a phone number configured, you're prompted to choose Voice Call or FaceTime Audio. When you make a choice, that call is placed. If the person only has an email address, an audio-only FaceTime call is placed over the Internet. You move into the Phone or FaceTime app and use that app to complete the call. (See Chapter 7, "Communicating with the Phone and FaceTime Apps," for the details about those apps.) Move to the Home screen and tap Messages or use the App Switcher to return to the Messages app.

12. Send a private message to one of the participants by tapping the Messages icon.

13. Place a FaceTime video call by tapping the Video Camera icon. You move into the FaceTime app to complete the call. When you're done, move to the Home screen and tap Messages or use the App Switcher to return to the Messages app.

14. To view a participant's contact information or send an email, tap

New group name

14

13

11

12

List of participants in the conversation

the person whose information you want to view.

15. Work with the contact information as described in Chapter 6.

16. Tap the back icon to return to the Details screen and click Done to return to the conversation screen.

Receiving and Reading Messages on an iPhone Plus

The larger screen on the iPhone Plus provides some additional functionality that is unique to it. You can access this by holding the iPhone Plus horizontally when you use the Messages app.

1. Open the Messages app and hold the iPhone so it is oriented horizontally. The window splits into two panes. On the left is the Navigation pane, where you can move to and select conversations you want to view. When you select a conversation in the left pane, its messages appear in the Content pane on the right.

2. Swipe up or down the Navigation pane to browse the conversations available to you. Notice that the two panes are independent. When you browse the left pane, the right pane doesn't change.

3. Tap the conversation containing messages you want to read. The messages in that conversation appear in the Content pane on the right.

List of conversations

Messages in selected conversation

Selected conversation

4. Swipe up and down the Content pane to read the messages in the conversation.

5. Work with the messages in the conversation just like when the iPhone is held vertically.

6. To add a message to the conversation, tap in the Send bar, type your message, and tap Send. Of course, you can embed audio, attach photos or video, add content from apps, or send your location just as you can when using Messages when you hold the iPhone vertically.

7. Work with the conversation's details by tapping the Info icon (i).

8. Change conversations by tapping the conversation you want to view.

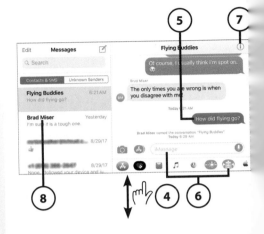

Using 3D Touch for Messages

You can use the 3D Touch feature (iPhone 6s and later models) with the Messages app as follows:

1. Browse your messages.

2. Tap and hold on a conversation in which you are interested. A Peek of that conversation appears.

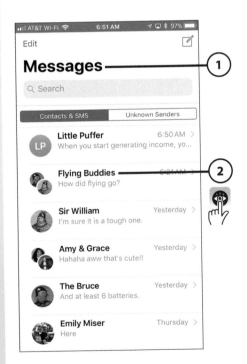

3. Review the preview of the messages that appear in the Peek.

4. Open the conversation so you can read all of its messages by pressing down slightly harder until it pops open. Use the steps in the earlier task to read it (skip the rest of these steps).

5. See actions you can perform on the message by swiping up on the Peek.

6. Tap the reply you want to make, which is based on the context of the previous message, such as responding to the question "How did it go?," to reply to the message with that message. If you tap Custom, you can create a custom reply to the message as you can when you view the conversation.

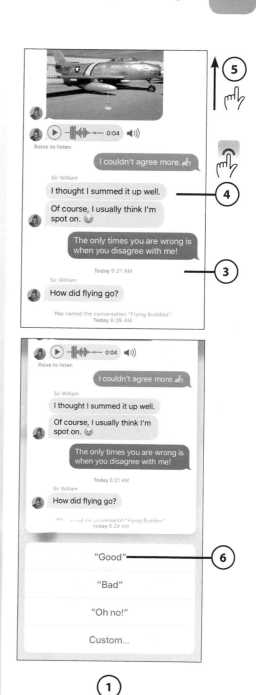

Browsing Attachments to Conversations

As photos, videos, and documents are added to a conversation, they are collected so you can browse and view them at any time:

1. Move to the conversation in which you want to browse attachments.

2. Tap the Info icon (i).

3. Swipe up until you see the Images and Attachments tabs.

4. Tap Images to see images attached to the conversation or Attachments to work with other types of attachments (such as PDF documents).

5. Swipe up and down on the attachments until you see one you want to view.

6. Tap the attachment you want to view.

7. View the attachment, such as looking at a photo.

8. Tap Done to return to the Details screen.

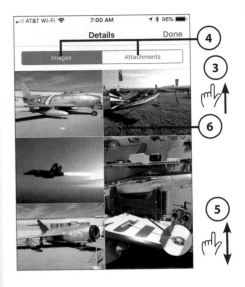

Keep Quiet!

You can disable notifications for a specific conversation by tapping its Info icon (i) to move to the Details screen. Set the Hide Alerts switch to on (green). You no longer are notified when new messages arrive in that conversation. Set the switch to off (white) to have notifications resume.

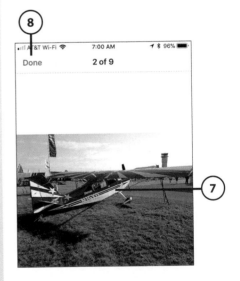

I'm Outta Here!

If you don't want to participate in a conversation any more, open the Details screen and tap Leave this Conversation.

Working with Messages from People You Might Not Know

As you use Messages, it is likely you'll receive messages from people who aren't in your contacts or who you haven't sent messages to before. Some of these will be legitimate contacts with whom you have messaged previously while some will just be because the person sending the message made a mistake, such as not typing the phone number correctly; others will be made for nefarious purposes. The Messages app can filter messages from unknown people for you and put them on the Unknown Senders tab so you can easily identify messages that are from people who you might not know.

To use this functionality, the Filter Unknown Senders switch on the Messages Settings screen must be turned on (green). (The details of configuring Messages settings are provided in "Setting Your Text and iMessage Preferences" earlier in this chapter.) When this switch is on, you see two tabs in the Messages app. The Contacts & SMS tab lists conversations with people who are contacts or with whom you have communicated previously. The Unknown Senders tab lists conversations from people who aren't contacts or with whom you haven't communicated previously. (If the Filter Unknown Senders switch is off, you don't see these tabs.)

If you enable the Filter Unknown Senders feature, you can work with "suspicious" messages as follows:

1. Open the Messages app.

2. Tap the Unknown Senders tab.

3. Tap a message to read it so you can determine if it is a legitimate message for you.

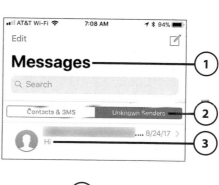

4. Review the identification of the sender as best Messages can determine it, such as an email address.

5. Read the message.

6. If the message is from someone you don't recognize and don't want to receive future messages from, tap Report Junk. The sender's message is deleted from the Messages app and the associated email address or phone number is blocked so you won't receive any more messages from the sender.

7. If you want to take other action on the sender, tap the Info icon.

8. Tap the contact information for the sender.

9. If you recognize the person, want to communicate with her, but don't have a contact configured for her, tap Create New Contact to create a new contact for the person. (For information about creating or updating contacts, see Chapter 6.)

10. If you recognize the person, want to communicate with her, and have a contact configured for her, tap Add to Existing Contact to update a current contact with new information.

11. If you don't want to receive future messages from the sender, tap Block this Caller.

12. Tap Block Contact.

Junk or Block?

When you report a message as junk, the contact is blocked from communicating with you, but their information is not stored on your iPhone. When you block the contact instead, messages don't reach you, but the contact information is stored on the list of people you have blocked. You can unblock people from this list if you want to resume communicating with them. You can't resume communicating with someone whose messages you have marked as junk.

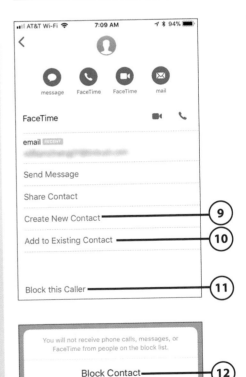

Responding to a Message with Icons

You can quickly respond to messages with an icon as follows:

1. View a conversation.

2. If you are using an iPhone with 3D Touch, press and hold on a message you want to respond to; if you are using a non-3D Touch phone, just touch and hold on a message. You can respond to any message, even if it's one you sent.

3. Tap the icon you want to add to the message; for example, tap the thumbs-up icon to indicate you like a message. The icon you select is added to the message.

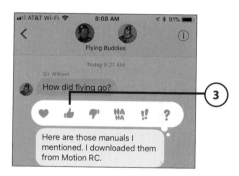

Deleting Messages and Conversations

Old text conversations never die, nor do they fade away (if you have your Keep Messages setting set to Forever, that is). All the messages you receive from a person or that involve the same group of people stay in the conversation. Over time, you can build up a lot of messages in one conversation, and you can end up with lots of conversations. (If you set the Keep Messages setting to be 30 Days or 1 Year, messages older than the time you set are deleted automatically.)

Long Conversation?

When a conversation gets very long, the Messages app won't display all its messages. It keeps the more current messages visible on the conversation screen. To see earlier messages, swipe down on the screen to move to the top and tap Load Earlier Messages.

When a conversation gets too long, if you just want to remove specific messages from a conversation, or, if you want to get rid of messages to free up storage space, take these steps:

1. Move to a conversation containing an abundance of messages.

2. If you are using an iPhone with 3D Touch, press and hold on a message you want to delete; if you are using a non-3D Touch phone, just touch and hold on a message to be deleted.

3. Tap More. The message on which you tapped is marked with a check mark to show it is selected.

Be a Copycat

Tap Copy to copy a message so you can paste it in other messages or in other apps.

Delete Them All!

To delete all the messages in the conversation, instead of performing step 4, tap Delete All, which appears in the upper-left corner of the screen. Tap Delete Conversation in the confirmation box. The conversation and all its messages are deleted.

4. Tap other messages you want to delete. They are marked with a check mark to show you have selected them.

5. Tap the Trash Can.

6. Tap Delete X Messages, where X is the number of messages you have selected. The messages are deleted and you return to the conversation.

Pass It On

If you want to send one or more messages to someone else, perform steps 1–4. Tap the Forward icon that appears in the lower-right corner of the screen. A new message is created and the messages you selected are pasted into it. Select or enter the recipients to whom you want to send the messages, and tap Send.

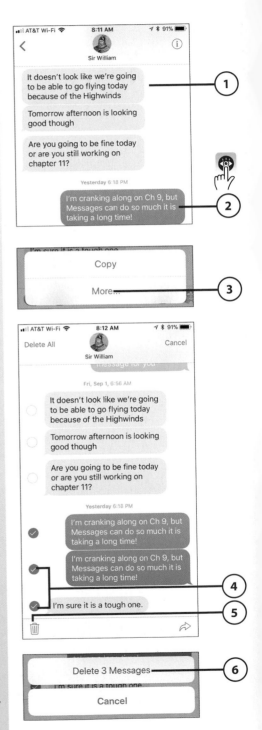

Deleting Conversations

If a conversation's time has come, you can delete it.

1. Move to the Messages screen.

2. Swipe to the left on the conversation you want to delete.

3. Tap Delete. The conversation and all the messages it contains are deleted.

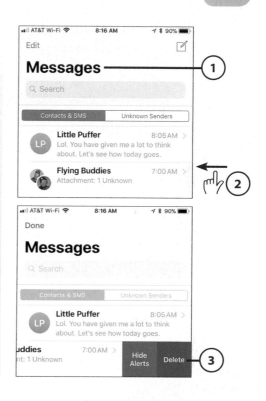

Gone, but Not Forgotten?

When you delete an iMessage conversation, it is removed from your iPhone. However, the actual conversation remains on the cloud and on other devices on which your iMessages account is configured. If you send a message to the same person or people who were on the conversation you deleted, it is restored to your iPhone.

>>>Go Further

TEXTING LINGO

People frequently use shorthand when they text. Here is some of the more common shorthand you might see. This list is extremely short, but there are many websites dedicated to providing this type of information if you are interested. One that boasts of being the largest list of text message acronyms is www.netlingo.com/acronyms.php.

- **FWIW**—For What It's Worth
- **LOL**—Laughing Out Loud
- **ROTFL**—Rolling On the Floor Laughing
- **CU**—See You (later)
- **PO**—Peace Out
- **IMHO**—In My Humble Opinion

- **TY**—Thank You
- **RU**—Are You
- **BRB**—Be Right Back
- **CM**—Call Me
- **DND**—Do Not Disturb
- **EOM**—End of Message
- **FSR**—For Some Reason
- **G2G**—Got to Go
- **IDK**—I Don't Know

- **IKR**—I Know, Right?
- **ILU**—I Love You
- **NM or NVM**—Never Mind
- **OMG**—Oh My God
- **OTP**—On the Phone
- **P911**—Parent Alert
- **PLZ**—Please

Tap here to configure your
date and time preferences

Go here
to figure
out where
and when
you're
supposed
to be

In this chapter, you explore all the calendar functionality your iPhone has to offer. Topics include the following:

→ Setting calendar, date, and time preferences
→ Working with calendars

Managing Calendars

When it comes to time management, your iPhone is definitely your friend. Using the iPhone's Calendar app, you can view calendars that are available on all your devices. You can also make changes to your calendars on your iPhone, and they appear on the calendars on your other devices so you have consistent information no matter which device you happen to be using at any time. You can also include other people in your events and manage events others invite you to attend.

Setting Calendar, Date, and Time Preferences

There are a number of time, date, and calendar settings that affect how you use your iPhone to manage your calendars and time. In most cases, you can leave these settings in their default configurations and start using the Calendar app right away (beginning with "Working with Calendars" later in this chapter).

Settings App Explained

To get detailed information on using the Settings app, see "Working with the Settings app" in Chapter 2, "Using Your iPhone's Core Features."

To be able to share your calendars among multiple devices, use an online account, such as iCloud, Google, or Exchange to manage your calendar information. Before working with the calendar app, ensure you have at least one online account configured to manage calendar information on your iPhone. See Chapter 3, "Setting Up and Using an Apple ID, iCloud, and Other Online Accounts," for information about configuring online accounts.

To change the calendar settings, open the Settings app and tap Calendar. Use the settings described in the following list to make changes to how the app works.

- **Siri & Search**—Set the Search & Siri Suggestions switch to on (green) to allow information in your calendars to be searched and used by Siri. Set the Find Events in Other Apps switch to on (green) if you want information that appears to be calendar related (such as someone mentioning a time and place to meet for lunch in an email) to be highlighted so you can easily add it to your calendars. These are both enabled by default.

- **Time Zone Override**—When disabled, the time for events is based on your current time zone. When enabled, the time zone for events on the calendars is overridden with the time zone for a city you select. This is useful if you always want event times to be based on a specific time zone. (See the Go Further sidebar at the end of this list for a more in-depth explanation of this setting.)

- **Alternate Calendars**—You can choose among different types of calendars, such as Chinese or Hebrew.

- **Week Numbers**—When this switch is on (green), week numbers appear on your calendars in the Month view.

- **Show Invitee Declines**—When enabled (the switch is green) and someone declines a meeting, they are shown on the Invitee list as having declined. When disabled (the switch is white), invitees who decline an event are removed from the list.

- **Sync**—Determines how far back events are synced onto your calendars. You can choose 2 weeks, 1 month (the default), 3 months, 6 months, or all events.

- **Default Alert Times**—Determines the default alert times for birthdays, events, and all-day events. When you set the Time to Leave switch to on (green), the Calendar app can use your travel time to configure an event's alert. You can change the alert time for any event on your calendar; these settings just determine the initial alert time.

- **Start Week On**—Determines the first day of the week.

- **Default Calendar**—Determines which calendar is used for new events by default (you can override this setting for any events you create).

- **Location Suggestions**—When this switch is on (green), the Calendar app makes suggestions about the location of events when you create them.

>>>*Go Further*

MORE ON TIME ZONE OVERRIDE

The Time Zone Override feature can be a bit confusing. If Time Zone Override is on, the iPhone displays event times according to the time zone you select on the Time Zone Override screen. When Time Zone Override is off, the time zone used for calendars is the iPhone's current time zone, which is set automatically based on your location or your manual setting. This means that when you change time zones (automatically or manually), the times for calendar events shift accordingly. For example, if an event starts at 3:00 p.m. when you are in the Eastern time zone, its start time becomes 12:00 p.m. if you move into the Pacific time zone.

When Time Zone Override is on, the dates and times for events become fixed based on the time zone you select for Time Zone Override. If you change the time zone the iPhone is in, no change to the dates and times for events is shown on the calendar because they remain set according to the time zone you selected for the Time Zone Override. Therefore, an event's actual start time might not be accurately reflected for the iPhone's current time zone because it is based on the fixed Time Zone Override city instead of the time zone where you are currently located.

To configure how your iPhone displays and manages the date and time, open the Settings app, tap General, tap Date & Time, and change the settings described in the following list:

- **24-Hour Time**—Turning this switch on (green) causes the iPhone to display 24-hour instead of 12-hour time.

- **Set Automatically**—When this switch is on (green), your iPhone sets the current time and date automatically based on the cellular network it is using. When it is off (white), controls appear that you use to manually set the time zone, time, and date.

Notifications

The Calendar app can communicate with you in various ways, such as displaying banners when something happens that you might want to know about; for example, you can be alerted with a banner when you receive an invitation to an event. The information you need to configure notifications is explained in Chapter 4, "Customizing How Your iPhone Works."

Working with Calendars

The Calendar app helps you manage your calendars; notice I wrote calendars rathe than calendar. That's because you can have multiple calendars in the app at the same time. To use the most cliché example, you might have a calendar for work an one for your personal life. Or, you might want a calendar dedicated to your travel plans, and then share that calendar with people who care about your location.

In most cases, you start by adding existing calendar information from an Exchange, iCloud, Google, or similar account. From there, you can use the Calendar app to view your calendars, add or change events, and much more. Any changes you make in the Calendar app are automatically made in all the locations that use calendars from the same account.

Viewing Calendars and Events

You use the Calendar app to view and work with your calendars, and you can choose how you view them, such as by month, week, or day.

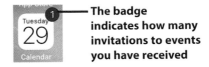

The badge indicates how many invitations to events you have received

To get into your calendars, move to the Home screen and tap the Calendar app (which shows the current day and date in its icon and a badge if you have at least one new invitation). The most recent screen you were viewing appears.

There are three modes you use in the app. The mode in which you'll spend most of your time is the one that displays your calendars in various views, such as showing a month, week, day, or event. Another mode is the Calendars tool that enables you to choose and edit the calendar information that is displayed. The third mode is your Inbox, which you use to work with event invitations you receive.

Configuring Calendars

To configure the calendar information you see in the app, perform the following steps:

1. If you have only one calendar, skip to step 2. Otherwise, tap Calendars to see all of your calendars. If you don't see this at the bottom of the screen, you are already on the Calendars screen (look for "Calendars" at the top of the screen) or you are on the Inbox, in which case, tap Done.

The Calendars screen displays the calendars available, organized by the account from which they come, such as ICLOUD, EXCHANGE, or GMAIL (the names you see are the descriptions of the accounts you created on your iPhone). By default, all your calendars are displayed, which is indicated by the circles with check marks next to the calendars' names. Any calendars that have an empty circle next to their names are not displayed when you view your calendars.

2. Tap a calendar with a check mark to hide it. The check mark disappears and the calendar is hidden. (The calendar is still available in the app, you just won't see it when you are viewing your calendars.)

3. To show a calendar again, tap its name. It is marked with a check mark and appears when you are viewing calendars.

4. Tap the info icon (i) to see or change a calendar's settings. Not all types of calendars support this function, and those that do can offer different settings. The following steps show an iCloud calendar; if you are working with a calendar of a different type, such as an Exchange calendar, you might not have all of the same options as those shown here. In any case, the steps to make changes are similar across all available types of calendars.

Calendars without check marks are hidden

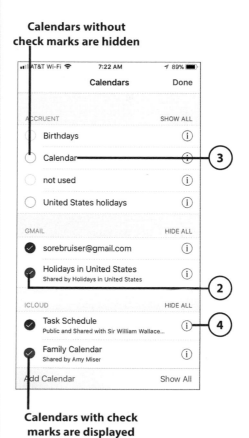

Calendars with check marks are displayed

5. Change the name of the calendar by tapping it and then making changes on the keyboard; when you're done making changes, swipe down the screen to close the keyboard.

6. To share the calendar with someone, tap Add Person, enter the email address of the person with whom you are sharing it, and tap Add. (Sharing calendars is explained in more detail later in this chapter.)

7. If the calendar is shared and you don't want to be notified when shared events are changed, added, or deleted, set the Show Changes switch to off (white). When this switch is enabled (green) and a change is made to a shared calendar, you receive notifications about the changes that were made. If the calendar is not shared, you won't see this switch.

8. Swipe up the screen.

9. Tap the color you want events on the calendar to appear in.

10. If you want alerts to be enabled (active) for the calendar, set the Event Alerts switch to on (green).

11. To make the calendar public so that others can subscribe to a read-only version of it, set the Public Calendar switch to on (green), tap Share Link, and then use the resulting Share tools to invite others to subscribe to the calendar (more on this later in this chapter).

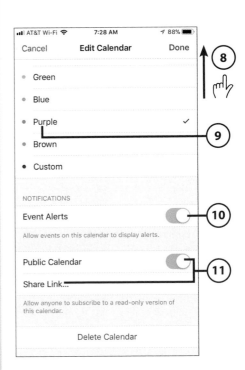

12. To remove the calendar entirely (instead of hiding it from view), tap Delete Calendar and then tap Delete Calendar at the prompt. The calendar and all its events are deleted. (It's usually better just to hide a calendar as described in step 2 so you don't lose its information.)

13. Assuming that you didn't delete the calendar, tap Done to save the changes you made.

14. Edit other calendars as needed.

15. Tap Done. The app moves into viewing mode, and the calendars you enabled are displayed.

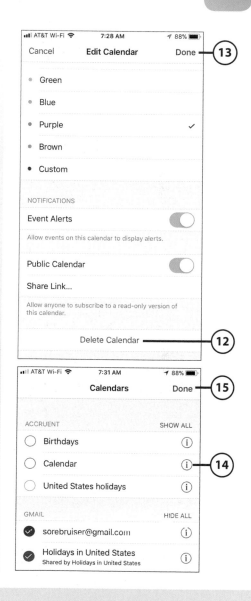

>>>Go Further

ALL OR NOTHING

You can make all your calendars visible by tapping Show All at the bottom of the screen; tap Hide All to do the opposite. After all the calendars are shown or hidden, you can tap individual calendars to show or hide them. You can show or hide all the calendars from the same account by tapping the SHOW/HIDE ALL command at the top of each account's calendar list.

Navigating Calendars

The Calendar app uses a hierarchy of detail to display your calendars. The highest level is the year view that shows the months in each year. The next level is the month view, which shows the days of the month (days with events are marked with a dot). This is followed by the week/day view that shows the days of the week and summary information for the events on each day. The most detailed view is the event view that shows all the information for a single event.

Viewing Calendars

You can view your calendars from the year level all the way down to the day/week view. It's easy to move among the levels to get to the time period you want to see. Here's how:

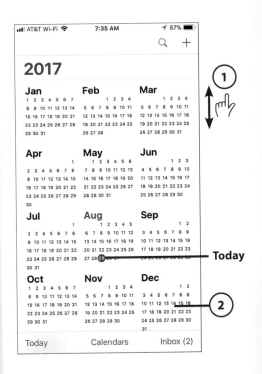

1. Starting at the year view, swipe up and down until you see the year in which you are interested. (If you aren't in the year view, keep tapping the back icon located in the upper-left corner of the screen until that icon disappears.)

2. Tap the month in which you are interested. The days in that month display, and days with events are marked with a dot.

3. Swipe up and down the screen to view different months in the year you selected.

4. To see the detail for a date, tap it. There are two ways to view the daily details: the Calendar view or the List view. Steps 5 through 8 show the Calendar view, whereas steps 9 through 11 show the List view. Each of these views has benefits, and, as you can see, it is easy to switch between them.

5. To see the Calendar view, ensure the List icon is not selected (isn't highlighted). At the top of the screen are the days of the week you are viewing. The date in focus is highlighted with a red circle when that day is today and a black circle for any other day. Below this area is the detail for the selected day showing the events on that day.

6. Swipe to the left or right on the dates or date being displayed to change the date for which detailed information is being shown.

7. Swipe up or down on the date detail to browse all its events.

8. Tap an event to view its detail and skip to step 12.

Dates with events

The date being displayed below

Today Is the Day

To quickly move to the current day, tap Today, which is located at the bottom-left corner of the screen.

9. See the events in List view by tapping the List icon so it is highlighted.

10. Swipe up and down to see the events for each day.

11. Tap an event to view its detail.

12. Swipe up and down the screen to see all of the event's information.

13. View information about the event, such as its location, repetition, and relationship to other events on the calendar.

14. Tap the Calendar or Alert fields to change these settings; tap the Invitees area to get information about people you've invited to the event.

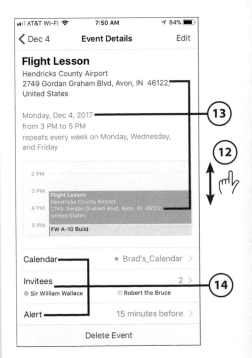

15. Tap attachments to view them.

16. Tap any links to move to information related to the event.

17. Read notes associated with the event.

18. Tap a location to get directions to it.

19. Use the Maps app to get directions (see Chapter 15, "Working with Other Useful iPhone Apps and Features," for more information).

20. Tap Calendar to return to the Calendar app.

21. Tap the date to move back to the week/day view.

22. Tap the back icon (labeled with the month you are viewing) to move back to the month view.

23. To view your calendars in the multiday view, rotate your iPhone so it is horizontal. You can do this while in the week/day view or the month view.

24. Swipe left or right to change the dates being displayed.

25. Swipe up or down to change the time of day being displayed.

26. Tap an event to see its details.

Current Time or Event

When you are viewing today in the Calendar view, the red line stretching horizontally across the screen indicates the current time, which is shown at the left end of that line. When you are viewing today in the List view, the current event is indicated by the text "Now" in red along the right edge of the screen.

Using 3D Touch for Events (iPhone 6s/6s Plus and Later)

You can use the 3D Touch feature on an iPhone 6s/6s Plus or later models with the Calendar app as follows:

1. Browse events, such as when you use the List view.

2. Tap and hold on an event in which you are interested. A Peek of that event appears.

3. Review the preview of the event that appears in the Peek.

4. To open the event so you can see all of its detail, press down slightly harder until it pops open and use the steps in the earlier task to work with it (skip the rest of these steps).

5. To see actions you can perform on the event, swipe up on the Peek.

6. Tap the action you want to perform, such as Delete Event, to delete the event from your calendar.

What's Next?

To quickly see the next event on your calendar, move to a Home screen or the Lock screen and swipe to the right to open the Widget Center. Find the UP NEXT widget, which shows you the next event on your calendar; you might want to move this to the top of the Widget Center if you use it regularly. (For more on configuring your widgets, see Chapter 4.)

What's Next...Even Faster?

You can find out what's next even faster by activating Siri and saying, "What's next?" Siri shows you your next event and speaks the time and name of the event. Siri can also help with many other calendar-related tasks. (See Chapter 11, "Working with Siri," for the details.)

Adding Events to a Calendar

There are a number of ways you can add events to your calendar. You can create an event in an app on a computer, website, or other device and sync that event onto the iPhone through an online account. You can also manually create events in the Calendar app on the iPhone. Your events can include a lot of information, or they can be fairly basic. You can choose to create the basic information on your iPhone while you are on the move and complete it later from a computer or other device, or you can fill in all the details directly in the Calendar app. You can also add an event by accepting an invitation (covered later in this chapter).

1. Tap the Add icon (+), which appears in the upper-right corner of any of the views when your phone is vertical (except when you are viewing an event's details). The initial date information is taken from the date currently being displayed, so you can save a little time if you view the date of the event before tapping the Add icon.

2. Tap in the Title field and type the title of the event.

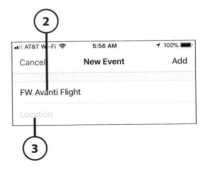

3. Tap the Location bar and type the location of the event; if you allow the app to use Location Services, you're prompted to find and select a location; if not, just type the location and skip to step 6.

Location Prompt

The first time you create an event, you might be prompted to allow the Calendar app to access your location information. When you allow the app to use Location Services, you can search for and select event locations. The app can use this information to include an estimate of travel time for the event and to display events on a map when you view their detail.

4. Type the location in the Search bar. Sites that meet your search are shown below. The results screen has several sections including Recents, which shows locations you've used recently, and Locations, which are sites that the app finds that match your search criteria.

5. Tap the location for the event; tap Current Location if the event takes place where you are. You return to the new event screen and see the location you entered.

6. To set the event to last all day, set the All-day switch to the on position (green); when you select the All-day option, you provide only the start and end dates (you don't enter times as described in the next several steps). To set a specific start and end time, leave this setting in the off position (white); you set both the dates and times as described in the following steps.

7. To set a timeframe for the event, tap Starts. The date and time tool appears.

8. Swipe up or down on the date wheel until the date on which the event starts appears in the center.

9. Swipe up or down on the hour wheel until the event's starting hour is shown.

10. Scroll and select the starting minute in the same way.

11. Swipe up or down on the hour wheel to select AM or PM.

12. If you want to associate the event with a specific time zone, tap Time Zone; if not, skip to step 14.

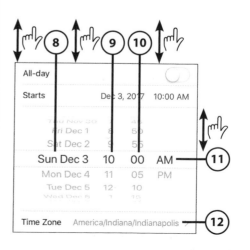

Your Results Might Vary

The fields and options available when you create a new event are based on the calendar with which the event is associated. For example, an iCloud calendar might have different options than an Exchange calendar does. If you aren't creating an event on your default calendar, it's a good idea to associate the event with a calendar before you fill in its details (to do that, perform step 30 before you do step 2).

13. Search for and select the time zone with which the event should be associated.

14. Tap Ends.

15. Use the date and time wheels to set the ending date and time (if applicable) for the event; these work the same way as for the start date and time.

Different Ending Time Zone?

The Calendar app assumes the time zone associated with the ending date and time is the same as for the starting date and time. If you want to set a different ending time zone, tap Time Zone below the Ends section and choose a different time zone as described in steps 12 and 13.

16. Tap Ends. The date and time tool closes.

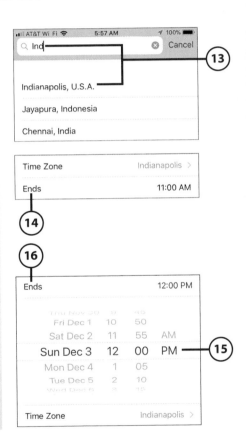

No Changes?

When you change a selection on most of the screens you see, you automatically return to the previous screen; for example, when you select a time zone, you immediately return to the New Event screen. If you don't make a change, you can return to the previous screen by tapping New Event in the upper-left corner of the screen. If you start to perform a search for something, such as time zone, but decide not to finish it, tap Cancel and then tap New Event.

17. To make the event repeat, tap Repeat and follow steps 18–23. (For a nonrepeating event, keep the default, which is Never, and skip to step 24.)

18. Tap the frequency at which you want the event repeated, such as Every Day, Every Week, etc.; if you want to use a repeat cycle not shown, tap Custom and create the frequency with which you want the event to repeat.

19. Tap End Repeat to set a time at which the event stops repeating.

20. Tap Never to have the event repeat ad infinitum, and then skip to step 23.

21. Tap On Date to set an end to the repetition.

22. Use the date wheel to set the date for the last repeated event.

23. Tap New Event.

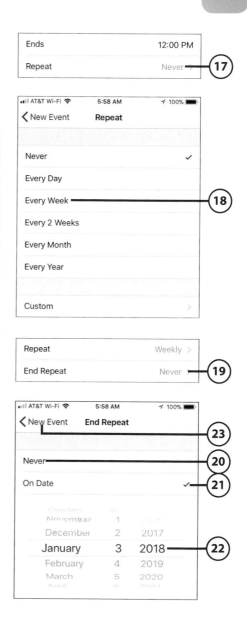

Custom Repeat

To configure a custom repeat cycle for an event in step 18, such as the first Monday of every month, tap Custom on the Repeat screen. Then use the Frequency (Monthly for the example) and Every (for example, On the first Monday) settings to configure the repeat cycle. Tap Repeat to return to the Repeat screen and then tap New Event to get back to the event you are creating.

24. To configure travel time for the event, tap Travel Time; if you don't want to configure this, skip to step 30.

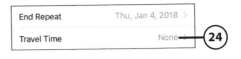

25. Set the Travel Time switch to on (green).

26. To manually set a travel time for the event, tap it and skip to step 29.

27. Tap Starting Location to build a travel time based on a starting location.

No Change Needed

If you don't make a change to one of the settings, such as on the Repeat screen, tap the back icon (labeled New Event) in the upper-left corner of the screen get back to the New Event screen.

---

28. To use your current location as the starting point, tap Current Location. Alternatively, use the search tool to find a starting location, and then tap it to select that location. This works just like setting a location for the event. The travel time is calculated based on the starting and ending locations entered for the new event. You can configure alerts based on this travel time as you see in later steps.

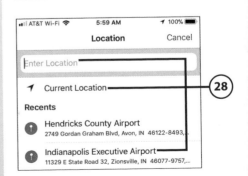

29. Tap New Event.

30. To change the calendar with which the event is associated, tap Calendar (to leave the current calendar selected, skip to step 32).

31. Tap the calendar with which the event should be associated.

32. To invite others to the event, tap Invitees; if you don't want to invite someone else, skip to step 37.

33. Enter the email addresses for each person you want to invite; as you type, the app tries to identify people who match what you are typing. You can tap a person to add him to the event or keep entering the email address until it is complete. You can also use the Add icon (+) to choose people in your Contacts app (see Chapter 6, "Managing Contacts," for help using that app).

34. Repeat step 33 until you've added everyone you want to invite.

35. Tap Done. You move to the Invitees screen and see those whom you invited.

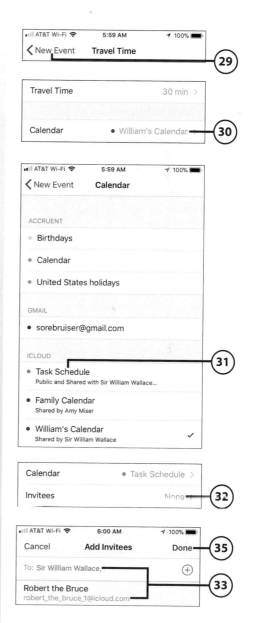

Automatic Sharing

When you add an event to a calendar that is shared with others, the people with whom the calendar is shared, see the event in their Calendar app automatically.

36. Tap New Event.

37. To set an alert for the event that is different than the default, tap Alert; if you want to use the default alert, skip to step 39.

38. Tap when you want to see an alert for the event. You can choose a time relative to the time you need to start traveling or relative to the event's start time.

39. To set a second alert that is different than the default, tap Second Alert; to use the default, skip to step 41.

40. Tap when you want to see a second alert for the event. If you have included travel time in the event, the At or before start of travel time options are useful because they alert you relative to when your journey should begin.

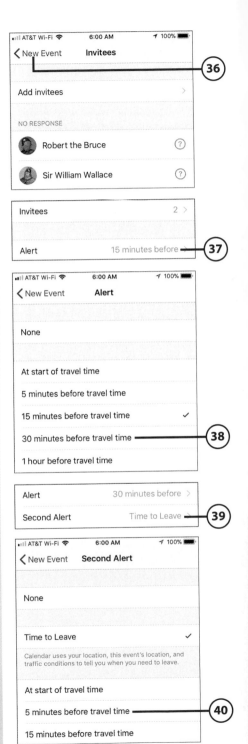

41. To indicate your availability during this event, tap Show As.

42. Tap the availability status you want to indicate during the event. If someone can access your availability through their calendar application, this is the status they see if they try to book an event at the same time.

43. Tap in the URL field to enter a URL associated with the event.

44. Type the URL.

45. Tap Done.

46. Tap in the Notes field.

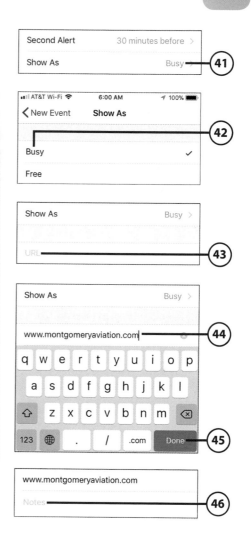

47. Type the information you want to associate with the event.

48. Tap Add. The event is added to the calendar you selected, and invitations are sent to its invitees. Alerts trigger according to the event's settings.

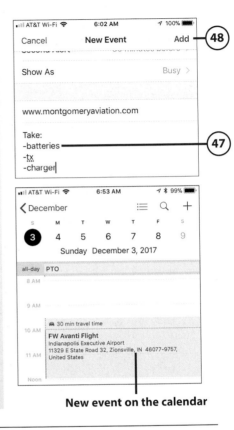

New event on the calendar

A Better Way to Create Events

Adding a lot of detail to an event in the Calendar app can be challenging. One effective and easy way to create events is to start with Siri. You can activate Siri and say something like "Create meeting with William Wallace in my office on November 15 at 10 a.m." Siri creates the event with as much detail as you provided (and might prompt you to provide additional information, such as which email address to use to send invitations). When you get to a computer or iPad, edit the event to add more information, such as website links. When your calendar is updated on the iPhone, via syncing, the additional detail for the event appears in the Calendar app, too. (See Chapter 11 for detailed information about using Siri.)

Using Quick Actions with the Calendar App (iPhone 6s/6s Plus and Later)

You can use the Quick Actions feature on an iPhone 6s/6s Plus or later models with the Calendar app as follows:

1. Press on the Calendar icon. The Quick Actions menu appears. At the top, you see the next event on your calendar.

2. To add a new event, choose Add Event and use the steps in the previous task to create the event.

3. Tap an event to view the event's details. You move to the event and can see all of its information.

Searching Calendars

You can search for events to locate specific ones quickly and easily. Here's how:

1. Tap the magnifying glass.

2. Type your search term. The events shown below the Search bar are those that contain your search term.

3. Swipe up or down the list to review the results.

4. Tap an event to see its detail.

5. Swipe up or down the event's screen to review its information.

6. Tap Back to return to the results.

7. Continue reviewing the results until you get the information for which you were searching.

8. Tap Cancel to exit the search mode or the Clear icon (x) to clear the search but remain in search mode.

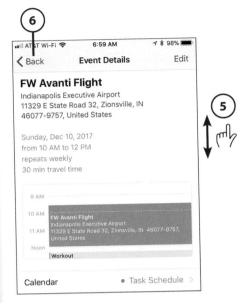

Working with Invitations

When someone invites you to an event, you receive an invitation notification in the Calendar app. You can accept these invitations, at which point the event is added to your calendar. You can tentatively accept, in which case the event is added to your calendar with a tentative status, or you can decline the event if you don't want it added to your calendar.

1. Tap the Calendar app icon when you see the badge on the app's icon indicating how many invitations you've received but not dealt with. (You may also receive notifications about new invitations according to your notification settings.)

2. Tap Inbox (the number in parentheses is the number of invitations you have received).

3. If you have multiple invitations, swipe up and down the screen to browse them.

4. If you see enough information about the event to be able to make a decision about it, tap Accept, Maybe, or Decline. The event is added to your calendar if you tap Accept or Maybe. If you tap Decline, it is not added to a calendar.

5. Tap an invitation to see its detail.

6. Swipe up and down the Event Details screen to see all its information.

7. To see how the proposed event relates to other events on the same date, look at the section of the calendar during which the event is being proposed. You see any events that might conflict with the one to which you have been invited.

8. To choose the calendar on which the event should be shown, tap Calendar, and on the resulting screen, tap the calendar on which you want to store the event. Tap the back icon located in the upper-left corner of the screen to return to the Event Details screen.

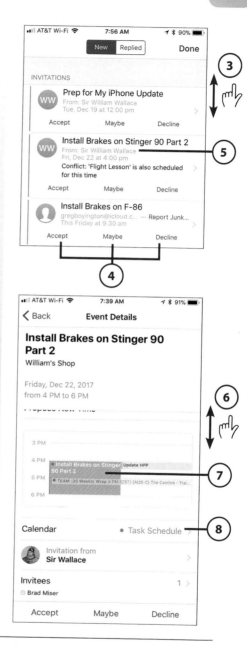

Invitation Notifications

You can use Notification settings to configure how the Calendar app informs you about invitations you receive. Refer to Chapter 4 for details. You can move to an invitation directly from its notification; for example, when a banner alert for an invitation appears on the screen, press it (3D Touch iPhones) or swipe it (non-3D Touch iPhones) to move to the invitation's details.

9. To view details about whom the invitation is from, tap the Invitation from bar. You move to the person's contact information (from Contacts if her information is stored there or as much as can be gleaned from the invitation if it isn't). Tap the back icon located in the upper-left corner of those screens to return to the Event Details screen.

10. Tap Invitees to see the status for each invitee to the event. You see a list of each person to whom the invitation was sent along with his or her current status. Tap Back to return to the Event Details screen.

11. If you want to change the event's alert, tap Alert and use the resulting Alert screen to choose an alert.

12. Review any attachments or notes for the meeting.

13. Use the Travel Time option to configure your travel time to the event. This works just like when you create an event (see "Adding Events to a Calendar" earlier in this chapter).

14. To set your availability during the event, tap Show As and then tap your status during the event; in most cases, you tap Busy so others who want to schedule time with you will see that you aren't available.

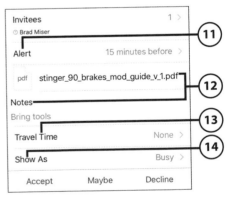

What You See Depends

Like when you create an event, the fields and options you see for an event to which you've been invited depend on the type of calendar the event is being sent from (for example, Exchange events may have different options than iCloud events do). Although the details for each type of calendar are slightly different, these steps help you deal with any invitations you receive.

15. Indicate what you want to do with the event by tapping Accept, Maybe, or Decline. If you tap Accept or Maybe, the event is added to the calendar with the status you indicated. If you tap Decline, the event is not placed on a calendar, and the recipient receives a notice that you have declined.

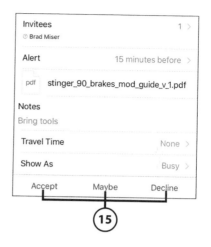

After you make a decision, you move back to the Inbox. Any events you have accepted, indicated maybe, or declined disappear from the list of events on the New tab. Events that you have accepted from another device, such as from a computer, are shown with an OK icon, which you can tap to remove the invitation from the list.

16. Use steps 5 through 15 to take action on other invitations you have received or tap OK to clear events you've dealt with on other devices.

17. To review the invitations to which you've responded, tap Replied.

18. Swipe up and down the screen to review all the invitations to which you have responded. The highlighted box indicates your status for each event, such as Accept for those you have accepted or Decline for those you declined (these are also marked with a strikeout through their titles).

Event you accepted

Event you declined

19. Tap an event to see its details.

20. To change your current status, tap one of the other status states. For example, to decline a meeting you previously accepted, tap Decline. The status changes immediately.

21. When you are done reviewing invitations, tap Done to close the Inbox. You move back to the calendar. If you accepted or indicated maybe for any events, they are added to your calendars.

Sharing Calendars

You can share your calendars with other people to enable them to both see and change your calendar, according to the permissions you provide. If you set the View & Edit permission, the person is able to both see and change the calendar. If you set someone's permission to View Only, she can see, but not change, the calendar.

1. Move to the Calendars screen. Calendars you are sharing are indicated by the Shared with *name*, text just under the calendar name, where *name* is the name of the person with whom you are sharing the calendar.

2. To see who is currently sharing a calendar, or to share a calendar, tap the Info icon (i) for the calendar to be shared. If the calendar is currently being shared, the SHARED WITH section appears on the Edit Calendar screen. This section contains the names of and permissions granted to the people who are sharing the calendar. The status of each person's acceptance is shown under his name (Accepted, Pending, or Declined).

Calendar you are sharing

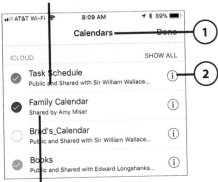

Calendar being shared with you

3. Tap Add Person to share a calendar with someone else (whether it is currently shared or not).

4. Type a person's name or email address, tap a name or email address that the app suggests based on what you are typing, or use the Contacts app to choose the people with whom you want to share the calendar (you can add multiple people at the same time).

5. Tap Add. You return to the Edit Calendar screen, and see the person you added on the SHARED WITH list. The person you invited receives an invitation to join the calendar you are sharing. If he accepts, the shared calendar becomes available in the calendar app he uses. As people make decisions about the calendar you are sharing, the status below each invitee's name changes to reflect the current status. You also see notifications when an invitee responds if you allow the app to provide notifications to you.

6. If you don't want a person to be able to change the calendar, tap View & Edit.

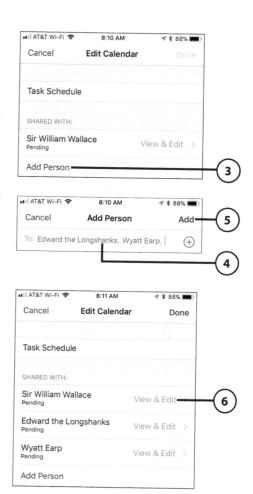

7. Slide the Allow Editing switch to off (white); the person will be able to view but not change the calendar.

8. Tap Edit Calendar.

9. When you're done sharing the calendar, tap Done.

10. When you are finished configuring calendar sharing, tap Done.

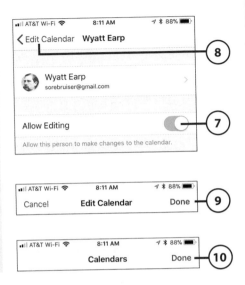

Managing Calendars, Events, and Invitations

Following are some more points about the Calendar app you might find helpful:

- You can also use the List view when you are viewing the calendar in month view. Tap the List icon (just to the left of the magnifying glass). The list opens at the bottom of the screen and shows the events on the day currently selected (the date is in a black circle unless the day selected is today, in which case the circle is red).

- You can see today's events at any time by opening the Widgets Center (move to a Home screen and swipe to the right) screen. In the UP NEXT box, you see information about the next event on your calendar. You can view the current day's calendar in the CALENDAR widget; tap an event in the widget to see its detail. (See Chapter 2 for more information about working with the Notification Center and widgets.)

- When an event's alarm goes off, an onscreen notification appears (according to the notification settings for the Calendar app) and the calendar event sound you've selected plays. When an alert notification appears, the event's title, location (if one is set), and time appear. If it is a temporary banner, you can ignore it and it moves off the screen after a few moments. If it is a persistent banner, you have to take action on it (such as viewing it) to clear it from the screen. To take action on a banner notification (persistent or temporary), you can press (3D Touch) or tap (non-3D Touch) the notification to view its details; you can tap the details to move into the Calendar app or close the notification by tapping the Close icon (x). You can swipe up from the bottom of a notification to manually close it without taking further action on it.

- If an event gets canceled after you accept it or indicated maybe, you receive a notification in your Inbox that displays a strikethrough through the event's title. Tap Delete to remove the event from your calendar.

- When you receive an invitation, the event is tentatively added to your calendar until you make a decision about it. The status changes as you accept, tentatively accept (Maybe), or decline invitations.

- Siri is useful for working with calendars, especially for creating events. See Chapter 11 for detailed information about using Siri.

- You can publish a calendar by making it public. When you do this, anyone who can access the shared calendar on the Web can view, but not change, the published calendar. To make a calendar public, move to its Edit Calendar screen and slide the Public Calendar switch to on (green). Tap Share Link. Then tap Mail to send the link via email, tap Message to send it via the Messages app, or tap Copy to copy the link so you can paste elsewhere. Tap AirDrop, Twitter, or Facebook to share the link in those ways. The link can be clicked to view your calendar or, if the person uses a compatible application, to subscribe to it so it appears in her calendar application.

>>>*Go Further*

OTHER USEFUL APPS FOR MANAGING YOUR TIME

Your iPhone includes a couple more apps that can help you manage your time. The Clock app enables you to easily see the current time in multiple locations, set alarms, set a consistent time for sleep every day, use a stopwatch, and count down time with a timer. The Reminders app enables you to create reminders for events, tasks you need to perform, or just about anything else. You can learn a bit more about these apps in Chapter 15.

Go here to set up Siri

Speak to Siri to send and hear messages, create and manage events, make calls, and much more

Dictate text input instead of typing

In this chapter, you learn about all the great things you can do with your iPhone by speaking to it. Topics include the following:

→ Setting up Siri

→ Understanding Siri's personality

→ Learning how to use Siri by example

→ Using dictation to speak text instead of typing

Working with Siri

Siri gives you the ability to talk to your iPhone to control it, get information, and to dictate text. Siri also works with lots of iPhone apps—this feature enables you to accomplish many tasks by speaking instead of using your fingers on the iPhone's screen. For example, you can hear, create, and send text messages; reply to emails; make phone and FaceTime calls; create and manage events and reminders; and much more. Using dictation, you can speak text into any supported app instead of typing. And, Siri can make suggestions as you perform tasks, such as searches, based on what you have done before.

In fact, Siri does so many things, it's impossible to list them all in a short chapter like this one; you should give Siri a try for the tasks you perform and to get the information you need, and, in many cases, Siri can handle what you want to do.

Think of Siri as your own personal, digital assistant to help you do what you want to do more quickly and easily (especially when you are working in handsfree mode).

You don't have to train Siri very much to work with your voice either; you can speak to it normally and Siri does a great job understanding what you say. Also, you don't have to use any specific kind of phrases when you have Siri do your bidding. Simply talk to Siri like you talk to people (well, you probably won't be ordering other people around like you do Siri, but you get the idea).

Your iPhone has to be connected to the Internet for Siri and dictation to work. That's because the words you speak are sent over the Internet, transcribed into text, and then sent back to your iPhone. If your iPhone isn't connected to the Internet, this can't happen, and if you try to use it, Siri reports that it can't complete its tasks.

Because your iPhone is likely to be connected to the Internet most of the time (via Wi-Fi or a cellular network when you have cellular data enabled), this really isn't much of a limitation—but it is one you need to be aware of.

Just start speaking to your iPhone and be prepared to be amazed by how well it listens! You'll find many examples in this chapter to get you going with specific tasks; from there, you can explore to learn what else Siri can do for you.

Setting Up Siri

There are several settings that affect how Siri works. In most cases, you can leave these settings in their default positions (including those you selected the first time you turned your iPhone on) and start using Siri right away (beginning with "Understanding Siri's Personality" later in this chapter).

If you decide you want to make changes to Siri's settings, you can use the information in the table that follows to understand the options available to you.

To access Siri's settings, tap Settings on the Home screen and then tap Siri & Search. For each of these settings, you see a description of what it does along with options (if applicable). (Siri must be enabled by setting the Siri switch to on [green] and then tapping Enable Siri before the rest of the settings become visible.)

The Settings App Explained
To get detailed information on using the Settings app, see "Working with the Settings App" in Chapter 2, "Using Your iPhone's Core Features."

Siri Settings

Setting	Description
Listen for "Hey Siri"	When this switch is on (green), you can activate Siri by saying, "Hey Siri" (along with the other options). The first time you turned your iPhone on, you were prompted to speak the five phrases Siri uses to recognize when you want its attention. When this switch is off (white), you can only activate Siri with the other options. When you enable it again, you might have to go through the recognition process again.
Press Home for Siri	This switch enables (green) or prevents (white) you from activating Siri by pressing and holding on the Touch ID/Home button. This setting doesn't apply to the iPhone X since it doesn't have a Touch ID/Home button.

Setting	Description
Allow Siri When Locked	When this switch is on (green), you can activate and use Siri without unlocking your iPhone. This can be convenient, but it also makes your phone vulnerable to misuse because someone else may be able to activate Siri (for example, to send a text message) without using a passcode or providing a recognized thumbprint. For some tasks, Siri requires the phone to be unlocked to complete them, but some can be done while the phone is still locked.
Language	Set the language you want Siri to use to speak to you.
Siri Voice	Choose the accent and gender of the voice that Siri uses to speak to you (the options you see depend on the language you have selected).
Voice Feedback	Choose when Siri provides verbal feedback as it works for you. When Always On is selected, Siri provides verbal feedback at all times. If you want to control Siri's voice feedback with the ring (Mute) switch, choose Control with Ring Switch. If you want voice feedback only when you are operating in handsfree mode, such as when you are using the iPhone's EarPods or a Bluetooth headset, tap Hands-free Only. Regardless of this setting, you always see Siri's feedback on the screen.
My Information	Choose your contact information in the Contacts app, which Siri uses to address you by name, take you to your home address, etc.
Suggestions in Search	When enabled (green), this switch allows Siri to make suggestions to you when you search. If you prefer not to have Siri make suggestions, set the switch to off (white).
Suggestions in Look Up	When enabled (green), this switch allows Siri to make suggestions when you use iOS's Look Up feature, that looks up information about a word or phrase you have selected on the screen. If you set this switch to off (white), Siri won't make suggestions when you use Look Up.
Apps	Toward the bottom of the Siri & Search screen, you see the list of apps installed on your iPhone. For each app, you can enable or disable Siri & Search Suggestions. When you enable this switch for an app, Siri can work within that app to make suggestions or learn from how you use the app. When you disable this switch, Siri is not able to work within the app for suggestions and search.

There are a couple of other settings that affect how you can speak to your iPhone:

- **Enable Dictation**—To access this setting, open the Settings app, tap General, and then tap Keyboard (you have to swipe up the screen to see it). At the bottom of the screen, you see the Enable Dictation switch. When this switch is on (green), you can tap the Microphone key on the keyboard to dictate text. When this switch is off (white), the Microphone key is hidden and you can't dictate text.

- **Cellular Data**—When enabled, this setting, located on the Cellular setting screen, allows your iPhone to access its cellular data network to connect to the Internet. This must be turned on for Siri to work when you aren't connected to the Internet via a Wi-Fi network.

iPhone X

The iPhone X doesn't have a Touch ID/Home button, so the Press Home for Siri setting doesn't apply. Refer to the online supplement *My iPhone X* by going to www.informit.com/myiphone11 for the details of using Siri on an iPhone X.

Understanding Siri's Personality

Siri works in two basic modes: when you ask it to do something or when it makes suggestions to you.

Telling Siri What to Do

When you ask Siri to do something, Siri's personality is pretty simple because it follows a consistent pattern when you use it, and it always prompts you for input and direction when needed.

If Siri is already active, tap the Listen icon at the bottom of the screen. Otherwise, activate Siri using one of the following methods:

- On all models except the iPhone X, pressing and holding the Touch ID/Home button until the Siri screen appears, you hear the Siri tone, and you feel the phone vibrate.

- On the iPhone X, pressing and holding the Side button for a couple of seconds until the Siri screen appears, you hear the Siri tone, and you feel the phone vibrate.

- Pressing and holding the center part of the buttons on the EarPods until the Siri screen appears and you hear the Siri tone.

- Saying "Hey Siri" (if you've enabled this setting).

This puts Siri in "listening" mode and the "What can I help you with?" text appears along with a line at the bottom of the screen that shows when Siri is hearing you. This screen indicates Siri is ready for your command; if you used the "Hey Siri" option to activate it, you don't see this text because Siri goes directly into listening mode. If you don't speak within a second or two, Siri starts prompting you for a request and presents examples of what you can do.

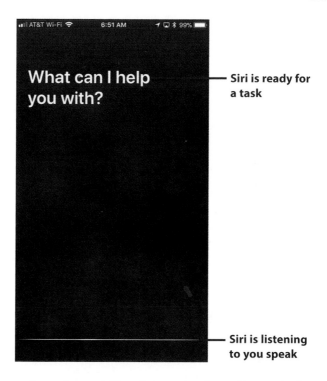

What can I help you with? — Siri is ready for a task

Siri is listening to you speak

Speak your command or ask a question. As you speak, the line at the bottom of the screen oscillates to show you that Siri is hearing your input, and Siri displays what it is hearing you say at the top of the screen. When you stop speaking, Siri goes into processing mode.

Show me my appointments today — What Siri heard you say

Tap to Edit

After Siri interprets what you've said, it provides two kinds of feedback to confirm what it heard: It displays what it heard on the screen and provides audible feedback to you (unless it's disabled through the settings you learned about earlier). Siri then tries to do what it thinks you've asked and shows you the outcome.

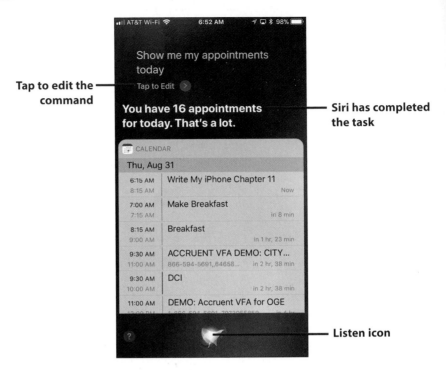

Tap to edit the command

Siri has completed the task

Listen icon

If it needs more input from you, you're prompted to provide it, and Siri moves into "listening" mode automatically. If Siri asks you to confirm what it is doing or to make a selection, do so. Siri completes the action and displays what it has done; it also audibly confirms the result (again unless audible feedback is disabled as described earlier). If you want Siri to do more for you, tap the Listen icon at the bottom of the screen and speak your command. If you want to work with the object Siri created for you in its associated app, tap the object Siri presents.

In some cases, you can edit the information you spoke to Siri to change it. For example, suppose you are sending a text message to Sir William Wallace but Siri didn't get the name quite right; you can tap Tap to Edit on the Siri screen and then change the name; this can sometimes be easier and faster than redoing the task from the beginning. You can also change the content of actions, such as what you are texting via Siri; if it isn't what you intended, you can tap the message to edit it before you send it.

Also, how Siri interacts with you can depend on how it was activated. For example, if you started the interaction using the verbal "Hey Siri" option, Siri assumes you want to interact verbally and might respond with other options than you would see or hear when you activate Siri manually. When you ask Siri to show you your appointments for the day in this mode, you see the summary, but then Siri asks if you want to hear the details; if you say yes, Siri reads each event to you. When you activate Siri by using the Touch ID/Home button with the same request, Siri stops after showing you the summary.

When you're done with Siri, press the Touch ID/Home button (all models except the iPhone X) to move back to the Home screen or to the app you were using. When you've finished with Siri on an iPhone X, swipe up from the bottom of the screen to move back to your previous location.

Siri uses this pattern for all the tasks it does, but often Siri needs to get more information from you, such as when there are multiple contacts that match the command you've given. Siri prompts you for what it needs to complete the work. Generally, the more specific you make your initial command, the fewer steps you have to work through to complete it. For example, if you say "Meet Will at the park," Siri might require several prompts to get you to tell it who Will is and what time you want to meet him at the park. If you say "Meet William Wallace at the park on 10/17 at 10 a.m.," Siri can likely complete the task in one step.

The best way to learn how and when Siri can help you is to try it—a lot. You find a number of examples in the rest of this chapter to get started.

Following are some other Siri tidbits:

- If Siri doesn't automatically quit "listening" mode after you've finished speaking, tap the oscillating line. This stops "listening" mode and Siri starts processing your request. You need to do this more often when you are in a noisy environment because Siri might not be able to accurately discern the sound of you speaking versus the ambient background noise.

- If you are having trouble with Siri understanding commands, speak a bit more slowly and make sure you firmly enunciate and end your words. If you tend to have a very short pause between words, Siri might run them all together, making them into something that doesn't make sense or that you didn't intend.

- However, you can't pause too long between words or sentences because Siri interprets pauses of a certain length to mean that you are done speaking, and it goes into processing mode. Practicing with Siri helps you develop a good balance between speed and clarity.

- If Siri doesn't understand what you want, or if you ask it a general question, it often performs a web search for you. Siri takes what it thinks you are looking for and does a search. You then see the results page for the search Siri performed, and you might have to manually open and read the results by tapping the listing you want to see. It opens in the Safari app. In some cases, Siri reads the results to you.

- When Siri presents information to you on the screen, you can often tap that information to move into the app with which it is associated. For example, when you tap an event that Siri has created, you move into the Calendar app, where you can add more detail using that app's tools, such as inviting people to an event, changing the calendar it's associated with, and so on.

- When Siri needs direction from you, it presents your options on the screen, including Yes, Cancel, Confirm, or lists of names. You can speak these items or tap them to select them.

- Siri is very useful for some tasks, such as creating reminders, responding to text messages, getting directions, and so on, but not so useful for others, such as inputting search criteria, because it can take longer to use Siri than to type your input.

- Siri is not so good at editing text you speak. You have to manually edit what Siri hears you say by tapping Tap to Edit and then using the keyboard to change what Siri heard or by selecting an option that Siri recommends. When you've finished making changes, tap Done. If you changed a command, Siri replaces the prior command with the edited version. If you changed content, Siri updates the content. After you've made changes, you can continue with the task.

- Siri might ask you to help it pronounce some terms, such as names. When this happens, Siri asks you to teach it to pronounce the phrase. If you agree, Siri presents a list of possible pronunciations, which you can preview. Tap the Select icon for the option you want Siri to use.

- To use Siri effectively, you should experiment with it by trying to say different commands or similar commands in different ways. For example, when sending email, you can include more information in your initial command to reduce the number of steps because Siri doesn't have to ask you for more information. Saying "Send an email to Wyatt Earp home about flying" requires fewer steps than saying "Send email" because you've given Siri more of the information it needs to complete the task, and so it won't have to prompt you for who you want to send it to, which address you want to use, or what the subject of the email is.

- When Siri can't complete a task that it thinks it should be able to do, it usually responds with the "I can't connect to the network right now," or "Sorry, I don't know what you mean." This indicates that your iPhone isn't connected to the Internet, the Siri server is not responding, or Siri just isn't able to complete the command for some other reason. If your iPhone is connected to the Internet, try the command again or try rephrasing the command.

- When Siri can't complete a task that it knows it can't do, it responds by telling you so. Occasionally, you can get Siri to complete the task by rephrasing it, but typically you have to use an app directly to get it done.

- If you have a passcode set to protect your iPhone's data (which you should), Siri might not be able to complete some tasks because the phone is locked. If that happens, Siri prompts you to unlock your phone, (which you can do by touching the Touch ID/Home button, using Face ID, or entering your passcode) and continue with what you were doing.

- Siri is really good at retrieving all sorts of information for you. This can include schedules, weather, directions, unit conversions, and so on. When you need something, try Siri first, as trying it is really the best way to learn how Siri can work for you.

- Siri sees all and knows all (well, not really, but it sometimes seems that way). If you want to be enlightened, try asking Siri questions, such as these:

  What is the best phone?
  Will you marry me?
  What is the meaning of life?
  Tell me a joke.

  Some of the answers are pretty funny, and you don't always get the same ones so Siri can keep amusing you. I've heard it even has responses if you curse at it, though I haven't tried that particular option.

Working with Siri Suggestions

When you enable the Suggestions in Search, Suggestions in Look Up settings, and the Search & Siri Suggestions setting for individual apps, Siri becomes pro-active and provides information or suggestions for you based on what you are doing and what you have done in the past. Over time, Siri "learns" more about you and tailors these suggestions to better match what you typically do. For example, when you create a text message and start to input a name, Siri can suggest potential recipients based on prior texts you've sent. Similarly, when you perform a search, Siri can tailor the search based on your history.

Because Siri works proactively in this mode, you don't do anything to cause Siri to take action. It works in the background for you and presents information or options at the appropriate times.

Learning How to Use Siri by Example

As mentioned earlier in this chapter, the best way to learn about Siri is to use it. Following are a number of tasks for which Siri is really helpful. Try these to get some experience with Siri and then explore on your own to make Siri work at its best for you.

Using Siri to Make Voice Calls

You can use Siri to make calls by speaking. This is especially useful when you are using your iPhone in handsfree mode.

1. Activate Siri (such as by pressing and holding the Touch ID/Home button [on all models except the iPhone X] or the Side button [iPhone X]).

Speeding Up Siri

You can combine these steps by saying "Hey Siri, call Pappy Boyington iPhone." This is an example where providing Siri with more information when you speak gets the task done more quickly.

2. Say "Call *name*," where *name* is the person you want to call. Siri identifies the contact you named. If the contact has only one number, Siri places the call and you move into the Phone app. If the person has multiple numbers, Siri lists the numbers available and asks you which number to use.

3. Speak the label for the number you want to call, or tap it. Siri dials the number for you and you move into the Phone app as if you had dialed the number yourself.

Siri Is Pretty Sharp

Siri can work with all kinds of variations on what you say. For example, if a contact has a nickname configured for him, you can use the nickname or the first name. If you want to call Gregory "Pappy" Boyington, you can say "Call Pappy Boyington" or "Call Gregory Boyington." If you say "Call Pappy" and there is only one contact with that nickname, Siri calls that contact. If more than one contact has "Pappy" as part of their contact information, Siri presents a list of contacts and prompts you to select one.

Placing FaceTime Calls

You can also use Siri to make FaceTime calls by saying "FaceTime *name*."

Siri has found multiple numbers for Gregory "Pappy" Boyington

Composing New Email with Siri

To create email with Siri, do the following:

1. Say "Hey Siri, send email to *name*," where *name* is the person you want to email. Siri creates a new email addressed to the name you spoke. (If the recipient has more than one email address, Siri prompts you to choose the address you want to use.) Next, Siri asks you for the subject of the email.

More Than One Recipient?

To send an email to more than one recipient, say "and" between each name as in, "Send email to William Wallace and Edward Longshanks." Siri adds each address before and after the "and."

---

2. Speak the subject of the email. Siri inserts the subject, and then prompts you for the body of the message.

3. Speak the body of the email. As you speak, you can include punctuation; for example, to end a sentence, say the word "period" or to end a question, say the words "question mark." When Siri completes the email, it displays the message on the screen and prompts you to send it.

4. Review the message.

5. Change the message by tapping Tap to Edit.

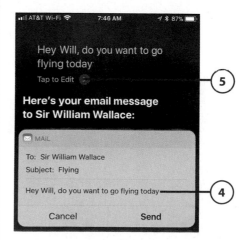

6. Use the keyboard to change the body of the email.

7. Tap Done. Siri updates the content based on your changes and presents the edited content to you; it again prompts you to send the message.

8. Say "send" to send the email or "cancel" to delete it. If you say "send," Siri sends the message, confirms it will be sent, and plays the sent mail sound when it is.

What Am I Editing?

When you tap Tap to Edit, you edit the last thing you spoke to Siri. If this was a command, you edit the command. If it was content, such as a text message, you edit the content. You can edit only the most recent thing you spoke.

Replying to Emails with Siri

You can also use Siri to speak replies to emails you've read. Here's how:

1. Open the message to which you want to reply.

2. Say "Hey Siri, reply to this email."
Siri prompts you for what you
want your reply to say.

3. Complete and send the reply; this
works just like when you create a
new message.

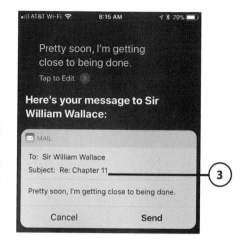

>>>*Go Further*

DOING MORE IN EMAIL WITH SIRI

Following are some other ways to use Siri for email:

- If you tell Siri to "Read email," Siri tells you how many emails are in your Inboxes
and starts reading the time and date of the most recent email message followed by the subject and sender of the message. Siri then does the same for
the next email until it has read a number of them. When it gets to the last message it reads, it prompts you to ask if you want to hear the entire list. On the
screen, Siri lists the emails; you can tap an email message to read it yourself.

- Siri can read the content of email messages to you when you speak commands
that tell it which email you want it to read, such as "Read most recent email," or
"Read last email from William Wallace." Siri reads the entire message to you.

- To edit an email Siri created, say "Change." Siri prompts you to change the
subject, change the message, cancel it, or send it. If you choose one of the
change options, you can replace the subject or the body of the message. To
change just some of the subject or body or to change the recipients, tap the
message and edit it in the Mail app.

- You can start a new and completely blank email by saying "New email." Siri
prompts you for the recipients, subject, and body.

- You can retrieve your email at any time by activating Siri and saying "Check
email." Siri checks for new email and then announces how many emails you
have received since the oldest message in your Inboxes was received. If you
don't have any new email messages, Siri announces how many emails you
have previously received and that remain in your Inbox.

- If you just want to know about new email messages, say "Check new email" instead. Siri reports back on new email you have received, but doesn't provide any information on email messages you've previously read.

- You can determine if you have emails from a specific person by asking something like, "Any email from William Wallace?" Siri's reply includes the number of emails in your Inboxes from William and displays them on the screen. Tap an email to read it.

- You can forward an email you are reading by saying "Forward this email" and then following Siri's lead to complete the process.

Having Messages Read to You

The Messages app is among the best to use with Siri because you can speak the most common tasks you normally do with messages. Especially useful is Siri's ability to read new messages to you. When you receive new text messages, do the following to have Siri read them to you:

1. When you receive a text notification, activate Siri.

2. Speak the command "Read text messages." (You can combine steps 1 and 2 by saying, "Hey Siri, read text messages.") Siri reads all the new text messages you've received, announcing the sender before reading each message. You have the option to reply (covered in the next task) or have Siri read the message again.

Siri is reading a text message

Siri reads each new message in turn until it has read all of them and then announces, "That's it" to let you know it has read all of them.

Siri only reads new text messages to you when you aren't on the Messages screen. If you've already read all your messages and you aren't in the Messages app, when you speak the command "Read text messages," Siri tells you that you have no new messages.

Reading Old Messages

To read an old message, move back to the conversation containing the message you want to hear. Activate Siri and say the command "Read text message." Siri reads the most recent text message to you.

Replying to Messages with Siri

You can also use Siri to speak replies to messages you've received. Here's how:

1. Listen to a message.

2. At the prompt asking if you want to reply, say "Yes." Siri prepares a reply to the message.

3. Speak your reply. Siri displays your reply.

4. Change the message before you send it by tapping Tap to Edit.

5. Use the keyboard to edit the message, or if you want to use Siri suggestions, skip to step 7.

6. Tap Done and skip to step 9.

7. Review Siri's suggestions for the message.

8. Tap a suggested message to use it.

9. At the prompt, say "Send" to send the message, "Cancel" to delete it, or "Change" to replace it. If you tell Siri that you want to send the message, Siri sends it and then confirms that it was sent.

Sending New Messages with Siri

To send a new message to someone, do the following:

1. Say "Hey Siri, send text message to *name*," where *name* is the person you want to text. Siri confirms your command and prepares to hear your text message.

2. Speak your message. Siri listens and then prepares your message.

3. If you want to send the message, say "Send." Siri sends the message.

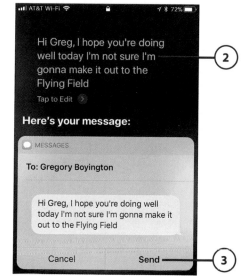

>>>Go Further

DOING MORE MESSAGING WITH SIRI

Following are some other ways to use Siri with messaging:

- If you say "Change" after you have created a new message, Siri prompts you to replace the message with a different one. If you say "Review" after creating a new message, Siri reads your message back to you. If you say "Cancel," Siri stops the process and deletes the message.

- You can use the Tap to Edit feature for any text message you are sending to manually edit it using the keyboard or to replace your message with one that Siri suggests.
- To send a text message to more than one recipient, say "and" between each name, as in, "Send text to William Wallace and Edward Longshanks."
- You can speak punctuation, such as "period" or "question mark" to add it to your message.
- You can tap icons that Siri presents on the screen, such as Send or Cancel, to take those actions on the message you are working on.
- Messages you receive or send via Siri appear in the Messages app just like messages you receive or send by tapping and typing.
- You can dictate into a text message you start in the Messages app (you learn about dictating later in this chapter).

Using Siri to Create Events

Siri is useful for capturing meetings and other events you want to add to your calendars. To create an event by speaking, use the following steps:

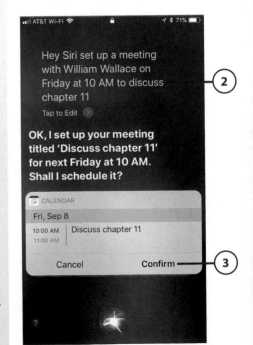

1. Activate Siri.

2. Speak the event you want to create. There are a number of variations in what you can say. Examples include "Set up a meeting with William Wallace on Friday at 10 a.m." or "Doctor appt on Thursday at 1 p.m." and so on. If you have any conflicts with the event you are setting up, Siri lets you know about them and asks you if you want to schedule the new event anyway.

3. Say "Confirm" if you don't have any conflicts or "Yes" if you do and you still want to have the appointment confirmed; you can also tap Confirm. Siri adds the event to your calendar. Say "Cancel" to cancel the event.

Invitees

If you include the name of someone for whom you have an email address, Siri automatically sends invitations. If you include a name that matches more than one contact, Siri prompts you to choose the contact you want to invite. If the name doesn't match a contact, Siri enters the name but doesn't send an invitation.

4. To add more information to an event Siri has created for you, tap it on the confirmation screen. You move into the Calendar app and can edit the event just like events you create within that app (see Chapter 10, "Managing Calendars" for information about the Calendar app).

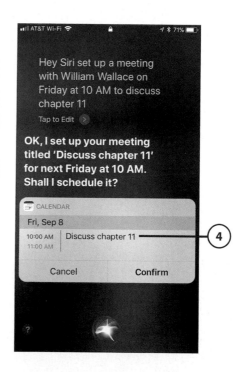

Using Siri to Create Reminders

Creating reminders can be another useful thing you do with Siri, assuming you find reminders useful, of course. Here's how:

1. Activate Siri.

2. Speak the reminder you want to create.

    Here are some examples: "Remind me to buy the A-10 at Motion RC," "Remind me to finish Chapter 10 at 10 AM on Saturday," or "Remind me to buy milk when I leave work."

    Siri provides a confirmation of what you asked. If you didn't mention a time or date when you want to be reminded, Siri prompts you to provide the details of when you want to be reminded.

3. Speak the date and time when you want to be reminded. If you included a date and time in your original reminder request, you skip this step. Unlike some of the other tasks, Siri creates the reminder without confirming it with you.

4. If you don't want to keep the reminder, activate Siri and say "Remove" or tap Remove.

5. To add detail to the reminder, tap it. You move into the Reminders app and can add more information to the reminder as you can when you create one manually.

>>>*Go Further*

GOING FURTHER WITH SIRI TO MANAGE TIME

Following are some other ways to use Siri with the Calendar, Reminders, and Clock apps:

- You can change events with Siri, too. For example, if you have a meeting at 3 p.m., you can move it by saying something like "Move my 3 p.m. meeting to Friday at 6 p.m."

- You can get information about your events with Siri by saying things such as

  Show me today's appointments.
  Do I have meetings on November 3?
  What time is my first appointment tomorrow?
  What are my appointments tomorrow?

  Siri tells you about the events and shows you what they are on the screen. You can tap any event to view it in the Calendar app.

- You can speak to your iPhone to set alarms. Tell Siri what you want and when you want the alarm to be set. For example, you can say something like "New alarm *alarmname* 6 a.m. tomorrow," where *alarmname* is the label of the alarm. Siri sets an alarm to go off at that time and gives it the label you speak. It displays the alarm on the screen along with a status icon so you can turn it off if you change your mind. You don't have to label alarms, and you can just say something like "Set alarm 6 a.m. tomorrow." However, a label can be useful to issue other commands. For example, if an alarm has a name, you can turn it off by saying "Turn off *alarmname*." Any alarms you create with Siri can be managed just like alarms you create directly in the Clock app.

- To set a countdown timer, tell Siri to "Set timer for *x* minutes," where *x* is a number of minutes (you can do the same to set a timer for seconds or hours, too). Siri starts a countdown for you and presents it on the screen. You can continue to use the iPhone however you want. When the timer ends, you see and hear an alert. You can also reset the time, pause it, and so on by speaking.

- You can get information about time by asking questions, such as "What time is it?" or "What is the date?" You can add location information to the time information, too, as in "What time is it in London, England?"

- Tapping any confirmation Siri displays takes you back into the related app. For example, if you tap a clock that results when you ask what time it is, you can tap that clock to move into the Clock app. If you ask about your schedule today, you can tap any of the events Siri presents to move into the Calendar app to work with them.

- When you use Siri to create events and reminders, they are created on your default calendar (events) or reminder list (reminders).

Using Siri to Get Information

Siri is a great way to get information about lots of different topics in many different areas. You can ask Siri for information about a subject, places in your area, unit conversion (such as inches to centimeters), and so on. Just try speaking what you want to learn to best get the information you need. Here's an example looking for Chinese restaurants in my area:

1. Activate Siri.

2. Say something like, "Show me Chinese restaurants in my area." (Or a faster way is to combine steps 1 and 2 by saying "Hey Siri, show me Chinese restaurants in my area.") Siri presents a list of results that match your query and even provides a summary of reviews at

If you like Chinese food (or just about anything else), Siri can help you find it

the top of the screen. (You must have Location Services enabled for this to work. Refer to Chapter 4, "Customizing How Your iPhone Works," for information about configuring Location Services.)

Siri prompts you to take action on what it found. For example, if you asked for restaurants, Siri tells you about the closest one and then asks if you want to try it. If you say yes, Siri offers to call it for you or gives you directions. You can tap other items on the list to get more information or directions.

Siri is also useful for getting information about topics. Siri responds by conducting a web search and showing you the result. For example, suppose you want to learn about the F-15 fighter plane. Activate Siri and say, "Tell me about the F-15 Eagle." Siri responds with information about your topic. You can have Siri read the information by activating Siri and saying "Read." Siri reads the results (this doesn't always work; it works best when the results are presented via Wikipedia or something similar).

Want to learn about something? Just ask Siri

 AT&T Wi-Fi 🛜   7:23 AM   ↑ ✳ 66% 🔋

Hey Siri tell me about the F-15 Eagle
Tap to Edit ❯

🔲 KNOWLEDGE

McDonnell Douglas F-15 Eagle
Air superiority fighter family

The McDonnell Douglas F-15 Eagle is an American twin-engine, all-weather tactical fighter aircraft designed by McDonnell Douglas (now Boeing) to gain and maintain air supremacy in aerial combat. Following reviews of proposals, the United States Air Force selected McDonnell Douglas' design in 1967 to meet the service's need for a dedicated air superiority fighter. The Eagle first flew in July 1972, and entered service in 1976.

See More on Wikipedia

Using Siri to Play Music

You can also play music by telling Siri
which music you want to hear.

1. Activate Siri.

2. Tell Siri the music you want to
   hear. There are a number of variations in what you can say. Examples include:

   Play album Time of My Life.
   Play song "Gone" by Switchfoot.
   Play playlist Jon McLaughlin.

   Siri provides a confirmation of
   what you asked and begins playing the music.

3. Tap Open Music to move into the
   Music app to control the music
   with your fingers.

>>>Go Further

MORE SPOKEN COMMANDS FOR MUSIC

There are a number of commands you can speak to find, play, and control music
(and other audio). "Play *artist*" plays music by the artist you speak. "Play *album*"
plays the album you name. In both cases, if the name includes the word "the,"
you need to include "the" when you speak the command. "Shuffle" plays a random song. "Play more like this" uses the Genius to find songs similar to the one
playing and plays them. "Previous track" or "next track" does exactly what they
sound like they do. To hear the name of the artist for the song currently playing,
say "Who sings this song?" You can shuffle music in an album or playlist by saying "Shuffle playlist *playlistname*." You can stop the music, pause it, or play it by
speaking those commands.

Using Siri to Get Directions

With Siri, it's easy to get directions—you don't even have to stop at a gas station to ask.

1. Activate Siri.

2. Speak something like "Give me directions to the airport." If you want directions starting from someplace other than your current location, include that in the request, such as "Get directions from the Eagle Creek Airpark to the Indianapolis International Airport."

3. If Siri needs you to confirm one or more of the locations, tap the correct one.

4. Tap Directions. Siri uses the Maps app to generate directions.

5. Tap Go to start turn-by-turn directions.

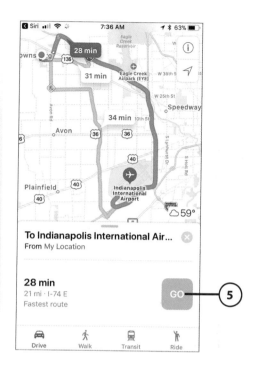

Using Siri to Open Apps

As you accumulate apps on your iPhone, it can take several taps and swipes to get to a specific app, such as one that is stored in a folder that isn't on the page of the Home screen you are viewing. With Siri, you can open any app on your phone with a simple command.

1. Say "Hey Siri, open *appname*," where *appname* is the name of the app you want to open.

2. If your phone needs to be unlocked to open the app, Siri prompts you to unlock it (such as by touching the Touch ID/Home button or using Face ID). Siri then opens the app for you, and you move to the last screen in that app you were using.

It's Not All Good

When Siri Misunderstands

Voice commands to Siri work very well, but they aren't perfect. Make sure you confirm your commands by listening to the feedback Siri provides when it repeats them or reviewing the feedback Siri provides on the screen. Sometimes, a spoken command can have unexpected results, which can include making a phone call to someone in the Contacts app. If you don't catch such a mistake before the call is started, you might be surprised to hear someone answering your call instead of hearing music you intended to play. You can put Siri in listening mode by tapping the Listen icon, and then saying "no" or "stop" to stop Siri should a verbal command go awry.

Using Siri to Translate

Siri can translate words and phrases from the language you are using into other languages. In the initial release of this feature, Siri supports the translation of English into French, German, Italian, Mandarin, and Spanish. Over time, Apple will add more capability to this, so you should try this translating function to see how it can work for you. Here's an example of translating an English phrase into Italian:

The phrase Siri is translating

1. Say "Hey Siri, translate How do I get to the airport in Italian." Siri does the translation for you and speaks the translated phrase.

2. Tap the Play icon to have Siri speak the translation again.

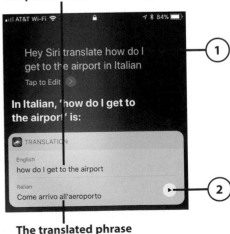

No Can Do

If Siri is unable to complete the translation you requested, it speaks what it can do. For example, it speaks a list of currently supported languages.

The translated phrase

Using Dictation to Speak Text Instead of Typing

You can use the iPhone's dictation capability to speak text into any app, such as Mail, Messages, and so on. In fact, any time you see the Microphone key on the keyboard, dictation is available to you. Here's how this works:

1. In the app you are using, put the cursor where you want the text you dictate to start. For example, if you are creating an email, tap in the body.

2. Tap the Microphone key on the virtual keyboard. The dictation pane opens at the bottom of the screen. The oscillating line indicates Siri is listening to you and you can begin speaking.

3. Speak the text you want to add. In addition to text, you can speak punctuation, such as saying "comma" when you want to insert a comma or "new paragraph" when you want to create a new paragraph. While you are speaking, you see the line that oscillates as you speak and the text you are speaking at the location of the cursor.

4. Tap the keyboard icon when you finish your dictation. The Dictation pane closes, and the keyboard reappears. The text you spoke is part of the message. From there, you can edit it just like text you've typed.

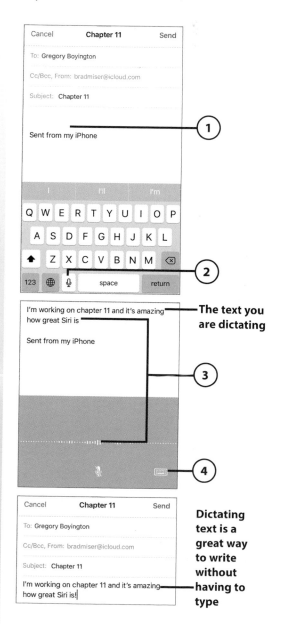

The text you are dictating

Dictating text is a great way to write without having to type

Tap to configure Safari

Tap to have the World Wide Web in the palm of your hand

In this chapter, you explore the amazing web browsing functionality your iPhone has to offer. Topics include the following:

→ Setting Safari preferences

→ Visiting websites

→ Viewing websites

→ Working with multiple websites at the same time

→ Searching the Web

→ Saving and organizing bookmarks

→ Using 3D Touch with Safari

→ Sharing web pages

→ Signing in to websites automatically

Surfing the Web

The Web has become an integral part of most of our lives. It is often the first step to search for information, make plans (such as travel arrangements), conduct financial transactions, shop, and so much more. Safari on the iPhone puts the entire Web in the palm of your hand. Safari is a full-featured web browser; anything you can do on a website in a browser on a computer can be done with Safari on your iPhone.

Setting Safari Preferences

Like most apps, Safari offers settings you can use to adjust the way it works. You can likely use Safari with its default settings just fine; when the time comes that you want to tweak how Safari works for you, use the following table as a reference for the available settings. To access these settings, tap the Settings icon on the Home screen, and then tap Safari.

Safari Settings

Settings Area	Location	Setting	Description
ALLOW SAFARI TO ACCESS	Siri & Search	Siri & Search Suggestions	Set this switch to on (green) to allow information from Safari to be used in searches, when you perform lookups, and in other places. It also allows Siri to learn from how you use Safari to make better suggestions over time. If you don't want Safari information to be used in this way, set the switch to off (white).
SEARCH	Search Engine	Search Engine	Enables you to choose your default search tool; the options are Google (default), Yahoo, Bing, or DuckDuckGo.
SEARCH	N/A	Search Engine Suggestions	When this switch is on (green), Safari asks your default search engine for suggestions related to what you type in the Address/Search bar. This makes search easier because you can type your search term in the bar instead of first moving to the search web page.
SEARCH	N/A	Safari Suggestions	When this switch is on (green), Safari makes suggestions related to what you type in the Address/Search bar. This makes search easier because you can type a term in which you are interested in the bar instead of first moving to the search web page.
SEARCH	Quick Website Search	Quick Website Search	When this switch is on (green), you can perform a search at a specific website by typing its name before your search term. For example, you can type "wiki william wallace" in the Address/Search bar and the first section of the results will be entries in the Wikipedia related to William Wallace; this saves you the steps of moving to the search engine results, and then tapping the articles you want to read because you can do this directly from the Search screen instead.
SEARCH	N/A	Preload Top Hit	When this switch is on (green), the sites you move to or find more frequently are loaded while you search, making accessing them faster.
GENERAL	Autofill	N/A	These settings enable you to automatically log in to websites and to quickly complete forms on the Web by automatically filling in key information for you. Set the Use Contact Info switch to on (green), tap My Info, and tap your contact information in the Contacts app. When you use the Auto-Fill function, this is the information that is entered for you.

Settings Area	Location	Setting	Description
GENERAL	Autofill	N/A	You can determine what data is saved on your iPhone by setting the following switches on (green) or off (white): Names and Passwords or Credit Cards. If you want to be able to automatically sign into websites, the Names and Passwords switch must be on. The Credit Cards switch enables you to store credit cards on your iPhone so you can more easily enter their information to make purchases.
GENERAL	Autofill	Autofill	Tap Saved Credit Cards to view or change existing credit card information or to add new credit cards to Safari.
GENERAL	N/A	Frequently Visited Sites	When this switch is on (green) and you move into the Address/Search bar, Safari shows a section of sites that you visit frequently, making them easier to return to.
GENERAL	Favorites	Favorites	Use this option to choose the folder of bookmarks for sites that you use most frequently. The bookmarks in the folder you select appear at the top of the screen when you move into the Address/Search bar, making them fast and easy to use.
GENERAL	Open Links	Open Links	This tells Safari the option you want to see when you tap and hold a link on a current web page to open a new web page. The In New Tab option causes Safari to open and immediately take you to a new tab displaying the web page with which a link is associated. The In Background option causes Safari to open pages in the background for links you tap so you can view them later.
GENERAL	N/A	Block Pop-ups	Some websites won't work properly with pop-ups blocked, so you can use this setting to temporarily enable pop-ups by sliding the switch to off (white). When the Block Pop-ups switch is on (green), pop-ups are blocked.
PRIVACY & SECURITY	N/A	Prevent Cross-Site Tracking	When enabled (green), this feature attempts to limit tracking of your browsing history by websites that you visit. Its purpose is to limit the exposure of your private information by websites that try to track you as you visit other sites to collect information about you.
PRIVACY & SECURITY	N/A	Block All Cookies	When enabled (green), Safari doesn't allow cookies to be stored; cookies are bits of information that websites store about you to use to tailor your experience at that website. If you block all cookies, some sites might not work correctly. Safari only accepts cookies for websites you visit, so, in general, you should leave this feature disabled (white) so websites you visit work correctly.

Settings Area	Location	Setting	Description
PRIVACY & SECURITY	N/A	Ask Websites Not To Track Me	Some websites track your activity in order to tailor the site based on your browsing history. When enabled (green), Safari includes a request not to track you to each website you visit. If the website honors that request, you won't be tracked. However, it's up to each website to implement this.
PRIVACY & SECURITY	N/A	Fraudulent Website Warning	If you don't want Safari to warn you when you visit websites that appear to be fraudulent, set the Fraudulent Website Warning switch to off (white). You should leave this switch enabled (green).
PRIVACY & SECURITY	N/A	Camera & Microphone Access	When this switch is on (green) Safari can access the iPhone's microphone and camera to enable you to present video and transmit and receive audio communication via a website.
PRIVACY & SECURITY	N/A	Check for Apple Pay	When you visit websites that support Apple Pay with this switch enabled (green), you can use your Apple Pay account to make payments for goods or services. (Refer to Chapter 15, "Working with Other Useful iPhone Apps and Features," for information about Apple Pay.)
PRIVACY & SECURITY	N/A	Clear History and Website Data	When you tap this command and confirm it by tapping Clear History and Data at the prompt, Safari removes the websites you have visited from your history list. The list starts over, so the next site you visit is added to your history list again—unless you have enabled private browsing. It also removes all cookies and other website data that have been stored on your iPhone.
READING LIST	N/A	Automatically Save Offline	The Reading List enables you to store web pages on your iPhone for offline reading. If you want to allow pages to be saved to your iPhone automatically, slide this switch to the on (green) position.
Advanced	Website Data	Website Data	Website Data displays the amount of data associated with websites you have visited; swipe up on the screen and tap Remove All Website Data to clear this data.
Advanced	N/A	JavaScript	Set this switch to off (white) to disable JavaScript functionality (however, some sites won't work properly without JavaScript).
Advanced	N/A	Web Inspector	This switch controls a feature that is used by website developers to see how their sites work on an iPhone.

Where, Oh Where Are My Passwords?

When you enable Safari to save your names and passwords, they are stored under the App & Website Passwords settings, which you can access by tapping Accounts & Passwords on the main Settings screen. When you tap App & Website Passwords, you see a list of the usernames and passwords stored on your iPhone sorted by the URL of the website with which they are associated. You can tap a URL to see the username and password for that site and a list of all websites using that information. To remove a URL and its associated username and password from the list, swipe to the left on it and tap Delete. The next time you move to that site, you will need to manually enter your username and password again.

Visiting Websites

If you've used a web browser on a computer before, using Safari on an iPhone is a familiar experience. If you've not used a web browser before, don't worry because using Safari on an iPhone is simple and intuitive.

Syncing Bookmarks

Using iCloud, you can synchronize your Internet Explorer favorites or Safari bookmarks on a Windows PC—or Safari bookmarks on a Mac —to your iPhone so you have the same set of bookmarks available on your phone that you do on your computer and other devices, and vice versa (refer to Chapter 3, "Setting Up and Using an Apple ID, iCloud, and Other Online Accounts"). You should enable iCloud's Safari switch before you start browsing on your iPhone, so you avoid typing URLs or re-creating bookmarks. When you enable Safari syncing via iCloud, you can also view tabs open in Safari on other devices, such as a Mac or an iPad.

Using Bookmarks to Move to Websites

Using bookmarks you've synced via iCloud or created on your iPhone (you learn how later in this chapter) makes it easy to get to websites.

1. On the Home screen, tap Safari.

2. Tap the Bookmarks icon.

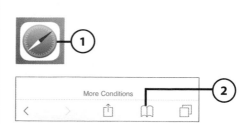

3. Tap the Bookmarks tab (the open book) if it isn't selected already. (If you don't see this tab, tap the back icon, which is labeled with the name of the folder from which you moved to the current screen, in the upper-left corner of the screen until you do.)

4. Swipe up or down the list of bookmarks to browse the bookmarks and other folders of bookmarks available to you.

5. To move to a bookmark, skip to step 10; to open a folder of bookmarks, tap it.

Back to the Bookmarks

The most recent Bookmarks screen is retained when you move away from Bookmarks and then come back. Each time you open your Bookmarks, you see the same screen you did when you left it.

6. Swipe up or down the folder's screen to browse the folders and bookmarks it contains.

7. Tap a folder to see the bookmarks it contains.

Change Your Mind?

If you decide not to visit a bookmark, tap Done. You return to the website you were previously viewing.

8. To return to a previous screen, tap the back icon in the upper-left corner of the screen, which is labeled with the name of the folder you previously visited (the parent folder); this disappears when you are at the top-level Bookmarks screen.

Your Favorites bookmark folder

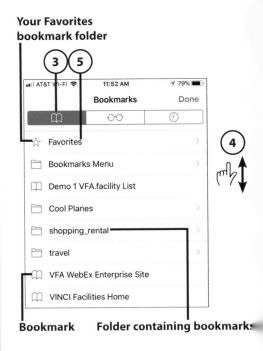

Bookmark   Folder containing bookmarks

The location Bookmar you are currently browsing

9. Repeat steps 5–8 until you see a bookmark you want to visit.

10. Tap the bookmark you want to visit. Safari moves to that website.

11. Use the information in the section "Viewing Websites" later in this chapter to get information on viewing the web page.

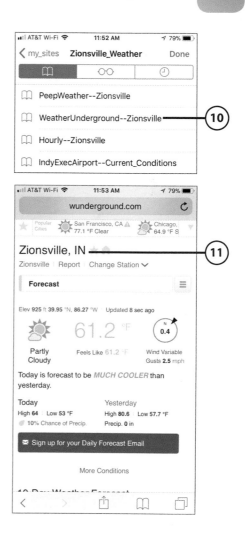

Playing Favorites

You might see two Favorites folders on the Bookmarks screen. The folder marked with a star is the folder you designated, using the Safari settings described previously in this chapter, as the place to store Favorites on your iPhone. If you use Safari on a computer, you can also configure bookmarks and folders of bookmarks on its Bookmarks bar. When these bookmarks are synced from your computer to the iPhone, they might be stored in a folder of bookmarks also called Favorites and shown with the standard folder icon. If you set this synced folder in your iPhone's Safari settings to also be its Favorites folder, you won't have to deal with this potentially confusing situation of having two Favorites folders.

iPhone Web Pages

Some websites have been specially formatted for mobile devices. These typically have less complex information on each page, so they load faster. When you move to a site like this, you might be redirected to the mobile version automatically, or you might be prompted to choose which version of the site you want to visit. On the mobile version, there is typically a link that takes you to the "regular" version, too. (It's sometimes called the Desktop, Full, or Classic version.) Sometimes the version formatted for handheld devices offers less information or fewer tools than the regular version. Because Safari is a full-featured browser, you can use either version.

Using Your Favorites to Move to Websites

Using the Safari settings described earlier, you can designate a folder of bookmarks as your Favorites. You can get to the folders and bookmarks in your Favorites folder more quickly and easily than navigating to it as described in the previous section. Here's how to use your Favorites:

1. On the Home screen, tap Safari. (If you are in Safari and have the Bookmarks screen open, tap Done to close it.)

2. Tap in the Address/Search bar (if you don't see the Address/Search bar, tap at the top of the screen to show it). Just below the Address/Search bar are your Favorites (bookmarks and folders of bookmarks). The keyboard opens at the bottom of the screen.

3. Swipe up and down on your Favorites. The keyboard closes to give you more room to browse.

4. To move to a bookmark, tap it and skip to step 8.

5. Tap a folder to move into it.

6. Continue browsing your Favorites until you find the bookmark you want to use. Like using the Bookmarks screen, you can tap a folder to move into it, tap a bookmark to move to its website, or tap the back icon to move to the previous screen.

7. Tap the bookmark for the site you want to visit.

Folder of bookmarks

Bookma...

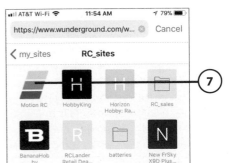

More Commands

At the top of the Favorites screen, you might see two more commands. Tap Add to Favorites to add a bookmark to the current site to your Favorites folder. Tap Request Desktop Site if you are currently viewing the mobile version of a site and want to see the "full" version; you move to that version after you tap the command.

8. Use the information in the section "Viewing Websites" later in this chapter to view the web page.

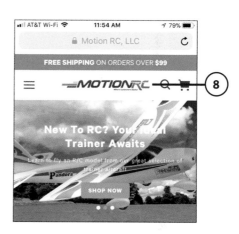

Typing URLs to Move to Websites

A Uniform Resource Locator (URL) is the Internet address of a web page. URLs can be relatively simple, such as www.apple.com, or they can be quite long and convoluted. The good news is that by using bookmarks, you can save a URL in Safari so you can get back to it using its bookmark (as you learned in the previous two tasks) and thus avoid typing URLs more than once. To use a URL to move to a website, do the following:

1. On the Home screen, tap Safari. (If you are in Safari and have the Bookmarks screen open, tap Done to close it.)

2. Tap in the Address/Search bar (if you don't see the Address/Search bar, tap at the top of the screen). The URL of the current page becomes highlighted, or if you haven't visited a page, the Address/Search bar is empty. Just below the Address/Search bar, your Favorites are displayed. The keyboard appears at the bottom of the screen.

3. If an address appears in the Address/Search bar, tap the clear icon (x) to remove it.

4. Type the URL you want to visit. If it starts with www (which almost all URLs do), you don't have to type "www." As you type, Safari attempts to match what you are typing to a site you have visited previously and completes the URL for you if it can. Just below the Address/Search bar, Safari presents a list of sites that might be what you are looking for, organized into groups, such as Suggested Websites.

5. If one of the sites shown is the one you want to visit, tap it. You move to that web page; skip to step 8.

6. If Safari doesn't find a match, continue typing until you enter the entire URL.

7. Tap Go. You move to the web page.

8. Use the information in the section "Viewing Websites" to view the web page.

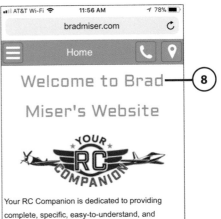

Shortcut for Typing URLs

URLs include a top-level domain code that represents the type of site (theoretically anyway) that URL leads to. Common examples are .com (commercial sites) and .edu (educational sites). To quickly enter a URL's code, tap and hold the period key to see a menu from which you can select other options, such as .net or .edu. Select the code you want on the keyboard, and it is entered in the Address/Search bar.

Using Your Browsing History to Move to Websites

As you move about the Web, Safari tracks the sites you visit and builds a history list (unless you enabled the Do Not Track option, in which case this doesn't happen and you can't use History to return to previous sites). You can use your browsing history list to return to sites you've visited.

1. Tap the Bookmarks icon.

2. Tap the History tab.

3. Swipe up and down the page to browse all the sites you've visited. The more recent sites appear at the top of the screen; the further you move down the screen, the further back in time you go. Earlier sites are collected in folders for various times, such as This Morning, or Monday Afternoon.

4. Tap the site you want to visit. The site opens and you can use the information in the section "Viewing Websites" to view the web page.

Erasing the Past

To clear your browsing history, tap the Clear icon at the bottom of the History screen. At the prompt, tap the timeframe that you want to clear; the options are The last hour, Today, Today and yesterday, or All time. Your browsing history for the period of time you selected is erased. (Don't you wish it was this easy to erase the past in real life?)

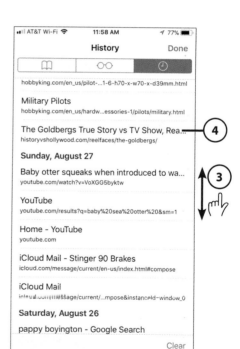

Viewing Websites

Even though your iPhone is a small device, you'll be amazed at how well it displays web pages designed for larger screens.

1. Use Safari to move to a web page as described in the previous tasks.

2. To browse around a web page, swipe your finger right or left, or up or down.

3. Zoom in manually by unpinching your fingers.

4. Zoom in automatically by tapping twice on the screen.

Where Did the URL Go?

When you first move to a URL, you see that URL in the Address/Search bar. After you work with a site, the Address/Search bar and the toolbar are hidden and the URL is replaced with the high-level domain name for the site (such as sitename.com, sitename.edu, and so on). To see the Address/Search bar and tool-bar again, tap the top or bottom of the screen. To see the full URL again, tap in the Address/Search bar.

Do More with Links

To see options for a link, tap and hold your finger down for a second or so. (If you are using an iPhone that supports 3D Touch, this can be a bit tricky. If you apply pressure, a Peek appears instead of the menu. To see the menu, place your finger on the screen and hold it there, but don't put any pressure on the screen.) A menu appears. Tap Open to open the page to replace the current page at which the link points (this is the same as tapping a link). Tap Open in Background to open the page in a new Safari window that opens in the background, or tap Open in New Tab to open the new page in the new tab. (The command that appears depends on the Open Links Safari setting that you learned about earlier in this chapter.) Tap Add to Reading List to add the page to your Reading List. If the link is an image, tap Save Image to save the image on your phone. Tap Copy to copy the link's URL so that you can paste it elsewhere, such as in an email message. Tap Share to open the Share menu that enables you to share the web page via email, a message, and so on. Tap Cancel to return to the current page and take no action.

5. Zoom out manually by pinching your fingers.

6. Zoom out on a column or a figure by tapping it twice.

7. Tap a link to move to the location to which it points. Links can come in many forms, including text (most text that is a link is in color and underlined) or graphics. The web page to which the link points opens and replaces the page currently being displayed.

8. To view the web page in landscape orientation, rotate the iPhone so that it is horizontal.

9. Scroll, zoom in, and zoom out on the page to read it, as described in steps 2–7.

10. Tap Refresh to refresh a page, which causes its content to be updated. (Note: While a page is loading, this is the stop icon [x]; tap it to stop the rest of the page from loading.)

11. To move to a previous page you've visited, tap the back icon (left-facing arrow). (If the arrow is grayed out, it means you are at the beginning of the set of pages you have visited.)

12. To move to a subsequent page, tap the forward icon (right-facing arrow). (If the arrow is grayed out, it means you are at the end of the set of pages you have visited.)

13. As you move around, the Address/Search bar at the top of the page and the toolbar at the bottom of the page are hidden automatically; to show them again, tap the top or bottom of the screen (on the iPhone 6/6s Plus or later models, tap the top of the screen when the phone is horizontal).

Different Phones, Different Look

The type of iPhone you are using to browse the Web affects how pages look and where controls are located. For example, when you use an iPhone 5s, you see black at the top and bottom of the screen whereas you see white there on an iPhone 7. Also, when you rotate an iPhone 5s, the tools are at the top and bottom of the screen, but on an iPhone 7, the controls are all at the top of the screen. Regardless of where the controls appear on the screen, they work in the same way.

Working with Multiple Websites at the Same Time

When you move to a web page by using a bookmark, typing a URL, or tapping a link on the current web page, the new web page replaces the current one. However, you can also open and work with multiple web pages at the same time so that a new web page doesn't replace the current one.

When you work with multiple web pages, each open page appears in its own tab. You can use the tab view to easily move to and manage your open web pages. You can also close open tabs, and you can even open web pages that are open on other devices on which your iCloud account has been configured and Safari syncing enabled.

There are two ways to open a new web page in a new tab. One is to touch and hold on a link on the current web page; you can use the resulting Open command to open the new page. There are two options for this approach; the one you use is determined by the Open Links preference set as described earlier in this chapter. The In Background option causes the new page to open and move to the background. This is most useful when you want to read the new page at a later time, such as when you are done with the current one. The In New Tab option causes the new page to open and move to the front so you see it instantl' while moving the current page and its tab to the background.

The second way to open a new web page in a new tab is by using the Tab Manager

These options are described in the following tasks.

Tapping Without Holding

When you tap, but don't hold down, a link on a web page, the web page to which the link points opens and replaces the current web page—no new tab is created. When you touch and hold down on a link, the behavior is determined by the setting you chose in the preferences as covered in a task earlier in this chapter ("Setting Safari Preferences"). To make things a bit more complicated, if your phone supports 3D Touch (iPhone 6s/6s Plus and later), don't apply pressure to the screen when you tap; if you do, a Peek appears instead (you learn about this in "Using 3D Touch with Safari").

Opening New Pages in the Background

If you enabled the In Background option for the Open Links preference, you can open new web pages by doing the following:

1. Touch and hold (but don't press) on the link you want to open in the background.

2. Tap Open in Background. The page to which the link points opens. The only result you see is the page associated with the link you touched "jumping" down to the Tab Manager icon in the lower-right corner of the screen.

3. Continue opening pages in the background; see "Using Tab View to Manage Open Web Pages" to learn how to use the tab view to move to pages that are open in the background.

Opening New Pages in a New Tab

If you enabled the In New Tab option for the Open Links preference, you can open new pages by doing the following:

1. Touch and hold on the link you want to open in the background.

2. Tap Open in New Tab. The tab view appears briefly, and a new tab opens and displays the page to which the link points. The web page from which you started moves into the background.

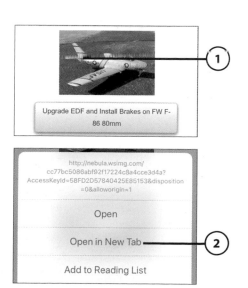

3. Continue opening pages; see "Using Tab View to Manage Open Web Pages" to learn how to use the tab view to manage your open pages.

Just Open It

If you tap the Open command on the menu in step 2 of the previous tasks, the new web page replaces the one you were viewing on the current tab. This is the same as tapping a link on the page rather than touching and holding (but not pressing) on it.

Using Tab View to Manage Open Web Pages

As you open new pages, whether in the background or not, new tabs are opened. Safari's tab view enables you to view and work with your open pages/tabs. Here's how:

1. Tap the tab view icon. Each open page appears on its own tab.

2. Swipe up or down on the open tabs to browse them.

3. Tap a tab/page to move into it. The page opens and fills the Safari window.

4. Work with the web page.

5. Tap the tab view icon.

Tabs Are Independent

Each tab is independent. So, when you are working with a tab and use the back/forward icons to move among its pages, you are just moving among the pages open under that tab. Pages open in other tabs are not affected.

6. Tap a close icon (x) to close a tab; alternatively swipe to the left on the tab you want to close.

7. To open a new tab, tap the Add icon (+) to create a new tab that shows your Favorites screen; navigate to a new page in that tab using the methods described in other tasks (tapping bookmarks or typing a URL).

8. Tap Done to close the tab view. The tab view closes, and the page you were most recently viewing is shown.

Opening Web Pages That Are Open on Other Devices

When you enable iCloud Safari syncing, iCloud tracks the websites you have open on all the devices on which you have Safari syncing enabled, including your iPhone, iPads, and Macs. This is really handy when you have pages open on another device and want to view them on your iPhone. (Web pages open on your iPhone are available on your other devices, too.) To view a page you have open on another device, do the following:

1. Open the tab view.

2. Swipe up the screen until you see the pages open on other devices. There is a section for each device; sections are labeled with the device's name. In each device's section, you see the pages open in Safari on those devices.

3. Tap the page you want to view. The page opens on the iPhone and becomes a new tab.

A Mac with op‍ web pag‍

Keep Private Things Private

If you aren't browsing in Private mode and tap the Private icon at the bottom of the tab view, Safari moves into Private mode and stops tracking the sites you visit. Tap the Private icon again to return to the previous state. If you are browsing in Private mode, tapping the Private icon shows or hides the tabs in the tab view.

Searching the Web

In the first section of this chapter, you learned that you can set Safari to search the Web using Google, Yahoo!, Bing, or DuckDuckGo. No matter which search engine you chose, you search the Web in the same way.

1. Tap in the Address/Search bar (if you don't see this bar, tap at the top of the screen). The keyboard appears along with your Favorites.

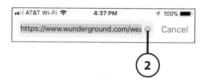

2. If there is any text in the Address/Search bar, tap the clear icon (x).

3. Type your search word(s). As you type, Safari attempts to find a search that matches what you typed. The list of suggestions is organized in sections, which depend on what you are searching for and the search options you configured through Safari settings. One section, labeled with the search engine you are using (such as Google Search), contains the search results from that source. Other sections can include Bookmarks and History, or Apps (from the App Store). At the bottom of the list is the On This Page section, which shows the terms that match your search on the page you are browsing.

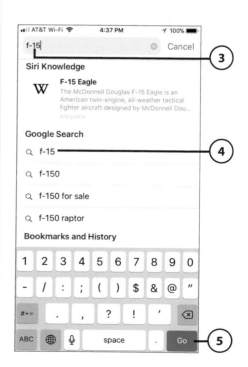

4. To perform the search using one of the suggestions provided, tap the suggestion you want to use. The search is performed and you can skip to step 6.

5. If none of the suggestions are what you want, keep typing until you have entered the entire search term, and then tap Go. The search engine you use performs the search and displays the results on the search results page.

6. Use the search results page to view the results of your search. These pages work just like other web pages. You can zoom, scroll, and tap links to explore results.

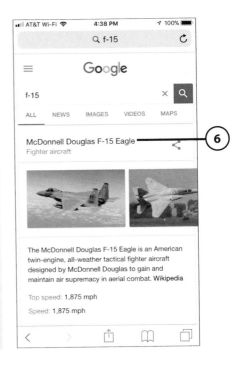

Searching on a Web Page

To search for words or phrases on a web page you are viewing, perform these steps, except in step 4, tap the word or phrase for which you want to search in the On This Page section (you might have to swipe up the screen to see this section). You return to the page you are browsing and each occurrence of your search term on the page is highlighted.

Quick Website Search

If you enabled the Quick Website Search feature, you can include the site you want to search in the Address/Search bar, such as "Wiki F-15." When you do this, the results from the site you entered appear at the top of the list and you can access them directly by tapping the information that appears (as opposed to having to move to the search engine site first as in these steps).

Saving and Organizing Bookmarks

In addition to moving bookmarks from a computer or iCloud onto your iPhone, you can save new bookmarks directly in your iPhone (they are synced onto other devices, too). You can also organize bookmarks on your iPhone to make them easier and faster to access.

Creating Bookmarks

When you want to make it easy to return to a website, create a bookmark with the following steps:

1. Move to a web page for which you want to save a bookmark.

2. Tap the Share icon.

3. Tap Add Bookmark. The Add Bookmark screen appears, showing the title of the web page you are viewing, which will also be the name of the bookmark initially; its URL; and the Location field, which shows where the bookmark will be stored when you create it.

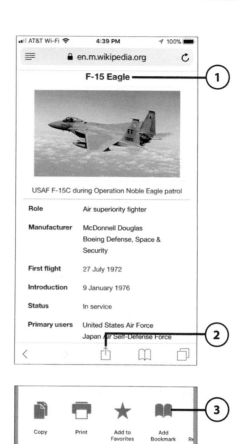

4. Edit the bookmark's name as needed, or tap the clear icon (x) to erase the current name, and then type the new name of the bookmark. The titles of some web pages can be quite long, so it's a good idea to shorten them so the bookmark's name is easier to read on the iPhone's screen.

5. Tap the current folder shown under Location. The Location section expands and you see all of the folders of bookmarks on your phone. The folder that is currently selected is marked with a check mark.

6. Swipe up and down the screen to find the folder in which you want to place the new bookmark. You can choose any folder on the screen; folders are indented when they are contained within other folders.

URL of web page   **Name of web page/bookmark**

Current bookmark location

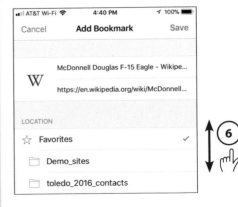

7. Tap the folder in which to store the new bookmark. You return to the Add Bookmark screen, which shows the location you selected.

8. Tap Save. The bookmark is created and saved in the location you specified. You can use the bookmark to return to the website at any time.

Organizing Bookmarks

You've seen how bookmarks can be contained in folders, which is a good thing because you're likely to have a lot of them. You can change the names and locations of your existing bookmarks and folders as follows:

1. Move to the Bookmarks screen showing the bookmarks and folders you want to change. (You can't move among the Bookmarks screens while you are in Edit mode so you need to start at the location where the items you want to change are located.)

2. Tap Edit. Unlock icons appear next to the folders and bookmarks you can change (some folders can't be changed and you won't see controls for those folders). The order icons also appear on the right side of the screen, again only for folders or bookmarks you can change.

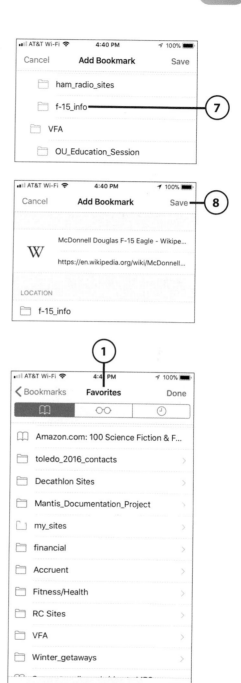

3. Drag the order icon next to the bookmark or folder you want to move up or down the screen to change the order in which it appears on the screen. When you drag a folder or bookmark between other items, they slide apart to make room for the folder or bookmark you are dragging. The order of the items in the list is the order in which they appear on the Bookmarks screen.

4. Tap a folder to change its name or location.

5. Change the name in the name bar.

6. To change the location of the folder, tap the Location bar, which shows the folder's current location.

Can't Move?

If you have only one bookmark you've added, you can't move them around as described here because Safari won't let you "disturb" the default bookmarks and folders (such as Favorites). You can only delete default bookmarks.

7. Swipe up and down the list of folders until you see the folder in which you want to place the folder you are working with.

8. Tap the folder into which you want to move the folder you are editing.

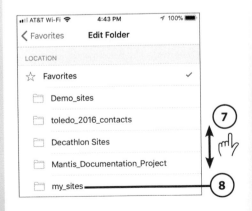

9. Tap the back icon, which is labeled with the location from which you came. You move back to the prior Bookmarks screen, which reflects any changes you made.

10. Tap a bookmark you want to change.

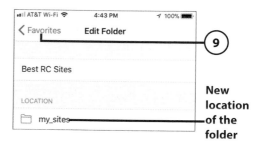

New location of the folder

Editing a Bookmark

If the bookmark you want to change isn't on the Bookmarks screen you are currently viewing, tap Done to exit Edit mode. Then open the folder containing the bookmark you want to change and tap Edit. You are able to change the bookmark.

11. Change the bookmark's name in the name bar.

12. If you want to change a bookmark's URL, tap the URL bar and make changes to the current URL. For example, you might want to change it to have the bookmark point to a site's home page rather than the page you are viewing.

13. To change the location of the folder or bookmark, tap the Location bar and follow steps 7 and 8.

14. Tap Done. You move back to the previous screen, and any changes you made—such as changing the name or location of a bookmark—are reflected.

15. Tap New Folder to create a new folder.

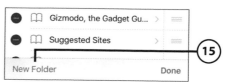

16. Enter the name of the folder.

17. Follow steps 6–8 to choose the location in which you want to save the new folder.

18. Tap Done. The new folder is created in the location you selected. You can place folders and bookmarks into it by using the Location bar to navigate to it.

19. Tap Done. Your changes are saved, and you exit Edit mode.

Browsing Both Ways

As you browse, make sure you try both the horizontal and vertical orientations. Safari sometimes offers different features in the two orientations on different models. For example, when you open the Bookmarks screen and rotate an iPhone 6 Plus, 6s Plus, or 7 Plus, the screen is divided into two panes. On the left is the Bookmarks pane you are viewing and the right pane shows the web page you were browsing. If you tap a bookmark, the web page in the right pane becomes the page at which the bookmark points.

Deleting Bookmarks or Folders of Bookmarks

You can get rid of bookmarks or folders of bookmarks you don't want any more by deleting them:

1. Move to the screen containing the folder or bookmark you want to delete.

2. Swipe to the left on the folder or bookmark you want to delete.

3. Tap Delete. The folder or bookmark is deleted. Note that when you delete a folder, all the bookmarks it contains are deleted, too.

Using 3D Touch with Safari

Like other default iPhone apps, Safari supports 3D Touch (iPhone 6s and later models), which you can use in a couple of ways.

Perform a Peek to see the Quick Actions menu

Move to the Reading List — Show Reading List

Show Bookmarks — Open the Bookmarks screen

Open a new tab in which the sites won't be tracked — New Private Tab

New Tab — Open a new tab and allow the sites to be tracked

When you press and hold on the Safari app's icon, you see the Quick Actions menu. You can select from among its options to quickly perform actions in Safari. For example, choose New Tab to open a new tab in which you can navigate to a web page, or choose Show Bookmarks to jump to the Bookmarks page.

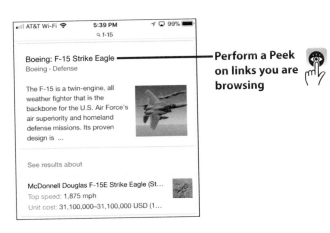

Perform a Peek on links you are browsing

When you see this, you can swipe up the screen to see options.

Perform a Pop to open the web page.

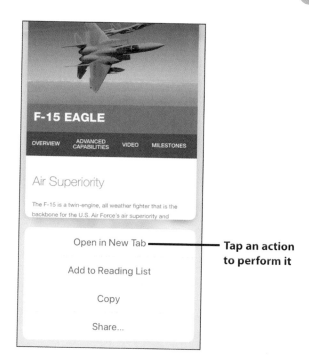

When you are browsing links, such as when you have performed a search, or your bookmarks, press on a link or a bookmark in which you are interested to perform a Peek on it. In the Peek window, you see the web page for the link or web page on which you peeked. If you continue to press on the Peek, it pops open so you can view the web page in Safari. When you perform a Peek on some screens, such as the links resulting from a search, you see an upward-facing arrow at the top of the screen; this indicates you can swipe up the screen to reveal a menu of commands. Tap a command to perform it. For example, tap Open in New Tab to open the web page in a new tab in Safari.

Sharing Web Pages

Safari makes it easy to share web pages that you think will be valuable to others. There are many ways to share, including AirDrop, Message, Mail, Twitter, and Facebook. A couple of examples will prepare you to use any of them.

Emailing a Link to a Web Page

You can quickly email links to web pages you visit.

1. Use Safari to navigate to a web page whose link you want to email to someone.

2. Tap the Share icon.

3. Tap Mail. A new email message is created, and the link to the web page is inserted into the body. The subject of the message is the title of the web page.

4. Complete and send the email message. (Refer to Chapter 8, "Sending, Receiving, and Managing Email," for information about the Mail app.) When the recipient receives your message, he can visit the website by tapping the link included in the email message.

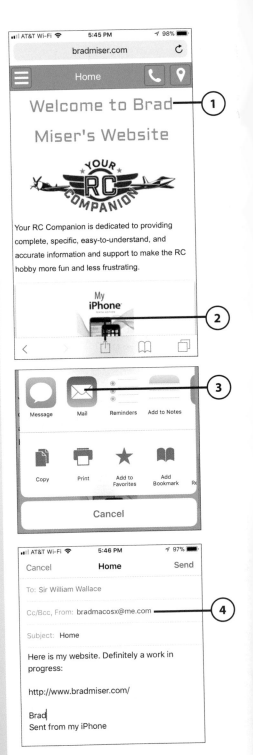

Messaging a Web Page

If you come across a page that you want to share with someone via Messages, Safari makes it easy.

1. Use Safari to navigate to a web page whose link you want to message to someone.

2. Tap the Share icon.

3. Tap Message. A new message is created, and the link to the web page is inserted.

4. Address the message.

5. Enter text you want to send along with the link to the web page.

6. Tap the Send icon. Your message is sent. The recipients can visit the web page by tapping the link included in the message.

>>>*Go Further*

MORE WAYS TO SHARE THE WEB

If you want to share a web page in the old-fashioned way, you can print it by opening the Share menu and tapping Print (assuming you have your iPhone set up to print, as explained in Chapter 2, "Using Your iPhone's Core Features"). If you tap Copy, the web page's address is copied to the clipboard, so you can paste it into documents, emails, notes, or messages. You can also share via Twitter and Facebook.

Signing In to Websites Automatically

If you enable Safari to remember usernames and passwords, it can enter this information for you automatically. When Safari encounters a site for which it recognizes and can save login information, you are prompted to allow Safari to save that information. This doesn't work with all sites; if you aren't prompted to allow Safari to save login information, you can't use this feature with the site you are visiting. When saved, this information can be entered for you automatically.

1. Move to a web page that requires you to log in to an account.

2. Enter your account's username and password.

3. Tap the icon to log in to your account, such as Continue, Sign In, Submit, Login, and such. You are prompted to save the login information.

4. Tap Save Password to save the information. The next time you move to the login page, your username and password are entered for you automatically. Tap Never for This Website if you don't want the information to be saved and you don't want to be prompted again. Tap Not Now if you don't want the information saved but do want to be prompted again later to save it.

>>>*Go Further*

LETTING SAFARI CREATE PASSWORDS FOR YOU

If you have enabled the Names and Passwords setting, Safari can create passwords for you. Go to a website that requires you to create a password, such as when you register for a new account. When you tap in a field that Safari recognizes as requiring a password, tap Suggest Password. Safari presents a password for you; most of these are not easy to remember, but that doesn't matter because it is saved for you automatically so you won't have to enter it manually. If you want to use the recommended password, tap Use Suggested Password; Safari enters the password in the password and verify password fields. When syncing is enabled, the password is stored on the synced devices, too, so you are able to sign in from those devices just as easily.

Take photos
and video

Configure
camera
settings

Take photos
and video and
quickly send
them to others

In this chapter, you explore all the photo and video functionality that your iPhone has to offer. Topics include the following:

→ Setting Camera preferences
→ Using the Camera app to take photos and video with your iPhone

13

Taking Photos and Video with Your iPhone

The iPhone's cameras and Camera app capture high-quality photos and video. Because you'll likely have your iPhone with you at all times, it's handy to capture photos with it whenever and wherever you are. And, you can capture video just as easily.

Whether you've taken photos and video on your iPhone or added them from another source, the Photos app enables you to edit, view, organize, and share your photos. (To learn how to use the Photos app with the great photos and video you take, see Chapter 14, "Viewing and Editing Photos and Video with the Photos App.") You'll likely find that taking and working with photos and videos are among the most useful things your iPhone can do.

Each generation of iPhone has had different and more sophisticated photo and video capabilities and features than the previous versions. All current versions sport high-quality cameras; in fact, there is a camera on each side of the iPhone. One takes photos of what you are looking at (the back-facing camera, located on the backside of the phone), whereas the other takes photos of what the screen is facing (the front-facing camera, which is usually for taking selfies, located on the face of the phone).

Current generations also have a flash; can zoom; take burst, panoramic, and time-lapse photos; and have other features you expect from a high-quality digital camera. The iPhone 6s and later models can also take Live Photos, which capture a small amount of video along with the photo.

The iPhone 7 and later models have image stabilization, more resolution, and other enhancements to enable them to take even higher quality photos and video with both the back-facing and front-facing cameras.

The iPhone 7 Plus, 8 Plus, and X have two back-facing cameras: one is the wide-angle camera that all models have (in different versions depending on the model), and the other camera has a telephoto lens. These two cameras give these models unique photo capabilities, which are a Telephoto mode that enables you to capture much better quality photos using both optical zoom and software zoom. It also enables you to take Portrait photos in which the subject is in very sharp focus and the background in a soft blur.

The iPhone's photo and video capabilities and features are probably the largest area of differences between the various models. Because of the fairly large variation in capabilities of iPhone models that can run iOS 11, it's impossible to cover all the differences in this chapter; the iPhone 7 and 8 are used for the step-by-step tasks in this chapter. If you have a different model, some of the tasks described might not be applicable to you, or some of the details in this chapter might be different than what you see on your iPhone if it is an older model. However, all models can do most of the tasks in this chapter so even if you don't have an iPhone 7 or 8, you can still take lots of different kinds of photos and videos using the information in this chapter.

Have an iPhone 7 Plus, 8 Plus, or X?

The iPhone 7 Plus, 8 Plus, and X have some amazing photographic features and are significantly more advanced than the iPhone 7 and 8 in this area. If you have one of these models, you can get detailed step-by-step tasks to help you learn to take advantage of their unique features in the online supplement *My iPhone X*. You can download this supplement from www.informit.com/myiphone11. Of course, these models can do all of the tasks described in this chapter, so its content will help you take great photos and videos just like the iPhone 7 and 8 do.

Additionally, the iPhone's photo and video capabilities have been increasingly tied into iCloud. For example, you can store your entire photo library under your iCloud account; this offers many benefits, including backing up all your photos, making it easy to access your photos from any device, and being able to quickly share your photos with others. Therefore, I've assumed you are using iCloud and have configured it to work with photos as described in Chapter 3, "Setting Up and Using an Apple ID, iCloud, and Other Online

Accounts." Like differences in iPhone camera capabilities, if you don't use iCloud with your photos, some of the information in this chapter doesn't apply to you and what you see on your phone might look different than what you see in this chapter.

Setting Camera Preferences

The following table describes options in the Settings app that you can access by tapping Settings, and then tapping Camera. The default settings allow you to take photos and video without making any changes to these settings, but it's good to know where they are and what they do if you decide to change how your apps work.

Settings App Explained

To get detailed information on using the Settings app, see "Working with the Settings App" in Chapter 2, "Using Your iPhone's Core Features."

iPhone 7 Plus, 8 Plus, and X

Because of their unique capabilities, these models of iPhone have slightly different camera settings than those shown in the table. Refer to the online supplement *My iPhone X* by going to www.informit.com/myiphone11 for the details to configure the Camera settings on these models.

Camera Settings

Section	Setting	Description
Preserve Settings	Camera Mode	When this switch is on (green), the Camera app retains the mode you most recently used, such as VIDEO or PANO. When off (white), the camera is reset to the PHOTO mode each time you move into the Camera app.
Preserve Settings	Filter	When this switch is on (green), the Camera app retains the filter you most recently used, such as DRAMATIC. When off (white), the camera is reset to the ORIGINAL filter each time you move into the Camera app.
Preserve Settings	Live Photo	When this switch is on (green), the Camera app retains the Live Photo setting you used most recently, such as Off. When off (white), Live Photo is turned on automatically each time you move into the Camera app.
N/A	Grid	When this switch is on (green), you see a grid on the screen when you are taking photos with the Camera app. This grid can help you align the subject of your photos in the image you are capturing.

Section	Setting	Description
N/A	Scan QR Codes	When this switch is on (green), you can use the Camera app to scan QR codes that provide information about the object to which they are attached or with which they are associated. For example, many zoos and museums put QR codes on their exhibits; you can use your iPhone's camera to quickly scan these QR codes to get information about what you are looking at. When this switch is off (white), this feature is disabled.
N/A	Record Video	Use the options under this menu to determine how video is recorded. The options available depend on the model of iPhone you have. You can choose from among different combinations of resolution and frame rate. Higher resolution and frame rates mean better-quality video, but also larger files.
N/A	Record Slo-mo	The selections under this menu determine the resolution and frame rate for slow-motion video. Like regular video, the higher the resolution and frame rate, the better quality the resulting video is and the file sizes are larger.
Formats	CAMERA CAPTURE	Choose High Efficiency if you want your photos to be captured in the HEIF/HEVC format so they use less storage space. Not all devices and apps can use this format, but any that are related to the iPhone (such as iPads and Macs) should be able to. This format results in smaller file sizes so you can store more photos on your iPhone. If you use photos on other types of devices or if you want to make sure your photos are compatible with as many devices and apps as possible, choose Most Compatible instead.
HDR (High Dynamic Range)	Keep Normal Photo	When this switch is on (green), the HDR (read more about this in a later sidebar) and the normal version of photos are stored. When this switch is off (white), only the HDR version of the photo is stored.

Photos Settings

You should use the Photos settings to determine what happens with your photos and videos after you capture them, such as if they are stored in your iCloud Photo Library and if photos are optimized for storage on your iPhone. See the section "Configuring Photos Settings" in Chapter 14 for a detailed explanation of these settings.

Using the Camera App to Take Photos and Video with Your iPhone

You use the Camera app to take photos and video with your iPhone. This app has a number of controls and features. Some features are easy to spot, whereas others aren't so obvious. By the end of this section, you'll know how to use these features to take great photos and video with your iPhone.

The general process for capturing photos or video follows:

1. Choose the type of photo or video you want to capture.

2. Set the options for the type of photo or video you selected.

3. Take the photos or video.

4. View and edit the photos or video you captured using the Photos app.

The information you need to accomplish steps 1 through 3 of this process is provided in tables and tasks throughout this chapter. The details for step 4 are provided in Chapter 14.

Type of photo or video being taken

Swipe to the left or right to choose the type of photo or video you want to take

The first step in taking photos or video is to choose the type of photo or video that you want to capture. You do this by swiping to the left or right on the selection bar just above the large shutter button at the bottom of the Camera app's screen, as shown in the previous figure. The option shown in yellow at the center of the screen just above the shutter button is the current type of photo or video you are capturing. The options available in the Camera app are explained in the following table.

Types of Photo and Video iPhones Can Capture

Type of Photo or Video	Description
TIME-LAPSE	Captures a video with compressed time so that the time displayed in the video occurs much more rapidly than "real time." This is what is often used to show a process that takes a long time, such as a plant growing, in just a few seconds.
SLO-MO	Takes slow motion video so that you can slow down something that happens quickly.
VIDEO	Captures video at a real-time speed. The steps to take video are provided in the task "Taking Video," later in this chapter.
PHOTO	Captures still photos (or Live Photos on iPhone 6s/6s Plus or later models). Step-by-step instructions showing how to use this option are provided in the task "Taking Photos," later in this chapter.
SQUARE	Takes "square" photos in which the height and width are the same.
PANO	Takes panoramic photos that enable you to capture very wide images. An example of capturing a panoramic photo is provided in the task "Taking Panoramic Photos," later in this chapter.

Telephoto and Portrait Photos

The iPhone 7 Plus, 8 Plus, and X can capture telephoto and portrait photos. The step-by-step instructions to take telephoto or portrait photos are provided in the online supplement *My iPhone X* that you can download by going to www. informit.com/myiphone11. The icons you see on the screen when capturing these types of photos are also explained in the supplement.

When you choose the type of photo or video you want to take, there are quite a few options you can select (the options available to you depend on the specific model of iPhone you are using). When you select options, the icons you see on the screen change to reflect your selection. For example, when you choose a self-timed photo, the Self-timer icon changes to show the time delay you have selected. And, not all options are available at the same time. For example, you can't set the flash and HDR to go on at the same time because you can't take HDR images with the flash.

The following table describes the icons and tools available on the Camera app's screen. (Remember that the specific icons and tools you see depend on the type of photo or video you are capturing and the model of iPhone you are using.)

Photo and Video Options and Icons

Icon	Description
⚡	**Flash**—When you tap this icon, you see a menu with the flash options, which are Auto (the app uses the flash when required), On (flash is always used), or Off (flash is never used). Tap the option you want to use and the menu closes. When the flash is set to on, the icon is yellow.
⚡	**Flash Being Used**—When this icon appears on the screen, it indicates the flash will be used when taking a photo or video.
HDR	**High Dynamic Range (HDR)**—Tap this to set the HDR options. (You learn more about HDR in the "More on Taking Photos and Video" Go Further sidebar later in this chapter.) The options are Auto, On, or Off. When the flash is set to on, this is disabled and you see a line through the HDR icon because you can't use the flash with HDR images.
◉	**Live Photo on**—When this feature is enabled, you take Live Photos (see the "Live Photos" note following this table) and the Live Photos icon is yellow. To turn Live Photos off, tap this icon.
⦰	**Live Photo off**—When disabled, you take static photos and the Live Photos icon is white. To turn Live Photos on, tap this icon.

Icon	Description
	Self-timer—When you tap this icon, a menu appears on which you can choose (3s or 10s) a 3- or 10-second delay for photos. When you choose a delay, the icon is replaced with one showing the delay you set. When you tap the shutter button, the timer starts and counts down the interval you selected before capturing the image.
	Filter—When you tap this icon, a filter selection bar appears above the Shutter button. You can swipe on this bar to see the filters available, with the name of the filter in the center box appearing above it. You can choose from such filters as DRAMATIC WARM and VIVID COOL. Then tap a filter to apply it to the photo or video you are capturing. For example, you can apply the NOIR filter to give the photo a cool Noir-movie look. When you apply a filter, you see the image with the filter applied and you see the name of the filter above its preview on the Filter selection bar. Generally, it's better to apply filters after you take a photo so that you have an original, unfiltered version of the photo (this is covered in the task "Applying Filters to Photos" in Chapter 14).
	Filter applied—When the Filter icon is in color, you know a filter is currently applied. You also see the filter highlighted on the selection bar. When you capture a photo using the filter, the filter preview is marked with a white dot. Tap the Filter icon to close the filter selection bar. To remove a filter, tap the Filter icon, select the ORIGINAL filter, and tap the Filter icon.
	Change Camera—When you tap this icon, you toggle between the back-facing and front-facing camera (the front-facing camera is typically used for selfies).
⬤	**Shutter**—This button changes based on the type of photo or video you are taking. For example, when you are taking a photo, this button is white as shown. When you take a video, it becomes red. It looks a bit different for other types as well, such as Time-Lapse. Regardless of what the button looks like, its function is the same. Tap it to start the process, such as to take a photo or start capturing video. If applicable, tap it again to stop the process, such as stopping video capture. To take burst photos, you touch and hold it to capture the burst.
00:00:06	**Timer**—When you capture video, the timer shows the elapsed time of the video you are capturing. The red dot on the left side of the time indicates you are currently capturing video.

Icon	Description
	Focus/exposure box—When you frame an image, the camera uses a specific part of the image to set the focus, exposure, and other attributes. The yellow box that appears on the screen indicates the focus/exposure area. You can manually set the location of this box by tapping on the part of the image that you want the app to use to set the image's attributes. The box moves to the area on which you tapped and sets the attributes of the image based on that area.
	Exposure slider—When you tap in an image you are framing, the sun icon appears next to the focus/exposure box. If you tap this icon, you see the exposure slider. Drag the sun up to increase the exposure or down to decrease it. The image changes as you move the slider so you can see its effect immediately.
AE/AF LOCK	**AE/AF Lock**—When you tap an image to set the location of the focus/exposure box and keep your finger on the screen after a second or so, the focus and exposure become locked based on the area you selected. This icon indicates that the exposure and focus are locked so you can move the camera without changing the focus or exposure that is used when you capture the image. Tap the screen to release the lock and refocus on another area.
	Faces found—When your iPhone detects faces, it puts this box around them and identifies the area as a face. You can use faces to organize photos by applying names to the faces in your photos.
	Zoom slider—You can unpinch on an image to zoom in or pinch on an image to zoom out. When you do, the Zoom slider appears on the screen. This indicates the relative level of zoom you are applying. You can also drag the slider toward the – to zoom out or drag it toward the + to zoom in to change the level of zoom you are using.

And Now a Few Words on Live Photos

The iPhone 6s/6s Plus and later models can capture Live Photos. A Live Photo is a static image, but it also has a few of what Apple calls "moments" of video around the static image that you take. To capture a Live Photo, you set the Live function to on (it is on by default and its icon is yellow) and take the photo as you normally would. When you are viewing a Live Photo you have taken (these photos have the LIVE icon on them), tap and hold on the photo to see the motion associated with that photo. When you aren't tapping and holding on a Live Photo, it looks like any other photo you've taken.

Taking Photos

You can use the Camera app to capture photos, like so:

1.   On the Home screen, tap Camera.

2.   To capture a horizontal photo, rotate your iPhone so that it's horizontal; of course, you can use either orientation to take photos just as you can with any other camera.

3.   Swipe up or down (right or left if the phone is vertical) on the selection bar until PHOTO is in the center and in yellow.

4.   If you want to change the camera you are using, tap the Change Camera icon. When you change the camera, the image briefly freezes, and then the view changes to the other camera. The front-facing camera (the one facing you when you look at the screen) has fewer features than the back-facing camera has. These steps show taking a photo with the back-facing camera.

5.   Set the Flash, HDR, Live, and Self-timer options you want to use for the photo; see the previous table for an explanation of these options.

Part of the image being used to set brightness, focus, and exposure

6. Frame the image by moving and adjusting the iPhone's distance and angle to the object you are photographing; if you have the Grid turned on, you can use its lines to help you frame the image the way you want it. When you stop moving the phone, the Camera app indicates the part of the image that is used to set focus, brightness, and exposure with the yellow box. If this is the most important part of the image, you are good to go. If not, you can set this point manually by tapping where you want the focus to be (see step 9).

7. Zoom in by unpinching on the image. The camera zooms in on the subject and the Zoom slider appears.

8. Unpinch on the image or drag the slider toward the + to zoom in or pinch on the image or drag the slider toward the – to zoom out to change the level of zoom until it's what you want to use.

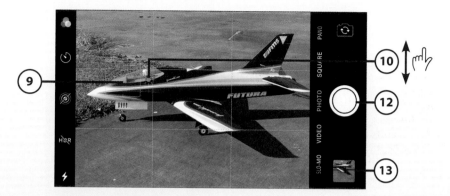

9. Tap the screen to manually set the area of the image to be used for setting the focus and exposure. The yellow focus box appears where you tapped.

10. To change the exposure, swipe up on the sun icon to increase the brightness or down to decrease it.

11. Continue making adjustments in the framing of the image, the zoom, focus point, and brightness until it is the image you want to take.

12. Tap the Shutter button on the screen, either Volume button on the side of the iPhone, or press the center button on the EarPods. The Photo app captures the photo, and the shutter closes briefly while the photo is recorded. When the shutter opens again, you're ready to take the next photo.

13. Tap the thumbnail to see the photo you most recently captured.

14. Use the photo-viewing tools to view the photo (see Chapter 14 for the details).

15. If you don't want to keep the photo, tap the Trash Can, and then tap Delete Photo.

16. Edit the photo by tapping Edit and using the resulting editing tools to make changes to the picture (see Chapter 14 for the details).

17. Tap the back arrow. You move back into the Camera app and can take more photos.

Taking Panoramic Photos

The Camera app can take panoramic photos by capturing a series of images as you pan the camera across a scene, and then "stitching" those images together into one panoramic image. To take a panoramic photo, perform the following steps:

1. Open the Camera app.

2. Swipe on the selection bar until PANO is selected. On the screen, you see a bar representing the entire image that contains a smaller box representing the current part of the image that will be captured.

3. Tap the Shutter button. The app begins capturing the image.

4. Slowly sweep the iPhone to the right while keeping the arrow centered on the line on the screen (if you move the phone too fast, you see a message on the screen telling you to slow down). The better you keep the tip of the arrow aligned with the line, the more consistent the centerline of the resulting image will be.

5. When you've moved to the "end" of the image you are capturing or the limit of what you can capture in the photo, tap the Shutter button. You move back to the starting point and the panoramic photo is created. You can tap the panoramic image's thumbnail to view, delete, or edit it just as you can with other types of photos.

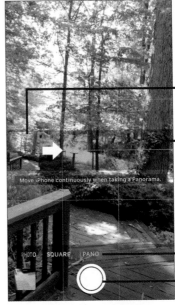

Current position in the image

The shade bar indicat the total possible area that c be include in the ima

As you mo the iPhon from the start of th image to t end, keep the arrow centered o the line

This box shows the image you've captured so far

Taking Video

You can capture video as easily as you can still images. Here's how.

1. Open the Camera app.

2. To capture horizontal video, rotate the iPhone so that it's horizontal; of course, you can use either orientation to take video just as you can with any other video camera.

3. Swipe on the selection bar until VIDEO is selected.

4. Choose the back-facing or front-facing camera, configure the flash, or zoom in, just like setting up a still image. (The Self-timer, Grid, and HDR mode are not available when taking video.)

5. Tap on the screen where you want to focus.

6. If needed, adjust the exposure by sliding the "sun" icon up or down just like a still photo (not shown on the figure).

7. Tap the Shutter button to start recording. You hear the start/stop recording tone and the app starts capturing video; you see the timer on the screen showing how long you've been recording.

Length of video

8. Take still images while you take video by tapping the white Shutter button. (If the Live Photos preference is enabled, the photos you take are Live Photos. If not, you take static images.)

9. Stop recording by tapping the red Shutter button again. Also, like still images, you can then tap the video's thumbnail to preview it as well as any still images you took while taking the video. You can use the Photos app's video tools to view or edit the clip. (These tasks are also explained in Chapter 14.)

Taking Photos and Video from the Lock Screen

Because it is likely to be with you constantly, your iPhone is a great camera of opportunity. You can use its Quick Access feature to quickly take photos when your iPhone is asleep/locked. Here's how:

1. When the iPhone is locked, press the Side button, touch the Touch ID/Home button, or lift your phone up (if you have a model that supports the Raise to Wake feature and it is enabled). The Lock screen appears.

2. Swipe to the left. The Camera app opens.

3. Use the Camera app to take the photo or video as described in the previous tasks. You can only view the most recent photos or videos you captured from within the Camera app when your iPhone is locked; you have to unlock the phone to work with the rest of your photos.

Taking Photos and Video from the Control Center

You can get to the camera quickly using the Control Center, too.

1. Swipe up from the bottom of the Home screen (all models except the iPhone X) or swipe down from the upper-right corner of the screen (iPhone X, not shown in the figure) to open the Control Center.

2. Tap the Camera icon. The Camera app opens.

3. Use the Camera app to take photos or video as you've learned in the previous tasks (not shown in the figures).

Taking Photos with Quick Actions (Models with 3D Touch)

On iPhone 6s/6S Plus and later models, the Quick Access menu offers a selection of photos and video commands that you can choose right from a Home screen.

1. Touch and hold on the Camera icon until the Quick Actions menu opens.

2. Tap the type of photo or video you want to take. The Camera app opens and is set up for the type you selected.

3. Use the Camera app to capture the photo or video (not shown in the figures).

Scanning QR Codes

QR (Quick Response) codes provide information about or enable you to take action on objects to which they are attached or associated. A QR scanner reads these codes and presents the information they contain. For example, rental cars usually have a QR code sticker on a window; when you scan this code, you get information about the car you are renting.

QR codes also enable you to take action, such as scanning the QR code for a Wi-Fi network and then joining it, scanning the code for an email address and then creating an email, and so on.

The Camera app can scan QR codes. After the code is scanned, you are prompted to take action on it.

The following steps show scanning a QR code for a rental car; scanning other types of QR codes is similar:

1. Open the Camera app and put it in either Photo or Square mode.

2. Frame the QR code in the camera.

3. Tap on the code to focus on it. You see a prompt about the code you scanned.

4. Tap the prompt to take action on it.

5. Complete the task you started in step 4 based on the type of code you scanned. For example, when you scan the QR code on a rental car, you might move to a website with information about the vehicle you rented. If the code is for a Wi-Fi network, you join that network. If the code contains an email address, you move into Mail and can complete the email to that address.

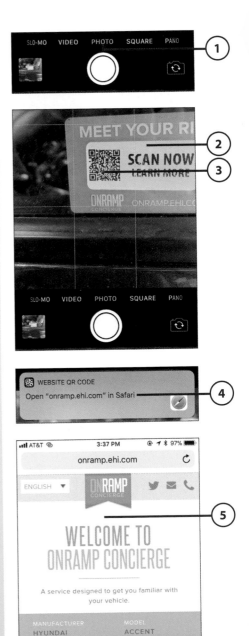

>>>Go Further
MORE ON TAKING PHOTOS AND VIDEO

The Camera app enables you to do all sorts of interesting and fun things with photos and video. Following are some additional pointers that help you make the most of this great app:

- **Set and forget**—You need to set the Flash, HDR, and most other options only when you want to change the current settings because these settings are retained even after you move out of the Camera app and back into it. The Camera Mode, Filter, and Live Photo behaviors are controlled by the Preserve Settings described earlier in this chapter.

- **HDR**—The High Dynamic Range (HDR) feature causes the iPhone to take three shots of each image, with each shot having a different exposure level. It then combines the three images into one higher-quality image. HDR works best for photos that don't have motion and where there is good lighting. (You can't use the iPhone's flash with HDR images.) Also, HDR photos take longer to capture.

  When the Keep Normal Photo switch in the Camera Settings is on (green), you see two versions of each HDR photo in the Photos app: One is the HDR version, and the other is the normal version. If you prefer the HDR versions, set the Keep Normal Photo switch to off (white) so that your photos don't use as much space on your iPhone, and you don't have twice as many photos to deal with.

  HDR photos display the HDR icon in the upper-left corner when you view them.

- **Location**—The first time you use the Camera app, you are prompted to decide whether you allow it to use Location Services. If you allow the Camera app to use Location Services, the app uses the iPhone's GPS to tag the location where photos and video were captured. Some apps can use this information, such as the Photos app on your iPhone, to locate your photos on maps, find photos by their locations, and so on.

- **Sensitivity**—The iPhone's camera is sensitive to movement, so if your hand moves while you are taking a photo, it's likely to be blurry; iPhone 6 Plus and later models have image stabilization that mitigates this to some degree. Sometimes, part of the image will be in focus and part of it isn't, so be sure to check the view before you capture a photo. This is especially true when you zoom in. If you are getting blurry photos, the problem is probably your hand moving while you are taking them. Of course, because it's digital, you can take as many photos as you need to get it right; delete the rejects as you take them and use the Photos app to periodically review and delete photos you don't want to keep (see Chapter 14), so you don't have to waste storage room or clutter up your photo library with photos you don't want to keep.

- **Burst photos**—When you touch and hold on the Shutter button while taking photos, a series of images is captured rapidly and you see a counter showing the number being taken. When you release the Shutter button, a burst photo is created; the burst photo contains all of the images you captured but appears as a single image in the Photos app. You can review the images in the burst and choose to keep only the images you want to save (this task is also covered in Chapter 14).

- **Self-timer**—When you set the Self-timer option, you choose either a 3- or 10-second delay between when you tap the Shutter button and when the image is captured. Like the other settings, the Self-timer is persistent, so you need to turn it off again when you want to stop using it.

- **Self-timer and burst**—If you set the timer, and then tap and hold on the Shutter button for a second or so, a burst of ten photos is captured when the timer expires.

- **Slow-motion video**—You can also take slow-motion video. Choose SLO-MO on the selection bar. Set up the shot and take the video as you do with normal speed video. When you play it back, the video plays in slow motion except for the very beginning and ending. (The speed of the video is determined by the Record Slo-mo setting, described earlier.)

- **Time-lapse video**—When you choose the TIME-LAPSE option, you can set the focus and exposure level and choose the camera you want to use. You record the video just like "real time" video. When you play it back, the video plays back rapidly so you seemingly compress time.

- **Screenshots**. You can take screenshots of your iPhone's screen by pressing and holding the Touch ID/Home and Side buttons at the same time (all models except the iPhone X) or pressing and holding the Side button and upper Volume button (iPhone X). The screen flashes white and the shutter sound plays to indicate the screen has been captured. You see a thumbnail of the screen capture. You can tap this to open the screen capture to edit it; when you're finished editing it, tap Done to close the preview (tap Save to Photos to save it or Delete Screenshot if you don't want to save it). If you don't tap the thumbnail, after a couple of seconds, it disappears (you can swipe it off the screen to get rid of it immediately).

If you didn't preview the screenshot, it automatically is saved. If that happened or you chose to save the preview in the editor, the resulting image is stored in the Screenshots album. You can view the screen captures you take, email them, send them via Messages, or other tasks as you can with photos you take with the iPhone's camera.

View, edit, and share photos, slideshows, and video

Use Messages, Mail, and other apps to share your photos and video

In this chapter, you explore all the photo- and video-viewing and editing functionality that your iPhone has to offer. Topics include the following:

→ Configuring Photos settings
→ Viewing, editing, and working with photos on your iPhone
→ Viewing, editing, and working with video on your iPhone
→ Using iCloud with your photos

Viewing and Editing Photos and Video with the Photos App

Chapter 13, "Taking Photos and Video with Your iPhone," explains how to take photos and video using the iPhone's Camera app. The photos and video you take with your iPhone's cameras are stored in your photo library, which you can access using the Photos app.

Configuring Photos Settings

The following table describes options in the Settings app that you can access by tapping Settings, and then tapping Photos. You can likely work with the Photos app without changing any of these, but it's good to know what and where these settings are in case you want to make changes.

Settings App Explained

To get detailed information on using the Settings app, see "Working with the Settings App" in Chapter 2, "Using Your iPhone's Core Features."

Photos Settings

Section	Setting	Description
Siri & Search	Siri & Search Suggestions	When this switch is enabled (green), information in the Photos app can be searched, used when you perform Look Ups on terms, and by Siri. If you set this switch to off (white), Photos information is not used for searches or Siri Suggestions.
N/A	iCloud Photo Library	When enabled, your photos and videos are stored in your iCloud account on the cloud so that they are backed up and you can access them from multiple devices. See Chapter 3, "Setting Up and Using an Apple ID, iCloud, and Other Online Accounts," for information about using iCloud with your photos and video.
N/A	Optimize iPhone Storage	If you select this option, only versions of your photos that are optimized for the iPhone are stored on your phone; this saves space so that you can keep more photos and videos on your iPhone. Full resolution photos are uploaded to the cloud.
N/A	Download and Keep Originals	This option downloads full resolution versions of your photos and videos on your iPhone. They consume a lot more space than optimized versions.
N/A	Upload to My Photo Stream	When enabled, all your photos are automatically uploaded to your iCloud Photo Stream when you are connected to the Internet with Wi-Fi. New photos are also downloaded from the cloud to your iPhone and other devices with this setting enabled.
N/A	Upload Burst Photos	This setting determines if all of the photos in a burst are uploaded to the cloud or only photos you tag as favorites are uploaded. Because burst photos can take up a lot of space, it's usually better to leave this disabled. If you leave this disabled, when you select favorite photos in a burst series, only those photos are uploaded.
N/A	iCloud Photo Sharing	When enabled, you can share your photos with others and subscribe to other people's Photo Streams to share their photos.
Cellular Data	Cellular Data	When enabled (green), photos are copied to and from your iCloud Photo Library when you are using a cellular Internet connection. If you have a limited data plan, you might want to set this to off (white) so photos are copied only when you are using a Wi-Fi network.

Section	Setting	Description
Cellular Data	Unlimited Updates	When enabled, updates to your photos are made constantly, which uses much more data. With this disabled, updates are made periodically, which lowers the data use.
PHOTOS TAB	Summarize Photos	When this switch is on (green), you see thumbnails for only some of the photos in a collection and the timeframe of each group is larger. If you set this to off (white), you see a thumbnail of every photo in your collections, which takes up much more screen space and you have to scroll more to move among your collections. This setting affects how you see Collections view and Years view only.
MEMORIES	Show Holiday Events	With this switch enabled (green), the Photos app attempts to collect photos taken on the holidays in your country into memories. When disabled (white), the Photos app ignores holidays when it creates memories for you.
TRANSFER TO MAC OR PC	N/A	If you select Automatic, when you sync photos to a Mac or Windows PC, the compatibility of the format is changed to improve compatibility with the computer you are transferring files to.
TRANSFER TO MAC OR PC	N/A	If you choose Keep Originals, the files are transferred without checking compatibility.

iCloud Settings

The iCloud-related settings on the Photos settings screen are the same as the Photos settings under the iCloud settings area (see Chapter 3 for details).

Viewing, Editing, and Working with Photos on Your iPhone

When you work with your photos in the Photos app, you first find and view the photos that you are interested in. You can then view those photos in a number of ways including individually or in memories. Should you want to make changes to photos, a couple of taps get you into the app's amazing editing tools so you can make bad photos better, good photos great, and, well, you get the idea.

Finding Photos to Work With by Browsing

The first step in viewing, editing, or doing other tasks with photos is finding the photos you want to work with. When you open the Photos app, you see four ways to access your photos: Photos, Memories, Shared, and Albums. You can browse these sources to find photos in which you are interested.

The Photos source automatically organizes photos based on the time and location associated with them (this information is automatically embedded in the photos you take with the iPhone's camera, assuming you haven't disabled Location Services for it). The top level is Years, which shows your photos grouped by the year in which they were taken. You can then "drill down" into a year where you find collections, under which photos are organized by location and date ranges, which are determined according to the time, date, and location information on your photos. When you tap one of these collections, you drill down and see moments, which show you the detail of a collection. At the moment level, you see and can work with the individual photos in the collection.

Memory based on people

Photos automatically collected into groups based on time, location, and even people

Memory based on place

The Memories source builds collections of photos for you automatically. These collections can be based on a number of factors, such as time, location, holiday, and even people. You can view the photos in a memory individually, and the app builds slideshows automatically to make viewing your photos more interesting.

Photos being shared with you

Photos you are sharing

Photos you are sharing and that are shared with you

Shared shows photos you are sharing with other people and photos other people are sharing with you. For each group of photos being shared, you see the name of the group and who is sharing it (you, for photos you are sharing, or the name of the person sharing with you). When you tap a shared group, you see the photos it contains and can work with them. (Working with photo sharing is covered in detail in "Using iCloud with Your Photos" later in this chapter.)

Where photos and videos you take are stored

Photos you've tagged as favorites

Album based on people

Album based on location

Use albums to organize photos just about any way you want

Albums allow you to organize your photos in a number of ways. Following are some of the albums or types of albums you might see:

- **All Photos or Camera Roll**—When you see the All Photos album, you have the iCloud Photo Library enabled so that you can use this album to see all the photos in your library. When this is not enabled, you see Camera Roll instead. When you use the iCloud Photo Library, all the photos that you've stored on the iPhone or other devices that are using the same iCloud account are stored here. If you don't use the iCloud Photo Library, the Camera Roll album contains photos and videos you've taken with the iPhone's camera or saved from other apps, such as attachments to email in Mail.

- **Favorites**—This folder contains images you have tagged as a favorite by tapping their heart icons.

- **Favorite Memories**—This folder contains memories you've tagged as favorites. This album makes it easy to get back to memories you want to view or use.

- **People**—This folder contains images based on the people in them (people are identified by the iPhone's facial recognition software).

- **Places**—This groups photos by the location at which they were captured.

- **Videos**—Videos you record are collected in this folder.

- **Live Photos**—This folder contains your Live Photos (which capture snippets of video along with the still photo).

- **Selfies**—Photos you take with the front-facing camera are stored here.

- **Panoramas, Slo-mo, Time-lapse, Bursts, and Screenshots**—These folders contain photos and videos of the types for which they are named.

- **Recently Deleted**—This folder is a temporary location for photos you have deleted recently. When you delete a photo, it is moved into this folder, where it remains for a period of time (how long depends on how many photos you have deleted and when you deleted them). You can recover photos from this folder if you change your mind. After the holding time passes, photos are permanently deleted and can't be recovered.

- **My Albums**—In this section, you see albums you create to manually organize photos. You can create albums for any reason and store photos within them.

Your Albums May Vary

Some apps, such as Instagram, might add their own albums to the Albums tab.

Although each of these sources looks a bit different, the steps to browse them to find the photos you want to work with are similar for most of these sources. The Memories source is a bit different and is covered separately. This example shows using the Photos source to browse for photos:

1. On the Home screen, tap Photos.

2. Tap Photos. On the Years screen, you see photos collected by the year in which they were taken. Under the year, you see a summary of the various locations where the photos were taken.

Start at the Beginning

If the title at the top of the screen isn't "Years," tap the back icon located in the upper-left corner of the screen until it is.

3. Swipe up and down the screen to browse all the years.

4. Tap the thumbnails in the year that contains photos you want to work with. You move to the Collections screen that groups the selected year's photos based on locations and time periods.

Memories

If you want to jump directly to memories for the photos, tap a group's heading, such as the locations for a group of photos. You move into the memory view of those photos (covered later in this chapter).

5. Swipe up and down the screen to browse all the collections in the year you selected.

6. Tap the collection that contains photos you want to see. Doing so opens the Moments screen, which further breaks out the photos in the collection by location and date.

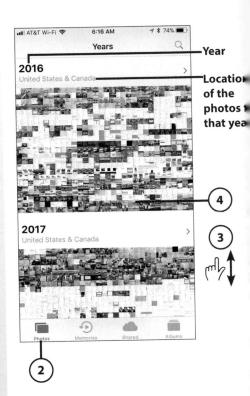

Year

Location of the photos f that yea

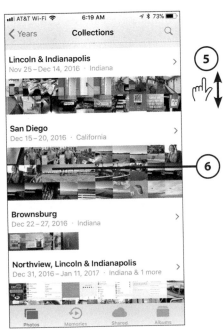

7. Swipe up and down the screen to browse all the moments in the collection you selected.

8. Tap a photo to view it.

9. You're ready to view the photos in detail as described in the task "Viewing Photos Individually" later in this chapter.

Go Back

You can move back to the screens from where you came by tapping the back icon, which is always located in the upper-left corner of the screen; this icon is named with the screen it takes you back to, it says Back, or it's just a left-facing arrow. To choose a different source, you might have to tap the back icon a time or two as the Photos, Memories, Shared, and Albums icons at the bottom of the screen are only visible on some screens.

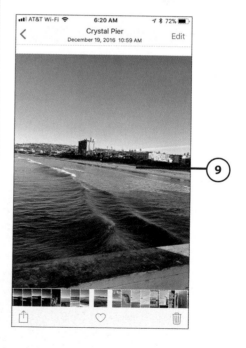

Finding Photos to Work With by Searching

Browsing photos can be a fun way to find photos, but at times you might want to get to specific photos more efficiently. The Search tool enables you to quickly find photos based on their time, date, location, and even content.

1. Continuing in the Photos app, tap the magnifying glass, which is available at the top of many of the app's screens. The Search bar opens.

2. Swipe up and down the current searches on the screen; these are created for you automatically based on your recent activity. For example, Nearby finds photos that were taken near your current location.

3. To use a current search, tap it and skip to step 5; if you don't want to use a current search, move to step 4.

4. Type your search term. This can be any information associated with your photos. As you type, collections of photos that match your search criteria are listed under the Search bar. The more specific you make your search term, the smaller the set of photos that will be found.

5. Swipe up and down the screen to browse all the results.

6. Tap the results you want to explore.

7. Tap a photo to view it.

8. View the photos in the group (covered in the next section).

9. Tap the back icon to return to the group of photos you were viewing.

10. Tap Back to move back to the Search screen.

11. Tap a different result to explore its photos.

12. To change the search, tap in the Search bar and change the current search term (you can delete the current term by tapping x).

13. Tap Cancel to exit the search.

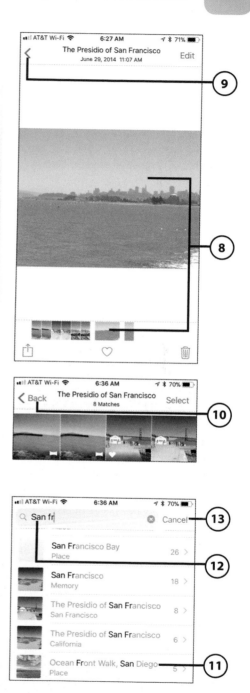

Viewing Photos Individually

The Photos app enables you to view your photos individually. Here's how:

1. Using the skills you learned in the previous tasks, open the group of photos that you want to view.

Orientation Doesn't Matter

Zooming, unzooming, and browsing photos works in the same way whether you hold your iPhone horizontally or vertically.

2. Swipe up and down to browse all the photos in the group.

3. Tap the photo you want to view. The photo display screen appears.

4. If it is a Live Photo, tap and hold on the screen to see the photo's motion.

My, Isn't That Special

If there is something unique about a photo, you see an icon indicating what it is on the photo when you view it. In this figure, you see the LIVE icon indicating it is a Live Photo. You might also see Burst for Burst photos, HDR for a photo captured with HDR, and so on. Keep an eye out for these icons as you explore your photos.

5. To see the photo without the app's toolbars, tap the screen. The toolbars are hidden.

6. Rotate the phone horizontally if you are viewing a horizontal photo.

7. Unpinch or double-tap on the photo to zoom in.

8. When you are zoomed in, drag around the image to view different parts of the zoomed image.

9. Pinch or double-tap on the photo to zoom out.

No Zooming Please

You can't have any zoom when you swipe to move to the next or previous photo so make sure you are zoomed out all the way before performing step 10. If not, you move the photo around instead.

---

10. Swipe to the left to view the next photo in the group.

11. Swipe to the right to view the previous photo in the group.

12. When you're done viewing photos in the group, tap the screen to show the toolbars again.

13. Swipe to the left or right on the thumbnails at the bottom of the screen to view all the photos in the current group. As you swipe, the photo you are viewing changes to be the one in the larger thumbnail at the center of the screen.

14. Tap a photo to view it.

15. Swipe up on the photo to get detailed information about it.

16. Tap Show Nearby Photos to see photos that were captured near the location associated with the photos you are viewing.

17. Tap the photo on the map to move to the map view (using the map view is covered in the "Working with Memories" section later in this chapter).

18. Swipe up the screen to see more details.

19. Tap a related memory to view it (details are provided later in this chapter).

20. Tap Show Photos from this Day to display the photos taken on the same day.

21. When you are done viewing the details, tap the back icon.

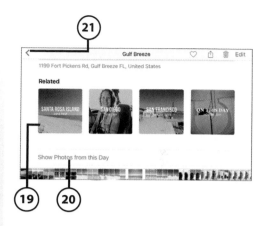

Using 3D Touch with Photos

You can use 3D Touch (iPhone 6s and later models) to preview and open photos as follows:

1. Browse a collection of photos in the Photos app.

2. Tap and hold on a photo in which you are interested. A Peek of that photo appears.

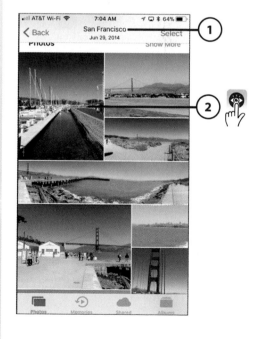

3. To open the photo, press down slightly harder until it pops open and use the steps in the previous task to view it. (If you pop the photo open, skip the rest of these steps.)

4. To see actions you can perform on the photo preview, swipe up the image.

5. Tap the action you want to perform, such as Favorite, to tag the photo as a favorite.

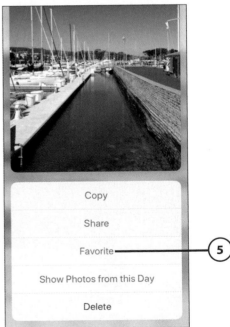

Copy

Share

Favorite

Show Photos from this Day

Delete

Working with Memories

The Memories feature automatically creates collections of photos for you to view in a number of ways. You can view them in a slideshow, individually, by selecting places, by selecting people, and so on. This feature provides lots of options and at times can be a very interesting way to view photos, because you might be surprised by some of the photos included in a particular memory.

There are a number of ways to access memories, including: tapping the Memories icon on the Dock at the bottom of the screen; tapping a heading for a group of photos when viewing years, collections, or moments; or tapping a Related item on a photo's Details page.

When you access a memory (no matter how you arrived), you see different options depending on the content of that memory. These can include:

- **Slideshow**—The photos collected in a memory play in a slideshow that plays using a theme, which has effects and a soundtrack. You can change the theme and length of the slideshow, and you can also edit it.

- **Photos**—All memories enable you to view the photos they contain just like photos stored in other places.

- **People**—If the photos in a memory include people, the app identifies those people by facial recognition and enables you to view other photos containing those people or groups of people.

- **Groups & People**—If the photos in a memory include people that are in consistent groupings, you can use these groups to view photos containing those groupings.

- **Places**—You can use the Places tool to view the photos in a memory on a map. You can tap locations on the map where photos were taken to view those photos.

- **Related**—This section of a memory presents other memories that are somehow related to the one you are viewing. This relationship can be based on location, people, and so on.

The Photos app creates memories for you dynamically, meaning they change over time as the photos in your library change. You can save memories that you want to keep as they are. Otherwise, the memories you see change as you take more photos or edit photos you have. This keeps memories a fresh and interesting way to view your photos.

Following are examples of different ways to access memories:

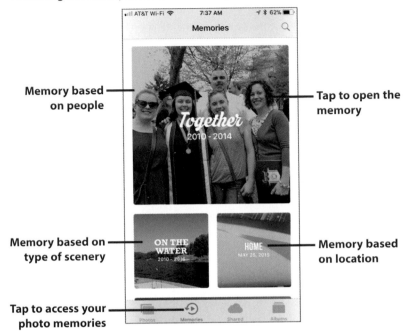

Memory based on people

Tap to open the memory

Memory based on type of scenery

Memory based on location

Tap to access your photo memories

- **Memories icon**—When you tap the Memories icon on the Dock, you see the Memories screen that contains the current memories the app has created and those you have saved. Tap a memory to open it.

Memory slideshow

Photos in the memory

On the memory's screen, you see different tools for viewing its photos, as described in the previous list, depending on the content of the memory. For example, if there aren't any people in the photos that the app recognizes via face recognition, there won't be a People section.

Tap to access a memory based on this group of photos

Memory containing photos in the selected group

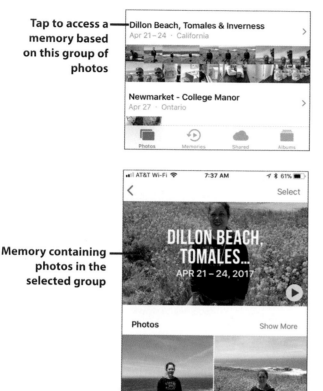

- **The heading of group of photos**—As you learned earlier, the Photos app collects photos based on the time and location at which they were taken. As you browse these groups, you can tap on a group's heading to view the photos it contains in a memory.

You can work with memories in a similar way no matter how you open them or what kind of photos they contain. Following are examples showing how to use several of the sections you see in memories.

Watching and Changing a Memory's Slideshow

All memories have slideshows that you can watch using the following steps:

1. Open a memory using an option described previously. Slideshows appear at the top of a memory's screen.

2. Tap the Play icon. The slideshow begins to play. If some of the photos in the slideshow aren't currently stored on your iPhone, there might be a pause while they are downloaded (you see the Downloading status on the opening screen while this is done).

3. To view the slideshow in landscape orientation, rotate the iPhone. As the slideshow plays, you see effects applied to the photos; videos included in the memory also play.

4. Tap the screen to reveal the slideshow controls.

5. To pause the slideshow, tap the Pause icon. (When paused, this becomes the Play icon that you can tap to resume the slideshow.)

6. Swipe to the right or left on the theme bar to change the slideshow's theme. As you change the theme you might see changes on the screen, such as a different font for the title, and hear different music while the slideshow plays.

7. Swipe to the right or left on the duration bar to change the slideshow's length. As you make changes, you see the slideshow's current length just above the theme bar.

8. Swipe to the left or right on the thumbnails at the bottom of the screen to move back or forward, respectively.

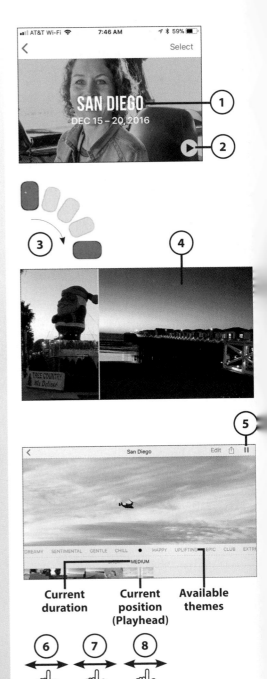

Current duration

Current position (Playhead)

Available themes

9. To restart the slideshow with the new settings, tap the Play icon.

10. Tap Edit to make manual changes to the slideshow and save the memory (see the Go Further sidebar "Make Your Own Memories" for more information).

11. Tap the Share icon and use the resulting menu to share the memory via AirDrop or an app; you can also save it to your iCloud Drive or Dropbox.

12. Tap the back icon to return to the memory.

Current runtime

>>>Go Further

MAKE YOUR OWN MEMORIES

You can edit a memory's slideshow to change how it plays. Tap Edit; you might see a prompt indicating that the memory is saved to your memories, tap OK if you see this. Tap Title to change the slideshow's name and title style. Tap Title Image to change the image shown in the video's opening thumbnail. Tap Music to change its soundtrack; you can choose None to remove the soundtrack, Soundtracks to use one of the default soundtracks, or My Music to use music in your iTunes Music Library. Tap Duration to set the slideshow's playing time. Tap Photos & Videos to manually select the photos that are included; tap the Trash Can icon to remove a photo from the video (this doesn't delete the photo from your library, only from the slideshow) or tap Add (+) to include more of the memory's photos in the slideshow (tap the back icon when you are finished selecting photos). Tap Done to save your slideshow. When you play the slideshow, the options you selected are used. Choose Custom on the Theme bar to view the video you created.

Viewing a Memory's Photos

You can view the photos contained in a memory using the following steps:

1. Open a memory using an option described previously.

2. Swipe up the screen until you see the Photos section. Here you see the photos in the memory.

Show All, Tell All

If the memory has lots of photos, you might see only a summary view of them on the Photos section. Tap Show More to see all the photos. Tap Summary to return to the summary view.

3. Swipe up and down the photos section to see all the photos the memory contains.

4. Tap a photo to view it.

5. Use the techniques you learned in "Viewing Photos Individually" earlier in the chapter to work with the photos in the memory.

6. Tap the back icon to return to the memory.

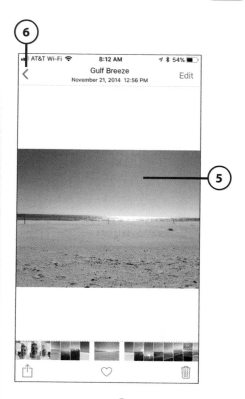

Viewing a Memory's Photos by Place

You can choose the photos in a memory to view based on the location using the Places section.

1. Open a memory using an option described previously.

2. Swipe up the screen until you see the Places section.

3. Tap a place. The map expands to fill the screen and you see more locations associated with photos in the memory.

Nearby Photos

Tap Show Nearby Photos to show other photos that were taken near the locations that you are viewing on the map, but that are not currently included in the memory. Tap Hide Nearby Photos to hide those photos again.

---

4. Unpinch your fingers on the screen to zoom in to reveal more detailed locations.

5. Swipe around the screen to move around the map.

6. Tap a location with photos to see the photos associated with it.

7. Swipe up and down the screen to browse the photos taken at the location.

8. Tap a photo to view it.

9. Use the techniques covered in "Viewing Photos Individually" earlier in the chapter to work with the photos you view.

10. Tap the back icon to return to the place.

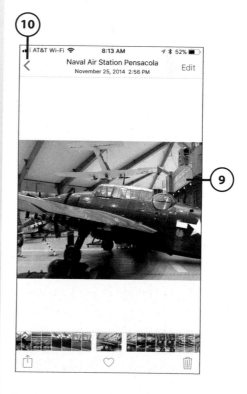

11. Tap Back to return to the map.

12. Tap other locations to view their photos.

13. Tap the back icon to return to the memory.

>>>Go Further
MAKING THE MOST OF YOUR MEMORIES

Here are a few more ways to make the most of your memories:

- To view memories based on people or groups of people, tap the person or group in the Groups & People or People section; you see a memory focused on the person or group you selected. Tap Add Name, enter and then tap the name of the person (if she is a contact), and tap Done. The person will be identified by name. When viewing photos containing a person, you can add more photos of a person by tapping REVIEW. You see more photos that might contain that person. Select the photos containing the person and tap Done. Any photos you confirm are added to that person's memory. (By the way, the Photos app can often identify pets in your photos and create memories focused on them.)

- Tap a memory in the Related section to see a memory that is related to the current one, such as one with photos containing the same people or in the same locations.

- Tap Add to Favorite Memories to add a memory you are viewing to the Favorite Memories album. Tap Remove from Favorite Memories to remove the memory from the Favorite Memories album.

- Tap Add to Memories to add a memory to the Memory screen. For example, when you are viewing a related memory and want to be able to get back to it quickly, tap Add to Memories. That memory appears on the Memories screen.

- Tap Delete Memory and then confirm you want to delete a memory by tapping Delete Memory again; the memory is deleted. When you delete a memory, only the memory is deleted; the photos that were in that memory remain in your photo library. (However, if you delete a photo from within a memory, that photo is deleted from your photo library, too.)

>>>Go Further

ROLL YOUR OWN SLIDESHOWS

The Memories feature creates slideshows that include effects and soundtracks for you automatically. However, you can create your own slideshows manually. View photos in a collection that you want to view as a slideshow; tap Select and then tap the photos you want to view in a slideshow. Tap the Share icon. Tap Slideshow. The slideshow plays. Tap the screen to show the slideshow controls. Tap Options to configure the slideshow, such as to choose music for it. When you're done configuring the slideshow, tap Done. Tap Done again when you are finished watching a slideshow.

Working with Burst Mode Photos

When you use the Burst mode to take photos, the Camera app rapidly takes a series of photos. (Typically, you use Burst mode to capture motion, where the action is happening too quickly to be able to frame and take individual photos.) You can review the photos taken in Burst mode and save any you want to keep as favorites; your favorites become separate photos just like those you take one at a time.

Here's how to identify which photos in a burst you want to keep:

1. View a Burst mode photo. Burst mode photos are indicated by the word Burst and the number of photos in the burst. (You can see all of the burst photos on your phone by opening the Bursts album.)

2. Tap Select. The burst is expanded. At the bottom of the screen, you see small thumbnails for the photos in the burst. At the top part of the screen, you see larger thumbnails of the photos; the photo in the center of the previews is marked with a downward-facing arrow. Photos marked with a dot are "suggested photos," meaning the best ones in the series according to the Photos app.

3. Swipe all the way to the right to move to the first photo in the series; swiping on the thumbnails at the bottom of the screen flips through them faster.

4. Tap a photo that you want to save. It is marked with a check mark.

5. Swipe to the left to move through the series.

6. Tap each photo you want to save.

7. Continue reviewing and selecting photos until you've gone through the entire series.

8. Tap Done.

Burst mode photo

Number of photos in the series

Photo in the center of the screen

Suggested photos

Number of photos currently selected

Selected photos

9. Tap Keep Only *X* Favorites, where
X is the number of photos you
selected, or tap Keep Everything
to keep all the photos in the burst.
Each photo you keep becomes a
separate, individual photo; you can
work with these just like photos
you take individually.

Burst Mode Photos and Uploads to the Cloud

If the Upload Burst Photos switch on the Photos Settings screen is set to off,
burst photos are not uploaded to the cloud until you go through the steps to
select and save photos from a burst. The photos you selected to keep are then
uploaded to the cloud just like individual photos you take.

Editing Photos

Even though the iPhone has great photo-taking capabilities, not all the photos you take are perfect from the start. Fortunately, you can use the Photos
app to improve your photos. The following tools are available to you:

- **Enhance**—This tool attempts to automatically adjust the colors and
  other properties of photos to make them better.

- **Straighten, Rotate, and Crop**—You can rotate your photos to change
  their orientation and crop out the parts of photos you don't want to
  keep.

- **Filters**—You can apply different filters to your photos for artistic or other
  purposes.

- **Red-eye**—This one helps you remove that certain demon-possessed
  look from the eyes of people in your photos.

- **Smart Adjustments**—You can adjust the light, color, and even the black-
  and-white properties of your photos.

- **Markups**—You can add markups, such as redlines, drawings, and magnification to photos.

Enhancing Photos

To improve the quality of a photo, use the Enhance tool.

1. View the image you want to enhance.

2. Tap Edit.

3. Tap the Enhance icon. The image is enhanced and the Enhance icon turns orange.

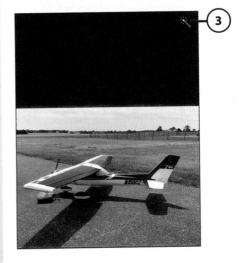

4. If you don't like the enhancements, tap the Enhance icon again to remove the enhancements.

5. Tap Done to save the enhanced image.

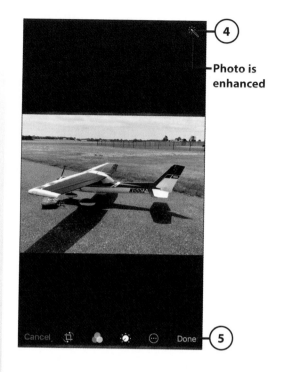

Photo is enhanced

Straightening, Rotating, and Cropping Photos

To change the alignment, position, and part of the image shown, perform the following steps:

1. View the image you want to change.

2. Tap Edit.

3. Tap the Rotate/Crop icon.

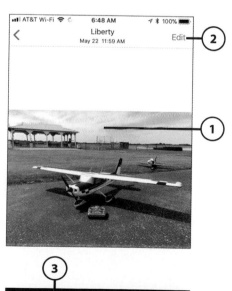

4. To rotate the image in 90-degree increments, tap the Rotate tool. Each time you tap this icon, the image rotates 90 degrees in the counterclockwise direction.

5. Rotate the image within its frame by dragging the triangle to the left or right. This is often useful to straighten photos that aren't aligned quite right, but can be used for artistic effects too.

6. When the image is straightened, lift your finger from the screen. The dial shows how much you've rotated the image.

7. Crop the image proportionally by tapping the Constrain icon; to crop the image without staying to a specific proportion, skip to step 9.

8. Tap the proportion with which you want to crop the image. You use this to configure the image for how you intend to display it. For example, if you want to display it on a 16:9 TV, you might want to constrain the cropping to that proportion so the image matches the display device.

9. Drag the corners of the crop box until the part of the image you want to keep is shown in the box. If you performed step 8, the app keeps the crop box in the proportion you selected.

10. Drag on the image to move it around inside the crop box.

11. When the image is cropped and positioned as you want it to be, tap Done. The edited image is saved.

More on Straightening and Cropping Photos

To undo changes you've made, tap RESET and the photo returns to the state it was in before you started editing it. To exit the Edit mode without saving your changes, tap Cancel.

Part of image that will be kept   **Part of image that will be cropped out**

Applying Filters to Photos

To apply filters to photos, do the following:

1. View the image to which you want to apply filters.

2. Tap Edit.

3. Tap the Filters icon. The palette of filters appears. If you haven't applied a filter, you see the current filter as Original.

4. Swipe to the left or right on the palette to browse all of the filters.

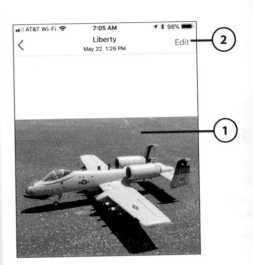

Undoing What You've Done

To restore a photo to its unedited state, tap Revert, which appears when you edit a photo that you previously edited and saved. At the prompt, tap Revert to Original, and the photo is restored to its "like new" condition.

The original version of photos is saved in your library so you can use the Revert function to go back to the photo as it was originally taken or added to the library, even if you've edited it several times.

However, you can't have the edited version and the original version displaying in your library at the same time. If you want to be able to have both an edited and original version (or multiple edited versions of the same photo), make a copy of the original before you edit it. To do this, view the photo, tap the Share icon, and tap Duplicate. You can do this as many times as you want. Each copy behaves like a new photo. If you edit one copy, the original remains available in your library for viewing or different editing.

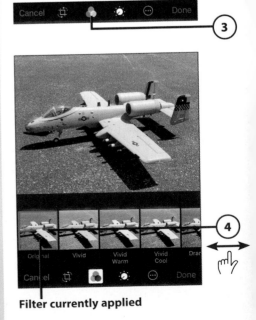

Filter currently applied

5. Tap the filter you want to apply. The filter is applied to the image and you see a preview of the image as it will be with the filter; the filter currently applied is high-lighted with a blue box. Keep trying filters until the image is what you want it to be.

6. Tap Done. The photo with the filter applied is saved.

Filter currently applied

Removing Red-Eye from Photos

When you edit a photo with people in it, the Red-eye tool becomes available (if no faces are recognized, this tool is hidden). To remove red-eye, perform the following steps:

1. View an image with people that have red-eye.

2. Tap Edit.

3. Tap the Red-eye icon.

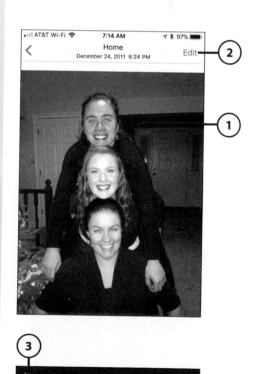

4. Zoom in on the eyes from which you want to remove red-eye; as you zoom in, drag the photo to keep the eyes you want to fix on the screen.

5. Tap each eye containing red-eye. The red in the eyes you tap is removed.

6. Repeat steps 4 and 5 until you've removed all the red-eye.

7. Tap Done to save your changes.

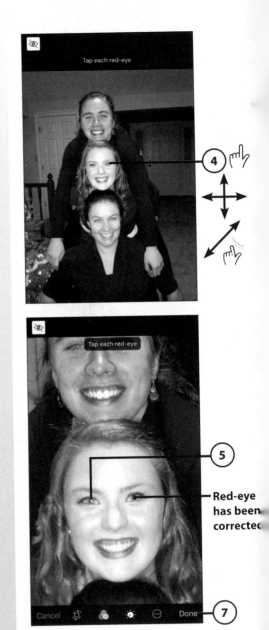

Red-eye has been corrected

Making Smart Adjustments to Photos

You can edit your photos using the Photos app's Smart Adjustment tools. Using these tools, you can change various characteristics related to light, color, and black-and-white aspects of your photos.

1. View the image you want to change.

2. Tap Edit.

3. Tap the Smart Adjust icon.

4. Tap the characteristic you want to change, such as Color.

Get Straight to the Point

To jump directly to a specific aspect of the area you are adjusting, tap the downward-facing arrow along the right side of the screen. On the resulting menu, tap the characteristic you want to adjust. For example, if you open this menu for Color, you tap Saturation, Contrast, or Cast to adjust those factors.

5. Swipe to the left or right to change the level of the parameter you are adjusting. As you make changes, you see the results of the change on the image.

Current setting

6. When you're done adjusting the first attribute you selected, tap the List icon.

7. Tap one of the options under the attribute you are already working with to adjust it; or tap the downward-facing arrow under one of the other attributes, and then tap the characteristic you want to change.

Curre**r** setti**n**

6

Curre**r** setti**n**

7

8. Swipe to the left or right to change the level of the parameter you are adjusting. As you make changes, you see the results of the change on the image.

9. Repeat steps 6 through 8 until you've made all the adjustments you want to make.

10. Tap Done to save the adjusted image.

Marking Up Photos

You can add markups to photos, including:

- **Draw**—You draw directly on top of photos, such as to indicate areas of interest or highlight something.

- **Magnify**—This tool magnifies a section of an image in a circle that looks kind of like an image you see through a magnifying glass.

- **Add text**—You can use the text tool to add words to an image.

With the drawing and text tools, you can choose the format of the markup, such as its color.

The following steps show the magnification and text markup tools; the drawing and other tools work similarly.

1. View the image you want to mark up.

2. Tap Edit.

3. Tap the Options icon (…).

4. Tap Markup.

But Wait, There Might Be More

The Markup tool is the default photo editor that comes with the Photos app. Over time, other photo-editing tools will become available (check the App Store). When installed, you see them on the Photo Editing menu. Tap a tool to use it. Tap More to configure the photo-editing tools you have installed—for example, set a tool's switch to off (white) to hide it. You can also change the order in which the tools are listed on the menu.

5. Tap Add (+).

Drawing Tools

Tap the pen or pencil icons to draw on the photo. You can change the size and color of the lines and drag them on the screen similar to how these steps show using the text tool.

6. Tap Magnifier. The magnification circle appears.

7. Drag the circle over the area of the image you want to magnify.

8. To change the size of the area being magnified, drag the blue dot away from the center of the circle to increase the area or toward the center to decrease the size of the area.

9. To change the amount of magnification being applied, drag the green dot clockwise around the circle to increase the magnification or counterclockwise to decrease it.

10. Tap Add (+).

11. Tap Text. A text box appears.

De-magnify

To remove a magnification mark-up, tap it and then tap Delete on the menu that appears.

12. Tap the text box.

13. Tap Edit.

14. Type the text you want to add.

15. Tap Done.

16. If it isn't selected already, tap the text.

17. Tap the font icon.

18. Use the font menu, size slider, and justification icons to format the text.

19. Tap outside the menu to close it.

20. If it isn't selected already, tap the text.

21. Tap the color icon (it starts as black so it is hard to see against the black background).

22. Tap the color you want to apply to the text.

23. Drag the text to where you want it to be on the photo.

24. Tap Done.

25. Tap Done to save your markups on the photo.

Editing Markups

To edit existing markups on a photo, edit the photo and open the markups tool using steps 1 through 4.

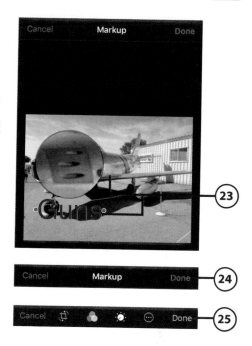

Working with Photos

Once you have photos on your iPhone, there are a lot of things you can do with them, including the following:

- Emailing one or more photos to one or more people (see the next task).
- Sending a photo via a text message (see Chapter 9, "Sending, Receiving, and Managing Texts and iMessages").
- Sharing photos via AirDrop (see Chapter 15, "Working with Other Useful iPhone Apps and Features").
- Sharing photos with others via iCloud (covered later in this chapter).
- Posting your photos on your Facebook wall or timeline.
- Assigning photos to contacts (see Chapter 6, "Managing Contacts").
- Using photos as wallpaper (see Chapter 5, "Customizing How Your iPhone Looks and Sounds").
- Sharing photos via tweets.
- Printing photos from your printer or (see Chapter 2, "Using Your iPhone's Core Features").
- Deleting photos (covered later in this chapter).
- Organizing photos in albums (also covered later in this chapter).

Copy 'Em

If you select one or more photos and tap the Copy icon, the images you selected are copied to the iPhone's clipboard. You can then move into another app and paste them in.

You'll easily be able to accomplish any actions on your own that are not covered in detail here once you've performed a couple of those that are demonstrated in the following tasks.

Individual Versus Groups

Some actions are only available when you are working with an individual photo. For example, you might be able to send only a single photo via some apps, whereas you can email multiple photos at the same time. Any commands that aren't applicable to the photos that are selected won't appear on the screen.

Sharing Photos via Email

You can email photos via iPhone's Mail application starting from the Photos app.

1. View the source containing one or more images that you want to share.

2. Tap Select.

3. Select the photos you want to send by tapping them. When you tap a photo, it is marked with a check mark to show you that it is selected.

4. Tap the Share icon.

Too Many?

If the photos you have selected are too much for email, the Mail icon won't appear. You need to select fewer photos to attach to the email message.

5. Tap Mail. A new email message is created, and the photos are added as attachments.

6. Use the email tools to address the email, add a subject, type the body, and send it. (See Chapter 8, "Sending, Receiving, and Managing Email," for detailed information about using your iPhone's email tools.)

7. Tap the size of the images you want to send. Choosing a smaller size makes the files smaller and reduces the quality of the photos. You should generally try to keep the size of emails to 5MB or smaller to ensure the message makes it to the recipient. (Some email servers block larger messages.) After you send the email, you move back to the photos you were browsing.

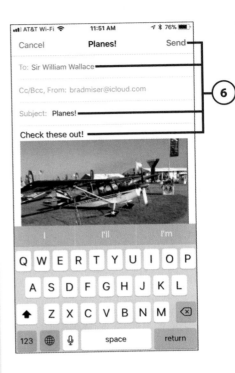

Images from Email

As mentioned in Chapter 8, when you save images attached to email that you receive, they are stored in the All Photos or Camera Roll photo album just like photos you take with your iPhone.

Organizing Photos in a New Album

You can create photo albums and store photos in them to keep your photos organized.

To create a new album, perform these steps:

1. Move to the Albums screen by tapping Albums on the toolbar.

2. Tap Add (+).

3. Type the name of the new album.

4. Tap Save. You're prompted to select photos to add to the new album.

5. Move to the source of the photos you want to add to the new album.

6. Swipe up and down to browse the source and tap the photos you want to add to the album. They are marked with a check mark to show that they are selected. The number of photos selected is shown at the top of the screen.

7. Tap Done. The photos are added to the new album and you move back to the Albums screen. The new album is shown on the list, and you can work with it just like the other albums you see.

Playing Favorites

To mark any photo or video as a favorite, tap its heart icon. It fills in with blue to show you that the item you are viewing is a favorite. Favorites are automatically collected in the Favorites album, so this is an easy way to collect photos and videos you want to be able to easily find again without having to create a new album or even put them in an album. You can unmark a photo or video as a favorite by tapping its heart icon again.

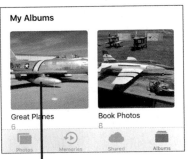

New album containing the photos you selected

Adding Photos to an Existing Album

To add photos to an existing album, follow these steps:

1. Move to the source containing the photos you want to add to an album.

2. Tap Select.

3. Tap the photos you want to add to the album.

4. Tap the Share icon.

5. Swipe to the left until you see Add to Album.

6. Tap Add to Album.

7. Swipe up and down the list to find the album to which you want to add the photos.

8. Tap the album; the selected photos are added to the album. (If an album is grayed out and you can't tap it, that album was not created on the iPhone, so you can't change its contents.)

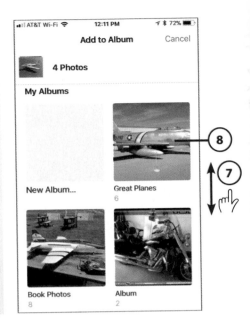

>>>Go Further
MORE ALBUM FUN

You can create a new album from photos you've already selected. Perform steps 1 through 6 and then tap New Album. Name the new album and save it. It's created with the photos you selected already in it.

You can change the order in which albums are listed on the Albums screen. Move to the Albums screen and tap Edit. Drag albums up or down the screen to reposition them. To delete an album that you created in the Photos app, tap its unlock icon (red circle with a –) and then tap Delete Album. (This only deletes the album itself; the photos in your library remain there.) When you're done making changes to your albums, tap Done.

To remove a photo from an album, view the photo from within the album, tap the Trash Can, and then tap Remove from Album. Photos you remove from an album remain in your photo library; they are only removed from the album.

Deleting Photos

You can delete photos and videos that you don't want to keep on your iPhone. If you use the iCloud Photo Library, deleting the photos from your phone also deletes them from your photo library and from all the other devices using your library. So, make sure you really don't want photos any more before you delete them.

1. Open the source containing photos you want to delete.

2. Tap Select.

3. Tap the photos you want to delete. Each item you select is marked with a check mark.

4. Tap the Trash Can.

5. Tap Delete *X* Photos, where *X* is the number of photos you selected. The photos you selected are deleted.

Deleting Individual Photos

You can delete individual photos that you are viewing by tapping the Trash Can, and then tapping Delete Photo.

Recovering Deleted Photos

As you learned earlier, photos you delete are moved to the Recently Deleted folder. You can recover photos you've deleted by opening this folder. You see the photos you've deleted; each is marked with the time remaining until it is permanently deleted. To restore photos in this folder, tap Select, tap the photos you want to recover, and tap Recover. Tap Recover *X* Photos, where *X* is the number of photos you selected (if you select only one, this is labeled as Recover Photo). The photos you selected are returned to the location from which you deleted them.

Deleted Means Deleted

Be aware that when you delete a photo from your iPhone, it is also deleted from your iCloud Library and all the devices sharing that library—not just from your iPhone. (After it has been deleted from the Recently Deleted folder of course.)

Viewing, Editing, and Working with Video on Your iPhone

As explained in Chapter 13, you can capture video clips with your iPhone. Once captured, you can view clips on your iPhone, edit them, and share them.

Finding and Watching Videos

Watching videos you've captured with your iPhone is simple.

1. Move to the Albums screen.

2. Tap the Videos album. Video clips display their running time at the bottom of their thumbnails. (Videos can also be stored in other albums, in collections, in memories, etc. This Videos album just collects videos no matter where else they are stored.)

3. Swipe up and down the screen to browse your videos.

4. Tap the video you want to watch.

5. Rotate the phone to change its orientation if necessary.

6. Tap Play. The video plays. After a few moments, the toolbars disappear automatically.

7. Tap the video. The toolbars reappear.

Deleting Video

To remove a video clip from your iPhone, select it, tap the Trash Can, and then tap Delete Video at the prompt.

8. Pause the video by tapping Pause.

9. Jump to a specific point in a video by swiping to the left or right on the thumbnails at the bottom of the screen. When you swipe to the left, you move ahead in the video; when you swipe to the right, you move back in the video.

Current frame

Watching Slow-Motion and Time-Lapse Video

Watching slow-motion video is just like watching regular speed video except after a few frames, the video slows down until a few frames before the end at which point it speeds up again. Watching time-lapse is similar except the video plays faster instead of slower than real time.

Editing Video

You can trim a video clip to remove unwanted parts. Here's how you do it:

1. View the video you want to edit.

2. Tap Edit. If the video isn't stored on your phone, it is downloaded. When that process is complete, you can edit it.

3. Drag the left trim marker to where you want the edited clip to start; the trim marker is the left-facing arrow at the left end of the timeline. If you hold your finger in one place for a few seconds, the thumbnails expand so your placement of the crop marker can be more precise. As soon as you move the trim marker, the part of the clip that is inside the selection is highlighted in the yellow box.

4. Drag the right trim marker to where you want the edited clip to end.

5. Tap Done.

6. Tap Save as New Clip to save the trimmed clip as a new clip or Cancel to leave the clip as it was. When you save it as a new clip, the frames outside the crop markers are removed from the clip and it is added to your library as a new clip.

There's an App for That

For more powerful video editing on your iPhone, download the iMovie app. This app provides a much more powerful video editor. You can use themes to design a video, add music, include titles and photos, and much more.

>>>*Go Further*

SHARING VIDEO

There are lots of ways to share your videos. Select the video you want to share. Tap the Share icon. Tap how you want to share the video. There are a number of options including Messages, Mail, iCloud, iCloud Photo Sharing, YouTube, and Facebook. Follow the onscreen prompts to complete the sharing process. The options available to you might depend on the size of the video; for example, you might not be able to email a large video.

Using iCloud with Your Photos

With iCloud, your devices can automatically upload photos to your iCloud account on the Internet. Other devices can automatically download photos from iCloud, so you have your photos available on all your devices at the same time. Using iCloud with your photos has two sides: a sender and receiver. Your iPhone can be both. Photo applications (such as the Photos app on a Mac) can also access your photos and download them to your computer automatically.

In addition to backing up your photos and having all your photos available to you on all your devices, you can also share your photos and videos with others and view photos and videos being shared with you.

Sharing Your Photos

You can share your photos with others by creating a shared album. This is a great way to share photos, because others can subscribe to your shared albums to view and work with the photos you share. When you share photos, you can add them to an album that's already being shared or create a new shared album.

To create a new, empty, shared album, do the following:

1. Open the Shared source. You see the Shared screen that lists the shared albums in which you are currently participating (as either the person sharing them or subscribed to them).

2. Tap Add (+).

3. Type the title of the new album.

4. Tap Next.

5. Enter or select the email address of the first person with whom you want to share the photos.

6. Add other recipients until you've added everyone you want to access the photos.

7. Tap Create. The shared album is created and is ready for you to add photos. The recipients you included in the new album receive notifications that invite them to join the album.

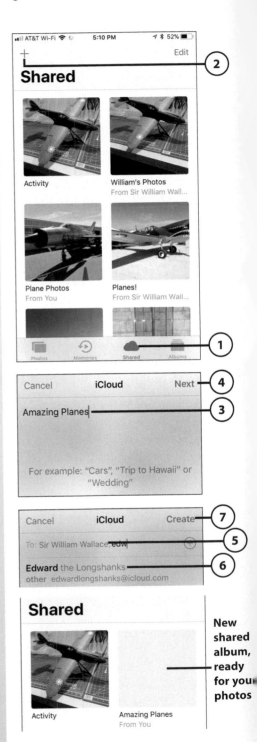

New shared album, ready for your photos

Adding Photos to a Shared Album

To add photos to an album you are sharing, perform the following steps:

1. Move to the source containing photos you want to add to a shared album.

2. Tap Select.

3. Tap the photos you want to share.

4. Tap the Share icon.

5. Tap iCloud Photo Sharing.

6. Enter your commentary about the photos you are sharing. (Note, this commentary is associated only with the first photo.)

7. Tap Shared Album.

8. Swipe up and down to browse the list of shared albums available.

9. Tap the album to which you want to add the photos.

New Shared Album with Photos

You can create a new shared album with the selected photos by tapping New Shared Album.

10. Tap iCloud.

11. Tap Post. The photos you selected are added to the shared album. People who are subscribed to the album receive a notification that photos have been added and can view the new photos along with your commentary.

iCloud Account Required

The people with whom you share photos must have an iCloud account.

>>>Go Further

MORE ON iCLOUD PHOTO SHARING

Following are a few more pointers to help you use iCloud photo sharing:

- You can add comments to photos you are sharing. Open the shared album and tap the photo to which you want to add comments. Tap Add a comment. Type your comment and tap Send. People with whom you are sharing the photo receive a notification and can read your comments.

- To add more photos to a shared album, open the album and tap Add (+). Use the resulting screen to select the photos you want to add, include commentary, and post the photos.

- To invite people to join a shared album, open the shared album. Tap the People tab at the bottom of the screen and then tap Invite People. Enter the email addresses of the people you want to invite and tap Add.

- You can configure various aspects of a shared album by opening it and tapping the People tab at the bottom of the screen. You can see the status of people you have invited, determine if the people with whom you are sharing the album can post to it, make the album a public website, determine if notifications are sent, or delete the shared album.

Working with Photo Albums Shared with You

You can work with albums people share with you as follows:

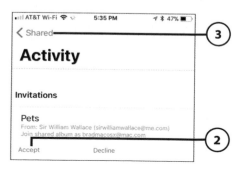

1. Tap the notification you received, or tap the Shared source when you see a badge indicating you have activity.

2. Tap Accept for the shared album you want to join. The shared album becomes available on your Shared tab.

3. Tap Shared.

4. Tap the new shared album.

5. Tap a photo in the album.

6. Tap Like to indicate you like the photo.

7. Tap Add a comment. (If you previously liked the photo, you see the number of likes for it instead; tap that number to add a comment.)

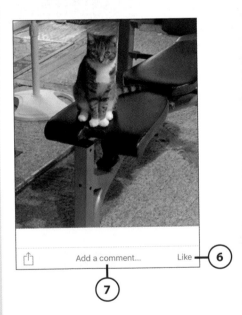

8. Type your comment.

9. Tap Send. Your comments are added to the album.

10. Tap the back icon.

11. If you were allowed to add photos to the shared album by the person who shared it, tap Add (+) and post your own photos to the album you are sharing. This works just like posting to your own albums.

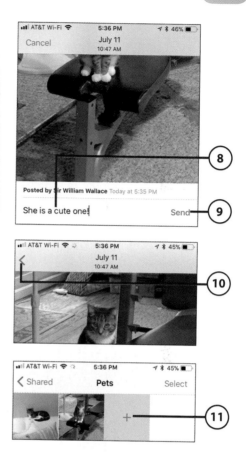

>>>Go Further

MORE ON PHOTOS SHARED WITH YOU

When you share other people's photos, keep the following points in mind:

- You can do most of the tasks with shared photos that you can with your own, such as emailing them, using them as wallpaper, and so on.

- To unsubscribe from an album, move to its People screen and tap Unsubscribe and confirm that is what you want to do. The shared album is removed from your iPhone.

- To see the activity associated with albums being shared with you, and those you are sharing, open the Activity Album on the iCloud Photo Sharing screen. You see new postings to the albums, when someone comments, and so on.

Be reminded about anything

Find your way

Check the time around the world, set alarms and timers, use a stopwatch

Capture notes containing text, attachments, lists, etc.

Get the news you want when you want it

Listen to or watch podcasts

Use Handoff to work seamlessly across devices

Take phone calls on Macs and iPads too

In this chapter, you learn about some other really useful apps and iPhone functionality. Topics include the following:

→ Touring other cool iPhone apps
→ Listening to music with the Music app
→ Finding your way with Maps
→ Using Bluetooth to connect to other devices
→ Connecting your iPhone to other iPhones, iPod touches, or iPads
→ Working with the Wallet app and Apple Pay
→ Working seamlessly across your devices

Working with Other Useful iPhone Apps and Features

In previous chapters, you learned about many of the iPhone's most useful apps, such as Phone, Mail, Messages, Photos, Safari, and Calendar. In this chapter, you learn about three more: Music to listen to your favorite tunes wherever you are, Maps to find and navigate your way to locations near and far, and Wallet that helps you manage and use various kinds of information such as boarding passes, reward cards, and so on.

In this chapter, you also learn how you can connect your iPhone to other devices in several ways. You can use Bluetooth to connect to speakers, headphones, fitness trackers, keyboards, and more. You can connect to other iPhones, iPads, and Macs using AirDrop, so you can quickly and easily share files across those devices.

You find out how Apple Pay enables you to safely and easily pay for purchases in online stores or in the "real world." You can store credit or debit cards in the Wallet app and then use them to pay for purchases with a wave of your phone or tap of a button.

The iOS Handoff feature makes it easy to work on the same tasks on Macs, iPhones, and iPads. For example, you create an email on a Mac, and see the same version on an iPad and your iPhone, too. When a phone call comes in to your iPhone, you can choose to answer it on your Mac, iPad, or Apple Watch.

Before getting into those details, take a tour of some of the other great iPhone apps you might want to explore on your own.

Touring Other Cool iPhone Apps

The following table provides an overview of a number of other apps (all of which are installed by default) that you might find useful or entertaining:

Other Cool iPhone Apps

Icon	App	Description
	Calculator	In portrait orientation, the Calculator is the equivalent of one you would get at the local dollar store. Rotate the iPhone to access scientific calculator options. Access the Calculator quickly by swiping up from the bottom of the screen to open the Control Center; then, tap the Calculator icon. You can also tap the Calculator icon on a Home screen to launch the app.
	Clock	Get the current time in multiple locations around the world, set alarms, set a consistent time to sleep every day, use a stopwatch, or count down time with a timer. Quickly access the Clock app by swiping up from the bottom of the screen to open the Control Center. Tap the Clock icon to open the Clock app. Or, tap the Clock icon on a Home screen.
	Compass (Extras folder)	Transform your iPhone into a compass. Using this app, you can see your current location on the analog-looking compass and with your exact position shown in latitude and longitude. If you swipe to the left, you transform your iPhone into a level that measures on the horizontal planes along with angles. Swipe to the right to get back to the compass.
	Files	When you enable the iCloud Drive under your iCloud account, use the Files app to access the documents stored there. (See Chapter 3, "Setting Up and Using an Apple ID, iCloud, and Other Online Accounts," for information on configuring your iCloud account.)
	Find Friends (Extras folder)	See the current location of "friends" who are part of your Family Sharing group or who you add to the app manually. You can also share your location with others.

Icon	App	Description
	Find iPhone (Extras folder)	Use this app to locate other iPhones, iPads, or Macs that have enabled Find My iPhone using the same iCloud account. (Learn about Find My iPhone in Chapter 16, "Maintaining and Protecting Your iPhone and Solving Problems.")
	Flashlight (Control Center)	Use your iPhone's flash as a flashlight. Open the Control Center and tap the Flashlight icon to turn the light on; tap it again to turn it off. Press and hold on the icon to pop up the brightness slider; drag the slider up to increase the brightness or down to decrease it. This is a very simple app, but also happens to be extremely useful.
	Health	Track and manage health-related information from multiple sources, such as other apps and devices, in one location. You can see your information on dashboards, or you can drill down into the details. You can configure the information you see by selecting the sources and types of information you want to track. You can also store your vital information in the Medical ID so that emergency workers can access it from your Lock screen in order to help you.
	Home	After you configure it to work with your home automation devices, use the Home app to control those devices.
	iBooks	Access and organize books and PDFs so that you always have something to read. The app enables you to change how the books appear on the screen, such as making the font larger or smaller. iBooks syncs across your devices so that you can read something on your iPhone and then pick it up later at the same spot on an iPad.
	iTunes Store	The iTunes Store enables you to browse or search for music, TV shows, movies, and other content. When you find something you want to listen to or watch, you can easily download it to your iPhone. You access the iTunes Store using your Apple ID; any purchases you make are completed using the purchase information associated with that account. Content you download to your iPhone is available in the associated app; for example, when you download music, you listen to that music using the Music app. This app works very similarly to the App Store app, which is covered in Chapter 4, "Customizing How Your iPhone Works."
	News	Read news from a variety of sources. You can search news and save items of interest to you. You can also choose your favorite news sources so that you can focus more on what you care about and avoid what you don't have any interest in.

Icon	App	Description
Notes	Notes	Capture different kinds of information, including text notes, lists, photos, maps, and more. You can also draw in the app and attach different types of objects to notes, and then use the Attachment Manager to view them. Using online accounts with the Notes app, such as iCloud, means that your notes are available on all your devices. If you want to share a note, tap the Share icon and choose how you want to share it.
Podcasts	Podcasts	This app enables you to subscribe to and then listen to podcasts on a wide variety of topics. Episodes of podcasts to which you are subscribed download to your iPhone automatically. You can configure how many episodes are saved on your phone globally and for individual podcasts. There are podcasts on any topic you can imagine so it's very likely you can find podcasts that are of interest to you. You can search for specific podcasts or browse for them based on category and topic.
Reminders	Reminders	Create reminders for just about anything you can imagine, such as to-do lists, items you need to purchase, etc. You can configure alarms for reminders that trigger notifications based on date and time or by location. You can set up repeating reminders, too. If that isn't enough, you can also create multiple lists of reminders, such as one for work and one for personal items. Like other apps, you can store your reminders on the cloud so that you can access them from multiple devices.
Stocks	Stocks	Use this app to track stocks in which you are interested. You can add any index, stock, or mutual fund as long as you know the symbol for it, and you can even use the application to find a symbol if you don't know it. You can see current performance and view historical performance for various time periods. Rotate the iPhone to see a more in-depth view when you are examining a specific stock. You can see the current "ticker" for the items you are tracking by opening the Widget screen and swiping up or down until you see the Stocks widget.
Tips	Tips (Extras folder)	Use this app to get a few pointers about working with your iPhone. Of course, because you have this book, you are way ahead of the game.
TV	TV	Use this app to watch TV shows and movies. You can sign in to a cable provider to watch TV content and you can subscribe to video services, such as HBO Now. Movies or TV shows you purchase or rent using the iTunes Store app are added to this app so you can watch them.
Voice Memos	Voice Memos (Extras folder)	Record audio notes using the Voice Memos app. Play them back, and, through syncing, move them onto your computer, or share them by tapping the Share icon. You can record through the iPhone's microphone or via the mic on the earbud headset.

Icon	App	Description
Watch	Watch	Use this app to pair and configure your iPhone with an Apple Watch. Once paired with your iPhone, you can configure how your Apple Watch accesses content from your iPhone's apps such as Mail, Calendar, Messages, Phone, Contacts, Photos, Music, Reminders, and more.
Weather	Weather	See current weather conditions and a high-level forecast for any number of locations. You can use the default locations, and if you tap the List icon in the lower-right corner of the screen, you can add, remove, and organize the locations you want to track. Swipe through the screens to see each location's forecast.

Your Control Center

You can configure some of the icons you see on the Control Center. See Chapter 4, "Customizing How Your iPhone Works," for details.

Listening to Music with the Music App

The Music app enables you to quickly move to and play any music in your personal music library, or you can access Apple's enormous music library through Apple Music and iTunes Radio. The Music app is quite powerful and offers lots of useful features for working with and listening to all types of music. The following tasks provide you with a good start toward making the most of this amazing app.

There are different sources of music to which you can listen. These include the following sources:

- **Music you own**—You can purchase music using the iTunes Store app, this music immediately becomes available in the Music app. You can buy individual songs or collections of songs. Once purchased, you can download this music onto any of your devices using the same Apple ID as was used for the purchase.

  You can also add music you own on audio CDs or in a digital format by first adding that music to the iTunes app and then syncing that music onto your iPhone. If you already own music like this, there is no additional cost to add it to your iPhone, but it does require some time and effort along with the use of the iTunes app on a computer.

- **Apple Music**—This subscription service from Apple enables you to access its huge music library. You use Apple Music to stream music onto your phone. You can also download it to the phone so that you can listen to it when your phone isn't connected to the Internet or if you want to avoid using cellular data to stream music.

  The benefit of Apple Music is that the amount of music available to you is both enormous and extremely diverse. Unless you have very niche musical tastes, you are likely to find any music you want to listen to in Apple Music. You can also access Apple Music on any of your compatible devices, such as an iPad or a Mac, at no additional charge.

  The downside of Apple Music is that it requires a monthly subscription fee. And you are only "renting" the music. If you let your Apple Music membership expire, you lose access to all of its music.

- **iTunes Radio**—This source, which is free to use, consists of streamed music organized in "stations." You can listen to existing stations or you can create your own stations based on songs or playlists that you like. You must have your phone connected to the Internet to be able to listen to iTunes Radio.

Of course, you can mix and match these sources. For example, you may already own music and also use Apple Music and iTunes Radio to expand the music available to you. Understanding which type of music you are working with is important because the source can change what you can do with that music. For example, you have to download Apple Music onto your phone to be able to listen to it when you aren't connected to the Internet.

There are lots of ways to use the Music app; the following tasks show you how to find and listen to music in your library and Apple Music. Working with iTunes Radio is similar.

Music Settings

Like most other apps you use, the Music app has settings you can configure to change some aspects of how the app works.

Finding Music in Your Library

The Library source contains music you own and music from Apple Music that you've added to it. There are a number of ways music in your library is organized and you can use these categories to find music to which you want to listen. Following are a couple of examples to get you started.

Finding Music by Artist

Finding music by a specific artist is a quick way to get to music you want to hear.

1. Open the Music app.

2. Tap Library. (Like other apps, Music remembers where you left off. If you don't move directly to the main Library page, tap the back icon located in the upper-left corner of the screen until you move to that page.)

3. Tap Artists.

4. Swipe up or down the list of artists to find the one you are interested in or tap the first letter of the artist's name on the index (tap # for artists whose name starts with a number).

5. Tap the artist whose music you want to explore.

6. Swipe up or down the screen to browse the artist's music.

7. Tap an album to see its contents.

8. Review and play the music you see (see "Playing Music" later in this chapter for details).

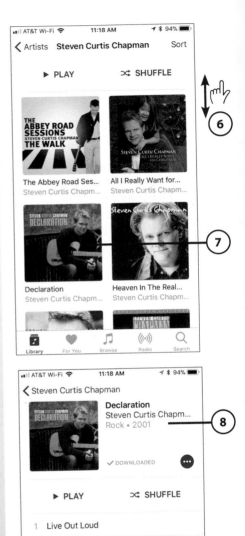

Finding Songs

Finding specific songs to which you want to listen is also simple.

1. Open the Music app.

2. Tap Library. (Like other apps, Music remembers where you left off. If you don't move directly to the main Library page, tap the back icon located in the upper-left corner of the screen until you move to that page.)

3. Tap Songs. On the Songs screen, you see a list of all the songs in your library organized by artist and song title.

4. Tap Sort.

5. Tap Title to have the songs sorted by title or Artist to have them sorted by the artist's name. If you know a specific song you want to hear, choose Title, or if you are looking for music from a specific artist, choose Artist instead. This example shows the Title option selected.

6. Swipe up or down the screen to browse songs.

7. To find a song by its title, tap the index on the first letter of the song's or artist's name and then swipe up or down the screen to find the song you want to hear.

8. Tap the song you want to hear (see "Playing Music" later in this chapter for details).

Other Library Categories

There are a number of other categories of music in your library. Playlists takes you to a list of your playlists. Albums shows you music grouped by album. Downloaded Music takes you to the music in your library that is currently stored on your iPhone so you can listen to it without an Internet connection. Home Sharing takes you to music you are sharing on a local network. The Recently Added section shows you music you've added to your library most recently.

Change Your Library Categories

You can edit the categories you see in your library as well as adding different ones by tapping Edit. Then add categories by tapping their circles, remove them by tapping their check marks, or reorganize them by dragging their List icons up or down the screen. When you're done making changes, tap Done.

Setting Up and Finding Music with Apple Music

Apple Music is Apple's subscription music service. Apple gives you the first three months for free to try it out, and after that you pay a monthly fee (currently $9.99 per month for an individual membership, $14.99 per month for a family membership of up to six people, or $4.99 for a student membership in the United States). The Apple Music Library is huge and you are likely to be able to find and listen to any music of interest to you. You can stream music to listen to it via the Internet or you can download it to your phone so that you don't have to be connected to the Internet to hear it.

Apple Music provides suggestions to you for music you might enjoy based on the music you listen to, or search for, and based on music you indicate that you like by tapping the heart icon while you view or listen to it. Over time, these suggestions get more specific to your musical tastes so that Apple Music's recommendations should help you discover and enjoy new music.

Apple Music is accessible on your iPhone, other iOS devices (such as an iPad), and any computer with the iTunes software on it. (Note that with a single membership, you can play Apple Music on only one device at a time.)

To access Apple Music, you must subscribe to the service.

Subscribing to Apple Music

You can subscribe to Apple Music as follows:

1. Open the Music app.

2. Tap For You.

3. Tap Try It Now.

4. Tap the type of account you want to create (Individual, Family, or College Student).

5. Tap Start Trial.

6. Follow the onscreen instructions to complete the process by first selecting an existing Apple ID to use or creating a new one. After you've completed the process, Apple Music is enabled in the Music app and you see its options on the Dock at the bottom of the screen. (These steps are not shown in figures.)

Browsing Apple Music for You

For You music is music that Apple Music has selected for you (hence the name) based on what you have listened to, what is already in your music library, and what you indicate that you like (you learn how to do this later). To browse the music Apple Music has selected, perform the following steps:

1. Open the Music app and tap For You. On the For You screen, you see a collection of playlists, albums, and songs that Apple Music recommends based on music you've listened to or that you indicated you like.

2. Swipe up and down the screen to browse the selected music. It is organized in different categories, and the content of each category changes over time.

3. Explore the contents of a playlist or album by tapping its artwork. You see the list of songs in the collection you tapped.

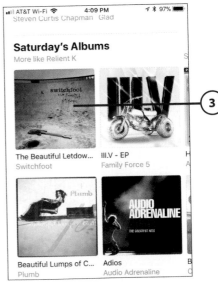

4. Review and play the music you see (see "Playing Music" later in this chapter for details).

5. Tap Back to return to the For You screen to browse for other music.

Browsing Apple Music

You can browse Apple Music to find music you want to hear.

1. Tap Browse.

2. Tap a category of music you want to browse, such as Genres.

3. Swipe up and down to browse all the genres.

4. Tap a genre to explore its contents.

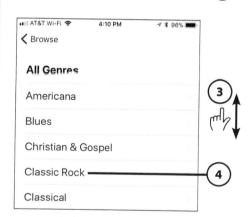

5. Swipe up and down and left and right to browse all the content available.

6. Tap a playlist, album, or other grouping to see the music it contains.

7. Review and play the music you see (see "Playing Music" later in this chapter for details).

Curated Playlist?

A curated playlist is one in which the music has been selected by a person (the curator) or a group of people (the curators). Other types of playlists are generated by software, such as a playlist based on a song you select; software then picks other songs that "go with" the selected song.

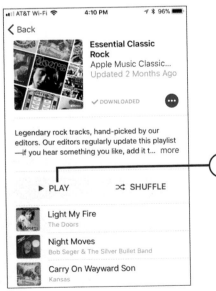

Adding Apple Music to Your Library

You can add Apple Music to your Library to make it easier to listen to again and so that it is downloaded to your iPhone so you can play it without an Internet connection. Here's how:

1. Using the information in the previous tasks, find Apple Music you want to add to your library.

2. To add all the songs you see to your Library, tap + ADD or to add an individual song to your library, tap its Add icon (+). You see the Added confirmation pop up briefly and then all of the songs in the current collection or the individual songs download to your iPhone. When the process is complete, you see DOWNLOADED at the top of the screen.

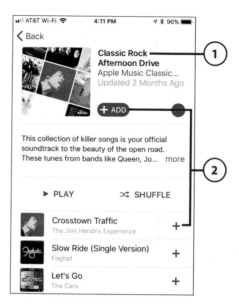

In Your Library, but Not on Your iPhone

If you see a collection of music that has the download icon (a cloud with a downward-pointing arrow) instead of + ADD, that means the music is in your library but hasn't been downloaded to your iPhone. When you listen to that music, it streams onto the phone, which requires an Internet connection. You can tap the download icon to download the music onto your iPhone.

Limited Data Plan?

If you have a limited data plan, you might want to disable music downloading when you are using a cellular Internet connection. Open the Settings app and tap Music. Tap Cellular Data. Use the controls on the Cellular Data screen to determine whether cellular data can be used at all (the Cellular Data switch), if it can be used for streaming, or if it can be used to download music. You also use the Cellular Data screen to choose the quality level of streamed music.

Limited Data Plan, Part II

If you have a limited data plan, you should consider downloading music if you think you'll listen to it more than once. That way, you can play it from the copy stored on your iPhone rather than streaming it over your cellular connection. You can always delete any music on your iPhone that you no longer want, so there's no downside to downloading it (especially if you download music when you are using a Wi-Fi network)—assuming your iPhone has plenty of free space of course.

Searching for Music

Searching for music enables you to quickly find music you want to hear. You can search music in your library or music available via Apple Music. To search for music, do the following steps:

1. Open the Music app.

2. Tap Search.

3. Tap a recent search to repeat that same search, and move to step 6.

4. Tap a trending search (one that other people are performing) to perform that search, and move to step 6.

5. Tap in the Search bar to perform a new search.

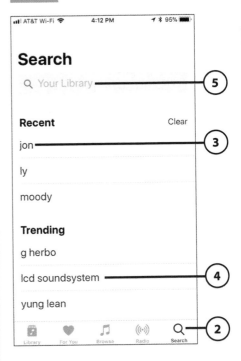

6. Search the music in your library by tapping Your Library, or search Apple Music by tapping Apple Music.

7. Type the term for which you want to search; this can be an artist's name, song title, album title, and so on. As you type, the results that meet your search term appear under the tabs.

8. Swipe up and down the screen to review the results of your search.

9. When you find something of interest, tap it. You move to that content's page. What this contains depends on what you tapped on. For example, if you tap an album, you move to the album's page. If you tap an artist, you move to a screen showing sections for top results, albums, songs, videos, and so on.

10. Browse the content of what you tapped in step 9.

11. Tap See All to see all the items in a group, such as all albums (not shown in the figure).

12. Tap an album, song, or other item to view it.

13. If you tapped an album, browse the songs it contains.

14. Tap a song to play it.

Playing Music

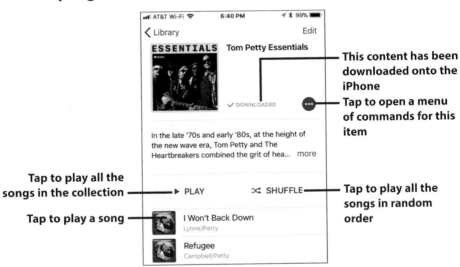

This content has been downloaded onto the iPhone

Tap to open a menu of commands for this item

Tap to play all the songs in the collection

Tap to play all the songs in random order

Tap to play a song

In the prior tasks, you learned how to find music to which you want to listen. No matter what you choose to listen to, such as a song, album, playlist, or other content, you use the same set of controls to listen to that music. When you find what you want to play, tap it to start it. The following sections describe several ways you can control music that is playing.

Playing Music on the Miniplayer

Miniplayer · Tap to open the Now Playing Screen · Song currently playing · I Won't Back Down · Skip to the next song · Pause/Play · Library · For You · Browse · Radio · Search

When you play music, the Miniplayer appears at the bottom of the screen. On this bar, you see the song currently playing and the art associated with the song playing. You also see the Pause/Play icon that you can tap to stop or start the music.

While the Miniplayer appears, you can use the upper part of the Music app's screen to find other music to listen to, to download more music, and so on. The Miniplayer remains on the screen as long as music plays so you can control what is playing while you are doing other things with the app.

To have more control over the music and to see other options, tap the Miniplayer. The Now Playing screen opens.

Playing Music on the Now Playing Screen

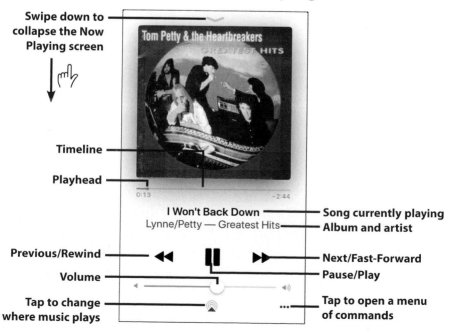

Swipe down to collapse the Now Playing screen · Timeline · Playhead · 0:13 · -2:44 · I Won't Back Down — Song currently playing · Lynne/Petty — Greatest Hits — Album and artist · Previous/Rewind · Next/Fast-Forward · Volume · Pause/Play · Tap to change where music plays · Tap to open a menu of commands

The Now Playing screen has many features, including:

- **Timeline**—Just below the art, you see the timeline. The elapsed time is on the left side, and the remaining time is on the right. The Playhead shows you where you are in the song. You can drag this to the left to move back in the song or to the right to move ahead.

- **Song information**—Below the timeline is the song's name (in larger, bold font). Under that is the artist and album title. If any of this information is too large to fit on the screen, it scrolls across the screen to display it all.

- **Previous/Rewind**—If the current song has been playing for more than a second or two, tap this icon once to move to the beginning of the current song. If you are at the beginning of the current song, tap it to move to the previous song in the current source (album, artist, and so on). Tap and hold to rewind in the current song.

- **Pause/Play**—Tap Pause to pause the song. Tap Play to play it again.

- **Next/Fast-Forward**—Tap once to move to the next song on the list (or the next randomly selected song, if you are shuffling). Tap and hold to fast-forward in the current song.

- **Volume**—Drag the slider to the left to lower the volume or to the right to increase it.

- **Output device**—Tap this icon to change where music is playing. When you tap this, a menu showing all the options appears. For example, if you have Bluetooth speakers paired with your iPhone, you can tap them to play the music there. If you have devices connected via AirPlay, such as an Apple TV, you can tap them to use them to listen to music. If you have EarPods connected to your iPhone, you can choose to play music over them. To return playback to the iPhone's speakers, tap iPhone.

- **Ellipsis**—Whenever you see the ellipsis icon (…), you can tap it to open a menu of commands as described in the following text and figure.

When you open an item's menu by tapping the ellipsis (…) icon, you see a menu of commands for that item. The commands you see depend on the item you are viewing at the time. For example, you see a different set of commands for an album than you do for an iTunes radio station. Also, the status of the item affects the commands you see. If you are viewing Apple Music that has been added to your library, you see the Remove command, which enables you to remove the music; if you are viewing music that hasn't been added, you see the Add to Library command instead.

Following is an example of this menu for an album that is part of my library.

Tap to move to album ——

Add the album to a playlist ——

Share the song ——

Tap to indicate you love the song and want to hear more like it ——

—— Tap to remove from the Library

—— Create an iTunes radio station based on the current song

—— Tap to indicate you don't like the song and don't want to hear more like it

Close the menu

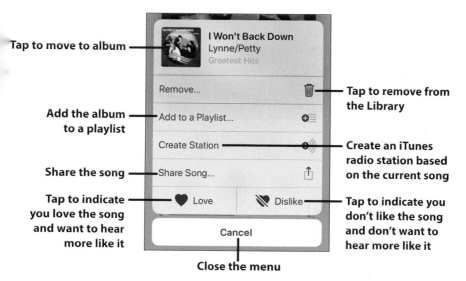

To collapse the Now Playing screen, swipe down from the top of the Now Playing screen. You return to the Miniplayer.

Turn It Up! (Or Down!)

No matter which technique you use to find and play music, you can control the volume using the Volume buttons on the left side of your iPhone. Press the upper button to increase volume or the lower one to decrease it. While you are pressing a button, a volume indicator appears on the screen to show you the relative volume level as you press the buttons. When you are on the Now Playing screen or viewing the Music control bar (covered later in this chapter), you can also use the Volume slider to set the sound level. If you listen with the EarPods included with your iPhone, you can use the buttons on the right EarPod's wire to crank it up (press and hold the top button) or down (press and hold the bottom button).

Sleep Timer

Here's a tip courtesy of my acquisitions editor. To cause your music to stop playing after a specific period of time, open the Control Center (by swiping up from the bottom of the screen), tap the Clock icon, and then tap Timer. Use the wheels to set the amount of time that you want the music to play. Tap When Timer Ends. Swipe up the screen and tap Stop Playing. When the timer expires, the music stops.

Playing Music from the Lock Screen

Lock screen

Information about the current music

Music controls

When audio is playing and your iPhone is locked, you can control music playback right from the Lock screen.

Press the Side or Touch ID/Home button or lift the phone (with Raise to Wake enabled). Your iPhone wakes up and you see the Lock screen, which displays information about and controls for the music currently playing. Use the controls you see; these work like they do in the Music app.

When you're done controlling the tunes, press the Side button again to prevent the controls from being on the screen (so that they don't accidentally get activated if you put your iPhone back in your pocket, for example).

Swipe down to open the Music controls

Information about the current music

Music controls

Swipe up from the bottom to return to the previous screen

If your phone is unlocked, you can open the same tool by swiping down from the top of the screen. You see the same music controls as on the Lock screen. The Notification Center is under those controls; you can swipe up and down the list of notifications to review them. Swipe up from the bottom of the screen to return to the previous screen.

Playing Music from the Control Center

Swipe up to open the Control Center

Press to open more music controls

Control the music

Tap outside the music controls to return to the Control Center

Tap the song/album information to jump to the Now Playing screen

The same controls as on the Lock screen

To get to some of the music controls quickly, swipe up from the bottom of the Home screen (all models except the iPhone X) or swipe down from the upper-right corner of the screen (iPhone X) to open the Control Center. In the upper-right corner of the Control Center, you see Audio tools. Press and hold on this area to open the same set of music controls as you see on the Lock screen. When you're done, tap outside the music controls to return to the Control Center. Use the controls you see; then, close the Control Center by tapping the downward-facing arrow at the top and continue what you were doing.

More Than Just Music

The controls in the Audio section of the Control Center change based on the app you are using to play audio. For example, when you are using the Podcasts app to play a podcast, these tools control the podcast's playback. Likewise, if you play audio with a different app, these controls work for that app.

Siri and Music

You can use Siri to select, play, and control music, too. For example, you can activate Siri and say "Play album Frank Sinatra's Greatest Hits" to play that album or "Play Song 'Free Bird'" to play that song. You can say, "Show me music by Switchfoot" to see music by that group. Refer to Chapter 11, "Working with Siri," for details.

Using 3D Touch with the Music App (iPhone 6s/6s Plus and Later)

Like other default iPhone apps, the Music app supports 3D Touch, which you can use in a couple of ways.

Perform a Peek to see the Quick Actions menu

Tap to search for music

Tap to play the Beats 1 station

Tap to play music

When you press on the Music app's icon, you see the Quick Actions menu. At the bottom of this menu, you see the Music widget displaying music you have played recently; tap an album cover or playlist art to play its music. You can tap Play Beats 1 to play that music or tap Search to jump to the search screen.

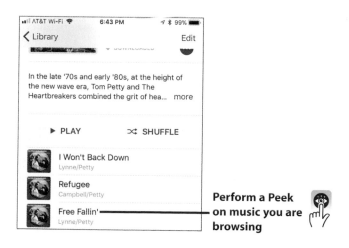

Perform a Peek on music you are browsing

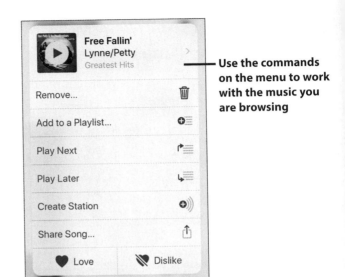

Use the commands on the menu to work with the music you are browsing

When you are browsing music, press on music in which you are interested to perform a Peek on it. In the Peek window, you view the music on which you pressed and you see a menu of commands. Tap a command to perform it. For example, tap the Play icon to play the music you are viewing.

Finding Your Way with Maps

The Maps app enables you to find locations and view them on the map. However, the real power of the Maps app is that you can then get detailed, turn-by-turn, voice directions to those places. You can use these directions to drive, walk, or even take public transportation to the places you find. Maps monitors your path; when there are issues that might be a problem, such as heavy traffic or an accident, the app attempts to reroute you to a better way.

Generating directions with the Maps app is easy and quick to do as the following steps demonstrate:

1. On the Home screen, tap Maps.

2. Tap in the Search bar.

3. Type in the location you want to find. You can type in an address, a place name (such as Indianapolis Executive Airport), or even a description of what you are looking for (for example, coffee). As you type, the app presents a list of locations that meet your search. Keep typing until you see the location you want to find on the list; if it isn't a public location, such as a business, you will likely have to type the entire address.

4. Tap the location you want to see on the map. The map appears and the location, or locations (if you do a more general search), for which you searched are marked with a pushpin. (If you found multiple locations, tap the one to which you want to navigate.)

5. To get directions to the selected location, tap Directions.

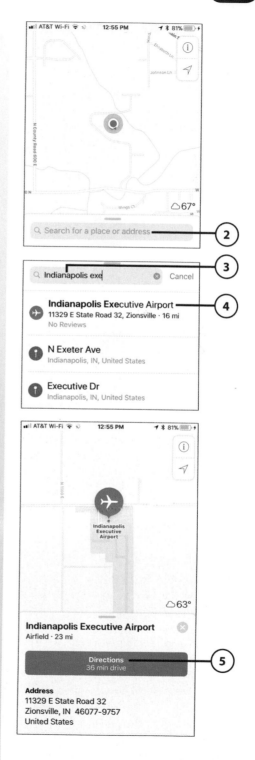

6. Tap how you want to travel to the destination, such as Drive, Walk, etc. The options you see depend on where you are going and where you are. The app generates alternative paths when possible. The primary or default path is shown in dark blue; alternative paths are in light blue. You see a time estimate for each path.

Don't Want to Get There from Here?

Maps assumes you want a path from your current location to the destination you selected. However, you can choose a different starting point by tapping My Location. Use the Change Route screen to search for and select a different starting location. Tap Route. Maps updates the route to start from the location you selected on the Change Route screen.

7. If you want to follow an alternate path, tap it. Maps re-generates the route.

8. Tap Go. The app shows you the part of the route you are on and announces what you need to do.

9. Follow the verbal or onscreen directions to start your journey. Maps shows you where you are on your route and what is coming next. As you approach the next step, such as a turn, the app starts to make announcements about what you need to do.

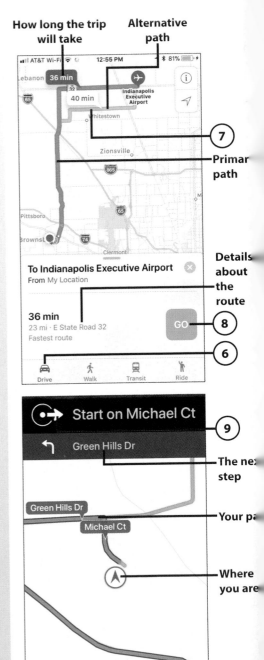

How long the trip will take

Alternative path

Primary path

Details about the route

Start on Michael Ct

The next step

Your path

Where you are

Arrival time, travel time, and distance

10. Listen for the app's instructions about the next step and follow the directions you hear.

11. To get more information or find interim locations (such as gas stations or restaurants), swipe up from the bottom of the screen.

The next step

The next step

Current speed limit

12. Tap the kind of service you need, such as Coffee (other options can include Gas Stations, Lunch, Breakfast, Dinner, or Restaurants). Maps locates services of that type that are "convenient" to your path and presents options on the map and in the panel at the bottom of the screen.

13. Swipe up and down on the list of options to review how far away from you they are and how much time will be added to the trip if you go to those locations.

14. To navigate to one of the locations on the list, tap GO. Maps reroutes you to that location. (After you arrive at that location, Maps prompts you to resume your previous route.)

15. If you don't want to choose one of the locations and just return to the directions to the original location, tap Done.

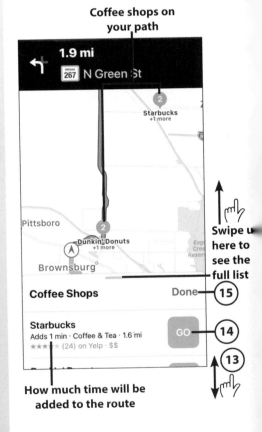

Coffee shops on your path

Swipe up here to see the full list

How much time will be added to the route

16. If you move out of the Maps app, you can tap the blue bar at the top of the screen to return to it. When the next step in your path approaches, you see that step in a pop-up box on the screen.

The next step

17. Continue following the directions until you arrive at your destination.

18. Tap End Route to reset Maps.

>>>Go Further

GET THERE WITH MAPS

Here are a few Maps pointers to help you along your way:

- If you want to stop the navigation before you reach the end, tap End and then tap End Route.
- On the Options panel (that appears when you swipe up from the bottom of the screen), tap Audio to change the volume of the instructions or pause the audio directions. You can also choose where the audio directions are played from, such as through the Dock connector or via your car's audio system.

- If you tap Overview on the Options panel, you see the overview of your route, similar to what you see at the beginning. Tap the black box that shows the next step to return to the step-by-step view.

- Tap Details to see a list of each step along the way.

- The Ride option shows your route using a ride-sharing service and app, such as Uber. When you choose Ride, your iPhone identifies the ride-sharing app configured on your phone. You see an estimate of wait time for your ride and cost for each service. Tap NEXT on the option you want to use. Maps then starts the ride-sharing process just like when you use the ride-sharing app directly.

- To repeat the current step you are on, tap it. The app speaks the current step.

- You can use the standard zoom and swipe motions on the map to change your view. For example, you can swipe down on the map to see further ahead on the path. Maps uses a "3D" view so you can see along your path as if you are flying above it.

- If you change the map so you can no longer see your location, tap the arrow icon and the map re-centers on your current location.

- If you get off the planned path, such as by taking a wrong turn, Maps reroutes you automatically.

- If Maps identifies a potentially faster route (perhaps because of traffic conditions on the current route), it prompts you to change to the updated route. If you allow that, Maps reroutes you. If not, you continue on your current path.

- If you tap the Info (i) icon, you can configure some aspects of how the app works or looks. For example, you can enable or disable the traffic re-routing function or change the view from a map to a satellite image.

- Maps remembers your recent searches and presents them on the search list when you move into search mode. You can tap a recent search to repeat it.

- Maps has a number of settings you can configure to tailor how the app works for you. For example, in the Driving & Navigation settings, you can choose to avoid tolls or highways or if the speed limit is displayed on the screen. Open the Settings app and tap Maps to see all its settings options.

- If you connect your iPhone to a car audio/video system that supports AirPlay, you see the Maps screen on the car's video screen and hear its directions over the car's audio system.

- If you connect your iPhone to a car stereo via Bluetooth or AirPlay and have the Show Parked Location switch on the Maps Settings screen enabled (green), the location of your parked car is shown on the map (assuming its location can be determined). This can eliminate the need to try to remember where you parked.

Using Bluetooth to Connect to Other Devices

The iPhone includes built-in Bluetooth support so you can use this wireless technology to connect to other Bluetooth-capable devices. The most likely devices to connect to your iPhone in this way are Bluetooth headphones, speakers, headsets, or car audio/entertainment/information systems, but you can also use Bluetooth to connect to other kinds of devices, most notably keyboards.

To connect Bluetooth devices together, you pair them. In Bluetooth, pairing enables two Bluetooth devices to communicate with each other. The one constant requirement is that the devices can communicate with each other via Bluetooth. For devices to find and identify each other so they can communicate, one or both must be discoverable, which means they broadcast a Bluetooth signal other devices can detect and connect to.

There is also a "sometimes" requirement, which is a pairing code, passkey, or PIN. All those terms refer to the same thing, which is a series of numbers, letters, or both, entered on one or both devices being paired. Sometimes you enter this code on both devices, whereas for other devices you enter the first device's code on the second device. Some devices, such as headphones or speakers, don't require a pairing code at all.

When you have to pair devices, you're prompted to do so, and you have to complete the actions required by the prompts to communicate via Bluetooth. This might be just tapping Connect, or you might have to enter a passcode on one or both devices to connect them.

Connecting to Bluetooth Devices

This task demonstrates pairing an iPhone with Bluetooth headphones; you can pair it with other devices similarly.

1. Move to the Settings screen. The current status of Bluetooth on your iPhone is shown.

2. Tap Bluetooth.

3. If Bluetooth isn't on (green), tap the Bluetooth switch to turn it on. If it isn't running already, Bluetooth starts up. The iPhone immediately begins searching for Bluetooth devices. You also see the status Now Discoverable, which means other Bluetooth devices can discover the iPhone. In the MY DEVICES section, you see devices to which you've previously paired your iPhone; their current status is either Connected, meaning the device is currently communicating with your iPhone, or Not Connected, meaning the device is paired with your iPhone, but is not currently connected to it. In the OTHER DEVICES section, you see the devices that are discoverable to your iPhone but that are not paired with it.

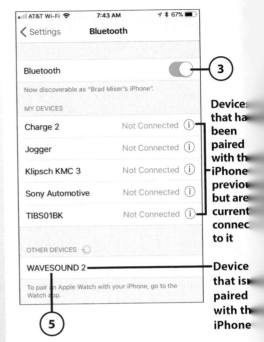

Devices that have been paired with the iPhone previously but are not currently connected to it

Device that isn't paired with the iPhone

4. If the device you want to use isn't shown in the OTHER DEVICES section, put it into Discoverable mode. (Not shown; see the instructions provided with the device.) When it is discoverable, it appears in the OTHER DEVICES section.

5. Tap the device to which you want to connect. If the device isn't currently paired with your iPhone, you might need to provide a passkey. If a passkey is required, you see a prompt to enter it on the device with which you are pairing; perform step 6. If no passkey is required, skip to step 7.

6. If it is required (not shown in a figure), input the pairing code, passkey, or PIN on the device, such as typing the passkey on a keyboard if you are pairing your iPhone with a Bluetooth keyboard.

7. If required, tap Connect (not shown in a figure)—some devices connect as soon as you select them or enter the passkey and you won't need to do this. You see the device to which the iPhone is connected in the MY DEVICES section of the Bluetooth screen, and its status is Connected, indicating that your iPhone can communicate with and use the device.

8. To manage a device, tap its Info icon.

9. Tap the command you want to use; for example, to stop working with a device, tap Disconnect. The options you see depend on the device and its current status.

When your iPhone is paired with a device that supports audio, such as headphones, you can open the device menu (such as the one on the Audio controls panel) and tap the device on which you want to hear that audio.

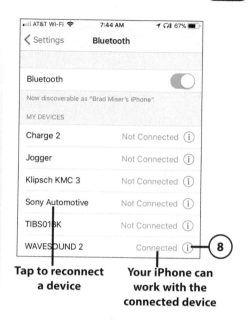

Tap to reconnect a device

Your iPhone can work with the connected device

When paired with Bluetooth headphones, choose the headphones to listen with them

>>>Go Further

MANAGING BLUETOOTH

Following are a few pointers for using Bluetooth with other devices:

- Like other connections you make, the iPhone remembers Bluetooth devices to which you've connected before and reconnects to them automatically, which is convenient—most of the time anyway. If you don't want your iPhone to keep connecting to a device, move to the Bluetooth screen and tap the device's Info (i) button. Tap Forget this Device and then tap Forget Device. The pairing is removed. Of course, you can always pair the devices again at any time. If you just want to stop using the device, but keep the pairing in place, you can tap Disconnect instead.

- If a device is already paired but has the Not Connected status, you need to connect it to use it. Move to the Bluetooth screen and tap the device to connect it to your iPhone. Once its status becomes Connected, your iPhone can communicate with the device again.

- You can use multiple Bluetooth devices with your iPhone at the same time. For example, you might want to be connected to a Bluetooth speaker and a keyboard at the same time.

Connecting Your iPhone to Other iPhones, iPod touches, or iPads

The iPhone (and other devices that run the iOS software, including iPod touches and iPads) supports peer-to-peer connectivity, which is the technical way of saying that these devices can communicate with one another directly via a Wi-Fi network or Bluetooth. This capability is used in a number of apps, especially multiplayer gaming, for information sharing, and for other collaborative purposes.

If the app you want to use communicates over a Wi-Fi network, such as a network you use to access the Internet, all the devices with which you want to communicate must be on that same network. If the application uses Bluetooth, you must enable Bluetooth on each device and pair them (as described in the previous task) so they can communicate with one another.

The specific steps you use to connect to other iOS devices using a collaborative app depend on the specific app you are using. The general steps are typically as follows:

1. Ensure the devices can communicate with each other. If the app uses Wi-Fi, each device must be on the same Wi-Fi network. If the app uses Bluetooth, the devices must be paired.

2. Each person opens the app on his device.

3. Use the app's controls to select the devices with which you'll be collaborating. Usually, this involves a confirmation process in which one person selects another person's device and that person confirms that the connection should be allowed.

4. Use the app's features to collaborate. For example, if the app is a game, each person can interact with the group members. Or, you can directly collaborate on a document with all parties providing input into the document.

Using AirDrop to Share Content with Other iPhones, iPod touches, iPads, or a Mac

You can use the AirDrop feature to share content directly with people using a Mac running OS X Yosemite or later, or using a device running iOS 7 or later. For example, if you capture a great photo on your iPhone, you can use AirDrop to instantly share that photo with iOS device and Mac users near you.

AirDrop can use Wi-Fi or Bluetooth to share, but the nice thing about AirDrop is that it manages the details for you. You simply open the Share menu—which is available in most apps—tap AirDrop, and tap the people with whom you want to share.

When you activate AirDrop, you can select Everyone, which means you see anyone who has a Mac running OS X Yosemite or later, or an iOS device running version iOS 7 or newer and is on the same Wi-Fi network as you (or has a paired Bluetooth device); those people can see you, too. (You can decline any request to share with you via AirDrop so even if you choose Everyone, you can still decide which content is moved onto your iPhone.) Or, you can select Contacts Only, which means only people who are in your Contacts app are able to use AirDrop to communicate with you. In most cases, you should choose the Contacts Only option so you have more control over who uses AirDrop with you.

Is AirDrop Safe?

Anything you share with AirDrop is encrypted, so the chances of someone else being able to intercept and use what you share are quite low. Likewise, you don't have to worry about someone using AirDrop to access your information or to add information to your device without your permission. However, like any networking technology, there's always some chance—quite small in this case—that someone will figure out how to use this technology for nefarious purposes. The best thing you can do is to be wary of any requests you receive to share information and ensure they are from people you know and trust before you accept them.

Enabling AirDrop

To use AirDrop, you must enable it on your iPhone.

1. Open the General screen of the Settings app.

2. Tap AirDrop.

3. Tap Receiving Off if you don't want to receive any content via AirDrop (you can still share your content with others), tap Contacts Only to allow only people in your Contacts app to be able to request to share content with you, or Everyone to allow anyone using a device running iOS 7 or later or a Mac running OS X Yosemite or later in your area to request to share content with you.

Another Way to Configure AirDrop

You can also configure AirDrop by opening the Control Center and pressing on the Airplane mode, Wi-Fi, Cellular Data, or Bluetooth icons. On the resulting panel, tap the AirDrop icon. Then choose the AirDrop status you want to set (these are the same as described in step 3).

Share and Share Alike?

You should choose the Receiving Off option when you aren't using AirDrop, especially if you usually use the Everyone option. By disabling it, you avoid having people in your area be able to try to communicate with you without you wanting them to do so. When you want to receive content again, you can quickly reset AirDrop to Contacts Only or Everyone again.

Using AirDrop to Share Your Content

To use AirDrop to share your content, do the following:

1. Open the content you want to share. This example shows sharing a photo using the Photos app (this app is covered in detail in Chapter 14, "Viewing and Editing Photos and Video with the Photos App"). The steps to share content from any other app are quite similar.

2. Tap the Share icon.

3. If the app you selected in step 1 supports it, you can swipe to preview other content and select it by tapping it. Each item you select is available for sharing. When marked with the check mark, the content will be shared.

4. Tap AirDrop (not shown on the figure) or just wait a couple of seconds. The AirDrop icon is replaced with icons for each person in your area who has AirDrop enabled that you have permission to access (such as being in her Contacts app if she is using the Contacts Only option).

5. Swipe to the left or right to browse all the people with whom you can share.

Content to be shared

Tap to share

6. Tap the people with whom you want to share the content. A sharing request is sent to those people's devices. Under their icons, the Waiting status is displayed. When a recipient accepts your content, the status changes to Sent. If a recipient rejects your content, the status changes to Declined.

7. If the app supports it, browse and select more content to share by tapping items that aren't selected; tap items currently selected if you don't want to send them again.

8. Tap the people with whom you want to share the content.

9. When you're done sharing, tap Done.

A sharing request has been sent and accepted

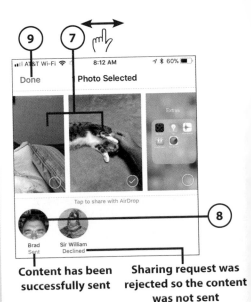

Content has been successfully sent

Sharing request was rejected so the content was not sent

Using AirDrop to Work with Content Shared with You

When someone wants to share content with you, you receive an AirDrop sharing request. (If you use AirDrop to share content among your own devices such as sending a photo from your iPhone to a Mac, it is accepted automatically.) Respond to sharing requests by doing the following:

1. Make sure you know the person attempting to share with you.

2. Make sure the content being shared with you is something you want. In this case, a photo is being shared.

3. To accept the content on your iPhone, tap Accept. To reject it, tap Decline.

4. Use the associated app to work with the shared content. For example, the Photos app provides tools to edit and share photos that are shared with you. In some cases, such as saving a contact shared with you, you need to tap Save to save the content on your iPhone or Cancel to not save it. (Other apps provide different controls depending on the type of content and the app it opens in.)

Working with the Wallet App and Apple Pay

The Wallet app manages all sorts of information that you need to access, from airline tickets to shopping and credit cards to movie tickets and rewards cards. Instead of using paper or plastic to conduct transactions, you can simply have your iPhone's screen scanned.

You use the Wallet app to access your Apple Pay information to make payments when you are in a physical location, such as a store or hotel (Apple Pay is covered in detail in "Working with Apple Pay" later in this chapter). You can also use Apple Pay when you make purchases online using some apps on your iPhone.

Working with the Wallet App

You can store a wide variety of information in your wallet so that it is easily accessible. Examples include boarding passes, membership cards (to a gym for example), store cards (such as Starbucks if you are an addict like I am), and loyalty or discount cards (like those loyalty cards that grocery stores or gas stations offer). The Wallet app eliminates the need to carry physical cards or paper for each of these; instead, your information is available to you digitally, and you can enter it as needed by scanning the iPhone's screen.

Tap to open your Wallet

Open the Control Center and then tap to open your Wallet

Cards available for Apple Pay

Passes, such as boarding passes or loyalty cards

Starbucks card

If necessary, swipe up or down to view all the cards in your Wallet

Boarding pass

Tap to make a card active

To open your wallet, tap the Wallet icon on a Home screen or first open the Control Center and then tap the Wallet icon. The Wallet app opens. At the top, you see the Apple Pay section that shows the cards you've enabled for Apple Pay. In the Passes section, you see other cards, such as boarding passes and loyalty cards.

As you add cards and boarding passes to your Wallet, they "stack up" at the bottom of the screen. Tap the stack to see the list of items available in your Wallet. The cards expand so that you can see at least the top of each card; if you have a lot of cards installed, swipe up or down on the screen to view all of them.

Boarding pass in the Wallet app

Scan this to board the flight

Tap to open the associated app

Tap to configure the boarding pass

Tap to open other cards available in your Wallet

To use a card in your Wallet, tap it. It becomes the active card and you can access its information. For example, you can quickly access a boarding pass by opening the Wallet app and tapping it. To board the plane, you scan the code on the boarding pass. Even better, boarding passes start appearing on the Lock screen a few hours before the take-off time. Press (3D Touch) or swipe to the right (non-3D Touch) on the boarding pass on the Lock screen and you jump directly to the boarding pass in the Wallet app (you don't even need to unlock your phone).

Some passes enable you to share them or information about them by tapping the Share icon and using the standard sharing tools that appear.

Others are connected to an app; you can tap the icon on the pass or card to move into the associated app.

Starbucks card ——

Starbucks Card

BALANCE
$15.02 —— Current balance

NICKNAME
My Card

Scan this to pay for
—— Starbucks goodies

Tap to open the
Starbucks app ——

—— Tap to configure
the card

—————————

AT&T Wi-Fi 🔋 10:24 AM 📶 ✳ 45% 🔋

Done —— Tap to save
changes and
close the
Configure
screen

Starbucks Card
Updated 27 minutes ago

Starbucks
Starbucks Coffee Company
INSTALLED

Open

Automatic Updates

Controls to
—— configure the
card

Share Pass

Tap to delete the
card from your
Wallet ——

Remove Pass

When you tap a card's info icon (i), you can use the controls on a card's Configure screen to adjust certain aspects of how the card works. If you set the Suggest on Lock Screen switch to on (green), for a card that works based on a location, such as your favorite stores, the card automatically appears on your Lock screen at the appropriate times. And, some cards can be automatically refilled from your bank account or credit/debit card so that they always have a positive balance.

To delete a card from your Wallet (such as a boarding pass when the flight is finished), tap its Info icon, tap Delete or Remove Pass, and then confirm that you want to delete or remove it. The pass or card is removed from your Wallet.

When you're done configuring a card, tap Done. The Configure screen closes and you return to the card you were configuring.

There a couple of ways to add cards to your Wallet. The most frequent way to add a card is by using the Add to Wallet command in the app associated with the card. In some cases, you might be able to scan the code on a card to add it.

Adding Passes or Cards to Your Wallet Using an App

If you are a frequent patron of a particular business (perhaps you are addicted to Starbucks coffee like I am) that has an iPhone app, check to see if it also supports the Wallet app. For example, when you use the Starbucks app configured with your account, you can add a Starbucks card to your Wallet as follows:

1. Open the app for which you want to add a pass or card to your Wallet.

2. Tap Pay. (These steps are specific to the Starbucks app, but you can add other cards to your Wallet in similar ways. Look for the command that enables you to configure how you pay for purchases associated with that card.)

3. Tap the app's command to manage its information; this command can be labeled with different names in different apps (it is the MANAGE command in the Starbucks app), or it might be accessed with an icon or menu.

4. Tap Add to Wallet.

5. Tap Add. The card or pass is added to your Wallet and is ready to use. (You might be prompted to do some additional configuration of the card, such as to indicate favorite locations.)

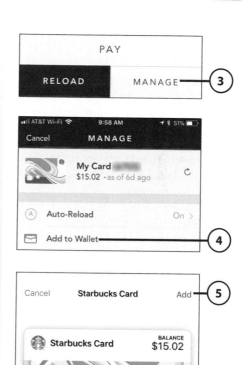

Finding Apps that Support the Wallet

You can search for apps that support the Wallet by opening your Wallet, tapping Edit Passes at the bottom of the Passes section, and tapping Find Apps for Wallet. This takes you into the App Store app and you see apps that support the Wallet. You can then download and install apps you want to use as described in Chapter 4.

Adding Passes or Cards to Your Wallet by Scanning Their Codes

In some cases, you can add a card or pass to the Wallet by scanning its code. To do so, follow these steps:

1. Open the Wallet app and swipe until you reach the bottom of the screen.

2. Tap Edit Passes.

3. Tap Scan Code.

4. Use the iPhone's camera to scan the bar code on the card by positioning the phone so that the white box encloses the bar code on the card (not shown on a figure). If the bar code is recognized and is available for the Wallet, the pass or card is added to the Wallet and is ready for use. If the bar code isn't recognized or doesn't support the Wallet, you see an error and you need to find an associated app for the card to use it with the Wallet.

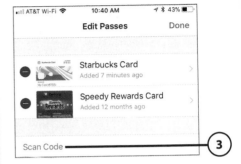

Working with Apple Pay

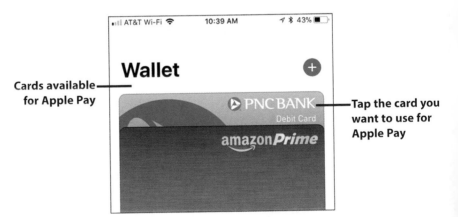

Cards available for Apple Pay

Tap the card you want to use for Apple Pay

Hold your phone near the reader and touch the Touch ID button to authorize payment

With Apple Pay, you can store your cards in the Wallet app, and they are instantly and automatically available to make purchases. Apple Pay enables you to pay for things more easily and securely than with physical credit or debit cards. (Note that Apple Pay requires an iPhone 6 or later.) When you are making a purchase in a physical store, you can simply hold your iPhone up to a contactless reader connected to the cash register and tap your finger on the Touch ID button. The iPhone communicates the information required to complete the purchase.

iPhone X

Using Apple Pay on an iPhone X is a bit different than on other models. Refer to the online supplement *My iPhone X* by going to www.informit.com/myiphone11 for the details of using Apple Pay on an iPhone X.

When you are making a transaction in an app that supports Apple Pay, tap this to pay

Apple Pay also simplifies purchases made in online stores. When you use an app or a website that supports Apple Pay, you can tap the Buy with Apple Pay icon to complete the purchase.

Apple Pay is actually more secure than using a credit or debit card because your card information is not passed to the device; instead, a unique code is passed that ties back to your card, but that can't be used again. And, you never present your card so the number is not visible to anyone, either visually or digitally.

Apple Pay Support

In addition to requiring an iPhone 6 or later model, a credit or debit card must support Apple Pay for it to work with that card. The easiest way to figure out if your cards support it is to try to add a card to Apple Pay. If you can do so, the card is supported and you can use it. If not, you can check with the credit or debit card company to see when support for Apple Pay will be added so you can use it.

Adding Credit or Debit Cards to Apple Pay

To start using Apple Pay, add a credit or debit card to it:

1. Open your Wallet by tapping its icon on the Home screen.

2. Tap Add (+) in the Apple Pay section at the top of the screen.

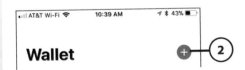

3. Tap Continue.

4. Position the iPhone so that the card is inside the white box. The app captures information from the card, which is highlighted in white on the screen. When it has captured all the information it can, you move to the Card Details screen.

Prefer to Type?

If you don't want to use the camera option, or if that option doesn't capture the information correctly, you can also type your card's information directly into the fields. To do this, perform step 3, and then tap Enter Card Details Manually, which is at the bottom of the Scan screen. You can use the resulting Card Details screens to manually enter the card's information.

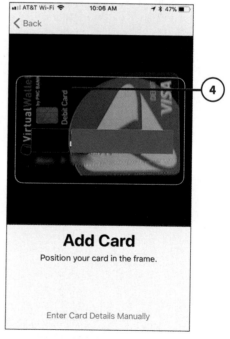

5. Use the keyboard or keypad to enter any information that wasn't captured or to correct any information that wasn't captured correctly.

6. Tap Next.

7. Use the keyboard or keypad to enter any information that wasn't captured or to correct any information that wasn't captured correctly.

8. Tap Next.

9. Tap Agree. The information for the card is verified. If it can't be verified, you see an error message. For example, if the card doesn't support Apple Pay, you see a message saying so. If this happens, tap OK to close the message and then wait for your card to support Apple Pay or enter a different card's information. When the card's verification is complete, you see it in your Wallet. Once the card is activated, you are ready to use it with Apple Pay.

After your card is activated, it is ready for Apple Pay

More Verification Required

In some cases, there might be an additional verification step after you tap Agree in step 9. When this is the case, the Complete Verification screen appears. Tap how you want to receive the verification code, such as via Email or Text Message, and then tap Next. The card configuration completes. You should receive a verification code. When you have the code, open the Settings app and tap Wallet & Apple Pay. Tap the card you need to verify, and then tap Enter Code. Enter the verification code you received; when you enter the correct code, the card is verified and becomes available for Apple Pay.

Managing Apple Pay

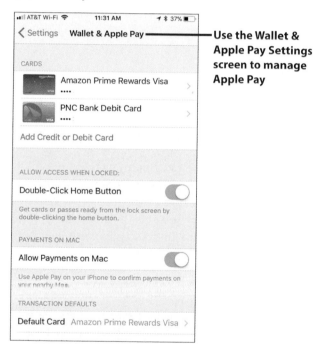

Use the Wallet & Apple Pay Settings screen to manage Apple Pay

To manage Apple Pay, open the Settings app and tap Wallet & Apple Pay. On the resulting screen, you can do the following:

- Tap a card to configure it, such as to determine if notifications related to it are sent. You also see a list of recent transactions for the card.

- Add a new credit or debit card.

- Use the Double-Click Home Button switch to determine whether you can access the cards in your Wallet by pressing the Touch ID/Home button twice when the phone is locked. This makes using your Wallet even easier because you press the Home button twice and your cards appear; tap a card to use it or touch the Touch ID/Home button to pay for something with Apple Pay.

- Set the Allow Payments on Mac switch to on (green) if you use a Mac computer and want to be able to use Apple Pay for online transactions.

- Set your default Apple Pay card. The default card is used automatically; you have to manually select other cards in the Wallet app to use one of them instead.

- Update your shipping address, email addresses, and phone numbers.

Ensure the Apple Pay switch is on so you can make payments using the Touch ID button

You should also make sure Apple Pay is set to use Touch ID because this makes it much easier and faster. Open the Settings app, tap Touch ID & Passcode, and then enter your passcode. Ensure that the Apple Pay switch is on (green). This enables you to complete Apple Pay transactions by touching the Touch ID/Home button. (See Chapter 4 for the steps to help you configure Touch ID.)

Paying People with Apple Pay

Apple Pay will enable you to send and receive money from other individuals; however, this feature was not active at press time. Refer to the online supplement *My iPhone X* by going to www.informit.com/myiphone11 to learn how you can pay individuals with Apple Pay and receive payment from them as well.

Working Seamlessly Across Your Devices

Your iPhone can work seamlessly with other iOS devices running iOS 8 and later (such as iPads) and Macs running OS X Yosemite and later. This enables you to change devices and keep working on the same tasks. For example, you can start an email on your iPhone and then continue it on your Mac without missing a beat.

You can also take phone calls on iPads or Macs.

Working with Handoff

Handoff enables you to work seamlessly between iOS devices, as well as Macs running OS X Yosemite or later. Each device needs to be signed into the same iCloud account and have Handoff enabled. If you do not have multiple iOS devices running iOS 8 or later, or a Mac running OS X Yosemite or later, then there is no need to turn on this feature.

Enable Handoff to work seamlessly across devices

Ensure that Handoff is enabled on all the devices with which you want to use it. On iOS devices, enable Handoff by opening the Settings app, tapping General, and then tapping Handoff. Set the Handoff switch to on (green).

To enable handoff on a Mac running OS X Yosemite or later, open the System Preferences app, and then open the General pane. Ensure that the Allow Handoff between this Mac and your iCloud devices check box is checked.

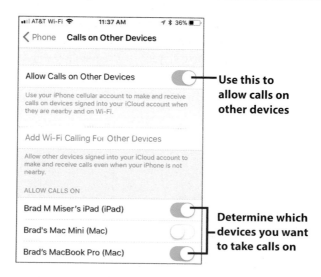

Use this to allow calls on other devices

Determine which devices you want to take calls on

If you want to be able to take phone calls on other devices, open the Phone settings and tap Calls on Other Devices. Set the Allow Calls on Other Devices switch to on (green). Set the switch to on (green) for each device on which you want to be able to take calls.

Using Handoff

When Handoff is enabled on your devices, you can work on the same items on any device, as the following example of working with email shows:

1. Start an email on your iPhone (note this only works for iCloud email).

2. To work on the email on another iOS device, swipe up on the Mail icon on its Lock screen and unlock the device or to work on a Mac, click the Handoff icon on the left end of the Dock.

3. Work on the email on the iOS device or Mac.

Handoff Goes Both Ways

This works in the other direction, too. For example, if you open a web page on your Mac, you see the Safari icon on the iPhone's Lock screen. Swipe up on it and unlock your iPhone, and the web page on your Mac opens on your iPhone.

Most Apple apps support Handoff, and Apple has made it available to other software developers so they can add support to their apps, too.

Taking Phone Calls on Macs or iPads

A call coming in on your iPhone appears on the iPad

Tap to be reminded to return the call

Tap to decline

Tap to respond with a message

Tap to answer

When your iPhone is on the same Wi-Fi network as an iPad running iOS 8 or later, or a Mac running OS X Yosemite or later, you can take phone calls on those devices. When a call comes in to your iPhone, you see the call screen on the other devices and can take the call on one of those devices (see Chapter 7, "Communicating with the Phone and FaceTime Apps").

An iPhone is easy to maintain and isn't
likely to give you much trouble

In this chapter, you learn how to keep an iPhone in top shape and what to do should problems happen. Topics include the following:

→ Maintaining an iPhone's software
→ Maintaining iPhone apps
→ Backing up your iPhone
→ Finding and securing your iPhone with Find My iPhone
→ Maintaining an iPhone's power
→ Solving iPhone problems
→ Getting help with iPhone problems

Maintaining and Protecting Your iPhone and Solving Problems

iPhones usually work very well, and you are unlikely to have problems with one, especially if you keep its software current. When problems do occur, you can usually solve them with a few simple steps. If that fails, there's lots of help available for you on the Internet or you can visit the Genius bar at an Apple store.

Maintaining an iPhone's Software

Like software on computers, the software on your iPhone gets updated periodically to fix bugs, solve issues, and introduce new features. For best results, you should ensure the software you use is current to the latest releases.

There are two types of software you need to maintain: the iOS software that runs your iPhone and the apps you have installed on it. Fortunately, maintaining both types is simple.

Maintaining the iOS Software with the Settings App

You can check for updates to the iOS using the Settings app. If an update is found, you can download and install it directly on the iPhone.

Update Notification

You might receive a notification on the iPhone when an update to iOS is available; you also see a badge on the Settings app's icon. You can tap Update in the notification to move to the Update screen (and so won't need to perform steps 1– 3).

1. On the Home screen, tap Settings.

2. Tap General.

3. Tap Software Update. The app checks for an update. If one is available, you see information about it and should proceed to step 4. If no update is needed, you see a message saying so and you can skip the rest of these steps.

4. If automatic update downloads are enabled, tap Install Now; if not, tap Download and Install. The update is downloaded if it hasn't been already and the installation process begins. You might see a brief prompt asking if the update should be installed; you can tap Install or just ignore it and the installation starts automatically. Depending on your iPhone's status, you might see different warnings, such as if you aren't connected to a power supply.

The iOS software is current; no update needed

An update to the iOS software available

5. Enter your iPhone's passcode.

6. Tap Agree.

7. Tap Agree at the prompt. The
software update installs on your
iPhone. As part of the update process, the iPhone restarts. When it
does, the updated iOS software is
ready for you to use.

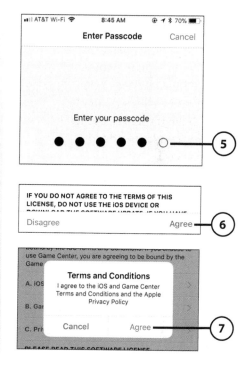

Maintaining iPhone Apps

iPhone apps are regularly updated to fix bugs or add features and enhancements. If you enable the AUTOMATIC DOWNLOADS setting for Updates in
the iTunes & App Store Settings (refer to the task "Configuring Your iPhone to
Download and Maintain Apps" in Chapter 4, "Customizing How Your iPhone
Works," for details), you don't need to worry about keeping your apps current because the iOS does that for you automatically whenever your iPhone
is connected to a Wi-Fi network. (Updates to the iOS software are also
downloaded automatically, but you have to start the installation process as
described in the previous task.) If you enable the Use Cellular Data setting
on the iTunes & App Store settings screen, the updates occur at any time
your iPhone is connected to the cellular network, too (except for very large
updates, which are only downloaded when your phone is connected to a
Wi-Fi network).

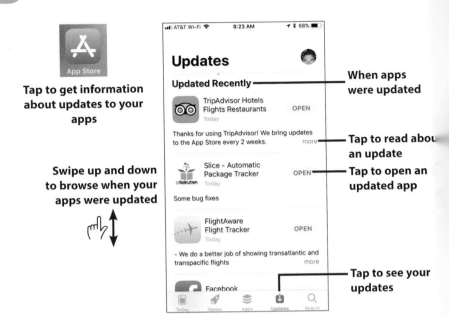

Tap to get information about updates to your apps

When apps were updated

Updated Recently

Tap to read about an update

Swipe up and down to browse when your apps were updated

Tap to open an updated app

Tap to see your updates

To see how your apps have been updated, tap the App Store app on the Home screen to open that app. Tap the Updates icon, and then swipe up and down to see the apps that have been updated. The updates are grouped by the date on which the updates occurred. To see details about an update, tap its more link. (Be aware that not all apps provide this link.) You can open the current version of the app by tapping OPEN. If an app's update is pending, tap UPDATE to update it, or you can tap Update All to update all your apps. (With automatic updates enabled, you don't need to manually update apps, but there might be times you don't want to wait for the automatic update to be done.)

Backing Up Your iPhone

Like all things data related, it's important to back up your iPhone's data. If you ever need to restore your iPhone to solve a problem or replace your iPhone with a new one, having a current backup can get you back to where you want to be as quickly and easily as possible.

There are two places where you can back up your iPhone. You can back up to your iCloud account or to your computer. In fact, you can back up to both places for maximum protection.

Ideally, you'll configure your iPhone to back up to iCloud so you can back up whenever your iPhone is connected to a Wi-Fi network that provides an Internet connection. Periodically, you can back up to your computer using the iTunes app.

To learn how to configure your iPhone to back up to your iCloud account, see "Configuring Your iCloud Back Up" in Chapter 3, "Setting Up and Using an Apple ID, iCloud, and Other Online Accounts." With this enabled, your iPhone is backed up automatically. You can manually back up at any time as described in the following task.

Manually Backing Up Your iPhone to iCloud

To manually back up your iPhone to your iCloud account, do the following:

1. Tap Settings.

2. Tap your Apple ID account.

3. Tap iCloud.

4. Swipe up the screen.

5. Tap iCloud Backup.

6. Tap Back Up Now. Your iPhone's data is backed up to iCloud. You can see the progress on the screen; however, you can continue using your iPhone because the process works in the background. You just need to start the manual back-up process, and then do whatever you want while it completes.

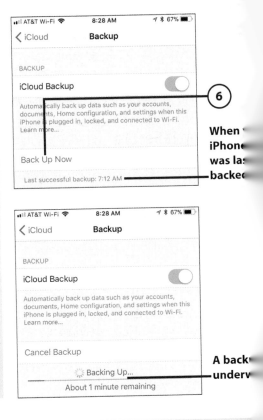

6

When iPhone was last backed

A backup underway

>>>Go Further

BACKING UP TO A COMPUTER

Using iCloud to back up your iPhone is good because the back-up process is done over the Internet, and it's automatic so you don't have to remember to do it. You can also manually back up your iPhone to a computer using iTunes. Connect your iPhone to a computer and open the iTunes app on the computer. Select the iPhone you want to back up. Click the Summary settings. Click Back Up Now. The iPhone's data is backed up and you can restore the iPhone using that backup should you need to.

If you don't want to back up your iPhone to iCloud for some reason (not recommended), click This Computer on the Summary screen in iTunes and click Sync. The iPhone is backed up only on the computer. You must connect the iPhone to the computer to back it up so if you choose this option, make sure you do so regularly and often.

Finding and Securing Your iPhone with Find My iPhone

If you lose your iPhone, you can use iCloud's Find My iPhone feature to locate your iPhone and to secure it by locking it or, in the worst case, erasing its data. Hopefully, you'll never need to use this capability, but it's good to know how just in case.

Keep It Secure

For better security, you should configure a passcode, as described in Chapter 4. When a passcode is required, it must be entered to unlock and use an iPhone. If you don't have a passcode, anyone who picks up your iPhone can use it. This section assumes you have a passcode set. If not, go back to Chapter 4 and set one before continuing—unless you've already lost control of your iPhone. If you don't have a passcode set and lose your iPhone, you're prompted to create a passcode when you put it in Lost Mode.

After you configure Find My iPhone and use it to locate your iPhone, you can perform the following actions on it:

- **Play Sound**—This does just what it sounds like. A sound is played on the iPhone and an alert appears on its screen. This provides information to whoever has the device—such as if you've loaned the device to someone and want it back. The sound can help you locate the device if it is in the same general vicinity as you.

- **Lost Mode**—This locks the iPhone so it can't be used without entering the passcode. This can protect your iPhone without changing its data. You can also display contact information on the iPhone's screen to enable someone to get in touch with you.

- **Erase Your iPhone**   This erases the iPhone's memory as the "last chance" to protect your data. You should only do this in the worst-case scenario because when you erase the iPhone, you lose the ability to find it again using Find My iPhone.

Keeping You Informed

Whenever you use one of the Find My iPhone actions, such as playing a sound or using the Lost Mode, you receive emails to your iCloud email address showing the action taken along with the device, date, and time on which it was performed.

To use Find My iPhone, it must be enabled on your iPhone using the iCloud Settings as explained in Chapter 3 (it is enabled by default so unless you have disabled it, it should be ready for you to use when needed).

Using Find My iPhone to Locate Your iPhone

To use Find My iPhone, perform the following tasks:

1. Use a web browser to move to and log in to your iCloud website located at icloud.com.

Two-Factor Authentication

If two-factor authentication is configured for your iCloud account, you need to enter an additional code after you perform step 1. This code appears on each device that is configured with your iCloud account. After you enter the code, click Trust so that you won't have to enter the code each time you sign in to iCloud on that device.

2. Click Find iPhone. All the devices associated with your Apple ID and on which Find My iPhone is active are located.

3. Click the All Devices menu. All your devices are shown on the My Devices list.

4. Click the device you want to locate. If the device can be located, you see it on a map. You can use the map's controls to zoom into the iPhone's location so you get the best idea of where it currently is. You also see a dialog box that enables you to perform the three actions described earlier. The details for each are provided in the following tasks.

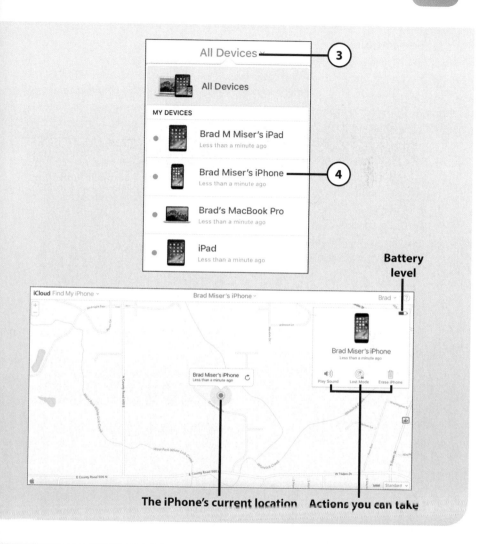

Battery level

The iPhone's current location   Actions you can take

Using Find My iPhone to Play a Sound on Your iPhone

Here's how to send a sound or message to an iOS device:

1. Locate your iPhone as described in the previous task.

2. Click Play Sound. The alert sound plays on the iPhone and the FIND MY IPHONE ALERT appears on the screen.

Passcode Required

When your iPhone is locked, a passcode is not required to stop the alert sound playing and to delete the alert. Therefore, anyone can do this. If you think someone else might have your iPhone, you should use the Lost Mode instead of playing a sound. The sound option is really only useful to help you locate the phone when you are certain no one else could have it—for example you know it is lost somewhere in your house, and the sound helps you to find it.

3. To stop the sound from playing on the iPhone when the phone is locked, press the alert if you are using a model with 3D Touch or swipe to the right on non-3D Touch models.

4. Tap X on models with 3D Touch or tap Clear on non-3D Touch models to stop the sound and delete the alert.

5. If the iPhone isn't locked when the alert plays, tap OK to stop the sound and close the alert.

The sound plays and the alert message appears on the iPhone

The Sound Remains the Same

When you send a sound to an iPhone, it plays even if the iPhone is muted.

Using Find My iPhone to Put Your iPhone in Lost Mode

You can put your iPhone into Lost Mode by doing the following:

1. Locate the device using the steps in the previous task.

2. Click Lost Mode. (If you haven't entered a passcode, you're prompted to create one by entering and verifying it.)

3. Enter the phone number you want someone to call if your phone is found.

4. Click Next.

5. Enter the message you want to appear on the iPhone. This can be your request that whoever has the device call you, instructions for returning the device, and so on.

6. Tap Done. The iPhone is locked and the message you entered displays on the screen. While the iPhone is in Lost Mode, the Lost Mode icon on the Find My iPhone screen rotates and you see the Lost Mode indicator.

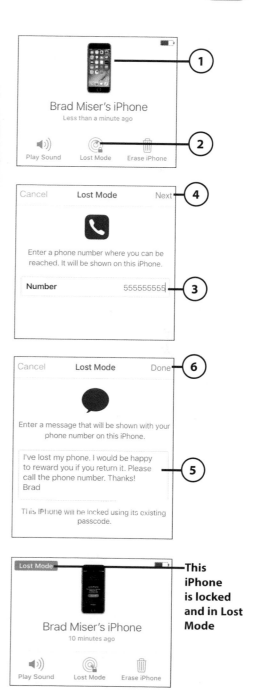

This iPhone is locked and in Lost Mode

When the device enters Lost Mode, it is locked and protected with the existing passcode. The phone number and message you entered appear on the iPhone's screen. The person finding your phone can tap Call to call the number you entered.

In addition to being locked, the phone is placed in Low Power Mode so the battery's charge lasts as long as possible. Apple Pay is also disabled.

The iPhone remains in Lost Mode until it is unlocked. You see the current status in the iPhone's window on the iCloud Find iPhone website. When you get your phone back, you can unlock it. You might need to re-enter your Apple ID password to restart iCloud services and re-enable Apple Pay.

This iPhone is locked

The message and phone number you entered

The phone can still be used for emergency calls

The person who finds the phone can tap to call the number you entered

Using Find My iPhone to Erase Your iPhone

If you decide you've lost control of your device and want to protect the information it contains, take the following steps to erase it:

1. Locate the device using the steps in the task "Using Find My iPhone to Locate Your iPhone."

2. Click Erase iPhone.

Finding and Securing Your iPhone with Find My iPhone **623**

3. Click Erase.

4. Enter your Apple ID password.

5. Click the right-facing arrow.

6. If you want to send a phone number to the device so that someone can call you about it, enter it at the prompt.

7. Click Next.

8. Enter the message you want to appear on the iPhone. This can be your request that whoever has the device call you, instructions for returning the device, and so on.

9. Tap Done. The iPhone is erased and the message you entered displays on the screen. The person who finds it can tap Call to call the number you entered in step 6, hopefully to return your iPhone. If it does get returned, you have to restore the iPhone using a backup from iCloud or iTunes on your computer (the steps to do this are later in this chapter).

Erase a Device

When you erase an iPhone, all its data is deleted and it's reset to factory conditions. This means you are no longer able to use Find My iPhone to locate it. Only do this when you're pretty sure the iPhone is out of your control or that you won't be getting it back any time soon.

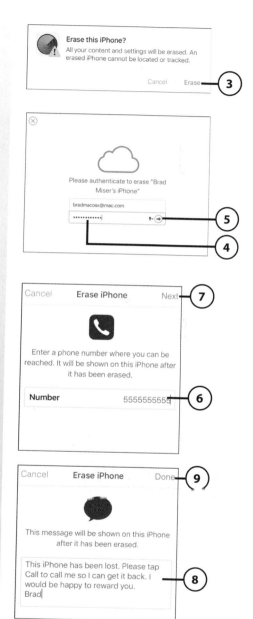

>>>Go Further
USING FIND MY iPHONE

Here are some more tips on using Find My iPhone:

- To update the locations of your devices, refresh the web page and reopen the A Devices list.

- When you send a message to an iPhone that is in Lost Mode or when you erase it, you might want to include additional contact information in the message, such as your name and where you are currently located. You could also offer a reward for the return of the iPhone. Include enough information so that if someone wants to return the device to you, she has what she needs to be able to do so.

- If you lose your iPhone, use an escalation of steps to try to regain control. Look at the iPhone's location on the map. If you are very sure no one else has the phone, play the sound because it might help you find it again. If the iPhone doesn't appe to be near your current location or it appears to be but you can't find it, put it in Lost Mode. This hopefully prevents someone else from using it while you locate it and allows someone who finds it to contact you. If you lose all hope of finding it again, you can erase the iPhone to delete the data it contains. When you do this, you lose the ability to track your iPhone and have to rely on someone finding it ar contacting you. This is a severe action, so you don't want to do it prematurely.

- Erasing an iPhone is a bit of a double-edged sword. It protects your data by erasir your device, but it also means you can't use Find My iPhone to locate it anymore. You should use this only if you're pretty sure someone has your device. After you erase it, there's no way to track the iPhone's location. How fast you move to erase your iPhone also depends on whether you've required a passcode. If you do requi a passcode, you know your device's data can't be accessed without that code, so i will take some time for a miscreant to crack it, and you can be slower on going to the point of erasing it. If your iPhone doesn't have a passcode, you might want to erase it sooner to prevent someone from accessing your content.

- As you use Find My iPhone, you receive email notifications about various events such as when a device is locked, when a message you sent is displayed, and so on. These are good ways to know something about what is happening with you iPhone, even though you might not be able to see the iPhone for yourself.

- If Find My iPhone can't currently find your iPhone, you can still initiate the same actions as when the iPhone is found, although they won't actually happen until the iPhone becomes visible to the Find My iPhone service again. To be notified when this happens, check the Email me when this iPhone is found check box. When the iPhone becomes visible to Find My iPhone, you receive an email and then can take appropriate action to locate and secure it.

- There's an app for that. You can download and use the free Find iPhone app on an iOS device to use this feature (it's installed on iPhones by default and is located in the Extras folder). For example, you can use this app on an iPad to locate an iPhone.

Maintaining an iPhone's Power

Keep your eye on the battery icon so you don't run out of power

Obviously, an iPhone with a dead battery isn't good for much. As you use your iPhone, you should keep an eye on its battery status. As long as the battery icon is at least partially filled, you're okay. As the iPhone gets low on power, the battery status icon becomes almost empty. Two separate warnings alert you when the battery lowers to 20% and then again at 10%.

This iPhone is in Low Power Mode

When you see the low-power warnings, you can tap Low Power Mode to have your iPhone run in this mode that reduces power use to extend the life of your battery. It does this by slowing down the phone's processor, stops automatic downloads, stops email push, and any other processes that consume lots of power. Although this reduces the performance of your phone, it can significantly extend the time until your iPhone runs out of power. While in Low Power Mode, the battery status icon is yellow.

Manual Low Power Mode

You can put your iPhone in Low Power Mode at any time by opening the Control Center and tapping the Low Power Mode icon (the battery). (If you don't see the battery icon on your Control Center, you can add it as explained in Chapter 4.) You might want to do this if you know you won't be able to charge your iPhone for a long time and don't need some of the functions it disables (such as push email).

This iPhone is being charged

If you keep going, whether you choose to run in Low Power Mode or not, the iPhone eventually runs out of power and shuts down. Once it shuts down because of a low battery, you won't be able to unlock or use it until you connect it to a charger and the battery has recharged enough for the phone to operate, which can take a few minutes. If you try to use it before it has enough power, you see the red, empty battery icon on the screen.

Fortunately, it's easy to avoid running out of power by keeping your iPhone charged. Connect the iPhone to the charger or a computer using the USB cable, and it charges automatically. Or, if you have an iPhone 8, 8 Plus, or X, you can place the phone backside down on a Qi wireless charger to charge it. While the phone is charging, you see the charging icon in the upper-right corner of the screen, and if you wake the iPhone, a large battery icon showing the relative state of the battery appears on its screen. When charging is complete, the battery status icon replaces the charging icon in the upper-right corner of the screen, the large battery icon disappears, and you see the iPhone's wallpaper if it's locked, or you see whatever screen you happen to be using if it isn't locked.

If your iPhone moved into Low Power Mode automatically before you started charging it, it also moves out of Low Power Mode automatically when it has been recharged sufficiently. When this happens, you see an onscreen message saying that Low Power mode has been turned off.

Topping Off

It's a good idea to keep your iPhone's battery topped off; this type of battery actually does better if you keep it charged rather than letting it run down all the way before recharging. Periodically, say every month or two, you might want to let your iPhone run completely out of power and then recharge it to maximize its life. The key point is, as Apple puts it, to "keep the electrons moving." So, don't let your iPhone sit with no activity for long periods of time.

Setting Low Power Mode and Getting Information About Battery Use

You can configure and get information about your iPhone's battery by doing the following:

1. Open the Settings app and tap Battery.

2. To manually activate Low Power Mode, set its switch to on (green); to leave it in automatic mode, skip to step 4.

For the First Time on this iPhone

The first time you manually activate Low Power Mode, you might see a warning prompt. Tap Continue to clear the prompt and activate Low Power Mode.

3. To return your phone to normal operation, set the Low Power Mode switch to off (white).

4. To see the percentage of charge remaining along with the battery icon, slide the Battery Percentage switch to on (green). The percentage of charge remaining appears to the left of the battery status icon at the top of the screen. (This happens automatically when you put the iPhone into Low Power Mode.)

5. Swipe up the screen to see the BATTERY USAGE section. This provides information about the percentage of power that apps have used over the last 2 hours, which can come in handy when you want to make your battery last longer (see the next task for details).

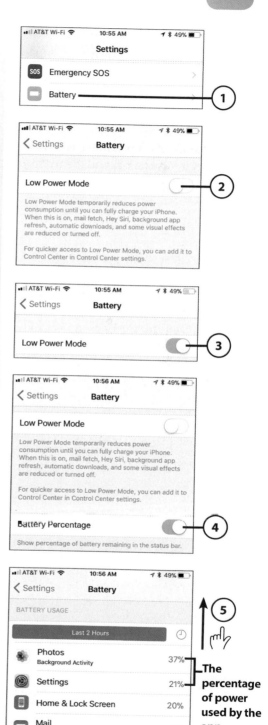

The percentage of power used by the app

6. Tap the Clock icon to see the amount of time the app has been running to use the percentage of power it has consumed. You see this both for on-screen or background activity.

7. Swipe all the way up the screen to see information about the time since the last full charge that your iPhone has been in use or has been in standby.

Making the Battery Last Longer

If your iPhone's battery doesn't seem to last very long, the issue is likely that a service is very active and is requiring near-constant activity. Common causes of this problem are Push being turned on for an account that has a lot of activity, an application using GPS capabilities, and so on. Try these steps to find and stop the source of the power drain:

1. Use steps 5 through 7 in the previous task to identify apps using a large percentage of power.

2. If you identify a power-hungry app that you don't want to use any more, press the Touch ID/ Home button twice (all models except iPhone X) or swipe up from the bottom of the screen and pause toward the middle of the screen (iPhone X) to open the App Switcher.

3. Swipe to the left or right on the App Switcher until the power-hog's screen is front and center.

4. Swipe up on the app's screen to shut it down. You can use your iPhone to see if that was the cause of the rapid power drain. If so, you're done. If not, you can continue with these steps to conserve power.

5. Open the Settings app and tap Accounts & Passwords.

6. Tap Fetch New Data (if you have a lot of accounts, you might need to swipe up the screen to see it).

7. Slide the status switch for Push to off (white). This disables Push functionality. To update your information, set a Fetch schedule using the controls on the bottom of the Fetch New Data screen or just open an app, such as Mail.

8. Turn off any transmitting and receiving functions that you aren't using, such as Bluetooth. Using the Control Center is a handy way to do this quickly.

9. Use your iPhone to see if the battery lasts longer. If it does, you know one of the changes you made was the reason; you can either leave the offending source of power drain shut down or just be aware when you are using it. If the battery still doesn't last very long, it might have a problem and you should contact Apple for assistance.

Battery Help

You can install apps on your iPhone that test the health of your battery. Use the App Store app to search for "battery life" and then download the app you want to use (see Chapter 4 for the details of using the App Store).

Solving iPhone Problems

Even a device as reliable as your iPhone can sometimes run into problems. Fortunately, the solutions to most problems you encounter are simple. If a simple solution doesn't work, a great deal of detailed help is available from Apple, and even more is available from the community of iPhone users.

The problems that you can address with the simple steps described in this section vary and range from such issues as the iPhone hanging (won't respond to commands) to apps not working as they should. Use the following tasks to address problems you encounter.

Restarting an App

If an app you are using locks up, displays an error, or isn't working the way it should, try shutting it down and restarting it.

1. Press the Touch ID/Home button twice (all models except iPhone X) or swipe up from the bottom of the screen and pause toward the middle of the screen (iPhone X). The App switcher opens.

2. Swipe to the left or right until you see the app that has frozen.

3. Swipe up on the app to shut it down.

4. Press the Touch ID/Home button (all models except iPhone X) or tap outside the App Switcher (iPhone X) to move back to the Home screen.

5. Open the app again. If it works normally, you're done. (It's generally a good idea to restart your iPhone when you've had to force an app to quit.)

Restarting Your iPhone

Whenever your iPhone starts acting oddly, restarting it should be the first thing you try. It's easy to do and cures an amazing number of problems. To restart your iPhone, do the following:

1. Press and hold the Side button (on 5s and SE models you use the Wake/Sleep button instead) until the slider appears on the screen.

2. Drag the slider to the right. The iPhone powers down and the screen goes completely dark.

3. Press and hold the Side button until you see the Apple logo on the screen. The iPhone restarts. When the Home screen appears, try using the iPhone again. If the problem is solved, you're done.

Can't Restart?

If your iPhone won't restart normally, press and hold the Side and Touch ID/Home buttons (all models except the iPhone X) or the Side and Lower Volume buttons (iPhone X) at the same time until the iPhone shuts off (about 10 seconds) and the screen goes completely dark. Then, press the Side button to restart it. (On the 5s and SE, you use the Sleep/Wake button with the Touch ID/Home button instead.)

Resetting Your iPhone

If restarting your iPhone doesn't help, try resetting your iPhone using the following steps:

1. On the Home screen, tap Settings.

2. Tap General.

3. Swipe up the screen until you see the Reset command.

4. Tap Reset.

5. Tap the Reset command for the area in which you are having problems. For example, if you are having trouble with Wi-Fi or other networking areas, tap Reset Network Settings, or if you decide your Home screens are a mess and you want to go back to the default layout, tap Reset Home Screen Layout. If you are having lots of issues in multiple areas, tap Reset All Settings or Erase All Content and Settings (be careful because this erases everything on your iPhone).

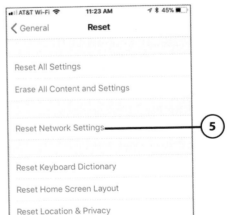

6. If prompted to do so, enter your passcode; if you don't see a passcode prompt, skip to the next step.

7. Tap the confirmation of the reset you are doing. The reset is complete and that area of the iPhone is reset to factory conditions.

8. Reconfigure the area that you reset. For example, if you reset your network settings, you need to reconnect to the networks you want to use. If you did a Reset All Settings or Erase All Content and Settings, you basically start from the beginning as if your iPhone was just taken out of its box.

Restoring Your iPhone

The most severe action you can take on your iPhone is to restore it. When this happens, the iPhone is erased, so you lose all its contents and its current iOS software is overwritten with the latest version. If you have added information to your iPhone since it was last backed up (when you last connected it to the computer or it backed up to your iCloud account), that information is lost when you restore your iPhone—so be careful before doing this. If none of the other tasks in this section corrected the problem, restoring the iPhone should.

Installing iTunes

If iTunes isn't installed on your computer, go to www.apple.com/itunes to download and install it.

To restore your iPhone, use the iTunes app on a computer and perform the following steps:

1. On the iPhone, turn off Find iPhone by opening the iCloud Settings screen, tapping Find My iPhone, setting the Find My iPhone switch to off (white), entering your Apple ID password, and tapping Turn Off. (If your iPhone has been erased using Find My iPhone or if iCloud services have previously been disabled, you won't need to perform this step.)

2. Connect the iPhone to your computer.

Where's the Trust?

The first time you connect an iPhone to your computer, you're prompted to trust the computer or not. Tap Trust to be able to connect it to iTunes; you need to input your passcode if the iPhone is locked. You also see a trust prompt in iTunes on the computer; click Continue to connect the iPhone to iTunes on the computer.

3. If iTunes didn't open automatically, launch the application.

4. If your iPhone is the only device connected to the computer, click the iPhone button at the top of the screen (not shown on the figure). (If you have more than one device connected to iTunes, this is the Devices button; click it and select your iPhone on the list of devices.)

5. Click Summary.

6. Click Restore iPhone. Remember that you lose everything on your iPhone when you restore it, so make sure that you have all its data stored elsewhere, such as backed up on iCloud, before you do this.

7. Click Back Up. This backs up your iPhone's contents to your computer. This is a critical step because it enables you to recover the data and settings on your iPhone. If you don't do this, some of your data and settings can be lost.

Backing Up Isn't Hard to Do

iCloud is the most convenient way to back up your iPhone because it happens automatically. You can also manually back up your iPhone to your computer at any time by using these steps to access the iPhone in iTunes and then clicking the Back Up Now button. If you use iTunes regularly, it's a good idea to use it to keep your iPhone backed up on your computer, too.

8. Click Restore in the dialog box. The Restore process begins, and iTunes extracts the software and prepares to install it.

Purchased Items?

If you have "purchased" items on the iPhone that haven't been synced to iTunes, you see a warning dialog box stating that you will lose these items and have to purchase them again. If you can, you should sync your iPhone to iTunes before performing the restore. If you do this, you won't see this dialog. Even if you haven't, you aren't likely to lose any content unless you purchased it from the iTunes Store very early in the iPhone's lifecycle. At that time, you could only download content once so if it wasn't in your iTunes library, you could lose it and would have to pay for it again. For the past several years, you are able to re-download content you purchase from the iTunes Store. If you can sync your iPhone, do so before completing the restore. If not, you'll have to proceed with the restore, though you might lose content if you purchased it long ago (in which case, you have probably synced it to iTunes long ago as well).

9. Read the information about the current version of the iPhone's software, and click Next. (This step is not shown in the figures.)

10. Click Agree (not shown). The current version of the iPhone's software is downloaded to your computer, and iTunes reinstalls it on your iPhone. You see several progress indicators along the way, both on the computer screen and on your iPhone. Early in the process, the iPhone restarts and iTunes begins reinstalling its software. (If a firmware update is needed, iTunes handles that, too.) When the process is complete, you see a message explaining what has happened.

11. Click OK (not shown). The iPhone is restarted, and you see the Welcome to Your New Phone screen.

12. Click the Restore from this backup radio button.

13. On the pop-up menu, ensure that your iPhone's name appears on the menu with no date and time. This indicates it is the most recent backup. If you don't see this or you want to choose to restore the phone from an earlier backup, open the menu and choose the backup you want to use to restore the phone.

14. Click Continue. iTunes restores the iPhone from the backup.

15. Click OK in the completion dialog box (not shown in the figure). The iPhone is synced according to the settings stored in the backup. When the sync process is complete, the iPhone should be back in working condition with all your content restored to it. If you have a lot of content, this process can take a while because the sync is performed starting with the iPhone's memory being "empty." You need to redownload any content that you've purchased from the iTunes Store to restore it, such as movies or TV shows.

Starting Over

If you want to start from the beginning, select the Set up as a new iPhone radio button in step 12 instead. Follow the onscreen prompts. When that process is complete, you're prompted to name and reconfigure the iPhone as you did when you first started using it.

How Does It Remember?

You might wonder how an iPhone can be restored. It's because critical iPhone data and settings are backed up on your iCloud account or on your computer. Each time you back up your iPhone, this information is saved so that it is available again when it is needed, such as when you restore your iPhone. iCloud backups happen automatically when your iPhone is connected to the Internet so you don't have to worry about backing it up manually. But, as described earlier, you can periodically back up your iPhone to your computer, too.

Restoring an iPhone Without iTunes

You can also restore an iPhone without using iTunes. Open the Settings app, tap General, tap Reset, and tap Erase All Content and Settings. After you enter your passcode and confirm the action, the data and settings on your iPhone are erased. You can then restore your iPhone from your iCloud backup as you had the option to do when you turned on your iPhone for the first time.

Finding a Missing App

I've had more than a few emails from people on whose phones an app icon seems to have disappeared. In many cases, these were core iPhone apps that can't be removed from the iPhone, such as Settings or Photos. In almost all of these cases, the app's icon had inadvertently been moved into a folder and so was not visible in its expected location. If this happens to you, perform the following steps to restore the app to where it should be:

1. Move to a Home screen.

2. Swipe down from the center top area of the screen. The Search tool opens.

3. Tap in the Search bar and enter the name of the app that is missing. As you search, you see a list of items that match your search. If the app is found, you know it is still on the iPhone and its icon was just accidentally misplaced; you can continue with these steps to find it.

   If the app you are looking for isn't found, it has been deleted from the iPhone and you need to reinstall it. Download and install it again using the App Store app (don't worry; if it has a license fee, you don't need to pay for it again). (Installing apps is covered in Chapter 4.)

4. Tap Search.

5. Note the current location of the app, which is shown on the right side of the screen. If no location is shown, the app is on one of your Home screens, in which case you need to browse through the screens to find it, and you can skip the rest of these steps.

6. Tap Cancel. You move back to the Home screen.

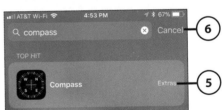

7. Open the folder where the app is currently located.

8. Touch and hold on the app icon until the icons start jiggling.

9. Drag the app's icon out of the folder and place the icon back where you want it to be (refer to "Customizing Your Home Screens" in Chapter 5, "Customizing How Your iPhone Looks and Sounds," for details of moving apps on the Home screens).

10. Press the Touch ID/Home button to lock the icons in their current positions (all models except iPhone X).

iPhone X

Refer to the online supplement *My iPhone X* by going to www.informit.com/myiphone11 for the details of locking icons on the Home screen on an iPhone X.

Making an iPhone's Screen Rotate Again

If your iPhone stops changing from horizontal to vertical orientation when you rotate the phone, you probably have inadvertently enabled the orientation lock. Unlock it again by doing the following.

The orientation of this iPhone is locked

1. Look at the top of the screen. If you see the Orientation Lock icon, the iPhone's orientation is locked.

2. Swipe up from the bottom of the Home screen (all models except the iPhone X) or swipe down from the upper-right corner of the screen (iPhone X) to open the Control Center.

3. Tap the Orientation Lock button. Note that when Orientation Lock is on, the button's graphic is red. When it is off, the button's graphic is white.

4. Confirm that the Orientation Lock icon at the top of the screen has disappeared. The iPhone now changes orientation when you rotate it.

Blocking Unwanted Calls, Messages, or FaceTime Requests

If you want to block calls, messages, or FaceTime requests from someone, do the following:

1. Open the app through which the person you want to block is trying to contact you; you can use Phone, Messages, or FaceTime. These steps show the Phone app, but blocking people with the others is similar.

2. Tap Recents.

3. Tap the Info (i) icon for the person you want to block.

4. Tap Block This Caller.

5. Tap Block Contact. The contact becomes blocked, and you no longer receive calls, messages, or FaceTime requests from them. When the person who is blocked tries to contact you, the attempt fails, but the person doesn't know that the reason it failed is that you blocked him.

Unblock

To remove the block on a contact, move to the contact's screen and tap Unblock this Caller. You will be available to the addresses or phone numbers that you unblock again.

Unblock Without a Contact

If you block a number for which you haven't created a contact, you need to unblock them from the settings for an app. For example, open the Phone settings screen and tap Call Blocking & Identification. You see a list of all blocked contacts. Swipe to the left on the person whom you want to unblock. Tap Unblock. The person will be able to contact you again. You can always block them again if needed.

Solving the Quiet iPhone Problem

If your iPhone stops ringing or making other sounds you believe it should, perform the following steps:

1. Make sure the iPhone isn't muted. The Mute switch on the left side of the iPhone should be in the position toward the front of the phone. If you see color in the switch, the phone is currently muted. Slide the switch toward the front of the iPhone to unmute it. You should hear sounds again.

2. With the iPhone unlocked, press the upper volume switch on the left side of the iPhone to make sure that the volume isn't set to the lowest level. As you press the button, a

visual indicator of the current volume level appears on the screen. As long as you see a few "dots" on this indicator, you should be able to hear sounds the iPhone makes.

3. Make sure that the iPhone is not in Do Not Disturb mode by opening the Control Center and ensuring that the Do Not Disturb icon is off (the moon is white); if it is turned on (the moon is purple), tap it to turn it off. In Do Not Disturb mode, sounds are not made, such as a ring when you receive a phone call.

4. Try a different app or task. If you aren't hearing sound from only one app and everything else sounds normal, you know there is a problem with that app. Try deleting and reinstalling it. If you still don't hear sound from any app, you know the problem is more general.

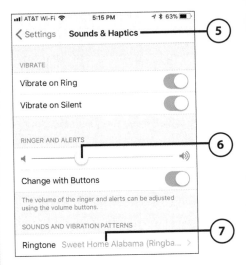

5. Move to Sounds & Haptics in the Settings app.

6. Make sure the volume slider is set to at least the middle position.

7. Tap Ringtone.

8. Tap one of the default ringtones. You should hear it. If you do, you know the problem is solved. If not, continue.

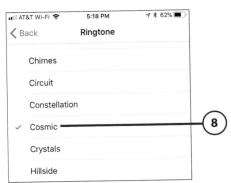

9. If you aren't hearing sounds when the EarPods aren't plugged in, connect the EarPods and repeat the sound you should be hearing. If you hear the sound only when the EarPods are plugged in, try removing the EarPods and plugging them back in a few times to see if that solves the problem. If not, your iPhone needs to be serviced by an Apple authorized repair center, or you can take it to the Genius bar in an Apple Store.

)o Disturb!

f Do Not Disturb was on, but you hadn't intended it to be, open the Settings app and
:ap Do Not Disturb to view its settings. Check to see if an automatic schedule has been
iet. If the Scheduled button is on (green) then a schedule for starting and stopping Do
Not Disturb has been active on the phone. Slide the Scheduled switch off (white) to
prevent it from automatically turning on Do Not Disturb.

Getting Help with iPhone Problems

If none of the previous steps solve your problem, including turning your
phone off and restarting it, you can get help in a number of ways:

- **Apple's website**—Go to www.apple.com/support/. On this page, you can
  access all kinds of information about iPhones, iTunes, and other Apple
  products. You can browse for help, and you can search for answers to specific problems. Many of the resulting articles have detailed, step-by-step
  instructions to help you solve problems and link to more information.

- **Web searches**—One of the most useful ways to get help is to do a web
  search for the specific problem you're having. Just open your favorite
  search tool, such as Google, and search for the problem. You are likely to
  find many resources to help you, including websites, forums, and such. If
  you encounter a problem, it's likely someone else has too, and has probably put the solution on the Web.

- **Genius bar at an Apple Store**—All Apple Stores have a Genius bar
  staffed with people who will try to help you with problems. If you can't
  resolve a problem on your own, going to an Apple Store is often a great
  solution because the Apple geniuses can help you with any problem,
  whether it's software or hardware. In many cases, the help they provide
  is free, too (though you might be charged for some hardware problems).
  You need to make an appointment before going to the Genius bar and
  can do so by going to www.apple.com/retail/geniusbar/.

- **Me**—You're welcome to send an email to me for problems you're having
  with your iPhone. My address is bradmiser@icloud.com. I'll do my best to
  help you as quickly as I can. (I do respond to every email I receive, though
  at times, it might take me a few days to get back to you. I am not able to
  respond to FaceTime or Messages requests, so please use email to reach me.)

Index

X-Y-Z

REGISTER YOUR PRODUCT at informit.com/registe

Access Additional Benefits and SAVE 35% on Your Next Purchase

- Download available product updates.
- Access bonus material when applicable.
- Receive exclusive offers on new editions and related products. (Just check the box to hear from us when setting up your account.)
- Get a coupon for 35% for your next purchase, valid for 30 days. Your code w be available in your InformIT cart. (You will also find it in the Manage Codes section of your account page.)

Registration benefits vary by product. Benefits will be listed on your account page under Registered Products.

InformIT.com—The Trusted Technology Learning Source

InformIT is the online home of information technology brands at Pearson, the world's foremc education company. At InformIT.com you can

- Shop our books, eBooks, software, and video training.
- Take advantage of our special offers and promotions (informit.com/promotions).
- Sign up for special offers and content newsletters (informit.com/newsletters).
- Read free articles and blogs by information technology experts.
- Access thousands of free chapters and video lessons.

Connect with InformIT—Visit informit.com/community

Learn about InformIT community events and programs.

informIT.com
the trusted technology learning source

Addison-Wesley • Cisco Press • IBM Press • Microsoft Press • Pearson IT Certification • Prentice Hall • Que • Sams • VMware Press